The
PORTABLE
MBA
in
MANAGEMENT

The Portable MBA Series

Forthcoming Titles

The

PORTABLE
MBA
in
MANAGEMENT

Allan R. Cohen

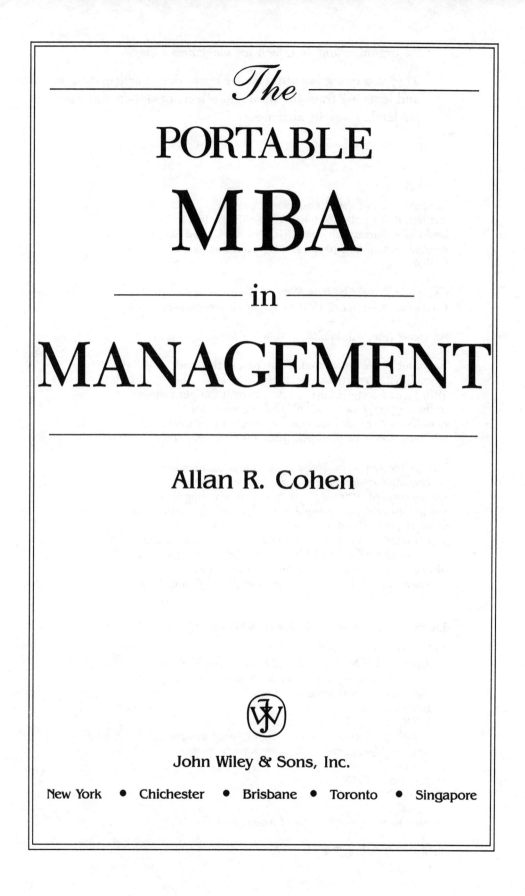

John Wiley & Sons, Inc.

New York • Chichester • Brisbane • Toronto • Singapore

For the organizations in which we work and consult

They are living laboratories for observing, participating in, and learning from the powerful effects of skilled management leadership—or its absence.

Library of Congress Cataloging-in-Publication Data

Cohen Allan R.
   The portable MBA in management / Allan R. Cohen
      p.   cm. — (The Portable MBA series)
   Published simultaneously in Canada.
   Includes index.
   ISBN 0–471–57379–5 (cloth : alk. paper)
   1. Industrial management. 2. Personnel management. 3. Work
groups 4. Management—Employee participation.   I. Title.
II. Series.
HD31.C586   1993
658.4—dc20   92-41917

Printed in the United States of America

10 9 8 7 6 5 4 3 2 1

Contents

v

PART ONE

PERSONAL AND INTERPERSONAL FRAMEWORKS

Contents

v

INTRODUCTION: THE NEW RELEVANCE OF LEADERSHIP, INFLUENCE, TEAMWORK, AND CHANGE MANAGEMENT

1

Allan R. Cohen

First a bit of ancient history: In 1959, when obtaining an MBA was far less common, I entered the MBA program at Harvard Business School. Although I came directly from college, I had grown up working in a family business and was very familiar with the kind of people problems that plague small businesses. Thus I was rather surprised at my classmates' disdain for the material in the "Administrative Practices" course, which attempted to raise questions about leadership, groups, and change. The general attitude was captured in the rapidity with which everyone adopted the verb to "ad prac" as shorthand for manipulating the behavior of others when they weren't behaving just as we enlightened managers knew they should. During the last part of the course, only about one-third of my classmates were attending class regularly; no one, however, dared miss marketing or finance classes because they promised the mastery of the real stuff that would make us successful. It wasn't necessary to know much about the "soft" (actually, soft-headed) territory of behavior. More accurately, my classmates, as inheritors of the managerial mantle, knew that *their* behavior was just fine; *everyone else* needed to be watched, tricked, or bullied into shaping up. In their desire to be hard-nosed leaders, there was no place for relationships, teams, openness, and trust—matters of character and heart.

I didn't agree with those views then, although I was singularly in-effective in arguing opposing views, which I could barely articulate, let alone prove. My classmates didn't see the need to change their convictions; they

3

were confident—correctly—of getting good jobs, and the captains of industry whom they emulated (and soon expected to displace) were not talking about interpersonal integrity or worker participation: The captains were talking about the benefits of huge conglomerates and about the glories of cash flow analysis. The times were stable enough, and employees docile enough, to make the more quantitative and strategic concepts appropriate.

Then came the sixties and the wave of disrespect for authority, the tough economy of the seventies, and the glorification of financial manipulation of the eighties; now has come the dawning realization of the nineties that the Japanese, Germans, and many others in the Pacific Rim and Europe are serious competitors that are carving away enormous chunks of what used to be the dominant economy in the world. The fifties-style U.S. business practices no longer are the envy of the world, and they no longer work. Too much has changed, and not even the most ostrich-like manager would argue that the rate of change will slow any time soon. Management practices need to change to fit the times.

What are the forces that make the so-called soft skills relevant and vital? Why do we see the surge of interest in leadership, influence, teamwork, and change management, even as managers must address tough tradeoffs, stringent financial goals, and increasing bottom-line concerns?

Global competition, as suggested above, is one important force. There's nothing like seeing whole industries shrink or disappear to get the attention of the captains of industry and of those who aspire to take their places. When competitive pressures force downsizing, reorganization, and company-preserving mergers and alliances, old models of managerial behavior begin to disintegrate. Furthermore, some management practices of other countries, especially Japan, seem to produce greater employee loyalty, more numerous ideas for improving processes and products, and higher quality and productivity. American managers are no longer so confident about their ability to gain cooperation and commitment from employees.

The rapid acceleration of technology in many fields is another major force driving the need for changed practices. When electronic products, for example, can barely be brought to market before they are superseded by the next generation of products, managerial responses geared to stable product life cycles are too sluggish. Information cannot slowly travel its way up and down the hierarchy, while layers of managers study and polish their recommendations. Decisions cannot be made by those who do not understand the rapidly shifting marketplace and technologies, which require either dramatic decentralization or delayering. In fact, one of the dirty little secrets of modern business life is that bosses no longer know the answers. It is not because they are dumb or lazy—if they are, they don't stay bosses for long—but because they *cannot* know.

In some cases even the boundaries between industries are crumbling because of the advent of new technologies. For example, telecommunications companies are competing with computer companies because digital computing is the core of modern telecommunications (thus AT&T sells computers now), and telephone companies are trying to gain permission to compete with cable-TV companies, which in turn want to provide telephone service. Meanwhile, cable companies have had competitive impact on TV networks and movie companies. Picturetel, a young company that makes low-cost telephone videoconferencing equipment, is a growing competitor for airlines and hotels, since meetings can be held over the videophone, eliminating some travel. Makers of fax machines also have an impact on the need to travel, as do low-cost long-distance providers. All of this is going on around AT&T, which only a few years ago used a 40-year depreciation life for its equipment! At this level of rapid technological change, managers are hard-pressed to keep up, and that's just one of the factors making it impossible for bosses to know.

As the AT&T example suggests, changing regulations have a profound impact on what managers must deal with. The breakup of the phone monopoly was more dramatic than some other regulatory changes, but everything from environmental-impact statements to accounting rules for pensions has an ongoing effect on companies. Politicians oscillate between wanting to reduce the constraints of government regulation and wanting to regulate corporate practices in order to protect the citizenry, the employees, or the environment. Politics makes predictability more difficult.

Customers too have become a source of unpredictability and change. No longer are they content to take what is offered and be grateful to the organization for providing the product or service; instead, customers are demanding better quality from the whole process: from the purchase through repairs when they are needed. Educated consumers vote with their purchases, and brand loyalty is far less a determinant of what will be bought than it used to be. As more companies figure out how to make the entire sales-service cycle more convenient and reliable for the customer, competitive pressures rise with rising expectations.

Another wave of change that makes managers' ability to have the answers difficult involves employee attitudes and beliefs. Not only has the population in general become less willing to take orders than it once was, but the recent recession and attendant layoffs and downsizing have made employees increasingly cynical, suspicious, and unwilling to invest themselves even in needed organizational change efforts. A leading company like GE went from the unwritten agreement that loyal and competent performance meant a lifetime job to public statements by CEO Jack Welch that loyalty was no longer relevant and that GE owed its employees challenging and exciting jobs, but only as long as they performed at top level. As realistic as his statements might be, the shock waves in GE and other companies that were forced to reconsider obligations to employees (including IBM, AT&T, and DEC) have spread everywhere, and it is harder to generate the kind of employee commitment and initiative needed to transcend competitive pressures and the fast pace of change that I have mentioned.

Commitment and initiative become more important when the world is moving too fast for bosses to have all the answers. Increasing numbers of companies are more dependent than ever on their smart, well-educated employees, since only they have the technical know-how, the imagination, and close touch with the market to keep companies competitive. In a period when expenses have to be kept low, yet the pressures to compete and innovate are great, companies are highly dependent on tapping the talents of all who are employed (including contract employees or allied suppliers and customers—even competitors—in order to spread costs, risks, and talent).

The picture is not a pretty one, though it is challenging and exciting. Managerial jobs were never easy, but they are far more loaded and complex than ever before. Managers used to be able to think of themselves and act heroically, taking responsibility for everything, having the answers, making bold decisions when needed, but spending most of their time keeping the corporate ship on an even keel. Now they must find a way to go beyond heroism and make everyone else heroes and heroines. They have to mobilize scarce resources and get employees to figure out how to do more with less. They must generate the willingness for employees to take responsibility, even when that is risky; for employees to speak out when they know what the manager needs to know; and to seek new and better ways of doing everything.[1]

Perhaps entrepreneurs in start-up companies can still act as if they know more than anyone else and maintain a command system of heroic decision making. Even if they do, as their companies begin to grow, they rapidly find that they must build a team of subordinates as committed to the company's success as they are. Such entrepreneurs either learn to share responsibility or get edged out by their financiers, who recognize that new, more collaborative leadership is needed.

Yet leadership is not just about being nice so that subordinates will want to cooperate. In a fiercely competitive world, initiative is required of all employees, whose knowledge is not easily duplicated or passed upward for others to act on. Employee initiative, however, can also cause its own problems, even when it works. Highly initiating employees can be competitive, looking out for their own interests as they perceive them. In pursuing their ideas they can trample over the ideas and interests of their colleagues, who inevitably will have differing perspectives on issues, differing bits of information, and differing goals that reflect their own responsibilities. So leadership requires more than setting people free to follow their own stars.

Establishing sufficient autonomy to allow the full use of each person's talents yet inspiring all to work together toward the overall objectives of the organization is the core human challenge of running a company. By definition, organizations consist of more than one smart person sitting alone and doing all the work; finding the means to get the most from a cooperative endeavor requires careful thought, application of concepts and theories from many disciplines, extraordinary interpersonal skills, support of flexible organizational design, ongoing commitment to change, and the ability to learn and continue learning from experience. That is why management can be an extremely challenging but thrilling profession.

HOW THIS BOOK ADDRESSES THE CHALLENGES OF LEADERSHIP AND MANAGEMENT

Because the problems of management are so universal, many authors, academics, and practitioners have filled many pages with advice about how to lead, organize, control, develop, and otherwise manage people. Some of what has been written is even useful. But it is rare to find material that is not too academic and sterile at one extreme or not too restricted to one person's experience at the other. Even courses in these subjects offered by many of the best MBA programs do not always find a way to combine the conceptual with the practical, to mix analysis with skills practice. Nor do they create balanced learning experiences that can carry forward into the work world and both guide behavior in new situations and provide a framework that enables continued learning.

Continued learning is necessary because everything is not yet known about the subtle art and science of leading and managing. Such constant learning can be very frustrating when faced with a work group that is sabotaging rather than problem solving, when challenged by an old-timer who refuses to change, or when puzzled by two subordinates who insist on attacking each other rather than working together. However, the managerial world is too complex to have been fully dissected and turned into a series of formulas. Even if a great deal of what managers need to know is codifiable, it still has to be carried out by you—a wonderful, intelligent, and caring person, no doubt, but an involved player with your own style and idiosyncrasies, which some louts have trouble with despite your best intentions. That's the nature of managerial work; it isn't scientific manipulation by remote control, but the handiwork of living, breathing, and all-too-human individuals who are part of the action. A very wise professor once noted: When a manager is pointing his or her finger at a subordinate who just won't do what the manager wants, it is as important to note the person to whom the pointing finger is attached as it is to analyze the one pointed at![2]

While no book can provide the classroom experiences that allow for the practice of the human skills needed to lead effectively, this one represents a rare combination of the conceptual and the practical. Contributors were found among those faculty members known to teach excellent elective courses at top schools, so that all have a base of solid experience from which to write. The chapters are not, however, written in the stifling jargon of the academic world; each is down-to-earth and loaded with advice based on research, classroom experience, and observations from consulting. Nevertheless, unlike most of the popular literature on management, these chapters have an underlying rigor based on the best current academic research. The results are all too rare: forefront knowledge delivered in an accessible, fun-to-read style.

THE CHAPTERS AND THEIR GOALS

As has been discussed, the old notion of a manager as hero with all the answers no longer works. If the manager can't know, then the essence of leadership requires the sharing of responsibility with subordinates who can collectively come closer to developing the answers. But sharing responsibility does not automatically get everyone on board, pulling toward the same goals. Thus a key task for leaders today is the articulation and selling of a transforming vision of what it is that the organization (or subunit) does that is special, unique, and exciting. A well-formulated vision can induce people to cooperate and can inspire their best work. Peter B. Vaill explores the ways of using vision, its potency and limitation, in Chapter 2, entitled "Visionary Leadership."

Part of what an effective vision makes possible is the building of a team that genuinely shares responsibility for the unit's success with the nominal leader. Teamwork is much easier said than done. In Chapter 3, "Building High-Performance Teams," David L. Bradford shows how powerful an effective managerial team can be, and he shows how to develop one.

In order to have an effective team, every subordinate needs to be working at full potential and willing to collaborate with peers. Unfortunately, not all subordinates come ready to fit the bill. Stephen L. Fink shows in Chapter 4, "Managing Individual Behavior: Bringing Out the Best in People," how to diagnose and deal with diverse and difficult subordinates.

In complex, rapidly changing organizations, managers must be effective not only with subordinates, but with peers and superiors. Managing is as much an activity aimed laterally and upward as downward. The cooperation of people who have their own tasks, goals, and agendas is far from automatic. Thus it is critical to understand how to use influence and power to accomplish organizational ends, as revealed by Anne Donnellon in Chapter 5, "Power, Politics, and Influence: The Savvy and Substance of Action in Organizations." Another way of thinking about influence and power is found by examining the everyday negotiations of organizational life. These transactions are not always called negotiations, but they involve getting others to agree to do something. Roy J. Lewicki summarizes the useful insights from his course on negotiations in Chapter 6, "Negotiating Strategically."

Managing others is hard enough; managing oneself is particularly difficult—and critical. How can you build a career without becoming so preoccupied with your own success that you lose sight of the needs of others and of the organization in which you work? In Chapter 7, "Managing Yourself: Building a Career," Douglas T. Hall brings the latest thinking on managing one's career.

Management and leadership, of course, involve more than personal and interpersonal dealings. It is necessary to make many arrangements of people and policies to create the organizational framework that enables cooperative work to be done. Employees do what is needed for their own personal reasons, but they also respond to the kind of organization they are in—its rules, structure, and mores. Part II of this book, "Organizational Frameworks," addresses these issues. Phyllis F. and Leonard A. Schlesinger spell out in Chapter 8, "Designing Effective Organizations," the complex elements needed in order to design organizations that match tasks and structure to imperatives derived from the competitive environment yet are flexible enough to change when the environment does. Looking at how organizations change over time, the authors introduce the concept of culture and show how to help direct its impact on behavior.

Charles J. Fombrun and Drew Harris use Chapter 9, "Managing Human Resources Strategically," to explore in detail the human resource systems that are part of an organization's design, which are needed to ensure that the right people are hired and developed. They show the difference between human resource systems that support the newer demands on organizations and those that are designed for previous conditions.

Effective organizations are dependent not only on the systems and structures that apply to managerial jobs, but also on the arrangements by which employees at all levels are encouraged to make the maximum contributions to the mission. *Empowerment* is more than a hot buzzword; it is a competitive necessity. As organizations have discovered this compelling need, they have begun to experiment with new structures affecting employees on the factory floor or employees who deliver service on the front lines. In Chapter 10, "Self-Managing Teams: The New Organization of Work," Harvey Kolodny and Torbjorn Stjernberg bring the latest discoveries about self-managing teams. They examine the key elements utilized in producing remarkable results, without a conventional supervisory system, in several countries.

From a different perspective, R. Roosevelt Thomas, Jr., shows in Chapter 11, "Managing Diversity: Utilizing the Talents of the New Work Force," the critical need for ways to utilize the skills and knowledge of increasingly diverse employees. It is no longer effective to limit the kinds of people who can make vital contributions to success. He shows that managers must go beyond accepting differences to promoting the mutual learning of all organizational members, including those who are in the majority.

No matter how carefully an organization is designed to create the right atmosphere, structures, procedures, and managerial behavior, the nature of the rapidly changing environment that I have described means that major changes will be needed—frequently. The art of managing the process of change is conveyed by Todd Jick in Chapter 12, "Managing Change."

The conclusion reminds us just how complex the managerial world has become; in a chapter entitled "Conclusion: Future Leaders Must Be Global Managers," Rosabeth Moss Kanter shows the impact of the new world order—or disorder—on contemporary organizations and managers. She lets us see how global managers must use all the ideas, concepts, and insights given in the other chapters to deal with the challenges arising from the highly permeable national boundaries that used to insulate managements. And she brings us full circle as she emphasizes the centrality in complex global economic life of soft skills—managerial qualities of the heart—requiring the creation of trusting relationships with people from other cultures who may seldom be available for face-to-face meetings or even speak English. Soft skills make hard challenges, especially since they must be wedded to tough business decisions in a tough environment.

By bringing together the best of current leadership and management theory and practice, the authors anticipate that the interested reader will be able to build on existing skills and insight and will immediately begin to add greater value to current (and future) employers. The intense competitiveness of today's economic world makes outstanding leadership a basic necessity, not a luxury. The ability and willingness to plunge forward and make things happen when you lack all the desirable facts or support and then to step back and learn from the outcomes so that the next plunge does not carry you into deeper trouble are critical talents for any manager's career. Personal and organizational survival depend on these capacities to make every experience count.

The authors wish you success in your managerial efforts and even more success in continuing to learn from your experiences. No less will suffice.

NOTES

1. These ideas on the limits of heroism were developed in the book by David L. Bradford and Allan R. Cohen, *Managing for Excellence* (New York: John Wiley & Sons, 1984).

2. The wise professor referred to, Fritz Roethlisberger, wrote about the pointed finger in Chapter 9 of *The Elusive Phenomena* (Boston: Harvard Business School Press, 1977).

2 VISIONARY LEADERSHIP
Peter B. Vaill

INTRODUCTION

To begin our consideration of leadership and vision, and their role in organizations, consider the following quotation. The question is, what sort of an organization would describe itself this way?

> Messenger of sympathy and love
> Servant of parted friends
> Consoler of the lonely
> Bond of the scattered family
> Enlarger of the common life
> Carrier of news and knowledge
> Instrument of trade and industry
> Promoter of mutual acquaintance
> Of peace and of goodwill
> Among men and nations.

There are probably several kinds of organizations that might describe themselves this way. In fact, these 10 lines are literally chiseled in stone across the facade of the main building of the U.S. Postal Service in downtown Washington, D.C. The building dates from 1912, that is, from a time when the Postal Service was the Post *Office*, from a time when UPS, Federal Express, and other private sector competitors did not exist, from a time when a first class letter cost a nickel to send and "special delivery" meant your package would get to its destination by the next day, from a time when "neither snow, nor rain, nor heat, nor gloom of night stays these couriers from the swift completion of their appointed rounds."

12

The fact that today's Postal Service may be having more difficulty fulfilling the vision embodied in the 10-line inscription than it once did does not detract from the importance of the subject of the role that vision plays in organizational life. In fact, that a vision can be "overtaken by events" is what has made the subject important! If visions could be articulated once and for all with no fear of becoming obsolete or irrelevant, the whole issue would not occupy the place it has come to occupy in management education over the past perhaps 20 years. This whole question of the durability of vision will receive extensive treatment later in this chapter.

For the moment, though, let us consider the inscription for its own sake. It captures an essential quality of *vision* as it will be discussed in this chapter. We define *vision* as an expression that does not merely describe why an organization exists and what products and services it intends to deliver. A vision is a portrayal of an organization's intended activities and character in vivid terms that capture the organization's human meaning and value. A vision is full of possibility. A vision is a motivational statement as much as it is a descriptive statement. It expresses the *feeling* that those who hold it have for the organization and its work. The bare statement of why the organization exists and of what it intends to do we will call the "mission." Its human meaning and the difference that the mission makes in the world we will call the "vision." If the mission is the words, the vision is the music.

This chapter treats the process of creating and effectively communicating vision as the essential characteristic of leadership. There are many things a leader must know and be able to do. I will argue that a vision of what the organization and its products and services mean to its customers, its employees, and its other key constituents needs to be interwoven in leadership. Put another way, leadership behavior that is not infused with vision is not truly leadership.

This chapter is organized in four broad sections. We first consider at greater length what role the vision plays in the organization. The guiding question is, what is vision and what does it do? Included in this section is a discussion of why the whole subject has recently become much more important in management education and management practice. The second section then discusses the creation of visions by leaders. What are they doing when they are "envisioning?" In particular, I elaborate on the statement above that for organizational behavior to be *leadership* it must have vision woven all through it. The third section of the chapter discusses in some detail various methods for making vision real for organization members. In many ways, it is the most important section of the chapter and covers one of the most important problems in management practice today: After a leader has created a vision, how does he or she make it meaningful to others in the organization and among its external constituents? In the final section I discuss certain special problems of vision in organizations—problems that are occasioned by other trends and events in organizations and in the wider world. A key premise of the section is that even as the subject of vision has become more and more important, it is also becoming more and more difficult. The chapter ends, therefore, with a somewhat paradoxical view of a world of organizations in greater need than ever before of men and women who can bring vision to their work as leaders.

Before proceeding with these topics, though, I would like to explain the tone of this chapter: I assume that the reader is interested in leadership and vision because he or she would like to be a person who leads with vision, that is, that the reader has a personal vision of actively using the ideas in this chapter. I assume that it is not just curiosity that brings you to this chapter and book, but a desire to give living meaning to these ideas.

This concept of the reader or learner in an action role is in fact the hall-mark of professional education—for management as well as for law, medicine, or engineering. Professional education, as distinct from purely academic ed-ucation, assumes that the learner is actually going to do what is being dis-cussed and will do it at a high-level of quality and in keeping with standards of the profession. Thus, the tone of this chapter is action-oriented, and I quite honestly intend to motivate as well as inform the reader.

WHAT IS VISION AND WHAT DOES IT DO?

The nature of vision and the role it plays in human organizations is not as elusive or exotic as one might think from listening to all the rhetoric about the need for men and women of vision in our society. Vision is very common and ordinary; indeed, vision's power lies in its commonness and ordinariness. Vision's common and ordinary quality can be illustrated by a simple exercise in reflection.

I invite you to think about the best experience you have ever had in an organization—the most memorable experience, one you look back on fondly, that you enjoy thinking and talking about, even bragging about. It doesn't matter what kind of an organization it was or is, how important its mission, or how famous or successful it was or is by the world's standards. Some to whom I ask this question are presently in the best situation they've ever been in, but many are not. Some hark back to college, their adolescence, or even childhood. Some mention their families, but most do not. For some it is a sports experience; others mention military experiences. Voluntary organizations, such as fund raising, political campaigns, or charities often get mentioned, as do performing arts troupes. The main thing is that you be able to say that this was the most meaningful or one of the most meaningful organizational experiences you have ever had. Take a moment before continuing and think as fully as you can of what was or is for you "the best organizational experience I've ever had."

I have asked this question of hundreds of people. Rather uniformly, nearly everyone has some experience that fits the above evocation. Some people have many experiences to choose from; others have relatively few. There is a huge range of experiences reported. Virtually every kind of organization imaginable gets mentioned by one person or another. Typically, people are in some kind of a membership role in the organization they are thinking of—an employee, a dues-paying member, a volunteer. Occasionally people mention being a customer of the organization they are thinking of; some remember classes in which they were students; others recall hospitals in which they were patients. Interestingly, though, such individuals *talk* like actual members of the organization, even though technically they were not. Sometimes people remember with awe not the organizations that they were members of, but rather organizations they *competed against*.

It is not uncommon for people to remember organizational experiences in which they had a primary leadership role, but seemingly just as many people remember experiences in which they were in a relatively lowly position.

The thing that is most striking about all these experiences, despite their concrete variety, is what prompts the writing of this chapter: In one way or another, all of these memories are infused with a *vision* of what the organization was, of what it was trying to do, of what it could be, of what it meant to the people involved with it. Ask someone to recall the best organizational experience they've ever had, and they don't just remember a "job," an "assignment," or something they did for awhile because they needed the money or because it was a stepping-stone to something else. They remember the fullness of the impact of the organization on them. They remember how it filled up their lives—how they lived, ate, slept, breathed it. They remember, not always fondly, how hard they worked on its behalf and the price they often paid to be involved with the organization. They shake their heads in wonderment even many years later that the organization could have had that strong an impact on them. Often there are tears and occasionally anger and regret. *Always* there are stories—stories that have to be told. Stories that are full of drama, humor, conflict, incredible demonstrations of talent and skill—of victory, of course—but of tragedy and defeat as well. I have inadvertently discovered that the reason soldiers tell war stories is that for many of them their experiences in battle are the most memorable things that have ever happened to them.

Stories are concrete, and concreteness is the hallmark of a vision that has taken hold deeply in the members' minds and feelings. Such a vision may start out merely as an idea or verbal statement, but, if you're talking about the best experience you ever had, the vision will have moved beyond a mere idea for you and will have truly become the *spirit* of the organization. It is this spirit that is remembered so positively and vividly. And indeed, it is often remembered wonderingly: "It's amazing when you think about it," someone will say, thinking back, "how we could ever have gotten so wrapped up in the work and in each other. There's no way to explain it."

"No way to explain it" embodies both the promise and the paradox of organizational visions. They exert an incredibly powerful tug on people's emotions and on their willingness to contribute, but exactly *how* this happens and whether it can deliberately be *made* to happen are quite different matters.

The point of this exercise has been to give the reader some sense of the role, the power, and the elusiveness of what we are calling vision. The principal thrust of this chapter is the challenge to leadership posed by this essential but rather mysterious phenomenon of *organizational vision.* For the moment, however, let me develop one more major theme that is present in the memories we have of our best organizational experiences.

One of the main reasons that the experience is so memorable for you is that there was some fit between the vision that existed in the organization and the personal needs, expectations, hopes, fears, and indeed visions of yourself that you brought to the situation. You may have had a hand in fashioning the vision that came alive, but your contribution was not geared purely to what was needed in the situation and to the organization's official mission. Your contribution also reflected what you wanted, were prepared to contribute, and were capable of: your potential and also your limits. The same can be said of everyone else who was in the situation with you.

The point is that organizational vision is not some independent thing, apart from the human beings in the situation. It partly reflects the official mission and the requirements of the situation, but it also reflects the personal aspirations and energies of those who are there. It draws its vividness and its force from people, not from "situations" or "problems." Vision is not a separate objective fact. It is instead a living expression of shared meaning and commitment. The power of vision lies not merely in its content and its appropriateness for the situation. The power lies with the content and appropriateness *combined* with the feeling among members of its being shared. No individual feels that "I'm the only one who is really committed to this project" in organizations for which the vision is truly working effectively. Instead, the feeling that an individual has is that "I am part of something larger than myself—something I personally believe in, but something that everyone else really believes in, too." The vision is glue, binding people together in common effort and common values.

The phrase "a sense of common purpose" is another phrase often heard in connection with the "glue" that binds people together in common effort. For instructive purposes, this chapter treats the notions of a common vision and a common purpose as being very closely related and as different. Both phrases imply that a group shares a common positive meaning about something and that this meaning is energizing. The notion of vision stresses the clarity of *what* is felt to be meaningful—be it something tangible, like a building or a new product, or a desired event. The idea of purpose places more emphasis on the *desirability of pursuing* this thing, whatever it is. Purpose is the *reason* the thing is felt to be meaningful and desirable. Leadership, as discussed in the next section, involves both of these two meanings: Leaders both portray desirable states of affairs (visions) and give us reasons (purposes) for seeking the states of affairs. Vision and purpose combine to give organization members *clarity, consensus,* and *commitment.*[1]

To return to the subject of our most memorable organizational experiences, there is another way to talk about all this—an approach that will connect this discussion to the challenges that organizational leaders are facing today. In modern management parlance, you, the participant, are a "stakeholder" in the organization. The term is a brilliantly memorable extension of the meaning of the term *stockholder*. It was coined in the 1960s to capture the idea that there are more persons and organizations than just those with an equity ownership stake (stockholders) who care deeply about how an organization does. Even though these other stakeholders don't legally own the organization, they are not prevented from coming to have expectations of it and from trying to influence its direction. A word was needed to describe all those having a stake in the organization, because the sixties was a decade of an enormous expansion of the number of persons and groups in society who had begun to assert their entitlement to influence society's institutions. The antiwar and civil rights movements were just two of the most visible and audible members of the rising chorus. Joining them were the women's movement, the free speech movement among students, various environmental protection groups, consumer advocacy groups, antismoking lobbies, gun control advocates, voter registration partisans, internationalists, advocates for the inner cities, white collar unions, radical free-enterprisers, and me-generation self-developers—just to name a few of the more prominent new sets of stakeholders in society's major institutions.

This unprecedented explosion of would-be stakeholders created for all organizations an enormous dilemma: how to respond in good faith to the claims these groups were making, without fragmenting in all directions the traditional visions of themselves that the organizations had been pursuing. I must emphasize that it was not just the business corporation that felt this upsurge of claims on visions of itself; it was any organization. No organizational leadership could afford to continue thinking of its organization in the way that it always had, once the exponential increase in the number and variety of stakeholders' demands really got underway. Some organizations were not able to adapt and either went out of existence or shrank into insignificance. But most major institutions were able to begin accommodating themselves—which is to say, refashion their vision—to the social changes that were occurring. The ongoing accomodation continues to this day, for we have truly become a global "entitlement society" in which there is no way to predict who will define themselves as stakeholders and what claims, legitimate or not, they will assert.

The stakeholder idea can be applied to all organizations—public and private, profit and nonprofit, large and small, domestic and international. As just noted, there is virtually no limit to the number of those who might become stakeholders in a particular organization, but the most common groups are customers, suppliers, owners, regulators, neighbors, competitors, and— significantly—employees at all levels, including managers up to the top of the organization. Some organizations might have unique groups of stakeholders. For example, Johnson & Johnson, the giant pharmaceutical company, declares *babies* to be one of its most important groups of stakeholders.[2] Or a nuclear power plant might have unborn generations as stakeholders, at least we would hope so, because of the long half-life of nuclear waste. Governmental agencies try to keep "the public interest" before them at all times, which is in effect a decision to define society at large as a stakeholder and to try not to let any single group of individuals (stakeholders) exercise undue influence. Governmental agencies, of course, do have continuing problems with special interest groups who seek special treatment. All the more reason for such agencies to be as clear as they can be in their "vision" of the public interest!

One of the key things about the stakeholder idea is that the stakeholders define their own stake in the organization; the organization doesn't define it for them. Each stakeholder is working within his or her own set of expectations of what the organization should do for it. It is not an exaggeration to say that these expectations themselves are a stakeholder's *vision*—a vision of how the organization ought to work. It is what you were remembering with your best organizational experience: how the organization fulfilled your own vision. That's what made it a best experience *for you*. However, *all* the stakeholders are seeking the same thing, whether they are succeeding or not. The stake is the meaning that the stakeholder wants the organization to have, that is, what the consequences will be of a satisfactory or an unsatisfactory relationship.

The leadership and managerial stakeholders, as is now clear, are in a special position. Unlike everyone else, they have an official responsibility for the fulfillment of the organization's mission, which earlier I said was the bare, unvarnished statement of why the organization exists and of what it intends to do. Leaders' and managers' principal stake is in the fulfillment of this mission. Their vision—their enrichment of the mission with energy and color—must be expressive of what the mission *means* to them. And their vision cannot ignore the visions of all the other stakeholders: all their expectations, needs, wishes, wants, aversions, prejudices, demands, and even threats.

Somehow, the vision of an organization's leadership must synthesize, integrate, and transform all the separate visions into an overarching one within which stakeholders can unite and cooperate effectively. The leadership's vision bears a constraint, in other words, that is true of no other stakeholder's: The leadership's vision must integrate as best it can all the *other* visions that are held. Even if the leadership is the first to articulate a vision, as in the case of a new business start-up, it must still take account of the other visions that stakeholders will come to have.

The task is sobering—to confront all the various visions of the organization that are held by its various stakeholders and to realize that they do not necessarily have anything to do with each other! In other words, it is easy for an organization's leaders to find themselves juggling the conflicting expectations (visions) of its various stakeholders as to what proper conduct is. When Harlan Cleveland, one of the most insightful of modern commentators, calls modern organizational leadership the "get-it-all-together profession," he is speaking of just this juggling act.[3] Organization leaders and managers frequently find themselves in an impossible cross fire, expected, as they say, to be all things to all people. It is not surprising that so many senior executives, especially profit-conscious business executives, resist new calls for social responsibility and increased service to their various stakeholders. It is not that they are irresponsible in some absolute sense, or that they necessarily deserve any of the other names they are frequently called, but rather that they are not eager further to complicate their lives with new stakeholders or higher levels of obligation to existing stakeholders. The job is already tough enough, in their view.

Thus, the stakeholder idea helps us to see the real leadership challenge that senior managers face. They are not free to ignore the idea of vision and to make do with specific objectives, because then their objectives will simply be caught in the cross fire of other stakeholders' demands (visions). Nor are they free arbitrarily to declare their personal vision of what the organization should be and do, for they inevitably will come into conflict with other visions. They have no choice but to think of vision as something that must come to infuse the whole, with themselves as the principal inventors of how this can happen. They have to learn to incorporate the new perspectives into their views of the organization, no matter how clumsily and haltingly. This learning process is the number-one challenge facing organization leaders today. In the next section, we take up in more detail just what leadership with vision entails.

LEADERSHIP WITH VISION

It will be difficult to talk about visionary leadership if we are constantly pausing to note its dangers and defects. A great deal can go wrong with visionary leadership; it is not a panacea. But let us discuss how its works ideally in a leader's actions and how it works when a leader is acting competently and in good faith. It will be easier afterward to note some of the key assumptions and dangers.

"An executive ought to *want* something," says David S. Brown, professor emeritus of public administration at George Washington University. Brown's remark is deceptively simple. Behind it are many years of observing executives in both the public and private sectors who don't seem to want anything in particular. They are content, apparently, to preside over the system pretty much as they found it. Their actions tend to be restricted to the problems that come *to* them. Of course, there is no dearth of such issues, so they can manage to stay very busy. However, quoting Russell Ackoff, one of the fathers of system theory and of strategic management, they are "reactive" leaders.[4] They are letting events—often crises—in the organization dictate their actions. They don't act until they have to. They are following a recipe without having exercised any choice over what dish they are cooking.

As noted in the previous section, the pace of change in the late twentieth century has rendered the reactive style obsolete. It is forcing all organizations to decide anew what dishes they want to cook. The recipes from their past are only partially useful at best, and sometimes former recipes (strategies) will take them in directions that they absolutely should not want to go. To put this point explicitly in managerial terms, David Hurst, a Canadian steel executive and management writer, has said "that the present challenge to management is to innovate—to find tomorrow's business."[5] This means disenthralling ourselves from present visions that may have served us for decades. It means looking beyond missions and objectives that already exist and formulating new visions of what the organization might be and do in the future.

We must be careful, however, not to set up a false dichotomy here. Just because events have rendered a purely reactive style obsolete, it does not mean that leaders should go to the other extreme and unilaterally impose their vision and will on the organization. As noted in the previous section, there are too many diverse stakeholders, and they are too smart and too well-funded and supported by societal values, for a leader to assume that his or her vision can just be announced and that everyone else (the stakeholders) will then docilely fall in line. Furthermore, in today's complex world, we probably would not even want a situation where a single person was the only source of vision for an organization. There is too great a chance of the vision being wrong, inappropriate for the circumstances, incomplete, out-of-touch. If a corporation's markets increasingly exist overseas, yet the CEO is not able personally to envision what the international possibilities are, would we not want that person to tap many other perspectives from inside and outside the organization in fashioning a vision? If a university is increasingly acquiring a graduate and professional student body, but its president's personal vision is primarily oriented toward the challenge of undergraduate education, would we not want that president to be open to other views (visions) of the institution's future?

An additional danger in heavy reliance on the creative vision of one person can be expressed with the question, where are these people when we need them? The idea of vision is strongly and popularly associated with a single "visionary leader" who somehow sees what is needed and possible and can inspire others with that vision. We know that there have been thousands of such men and women throughout history. The problem is that we can't call them forth on demand, that is, we can't plan their emergence at the moment in time when they are needed. Because of this association of "vision" with a single person, it is easy to believe that without one an organization is doomed to mediocrity at best. That need not be the case, but it does leave open the question of how vision can arise in an organization even though there is no single charismatic source. I will have more to say about it.

So, even as the day of the purely reactive, firefighting executive is over, so too has the modern world called into question the tradition of the single "man on a white horse" who boldly and charismatically cries "That way!" and then leads the charge. There are still both sorts of leaders around, to be sure, but we cannot limit our discussion of vision to the magic of a single person. With the sophisticated, well-funded stakeholders noted above surrounding and permeating the organization, the *process* of developing and implanting a vision is becoming more and more complicated as time goes on. Yet the *need* for vision continues undiminished.

In the previous section I described the similarity of the notions of common vision and common purpose. Those who create vision we say are "visioning." In the same sense, we may say that those who articulate purposes are engaged in "purposing," even though the term is not often heard. In an earlier essay, describing what leaders do in high-performing organizations, I defined *purposing* as that continuous stream of actions by an organization's formal leadership that has the effect of inducing clarity, consensus, and commitment regarding the organization's basic purposes.[6] *The visions— the vivid and memorable stories, pictures, images, metaphors, slogans, and other symbols—that leaders offer should have the effect of crystallizing a sense of purpose.* Vision, in other words, doesn't guarantee a sense of common purpose. A vision could merely entertain people, it could cause fear among them, or it could create conflict among them; it helps create a common *view* of a given subject but not automatically a common commitment. The essential *leadership* act is to create visions that bring people together and give them a sense of common purpose. "The inculcation of belief in the real existence of a common purpose," said the pioneer management theorist Chester Barnard, "is an essential executive function."[7] It is not any old vision that a leader should be interested in, but rather one that reinforces the kinds of purposes that are needed in the organization in order for it to prosper and fulfill its reason for existing. That explains why David Brown's remark about the executive *wanting* something is so important.

Effective acts of visioning and purposing need not necessarily be elaborate statements. They can be very simple—*if* they convey a mission-relevant message and convey it in a way that everyone can understand. "Nuts!" was General Anthony C. McAuliffe's famous reply to the Nazi ultimatum to surrender at Bastogne. The *vision* and purpose that the epithet conveys is that surrender is unthinkable. "Threepeat!" was a word that Los Angeles Lakers coach Pat Riley came up with to launch the 1988–1989 season after the team had won the professional championship the two previous seasons. Although the team was not successful because of the determination and inspired play of the Detroit Pistons, "Threepeat!" was a guiding image for the Lakers throughout the season. It and General McAuliffe's call are about as vividly compact vision statements as one could ask for. As another example, AMF Inc.—a conglomerate that included Alcort Sailboats, Brunswick bowling equipment, Spaulding athletic equipment, as well as other recreational products—came up with the phrase "We Make Weekends" as an overarching vision of what the whole company was about.

Interestingly enough, the AMF vision was originally an advertising slogan; but that does not disqualify it as a possible vision statement for other stakeholders, such as employees. One of the most famous examples of a vision aimed at customers that was probably also a powerful motivating influence for employees was Lee Iacocca's personal guarantee, in Chrysler TV ads, accompanied by an authoritative slap on the hood of a car: "If you can find a better car built in America, buy it!" Iacocca's proclamation was aimed at Chrysler customers, but it is likely that employees were watching the ad, too. Given that Chrysler was struggling back from the brink of bankruptcy, it may well have fostered pride and hope in them, even as it stimulated demand for the company's cars. It is a powerful vision: "Our boss actually believes we can make it!" Similar corporate slogans that can potentially have a powerful motivating effect on employees might be Weyerhauser's description of itself as "the tree-growing company," Du Pont's "better things for better living through chemistry," an early motto of International Harvester—"our field is the world," GE's well-known "we bring good things to life," and Ford's "quality is job one."

If—and it is a big if—employees can see these vivid phrases being valued and lived up to in their daily experience of company operations, then these phrases can function as authentic vision statements. However, if employees see these phrases being violated, not only does it make them cynical about the phrases, it becomes less likely that they will believe *any* "calls to arms" that the organization leadership offers. The message to corporate leadership is a simple one: *Do not proclaim a vision you do not believe in. Do not proclaim a vision just for effect. Be aware that people have a deep need for this sort of inspiration, but that if they become disappointed and cynical, it can be worse than if you had not tried to inspire them with vision in the first place.*

One of the most famous vision statements by a corporate leader, which was believed by its creator and which came to galvanize an entire company, was Theodore N. Vail's vision for the original AT&T, enunciated in the 1920s: "We will build a telephone system so that anyone, anywhere in the world, can talk with anyone else, cheaply, quickly, and satisfactorily." This became the Bell System's vision of "universal service." It rivals all other organizational visions for the power it came to exert over the thinking and actions of Bell System employees. Perhaps only "Semper Fidelis," the motto of the Marine Corps, and the "We the People" preamble to the U.S. constitution could be said to have exerted influence of similar depth.

It is not just the rhetoric, however, for rhetoric is not by itself the act of leadership. The *leadership* is composed of the combination of clarity and commitment: These two ingredients then make possible the third—consensus. If the top leadership is unclear and uncommitted, it will not be able to foster organization-wide commitment. In the early 1980s, for example, the CEO of one of the nation's largest consumer products companies spoke to his top 100 executives and offered this vision: "We will build the business through providing superior consumer satisfaction and value." This vision occurs on page 1 of a 20-page prepared text. Its literal meaning is that they would focus on the consumer and that the health of the business (sales, shares of market, profits, and so on) will follow. The remaining 19 pages never again mention the consumer or providing products of the highest quality. The entire remainder of the text is taken up with setting performance targets in terms of increases in sales, shares of market, profit margins, and the like—the "build the business" factors. It is important to understand that a focus on consumer satisfaction and a focus on maximizing financial performance can lead to very different actions by executives. Not surprisingly, people walked out of that meeting quite confused about what the boss really wanted. If there was a vision, it was of a financially successful organization, not of one that was willing to do whatever necessary to provide "superior consumer satisfaction and value."

In short, vision is not rhetoric. Vision may use rhetoric, but it is not the same thing. An example of a relatively nonrhetorical vision is that of Tandem Computer, as envisioned by CEO James Treybig.[8] Treybig expresses his vision in five operating principles, all of which are phrased in a very down-to-earth way:

1. All people are good.
2. "People," "workers," "company," and "management" are all names for the same thing.
3. Every single person in the company must understand the essence of the business.
4. Every employee must benefit from the economic successes of the business.
5. Management must create an environment where all of the above can happen.

There is a multiplicity to these five statements. They form a collage of meaning. They include ideas about how people are regarded, how they will be treated, what they must understand, and what the leadership responsibility is for making it all happen. Interestingly, Treybig's fifth principle is anticipated in an early list of operating principles of Lincoln Electric Company, arguably the most continuously successful U.S. corporation of the twentieth century. Lincoln has as its fundamental vision this remarkable notion: "A better and better product at a lower and lower price." Lincoln's specific values differ a bit from Treybig's, but they also have on their list, "non-stop repetition by management of the corporate operating philosophy." I stated that *purposing* generally is a *continuous stream of actions by an organization's leadership*; Treybig's and Lincoln Electric's insistence that management live the corporate philosophy reflects that definition.

What about the organizational conditions that encourage or discourage the emergence of visionary leaders? I have stated that visionary statements and actions are not purely products of the overwhelming will of single individuals. Are there some kinds of organizational conditions that make it more likely that a person's or group's vision might come to have meaning in the organization as a whole? Not a great deal is known on this subject, but it is possible to speculate a bit. In Table 2-1, I have listed eight kinds of factors that may influence a person's or group's potential for visionary leadership.

Each of the factors can be viewed as a continuum, the two ends of which are listed. The hypothesis is that the more each factor lies at the "encouraging" end of the continuum, the greater the likelihood that these persons or groups will be able to make their visions meaningful to others in the organization. The table helps explain why so many visionary leaders never have the impact in their organization that they would like to have. They may

TABLE 2-1

Factors Possessed by Potentially Visionary Person or Group	Effect on Vision Effectiveness	
	Encouraging	Discouraging
Credibility with others	High	Low
Positioning relative to the top of the unit in question	At or near	Far from
Relevance of ideas to main mission of unit in question	Clear or close	Unclear or not close
Ability to draw others in	High	Low
Likelihood of long-term commitment to vision	High	Low
Organization members' readiness for new vision	High	Low
Other encouraging factors	Many	Few
Other discouraging factors	Few	Many

have a powerful personal vision, which may in time be proved dead right, but if there are not enough of the "encouraging" factors above lined up in their favor, they might as well be shouting into the wind.

The words "unit in question" are used in Table 2-1 to signal that we need not consider only the total organization. We could be talking about a division or department. Vision is needed at all levels of an organization. The vision articulated from the very top should encompass the whole, as has been said, but there may well be a need for bringing the overall vision to a sharper focus in specific component units. This is the responsibility of the leadership of those units. Such leaders shouldn't depend on the very top people to provide all the inspiration. Vision doesn't automatically just cascade down the hierarchy; at each level it needs to be revivified by leaders who have thought deeply about what the vision means for them and their people. If the vision from the top is vague or confusing, it is even more important that leaders of component units take responsibility for clarifying the vision and focusing it on the main mission of the unit.

I draw this section to a close with observations on a subject of great contemporary importance in organizations: *empowerment.* The term embodies a vision that calls for a substantial increase in the influence that lower-level employees will have in an organization that adopts an empowerment philosophy. In the early nineties, it is an idea that many hundreds of organizations in all sectors of society are experimenting with. The surge of interest is due partly to the ideas of so-called total quality management systems, as fathered by W. Edwards Deming and others;[9] is due partly to the Malcolm Baldrige award's specific support for employee empowerment; is due partly to excellence guru Tom Peters's emphasis on pushing decision-making authority to the lowest possible level;[10] and is due partly to the preparation that research on the delegation of authority and on so-called participative management has provided over the past forty years. In other words, it is not as if managers are hearing for the first time about the value of trying to create more autonomy and initiative at lower levels of the organization. Still, empowerment has an appeal, and it has received a commitment from line managers that these earlier concepts never quite achieved.

But what, employees are asking, does empowerment really *mean?* What picture (vision) of life at lower levels of the organization does the word convey? What picture of relationships *between* various levels of the hierarchy does the word convey? Employees everywhere are asking, "Is management really serious?" We can see in empowerment a very important vision that is in the process of being born—or sadly, in many organizations, in the process of becoming an empty promise that does not inspire anyone and in fact may be creating cynicism and resistance. The leadership challenge with empowerment is to "fill out the story" in a way that intrigues, inspires, and excites employees and then begin quickly to take the specific actions that employees will perceive as actions that reinforce the vision.

Here is a definition of empowerment that I have tried out on several top management teams who say they are committed to the concept:

> Empowerment exists in an organization when lower level employees feel that they are *expected* to exercise initiative in good faith on behalf of the mission even if it goes outside the bounds of their normal responsibilities; and if their initiative should lead to a mistake—even a serious one—they trust that they will not be arbitrarily penalized for having taken that initiative.

In other words, this definition supports a vision that might thus be phrased: When you see something that needs to be done, do it! Don't wait to be told to do it, don't sweep the problem under the rug, don't blame it on someone else.

Most of the senior managers who have read this definition are uncomfortable with it. It seems to them to be a license to act irresponsibly. A careful reading will show that it does not encourage that at all, but the point is that it does trigger a *vision* of irresponsible action in the minds of at least some executives who are interested in empowerment philosophy. As one executive vice president of a Fortune 50 company said after reading this definition, "No, that's too extreme. Real empowerment is telling the people what you want from them, giving them the tools to do it, and leaving them alone." Notice what a very different "vision" of empowerment this is, and notice how much more managerial control it retains compared to the first definition. It leaves management in charge of setting the tasks, determining the relevant tools, and determining the people who will be involved. It also leaves the initiative for communication in management's hands.

The contrast between these two definitions illustrates the problem that a managerial leader faces with any new idea or program. As soon as it is announced, various stakeholders inside and outside the organization begin to envision what it means for them, that is, to see themselves affected in various ways by it. Too many managements forget or underestimate this often feverish visioning that is going on throughout the organization. They don't realize that it is unlikely that clarity, consensus, and commitment will spontaneously and naturally emerge. This is the real meaning of leading with vision: transforming all the various images, hopes, fears, expectations, and desires to contribute toward a way of talking about the organization and its affairs that the majority can commit to.

MAKING VISION REAL

"Each of us sits in a long, dark hall," wrote Herbert Simon, Nobel Prize–winning decision theorist and one of the fathers of organization theory and of artificial intelligence, "within a circle of light cast by a small lamp. The lamp light penetrates a few feet up and down the hall, then rapidly attenuates, diluted by the vast darkness of future and past that surrounds it."[11] Vision, one might say, is the attempt to extend, even a little bit, Simon's lamp light and to provide members of an organization with a feeling for the reality and the significance of what the organization is trying to do. In this section, attention turns to some specific things leaders can do to *make the vision real* for others.

Probably the two most common methods by which leaders make their personal vision real for others are inspirational speech making and personal, intimate conversation with individuals. We see politicians employ such methods constantly, but organizational executives use them effectively as well. Leaders have been making dramatic speeches, filled with vivid and inspiring images, throughout history. Likewise, they have been exercising a personal touch with their followers. Shakespeare, for example, has Henry V on the night before the Battle of Agincourt "walking from watch to watch, from tent to tent . . . That every wretch, pining and pale before,/Beholding him, plucks comfort from his looks." Tom Peters has made MBWA (management by wandering around) a strategic activity for one who would lead toward excellence.[12]

The speech to a large group gives the leader the opportunity to develop the vision in detail, to provide the stories and the metaphors and to link them to the reality that people are experiencing, and to infuse the words and images with personal energy and feeling. By contrast, the close-up, one-on-one contact gives the leader the chance to adjust the vision to the particular concerns of individuals; and equally important, close contact gives the leader a sense of how people are reacting to the vision. Additionally, it sends a powerful message to everyone that the leader cares enough about the vision to take the time to deliver it personally.

These two tried-and-true methods are still probably the most effective methods that we have. But over the past few decades an additional class of methods has evolved that does not depend so heavily on a single leader having the vision and imparting it either in spellbinding oratory or the tête-à-tête. We might call these *group-centered* methods, because their essence is that the vision at least partially—and often entirely—grows out of the ideas and vision of organization members, rather than originating with the leader. The leadership that the leader provides is in helping vision to emerge from the members—and it is important leadership indeed. The premise of the many varieties of group-centered approaches is that people support what they have a hand in creating; since vision is so important, the argument goes, the more people that can be part of creating it, the more likely they will be to support it.

On the assumption that speeches and tête-à-têtes are well-understood leadership methods, I will say no more about them in this section and instead devote attention to further comments on group-centered methods. It should be noted that, in the discussion that follows, we are thinking of a variety of different organizational configurations when we define *group-centered*. It could be the top management of an organization; it could be the leadership of a division of an organization; it could be all members of the organization (although involving more than about one hundred people can get quite unwieldy); it could be two or three groups who are coming together for the first time, as in a corporate merger or reorganization; it could in fact be any set of people who need a common vision.

There are two aspects of group-centered methods, each of which is quite important. The first has to do with the circumstances in which a group of organization members, such as a top executive team, are brought together to engage in joint visioning. The second aspect deals with the specific activities that they engage in to produce a common vision. There is a great deal of quite creative work going on presently in both areas, because both are integral to the emergence of a vision that possesses clarity, consensus, and commitment.

With regard to the first aspect, there is general agreement that the office with its normal modes of conduct is not an effective place for meeting to create a vision. There are too many interruptions, too many competing items on the group's agenda, or too many temptations to duck out of the meeting for phone calls or other personal business. Furthermore, the office culture, with its consciousness of roles, responsibilities, and reporting relationships can get in the way of the egalitarian mood a group needs to develop a shared vision. Even such things as the relatively formal attire that pervades most office environments can be a hindrance to the kind of creative thinking that is needed to evolve a common vision. Finally, most office environments do not have the physical spaces and resources that we have learned we need for effective group interaction: open, flexible rooms with lots of wall space; a variety of possible seating configurations; availability of materials with which visual models can be built; and an ambience that invites and stimulates creative thinking. It is quite sobering, in fact, to consider just how much the typical office environment *discourages* collaborative visionary thinking. Perhaps if the modern office had not evolved as a place so unfriendly to visioning work, there would not be so many organizations today that lack a strongly shared vision of who they are and what they can accomplish.

With the office not a felicitous place for visioning work, most organizations have come to make more and more use of retreats or off-site meetings. Conference facilities of commercial hotels have been most often used, but organizations increasingly are building their own facilities. Organizations whose business is to conduct retreats are also springing up. There is presently a great deal of innovation going on in the design of learning environments in which visioning work as well as other kinds of creative problem solving can take place. In fact, it is not an exaggeration to say that the design of these settings is becoming so elaborate that there is a danger of a reverse effect, occurring when the setting is so self-consciously designed for creativity that participants can't get their minds off it—with the creative work they are there to do correspondingly inhibited!

Closely related to the nature of the setting within which the vision work is to occur are the actual activities that the participants engage in. This is the second key aspect of group-centered methods for generating vision. There has been much experimentation and many innovations. Increasingly, completely worked-out approaches have been developed in which a set of activities has been carefully designed and sequenced and supporting workbooks and software developed. The claim is that a team that goes through the steps under the guidance of a trained workshop leader will end up with a shared vision for its organization. I cannot undertake in this chapter to critique all the various approaches that are proliferating. Instead, I will briefly describe eight kinds of processes that arise with most methods. By implication, we are saying that whether an organization uses a predesigned approach or invents one as it goes along, the following factors can be expected to play an important role in a successful visioning workshop:

1. *Create fruitful interaction.* This includes talking to people in the organization one normally doesn't get to talk to; talking about things one normally doesn't get to talk about; talking at a more personal level than one often does; talking in settings, such as mountain hikes or midnight bull sessions, that one usually doesn't share with other organization members.

2. *Create greater team feeling.* This is one result of increased interaction, but it is an objective in its own right. Too often, organization members need to develop greater team feeling and sense of a common fate before it makes sense to generate a common vision. Team feeling is fostered by performing various tasks, often under competitive conditions, that bring people into much closer relations with each other.

3. *Create perspective on organization issues.* Vision needs to be created from a perspective that is broader than usual for members collectively to have. Various exercises get members looking at where the world is

going and what roles the organization might play in the emerging conditions. Analysis of the nature and needs of various stakeholders can be carried out in detail. If tradition is important, attention will also be given to where the organization has been and what it means for the future. Often members of the organization learn things about the organization and its environment that they have never heard before—both opportunities and threats. The experience is genuinely enlightening and can be a powerful stimulus to clearer vision.

4. *Make leaders accessible.* This is one of the most important benefits of these off-site workshops: giving the persons in authority an opportunity to show sides of themselves that are hidden by the ordinary office culture. What the boss really thinks about the organization can be a crucial stimulus to vision. Sometimes the boss needs quite a bit of coaching on this matter, of course, because it is a fine line between saying clearly what one thinks and feels and dominating the meeting or suppressing other views. When properly done, though, some reflections from the boss on what he or she sees for the future and wants for the organization can empower people to take risks, say things out loud, or make public commitments that they might otherwise withhold.

5. *Expose and work through conflicts.* Inevitably, any discussion of something as fundamental as the organization vision will probably produce differences of opinion and often quite pointed conflict. If these differences aren't recognized and worked through, they will reappear in people's interpretations of the vision itself and the common commitment that is so important will not be achieved.

6. *Uncover and highlight feelings.* Enthusiasm is not just a frequent by-product of these sessions; it is an essential element. As has been repeatedly said about vision, it is more than just an abstract idea about the organization. It is a personally meaningful picture of what the organization can be, of what its human value can be, and of the role the person who holds the vision can play in helping all this to happen. Enthusiasm, passion, commitment, optimism, a sense of urgency—these feelings are key. If they are not emerging in a workshop devoted to creating vision, it is likely that whatever is being discussed is not very interesting to participants.

7. *Determine next steps and reentry back home.* It is easy to forget in the excitement of visioning that the success of the event depends on what participants take back to the workaday organization, what they tell those who did not attend, what steps they take to begin implementing the vision, and so on. If participants don't spend some time at the workshop talking about this, it is less likely to get done once everyone is back on

the job. If a vision is not having much impact on the organization, it is likely that too little attention was given to follow-up work after the vision workshop.

8. *Institutionalize this process for creating and re-creating vision.* One frequently hears participants at these workshops ask, why don't we work this way more often? In other words, the experience does show participants a different way of working. It can give them ideas for how they might modify their regular organizational culture, and it can give them ideas for future retreats. This is important learning, for there may also be counterforces at work that suggest that a successful off-site vision workshop need never be repeated.

These eight processes arise repeatedly in vision workshops. The first seven are necessary to a successful single event; the eighth factor is needed for an organization to keep its vision fresh and meaningful over time. Highly effective vision workshops will give attention to all eight of these factors. Less successful workshops will ignore or downplay one or more of these eight.

The role of the organization's leadership in a group-centered process of creating vision is very important. It is the leadership that decides that a group's time on the issue of vision is important, that makes resources available, that models by its own actions the significance of the effort, that uses its visibility and authority to articulate the vision openly and forcefully, that provides "push" and support for subsequent efforts to implement the vision once it has been formulated, that takes on the inevitable cynics and the naysayers. At virtually every step along the way, it is critical that the formal leadership understand and show how important it is to have a vision for which there is clarity, consensus, and commitment. This is an emerging leadership role. As recently as the early eighties it was hardly understood as a way to exercise leadership. It is a role that has become more and more important as complexity and uncertainty have increased and as more and more stakeholders have sought involvement in the creation of vision for the organization.

The leader's *personal* vision, we might say, is to foster and sustain an organization that possesses vision. This does not mean that the leader plays no role in creating the substantive vision itself, but rather that the leader's own vision needs to actualize *both* the content of the vision *and* the process of making it meaningful to others.

In today's turbulent organizational world, leaders who possess only substantive vision for what the organization should be and do are seriously handicapped, because they will not understand the process by which their ideas can become meaningful to others. They need what might be called a "process vision" of how their substantive ideas and those of others can come to inspire people in the organization. And "process vision" is not too flowery a term, because the process cannot merely be a series of mechanical steps. These vision workshops and other off-site retreats must feel to participants like a good use of time. They must engage and inspire the participants. They must uplift participants beyond the normal frame of mind adopted for organization meetings. The various activities participants are asked to undertake must have credibility.

It is not an exaggeration to say that the leadership role in the process of visioning is becoming more important than its role in the actualization of the vision. The latter will always be important, of course, particularly in smaller organizations, but the organizations of the future that achieve and then fulfill their visions will be ones whose leadership understands the process of visioning.

SPECIAL PROBLEMS OF VISION IN ORGANIZATIONS

Enough has been said up to this point for the reader to realize both how important and how complicated vision is. Leadership with vision is by no means just another management skill. The visioning process can be quite fragile, even in the most well-led and successful organizations. Moreover, because the organizational world is so dynamic, it is unlikely that we will ever solve the problem of vision, making it less elusive. In this final section, I have identified five kinds of special problems that organization leaders can expect will mark the next few years of work on creating and implementing vision in organizations.

1. Multiculturalism and Diversity

All organizations are becoming more demographically heterogeneous (diverse in terms of race, religion, national origin, ethnicity, gender, age, physical ability, and language preference). Multiculturalism and diversity pose challenges to managerial leaders on all fronts because so many of the ideas that we think make up a good organization and a good management are in fact culture-bound. I have written about this problem at some length elsewhere.[13]

Vision is affected by increased heterogeneity quite directly and deeply. I have stated repeatedly that the vision needs to appeal to people at the level of their personal needs for meaning. Yet the wider the range of their values and experience, the more difficult that is to do. We are at the beginning of understanding what *intercultural* visioning may be like. There is certainly plenty of experience with the *failure* to achieve a vision that spans culture, as can be seen from the history of racial conflict in North America and the religious conflicts of the Middle East. It is tempting, apparently, to develop a vision that sets your group *against* another group, rather than one that bridges the groups. More and more we are going to see this problem inside organizations as well as in society at large.

2. Loss of Vision

The very rapid pace of technical, economic, and social change has created a situation in which many organizations that once had a clear and powerful vision have lost it. It is doubtful, for example, that the old Post Office vision with which we began is very meaningful to the current work force. Theodore N. Vail's vision for AT&T of universal service was also cited. That vision has now been rendered obsolete by AT&T's divestiture of its operating companies in 1984. Countless other organizations, including some of society's noblest institutions, have seen their vision overtaken by events.

Because of the nature of vision, its loss can be traumatic. Vision is not a mere fact about the organization; it expresses the human meaning and value of the organization. When the vision dies, in the eyes of some the organization has died; *they* might as well have died, some may feel. William Bridges has written movingly about the need for people to have time to grieve over the loss of old ways of working and valuing.[14] They cannot be expected to quickly adopt a new vision to go with their changed circumstances. If the psychological significance of vision loss is not taken into account, the entire subsequent process of renewal can be affected.

3. The Need for Transforming Vision

In this chapter I have written of vision as something that undergirds all organizational operations. I have not insisted that vision necessarily be heroic or an order of magnitude different from the organization's ordinary mode of operations. However, the rapid rates of change and the increasing turbulence that organizations are living with and will continue to live with are forcing them to produce visions that take them substantially beyond anything they may have done before. They are finding the need to envision a whole new mode of operations—new missions, new customers, new technologies, new ways of acting toward employees and other stakeholders. The word *transformation* has become the popular name for what needs to happen to the thinking of organization members, especially leaders.

Although there is a great deal of excitement and romance associated with the idea of organizational transformation, we don't know very much about how to do it.[15] The *vision* of transformation has not yet been fulfilled.

Probably the closest thing to transformation are the changes that American corporations have made in response to the Japanese challenge. Such forced changes, however, may be primarily driven by a negative vision, a vision of "extinction." The positive view of vision that has been taken in this chapter is much more difficult to come by. This may be an appropriate place to note that the pride that the American businessperson seems to take in "running scared" is not actually a very wise strategy for leading an organization: Only so much motivation can be squeezed from fear before people either become inured to the alarms or else find ways of protecting themselves from the thing that is feared. Leaders who create visions designed to frighten employees into heroic acts are being very shortsighted.

4. Cynicism

Vision is about hope. Vision involves a measure of trust and of willingness to believe that things can be dramatically better. It involves trusting those who are creating vision—trusting their motives, trusting their moral character. Modern society contains many people who have been bitterly disappointed—by their families, their employers, their government, their friends. Furthermore, there have been many colorful leaders of the past half-century whose visions have not brought the good things that they promised. The developed world has become a society within which it is harder and harder to articulate a vision and be believed; it may even be harder and harder to generate the faith within oneself, as discussed in the following. But if vision is to continue to have the inspiring effect that is needed, we have to find ways of combating the doubters and the naysayers. Some years ago, the political scientist Norton Long remarked that "leadership is concerned with the transformation of doubts into the psychological grounds of cooperative common action."[16] As time goes on, this becomes a more and more significant insight.

Integrity has for years been on every list of qualities that executives consider most important. The pervasiveness of doubt and cynicism about vision only underlines the importance of integrity. Leaders should associate themselves only with visions they can put their heart into. To articulate a vision just because one thinks the organization needs one is a tragic mistake, for it will only produce more cynicism and despair when the leader's lack of real commitment is revealed.

5. Vision and the Leader's Spiritual Development

I have said that vision deals with fundamental meanings of the organization, that in the turbulent modern environment vision is constantly in need of renewal and revitalization, and that vision must appeal to increasingly diverse groups of stakeholders. Clearly, it would appear that leaders who are going to offer new visions and support others' efforts to do the same need to be men and women of strong character and well-formed personal values. But that is not quite the right way to frame the issue. The leader's character and personal values are not immutable, not the only stable elements in an otherwise totally fluid situation. The leader's values and character are in a process of growth, change, and development. The older view of the leader as the rock on whom everyone leans is being replaced by a view of the leader as the one who demonstrates the *way of being* appropriate for our turbulent days as well as for what our organizations should do. The leader takes the lead in humility, in being a learner—and on the subject of vision the most important area of learning is in values, priorities, and meanings. One who is learning in these areas has traditionally been seen as a person in a process of spiritual growth. Thus, as I have noted elsewhere, "executive development is spiritual development" when it comes to maintaining an ability to offer vision that *inspires* others.[17] There is a growing consensus that learning for leadership needs to occur at this quite personal and profound level of spirituality if a person is to have the resources and the resilience to lead under the trying modern conditions.

CONCLUSION

Our twin themes throughout this chapter have been the nature of vision in organizations and the meaning it has for the work of organizational leadership. Vision, I have said, is expressive of the feelings held for the organiztion and its work. Vision is not magic, but it is not exactly logical and clear-cut either. In the short run, an organization can operate on habit and past successes. However, in the longer run, vision is indispensable: It is the basis on which an organization acquires and maintains personal meaning for all those who are associated with it. Vision arises in people who care about the situation they are involved in. The leadership role is to help people *understand* the caring and to express it in terms that will bring them forward into the future.

NOTES

1. Peter B. Vaill, "The Purposing of High Performing Systems," *Organizational Dynamics*, Autumn, 1982.

2. A. J. Rowe, R. O. Mason, and K. E. Dickel, *Strategic Management and Business Policy* (Reading, MA: Addison-Wesley, 1986), p. 558.

3. Harlan Cleveland, *The Knowledge Executive* (New York: Truman Talley, 1985), Chapter 1.

4. Russell L. Ackoff, *Redesigning the Future* (New York: John Wiley & Sons, 1974), p. 24.

5. David Hurst, "Why Strategic Management Is Bankrupt," *Organizational Dynamics*, Autumn 1986: p. 24.

6. Peter B. Vaill, *Managing as a Performing Art*, p. 29.

7. Chester Barnard, *The Functions of the Executive* (Cambridge, MA: Harvard University Press, 1938), p. 87.

8. Myron Magnet, "Managing by Mystique at Tandem Computers," *Fortune* June 28, 1982: p. 84ff.

9. W. Edwards Deming, *Out of the Crisis* (Cambridge, MA: MIT Center for Advanced Engineering Study, 1986); and Joseph M. Juran, *Juran on Planning for Quality* (New York: Free Press, 1988).

10. Thomas J. Peters and Robert H. Waterman, *In Search of Excellence* (New York: Harper & Row, 1982), Chapter 7.

11. Herbert Simon, *The Sciences of the Artificial*, 2nd ed. (Cambridge, MA: The MIT Press, 1981), p. 178.

12. Thomas J. Peters and Nancy Austin, *A Passion for Excellence* (New York: Random House, 1985), Chapter 2.

13. Peter B. Vaill, *Managing as a Performing Art* (San Francisco: Jossey-Bass, 1989), Chapters 1 and 10.

14. William Bridges, *Surviving Corporate Transition* (New York: Doubleday, 1988), Chapter 3.

15. Marvin Weisbord, *Productive Workplaces* (San Francisco: Jossey-Bass, 1987), Chapter 14; and Harrison Owe, *Riding the Tiger* (Potomac, MD: Abbott, 1991).

16. Norton Long, "The Political Act as an Act of Will," *The American Journal of Sociology*, 69 (July 1963), p. 4.

17. Suresh Srivastva, et al. *Appreciative Management and Leadership* (San Francisco: Jossey-Bass, 1990), Chapter 12.

3 BUILDING HIGH-PERFORMANCE TEAMS

David L. Bradford

THE MEETING AT INTEGRATED SOFTWARE

Integrated Software is a young, highly successful software company that specializes in developing complicated information systems.* Their approach has been to build a base system that meets the key needs of a particular target industry and then to adapt this core product to each client's specifications. The company has succeeded in resolving the challenge of developing sophisticated state-of-the-art systems that are user-friendly and that meet the special requirements of each customer.

Although Integrated Software has experienced greater than expected growth over each of the seven years of its existence, management finds it difficult to predict yearly sales with any degree of certainty. Since their products tend to be big-ticket items, customers often hold off placing a firm order until they themselves know what their year-end financial picture will be like. This pattern leaves Integrated with three modest quarters and then a flurry of orders for the fourth quarter. Needless to say, the tension of wondering if that final rush of orders will materialize is quite disconcerting and makes any long-range planning difficult to do.

The particular meeting that we focus on was the monthly, all-day session involving the executive team. The group was comprised of the president (David Fletcher), the chief financial officer (Jayne Simmons), the director of

---

*Although the names have been changed, the case study relates actual events.

38

technology (Dale Wilber), and the three sales vice-presidents (Rob Prescott for the Americas, Jacques Prudoe for Europe/Middle East, and Asoko Somo for the Pacific). It was mid-June and near the end of the second quarter, so the purpose of this meeting was to review sales progress and its impact on plans.

The immediate concern was a projected $14 million shortfall in sales for the year. Although they had met the plans for the first two quarters, when Jayne—the chief financial officer—checked with regional sales managers about potential orders, it appeared that future sales were likely to be down for the final two quarters. In addition to this being the first time in their history that they might not meet their yearly financial targets, it posed cash-flow problems in funding some of their expansion objectives.

After Jayne reported her findings, the president talked about how important it was that they achieve their financial targets. "Not only do we need the income for our growth plans, but, if we go public in 18 months, the financial analysts will be looking at us closely in terms of our financial stability." He then went on to press for increased sales: "It is crucial if we are to meet our goals to significantly increase the number of serious leads." David turned to the European sales VP and asked, "Jacques, what could your area do?"

Jacques said it was difficult to promise anything, because the spate of actual and projected mergers in Europe meant that companies were hesitant to invest in software. David (and Jayne) pushed Jacques about some of their key customers: "Would it help if we offered discounts for immediate purchases?" Jacques was doubtful that it would work; the president and the CFO (Jayne) continued to offer suggestions, which were received without much enthusiasm. Finally, after much pressure, Jacques said that he could probably guarantee about $3 million against the $14 million shortfall but no more.

Attention then turned to Asoko, who was queried about possibilities in Japan and the Far East. He was even more uncertain than was Jacques about new leads. As the discussion went on, Asoko appeared to have difficulty understanding some of the questions, and the level of misunderstanding between him and David increased. After about twenty minutes of this, Asoko said that although he could not guarantee any increased revenues, he would go back and talk to his people about renewed effort. In frustration, the focus shifted to Rob Prescott, the sales VP for the Americas.

David: "Rob, you have just added four new salespeople; shouldn't that be reflected in increased orders?"

Rob: "Not immediately; remember that they need to get up to speed on our product line. Also, it takes time to make contact with the senior decision makers in the companies."

David: "But you said that you were hiring experienced people just so that we wouldn't have this problem."

Rob: "Yes, but there is always start-up time. And remember that we have just reorganized the territorial assignments and it will take a while for the sales force to settle in."

The conversation continued in a similar vein for another 15 minutes. Jayne joined in to pressure Rob, who slowly gave way and agreed to match Jacques's added contribution. But there was still more than half of the projected shortfall to make up. It was now midmorning, and in frustration David called a break while he pondered what to do next. Unfortunately, this felt like a familiar spot for the group to be in; too many meetings in the past had stalled like this one. David wondered what could be done to get the group to address the core problems more constructively and to work effectively as a team.

What's Going On?

What is causing this group to be so unsuccessful in solving this problem? Clearly, members are acting in dysfunctional ways; each of the vice-presidents is protecting his own turf, stressing problems—not opportunities—in developing new business and not working collaboratively. In fact, they are in a negative cycle with the president and CFO. The more that the latter two push, the more the sales VPs resist; and the more that the VPs resist, the more the others push. Furthermore, two members have withdrawn from the discussion: The director of technology was silent during that entire period and Asoko conveniently "forgot" his English language skills. This is certainly not a model of a productive team.

But why is this going on? What are the underlying causes of this nonproductive behavior? Do we just have a unique collection of recalcitrant individuals who are unable to take a larger viewpoint, who are passive and shun responsibility? Probably not. Instead of seeing this situation as representing individual deficiencies, it can be viewed as reflecting problems with the way the team is operating as a group. More specifically, there are three underlying core difficulties that exist with this group and with so many others that I have observed in a wide range of organizations.

1. *The group is operating as a "federation."* Members are defining their primary responsibilities as representing their separate areas rather than as being committed to the common enterprise. They are more a

federation of (non)cooperating parts than an integrated "union." It is only the leader, with some help from the chief financial officer, who feels responsible for the overall good of the company.

2. *The problem-solving process is not being adequately handled.* Specifically, they have jumped into trying to implement *one solution* rather than clearly defining the problem, exploring the range of alternatives, and objectively assessing the pros and cons of the various options.

3. *They are not examining and dealing with the way they are operating as a group.* Although each member, if interviewed privately, could point out the dysfunctional modes of behavior, they are not raised and confronted in the group. The members are not looking at whether their *norms* are functional or dysfunctional, at the appropriateness of the *roles* that members are playing, and at their *mode of operation* as a decision-making group.

Difficulties of not being a cohesive team, of not managing the problem-solving process, and of not paying attention to how they are operating as a group are not unique to Integrated Software but are endemic in most small face-to-face groups. They contribute to the common complaint of low productivity, high frustration, and poor morale. Members complain about hidden agendas with the real issues not being put on the table, endless discussions, sniping and noncooperation, mediocre decisions, and less than full commitment to implementation. "We keep minutes but waste hours" is a frequent charge.

FOCUS OF THIS CHAPTER

Before proceeding further, it is important to delineate the territory that this chapter covers. First, we are dealing with small face-to-face groups (those ranging in size roughly from five to twelve members). Less than five removes much of the complexity of interaction; three or four people do not evoke the complicated group dynamics found in larger groups. Conversely, greater than a dozen makes it difficult to handle the myriad interactions in a timely fashion. Groups of sixteen or more tend to become an impersonal crowd where people can "blend in with the woodwork."

Second, we focus on groups that have continuity over time, rather than a temporary collection of individuals thrown together for three or four meetings. Somewhat arbitrarily, we set a minimum of a dozen meetings (or weekly for three months); that is sufficient to allow the group's dynamics to develop and to make it worthwhile for members to commit the energy to develop the team. Even though many of the points in this chapter are relevant to shorter-lived groups, it is difficult to obtain sufficient investment to deal with them. (See Chapter 2, "Visionary Leadership," by Peter B. Vaill and Chapter 5, "Power, Politics, and Influence," by Anne Donnellon for useful ideas relevant to short-term teams.)

Lastly, the emphasis is on *decision-making* groups. A myriad of kinds of groups is formed in organizations—from work teams to task forces to problem-solving groups. People can get together to turn out a product, such as assembling a washing machine or just to exchange information, but neither taps into the potential of groups when formed to problem solve complex issues. Increasingly in our fast-changing and interdependent world, yesterday's answers do not fit today's problems. Individuals with diverse viewpoints and expertise must come together to form teams that can effectively develop new solutions. This chapter is about how to build such teams.

THE POTENTIAL POWER OF GROUPS

Although folklore often disparages the potential of groups ("a camel is a horse made by a committee"), in actuality, a team that works well is unsurpassed in its ability (a) to produce quality solutions, (b) to guarantee their implementation, and (c) to be a source of learning for the members. Let us take each of those three outcomes and explore them in depth.

A. The Quality of Group Problem Solving

Groups do not always make decisions superior to those made by individuals. Research indicates that when the problem is simple and when there is one expert, individuals make decisions that are of equal or superior quality to those made by a group—and in a much shorter time period. However, when the problem is complex and multifaceted, when there is no one expert, and when the team is working well as a group, the group will almost inevitably make a higher quality decision than even the best member.[1]

Why is this so? Although having more people join in problem solving increases the range of ideas being considered, of equal importance is the ability of other members to spot and weed out poor ideas. The idea initiator tends to be overenthusiastic about the possibilities and blind to the defects. Even more important, the various viewpoints that different members bring can lead to synergistic solutions: The best points of each are brought together to form a new creative solution superior to the ideas of any one member. Thus, when properly utilized, more heads can be better than one in generating and evaluating ideas and in developing truly innovative outcomes.

B. Implementation

Decisions are more likely to be effectively implemented when made by a well-working group than by an individual acting autonomously. A group provides more *support*; other members are there to give assistance and encouragement. That is increasingly important as problems become complex and cross-functional. Rarely in organizations today can one person carry out decisions by acting alone. Instead, there is the need for others to buy in (not just "to be bought off"), that is, to invest in contributing information and tangible assistance, rather than merely agreeing to go along because a particular need is met.

Members are more likely to put in the extra effort if they know they will be *held accountable*. Although the leader of the group is a force to be reckoned with, especially if that person has the power to fire or promote, even more powerful is a committed group. Having to face one's colleagues and explain why a jointly agreed-to task was not accomplished can be daunting. It comes not just out of fear but out of loyalty; not wanting to let the team down dramatically increases the chance that decisions will be implemented.

C. Learning

The group can be an important source of learning in several areas. First, individuals can increase their competence on the task or technical level. As problems grow in complexity and knowledge becomes more specialized, individuals come with different experience and expertise. If group norms can support learning from each other (rather than members having to pretend that they are all-knowing themselves), then as the group struggles through the problem-solving process, members will pick up new information and knowledge.

A second crucial area for individual learning involves interpersonal and group skills. To be an effective team member demands a range of abilities many people do not have: how to take the larger viewpoint and not be trapped in the specifics of one's area, how to problem solve creatively with others who come with different orientations, how to be both influential and open to influence, and how to build appropriate group norms and procedures. The key point is that it is one's peers who have the information about how a member can increase his or her interpersonal and group effectiveness. Our co-workers know what we do that makes us a valuable group member and what we do that diminishes our effectiveness. Sharing that information feels risky: "Will expressing that hurt our relationship and invite retaliation?" Of course, the ability to give constructive feedback is still another group skill that is necessary if members are to build high-performance teams.

Finally, there is a third area of group learning. Even if members come with all the requisite skills, the group needs to develop as a learning group. The norms and procedures need to fit the needs of the individual members and the special requirements produced by the task of the group. Although this third area speaks to group learning, it is interdependent with the first two areas. Learning about other areas and about one's behavior in a group occurs best when members can openly examine the group's process. And in examining factors that inhibit the free flow of ideas, individuals will gain insight on how they are operating as group members.

The Interrelationship of the Potentials with the Problems

The three core problems identified in the Integrated Software case affect the extent to which groups can achieve their potential. If a group is a federation, there is less motivation to work together to solve problems and implement agreed solutions. Rather than searching for the synergistic solutions, there is a greater tendency to block ideas or revert to compromises. Likewise, not being a union lowers allegiance to the group, reducing commitment to take the risks of openly looking at individual and group behavior.

The effects are, of course, circular. Having a flawed problem-solving process not only lowers the quality of the decision and correspondingly decreases commitment to implementation, but it lessens the attractiveness of the group. There is not much incentive to give up one's own self-interest to a group that has meeting after meeting without producing anything of quality.

Finally, not examining the group's process prevents corrective action from being taken to remove the barriers to effective team performance. There is no self-corrective mechanism to deal openly with problems. Furthermore, appropriate norms that legitimize members' accountability are probably lacking. Improper implementation is therefore not confronted and corrected, which further lowers the value of the group and encourages members to push their own self-interests.

Thus to achieve the full potential in terms of the quality of the decision, the commitment to implementation, and the teams' capability for member and group learning, the leader and members need to deal with the three core problems identified. But before turning to the specific steps needed to deal with these three areas, I must address a false dilemma. Too often people feel blocked because they think that they must choose between team development and performance. "We don't have time for working on how we operate; we'll muddle through because we have to get this decision made." In the following sections, I will attempt to demonstrate that the same processes used for increasing team productivity are the ones necessary for individual and team development. You truly can "get two for the price of one." But achieving both benefits demands knowledge and skill and, most of all, a willingness to take (prudent) risks.

THE THREE CORE AREAS FOR BUILDING EFFECTIVE TEAMS

A. Federation or Union?: Issues of Cohesiveness

One dimension along which groups can be arrayed is the extent to which members represent their separate areas versus identify with a common goal. An example of the former would be a task force whose members were purposely selected to bring the concerns of their departments to the table. Such representation can be from one's work area ("we in Marketing feel that . . ."), from a discipline ("as chemists in this company, . . ."), from a demographic group ("women in this organization are concerned about . . ."), or from a value system ("I think that the exhibit should represent only local artists").

Such a representational group can be highly desirable when it is crucial that these different interests have a forum to express their viewpoints, and when a negotiated settlement is sufficient. However, being a federation of separate interests diminishes the potential that groups can provide. Under these conditions, rather than objectively exploring the issues, individuals promote their predetermined positions. Rather than increasing areas of interdependency, members protect their turf. And rather than creative problem solving, the decision tends to be made by compromise. This may permit individual (or subgroup) special interests to be achieved, but doing so can interfere with accomplishing organizational goals.

Although leaders of most groups "talk" as if the team were a union, the individuals operate more as in a federation if one watches the interactions closely. Each member primarily represents his or her area, and, as long as those subgoals are met, that person is satisfied. If a peer is pushing a position that doesn't interfere with a colleague's area, that colleague is likely not to oppose ("after all, it's no skin off my nose"). A second indication is the tendency for members to "delegate upward" the responsibility for the overall good. As one executive put it, "we are a series of 'silos'—I look up [to the boss] and down [to the subordinates] and as long as the decision doesn't infringe on my area, I don't look sideward that much." Note that compensation systems that reward "producing in your area" support this federation orientation.

Moving Beyond Federation

Insofar as tasks are highly interdependent and members come with different knowledge and expertise, a quality solution is more likely to be produced if the team moves beyond being a federation. A negotiated solution is rarely as good as an integrative one, which is more likely to result when members leave their entrenched positions and collaborate as a team. Moving toward more of a union can be achieved by increasing the centrality or cohesiveness of the group. *Cohesiveness* is defined as the extent to which members are attracted to the group. Such attractions can arise from many sources: from the group being used as a vehicle for getting *tasks accomplished,* as a source of *prestige,* as a way of providing *access* to key people in the organization, by giving *visibility* to members, as a source of *support* and *affiliation,* and so forth.

Of the various sources of attractions, some are more relevant to the task than others. In fact, it is possible that some sources can actually interfere with work effectiveness. If an individual values membership in a certain group because it conveys status, that individual may be hesitant to raise valid but unpopular points of view for fear of exclusion. For these reasons, the cluster of attractions on which we want to focus is the ability to have influence on core decisions.[2]

Groups that only share information are less attractive than groups that make decisions. Groups that make minor decisions ("how are we going to publicize this event?") are less attractive than those that make the core strategic decisions ("what should be our role in the major change effort this organization is going through?"). And groups that make decisions by consensus are more attractive than those whose members provide only advice and consultation to the leader, who makes the final choice.

Changing a group from being a federation, in which members feel responsible primarily for their subareas, to a union, in which they share responsibility for the success of the group, requires the following:

- Redefining the purpose of the group
- Building commitment to the group's objectives, by dealing with the core issues
- Making decisions by consensus

Clearly, if members come in with the expectation, as did the vice-presidents at Integrated Software, that their job is just to represent their area and pass upward to the leader the task of taking responsibility for the overall good, then it is impossible to move beyond a federation. Thus the first step is to redefine the purpose of the group so that members take on this larger perspective. Although necessary, that by itself is not sufficient unless there is a pull that makes the group's objectives more attractive than the individual's interests.

There are many ways to provide the pull. Sometimes the group's goals are so clear and exciting that members immediately feel a commitment: For example, a task force has been given the assignment by the president to change the entire compensation system in the company. But with a group that has a history of having secondary and often trivial items on its agenda, it may be necessary to identify explicitly the core issues as a way to signal that future practice will be different.

Finally, when decisions are made by consensus, not only does quality improve, but commitment to the team and its decision increases. *Consensus* is a joint decision-making process in which each person's ideas are considered and through which a solution is one that all can support even if it is not their first choice. This is very different from a *consultative* decision-making style, in which the leader may be swayed by members' arguments but in which the final decision would be the leader's first choice. Consensus also differs from *unanimity*, in which the decision has to be everyone's first choice, thus giving any individual veto power. Since consensus involves mutual influence, high-quality synergistic solutions emerge from that give-and-take.

The distinction between consultative and joint decision making is important because of the impact it has on building a cohesive group. Even though most managers may talk participation, they use a consultative style because it allows them to hold on to personal control. Even though they are open to influence, they know that the decision will be their first choice. The downside of a primary reliance on consultative decision making is that it fosters a federation orientation. When members know that the leader is the crucial person to influence, they tend to advocate their personal interests and pass up to the boss the responsibility for developing an integrative solution. Conversely, joint decisions force all to take responsibility for the optimal solution.[3]

An Example of Movement Toward Cohesion: Sue Williams's Team

To give a sense of how the change from a federation to a more cohesive team can occur in practice, here is what Sue Williams, director of information systems in a large company, did with her group. She had been feeling for some time that her team was not working up to its potential. Members were representing primarily their individual areas, too much of the time in meetings was spent just on sharing information, and those decisions that were made tended to be of relatively low importance, Near the end of one such meeting, Sue said, "I have been thinking about how we have been operating as a team, and I'm not fully satisfied that we are getting the value that we could from our meetings. As you know, the company is going through some major changes and our division will play a major role in that. Up to now, I have taken on most of the responsibility for trying to figure out the actions our department should take. But I think that if we could work on this collectively we could come up with better solutions. What do you think?"

What followed was a surprisingly rich discussion in which members also expressed their dissatisfaction with the meetings. They complained that the discussions did not focus on the more strategic issues, concerning where the division should be heading. After exploring the pros and cons of taking on those larger issues, the members agreed to shift their emphasis. In the change, they also agreed to be less parochial in their orientation and to jointly own responsibility for the success of the division. Sue ended the session by suggesting the following: "In preparation for our next meeting, will each of you think about the role that our division should play in the major change our company is going through? Then list what you think are the core problems we need to resolve in the next nine to twelve months. We will start by listing and then prioritizing, to see what our focus should be."

At the next week's meeting, the group discussed and gained agreement on their vision of the strategic thrust of the information systems division. They then looked over their list of core problems and decided, starting with the most important, to tackle one item each meeting. For the first several items, they assigned individuals to do background research and to bring relevant information to that particular meeting (but not to come with a recommendation, since that could lead into the trap that Integrated Software fell into: arguing solutions rather than problem solving).

Near the end of the meeting, one member asked, "but what do we do with the information-transmittal items; don't we need to keep each other informed about what we are doing?" Before Sue could respond, one member noted that in solving the core problems they would have to share information. Much of what they had laboriously described in their previous "show and tell" sessions would now be conveyed in the process of making decisions. But others felt that that might not be sufficient to keep each other informed of ongoing activities. The group therefore decided to extend their normal 10:00 to 12:00 meeting through lunch and update each other over sandwiches.

Difficult Transition: Issues of Control and Influence

Although these steps appear relatively clear-cut and not that difficult to implement, they don't always go as smoothly or quickly as in Sue's group. Why are so many groups stuck in the federation mode? Resistance for the transition comes from both the leader and members, and I believe that it has to do with issues of influence and control.

For the leader, making the change requires letting go of personal control in two areas: (a) around the specific outcome and (b) around what goes on in the group, for example, the running of the meeting. Such control can be exerted through a relatively rigid differentiation between the role of the leader and members ("one chief and many indians"). A second form of control is through the selection of items for the agenda ("if they are minor, I can live with any decision the group wants"). A third control is exerted through the decision-making process. As I have noted, using a consultative mode gives the leader final control—but at a cost most leaders are unaware of.

These tendencies are especially likely to exist when the group is embedded in the hierarchy of a larger organization, so that the leader and members of the group are bosses and subordinates, respectively, in the larger system. The leader feels held accountable by the larger organization ("after all, the buck stops here"), and job descriptions of the members encourage them to focus on their subarea, because that is how they are evaluated and rewarded.

The leader's preoccupation with control is not unwarranted. Fears that the decision may not be the right one, that members won't take the larger perspective, and that the team might not pull together are realistic concerns. But moving from a consultative decision-making style, which is the most common under a federation approach, to a consensus style does not mean letting go of all control. What it does is change the *bases* of control. Rather than having to rely on the leader to hold the reins tightly, control now rests in the *purpose* (and vision) of the group, in the increased *cohesiveness* of the team, in the discipline of the *problem-solving process*, and in norms that legitimize *mutual influence* among the members.

If member agreement on the group's objectives can be achieved, it serves as a common framework around which decisions can be made and member activities coordinated. Another benefit from the group dealing with core issues, in addition to being the most cost-effective use of time, is that it starts to develop common understanding and commitment, which serve as a force for the coordination of members' activities. Likewise, as teams become more cohesive, this very attractiveness means that members are more willing to be influenced by their peers. (The other two forces that increase coordination and control, the quality of the group's decision-making process and the ability of members to influence each other, are the topics of the next two sections.)

Resistance from members in moving beyond a federation comes from ambivalence about increased responsibility and about letting peers have influence in their area. People may want to have more influence about what the group does, but with that comes responsibility for making tough decisions, about which members may have ambivalence. Although "delegating upward" is disempowering, there is a certain comfort in pushing off responsibility—and perhaps in complaining behind the leader's back when the decision is not liked. Likewise, members may want to influence their colleagues but not want the same in return! So what develops with the federation mode is a "mutual-protection-society," in which members collude not to raise questions or "interfere" too directly in another's area. Note how the federation encourages this: If members' comments come only from the perspective of what is best for their subarea, then it is natural for other members to resist their involvement.

To summarize this section, I have described the advantages of increasing group cohesiveness through encouraging members to pull together around common objectives. There are many ways to do that; the method I have stressed, that of sharing the responsibility for making the core decisions, is only one of them. But consider how the discussion at Integrated Software could have gone if members had taken this larger perspective. Rather than just defending their areas and being concerned with meeting their sales targets, they would also have been concerned with the company as a whole. They would have felt that, even if their subunit had been successful, the failure of the company to close the $14 million shortfall was their failure as well.

B. The Problem-Solving Process

One of the concerns leaders have about building a highly cohesive group that makes core decisions is whether the team actually will produce quality solutions. And part of what determines the quality is how well the group handles the problem-solving process. Table 3-1 summarizes the stages and common traps of that sequence.

TABLE 3-1   Steps and common traps of the problem-solving process

Steps	Common Traps
Identifying & diagnosing the problem	• Focusing on *symptoms,* not problems • Assuming a knowledge of *causes*
Generating alternatives	• Seizing the *first suggestion* rather than seeing range of options • Being highly *evaluative* about the ideas before they are fully understood
Evaluating options	• Overreliance on *subjective* data • Number crunching *without judgment* • *Not* searching for *integrative* solutions
Making a decision	• *Closing* too quickly on the first attractive option • *Smoothing over disagreements* • *Not* getting full commitment from all members
Implementing the decision	• *Not* agreeing on "*who* will do *what* by *when*" • Not getting *support* from other members

One of the drawbacks of a stage model is that it can imply a strict sequential flow, in which the discussion moves in lockstep from one stage to the next. But groups—and life—are more complicated. In reality, there is a movement back and forth among these stages. For example, often it is only when one explores alternatives that the nature of the problem becomes clear; the evaluation process may generate new alternatives; or closing on a solution may raise some concerns that identify new problems with the options being considered. Thus there are inevitable loops back to early steps. But the five-part model given in Table 3-1 can be helpful to members in identifying where they are and in judging whether that stage has been adequately addressed or whether it has become time to move on or return to a previous point.

Note how Integrated Software got into their impasse: They inadequately handled the first stage by failing to correctly diagnose the situation. First, was there really a problem? After all, the pattern of slow sales until the final quarter had existed in previous years. Why was this year any different? Even if there was a problem, what was it? The issue they worked on was a symptom, that of not enough orders in the pipeline. But what was the real cause of that? Was it changing market conditions, an improperly trained sales force, the compensation system, new competition, product obsolescence, lack of technical support to the field—or some combination? Instead of an appropriate diagnosis, the president came in with his solution and tried to impose it on the members.

Unless the problem is accurately defined, the appropriateness of any solution has to be hit or miss. One useful management adage is the following:

> It's better to find the wrong solution to the right problem than the right solution to the wrong problem. If the former, you soon know it is the wrong solution but if the latter, it can be a long time before you realize it's the wrong problem.

One of the reasons that Japanese managers are perceived as making superior decisions compared to Western managers is that they spend a great deal of effort determining that the problem is correctly defined. Up to half the time in meetings is spent asking, "is this the *real* problem?" Unfortunately, too often in the West, managers assume that the initial definition of the situation is correct. Much of the arguing that goes on around alternative solutions occurs because people hold different perceptions of the problem. Spending that initial time gaining agreement on problem definition can dramatically save time later on. Not infrequently, when the problem has been accurately defined, the solution becomes self-evident.

When David Fletcher, president of Integrated Software, came in with his solution of increasing orders through having the sales force move more aggressively he cut off the exploration of alternatives. This trap is especially likely to occur when the leader pushes his or her pet solution. The group argues the pros and cons of that position—or too quickly accepts the erroneous diagnosis—rather than stepping back for a moment and exploring for alternatives that should be considered.

When moving on to the evaluation stage, intuitive and subjective reactions are legitimate processes: We appropriately make hunches before we can produce the data to support them, but the trap here is to overrely on subjective data and not see if there is objective evidence to corroborate intuition. Maybe sales are down because of product obsolescence—but is there any market data to support that notion? Groups can bog down because members just argue their different viewpoints rather than make an objective assessment of each option and determine what information would confirm or disconfirm the alternatives.

Especially with new and complex problems, it is unlikely that one solution will exactly solve the problem. Rather, several of the proposed options can each carry a bit of the truth. Thus, groups can become trapped into seeing alternatives only in *either-or* terms rather than trying to develop a new, integrated option that pulls out the best idea of each proposal. Note that this process of building a creative solution that is synergistic is very different and usually far superior to splitting the difference through compromise.

Quickly grabbing the first solution rarely produces creative outcomes, which may be exactly what is needed in new and fast-changing conditions. First ideas tend to be along the lines of what has been tried before. Thus, if the group is highly evaluative, members will feel inhibited from thinking in new and creative ways that break out of established frameworks. What is important is to build a climate in which new and divergent thoughts are encouraged.[4]

Too often teams measure how good they are by the harmony in their ranks. Disagreement and even conflict are defined as rocking the boat; dissenters are punished. Doing so can produce a "groupthink" mentality with which individuals keep their doubts to themselves. The majority may actually oppose an outcome, but each member thinks that only he or she disagrees.[5] Research shows that when the leader and members value task disagreements, solutions tend to be more creative than when such disagreements are suppressed.[6]

Another way that disagreements are inappropriately handled occurs when the majority, perhaps under time pressure to reach a decision, coerces agreement from the minority. Not only does it tend to lower the quality of the outcomes, because dissenting viewpoints can hold validity, but it can also lower commitment. Instead of striving for a mere majority, which tends to produce "her majesty's *not-so-loyal* opposition," the goal for important decisions is consensual agreement. The danger becomes wishfully seeing silence as assent rather than as silence! (Perhaps opposition has been driven underground.) It is important to check carefully that everybody buys in (and not just "buys off") on the decision.

Even if a high-quality decision is made, there is no guarantee that it will be fully implemented. Is there agreement on who is going to take the lead in carrying out the decision? Do all agree on exactly what steps have been committed to, and is there joint understanding about the time frame? Furthermore, if there is shared responsibility, what assistance do the implementers need from other members?

As noted at the beginning of this section, the stages in the problem-solving process are not rigidly carried out by lockstep; effective groups show flexibility in moving back and forth as needed. If members keep this model in mind, they can move back or move on as needed to make decisions efficiently.

Whose Responsibility?

One question is, whose job is it to make sure that this sequence is adequately handled? So often it is seen as solely the leader's responsibility. But teams tend to be more successful when all members feel that obligation. Taking the problem-solving sequence as an example, can't the members do as much as the leader to make sure the steps are adequately handled? Following are examples of comments that any member can make to help the group deal with the various steps.

1. **Defining the Problem**

   "I think we are discussing more the symptom than the real problem. Isn't the core problem . . . ?"

   "Have we really diagnosed what caused this difficulty? I think there are some other causes we need to look at."

   "I think that the two of you have defined the problem differently: Joe, it sounds as if you see it as X, while Mary, it seems that you are defining it in terms of Y."

2. **Generating Alternatives**

   "We seem to be debating the pros and cons of only two options. Could we hold off evaluating them and continue brainstorming more possibilities?"

   "Three of us have been doing most of the talking; before moving on to the evaluating stage, let's hear from the other members to make sure we have all ideas out."

3. Evaluating Options

"Let's list on the board the pros and cons of each of the options; I think we are starting to argue the two sides of just one alternative and we need to evaluate all of them objectively."

"I am hearing a lot of opinions; what we need are facts. Could we list the evidence needed to assess these options?"

4. Making a Decision

"Seems to me that we are getting close to a decision; could we check to see if we have agreement?"

"I am not sure that all of us really buy in to this decision. I think you, Harry, and Jane, have some qualms. What would have to change in order for you really to support this decision?"

5. Implementing the Decision

"I don't know if we have agreed who is going to carry this out. And what specifically do we expect that person to do?"

"Jim, in taking responsibility for this, what do you need from the rest of us to make our decision fly?"

These comments aren't profound, highly sophisticated types of interventions; in fact, they are just verbalizations of the thoughts most members carry around in their head but don't feel free to state. How often does one member think "we are beating a dead horse, why don't we move on?" but keeps it inside? Such private observations would frequently be beneficial if directly expressed.

Factors That Inhibit Effective Problem Solving

Even if one has a clear understanding of the problem-solving process and a sense about the kind of comments that would be helpful, there are other forces that inhibit their utilization. When I have seen members hold back and have asked them why, they report that they consider it "the leader's job" and fear that it would be seen as presumptuous for them to make such comments. Another concern they report is that such statements would be seen as critical of the chairperson's abilities and therefore a personal attack.

Another cause is that few people are trained in *collective* problem solving. Most of the emphasis in our education and in organization life has been on the individual as problem solver. Throughout school, students are rewarded for personally figuring out the answer—after all, using others is cheating! In organizations, think of how leadership has been defined, at least traditionally. The Leader was one who took charge, had the answer, and exhibited no uncertainty. Collaborative problem solving, on the other hand, works best when there is more of a joint exploratory process, in which members can admit what they don't know and can build off the ideas of others.[7]

A member's personal needs can interfere with effective problem solving. Even though such needs (or "ego," as commonly used) can become dominant when individuals solve problems alone (familiar to all of us are occasions when people overinvest in their proposals), there is a set of self-oriented needs that are especially likely to be activated in groups. When an individual enters a group that is attractive, the following four personal concerns tend to get aroused.

1. Will I be *accepted*?
2. What sort of person do I have to be in this group? What *identity* can I show and what parts of me will I have to hide?
3. Will I have *influence* in this group?
4. Is there congruence between my needs (and interests) and the goals of the group? Will I get my *personal objectives* met here?[8]

It is not that these are illegitimate needs, for we all want acceptance, to be ourselves, to have influence, and to achieve personal goals. Instead, the problem is how they play themselves out. It is extremely rare for members openly to state such needs. To do so feels too vulnerable, and we fear rejection. Unfortunately, the needs are expressed through the task in indirect ways and in so doing interfere with the productivity of the team.

For example, does feeling valued become intertwined with the acceptance of one's point of view—"love me, love my ideas"? Does wanting one's ideas accepted become a marker of having influence in the group? Is accepting another's point of view felt as losing one's individuality? And does the decision-making process become subverted into win-lose battles around dominance and power? Do members take disagreement as a personal attack? These are the issues that can cause a meeting to be marked by hidden agendas, people not stating their real issues, and egos becoming intertwined with task efforts.

We can only guess at the extent to which personal issues were part of the driving forces behind the executives' behaviors during the meeting at Integrated Software. Did the president push his solution so hard because he felt a need to demonstrate that he could act decisively? Did the CFO come in with support (being a relatively new member of the team) because she wanted to demonstrate her value? Did Asoko withdraw (coming from a different culture) because he didn't feel fully accepted in the group? Being outside observers prevents us from knowing, but we are all human, so it is only to be expected that such needs will arise when people work together.

Adhering to the problem-solving stages can do much to alleviate these problems. However, a more direct (and therefore time-efficient way) is to have the group examine how it is operating and correct the dysfunctions. And that is the topic of the next section.

C. Managing How the Group Operates as a Group

Ironically, one of the advantages of groups, different people with different viewpoints and approaches, is also the cause of one of the core difficulties: How do we mesh individual talent to achieve coordinated action? Furthermore, the benefit from diversity can only be realized if these differences are integrated. This issue of integration refers not only to the diversity of ideas but also to different work styles, and temperaments, of the various members.

Organizations, from societies to intimate relationships, have to handle issues of coordination and control. To a high degree, managing differences is done by developing regulations and procedures governing how that system operates. Likewise, small groups develop rules, norms, and patterns of interaction. *Rules* are explicit statements of how the group will operate—for example, we will meet every Monday at 10:00 to deal with these topics.

Norms, on the other hand, are more likely to be implicit and to define what is appropriate and inappropriate behavior—for instance, it is understood that the way to disagree is first to point out the positive aspects of another's statement. Norms are not only more numerous than formal rules but tend to be more powerful, partially because they are often implicit. It is what is unexamined that can have so much control.

The term *patterns of behavior* refers to the routines that develop over time and that organize how the group functions. Does the group tend to start its meetings with fifteen minutes of small talk? Does it handle the safe items first? Is there a pattern in which first the members state their opinions and then turn to the leader for clues about the "right" direction to go? Such patterns are rarely explicitly determined and emerge as "the natural way we do things here."

These rules, norms, and patterns of behavior influence how the group operates and the procedures it uses to get work done. The major areas that groups must deal with involve the following:

- *Domain and Purpose.* Even if there is formal agreement indicating the group's jurisdiction, there can still be great leeway within the purview. Are there certain areas not to touch ("sacred cows") or others in which members can push just so far before a barrier is reached (for example, "we can question the leader about going to top management for more resources but once he acts hesitant, we drop the issue")?

- *Influence and Power.* What is the basis of power in this group—expertise, seniority, dominance, or external-role position? How can members influence each other and in what areas is influence legitimate (for example, "we can pressure others about *what* they do but not about *how*")? How is influence distributed in this group; do only a few people have it or is it relatively evenly dispersed?

- *Conflict and Disagreement.* How are disagreements and conflicts handled? Are they suppressed, dealt with indirectly (through innuendo), or raised outside the meeting? Are there certain areas in which disagreements can and cannot be expressed (for example, "we can disagree on task issues but cannot confront each other when someone has not fulfilled their obligations")? When expressed, does it have to be done in a certain way ("we don't raise our voices in this organization")?

- *Decision Making.* This refers not just to *what* is decided ("we make only the minor decisions here") but what decision-making style is used (by consensus or does the leader have the final say, with the members' role only to advise and consult). Even if the decision-making style appears consensual, how does the group go about it ("we talk things to death until the opposition gives up")?

- *Group Roles.* There are both *task roles* and *maintenance roles* that must be fulfilled if a group is to operate successfully. The former facilitate the decision-making process, such as by initiating ideas and proposing solutions, whereas the latter maintain the proper functioning of the group, such as by monitoring the inclusion of all members' opinions and supporting minority opinions. The issue is not only whether all the roles are being adequately carried out but whether the responsibility moves among the members rather than being relegated as the sole responsibility of one person. When only one individual is charged with raising the tough questions, not only does that person become pigeonholed into that narrow function but the skills of other members in that area are not being utilized.

- *Members' Rights and Responsibilities.* What rights do members have in this group? Can they be coerced by the majority or are there legitimate areas in which they can deviate without fear of rejection or loss of status? And what are their responsibilities? What are the expectations around involvement and commitment? What is required to be a good group member ("valued members always volunteer for extra tasks")?

How are decisions around the preceding areas made? The few formal rules that develop cover only a small part of the territory, so how do the (usually) implicitly derived norms and patterns evolve? In some cases they reflect (key) members' personal proclivities. Jack, one leader with whom I have worked, had a difficult time with conflict. He smoothed over disagreements any time they arose, and soon that became the pattern for how the team operated. Norms and practices develop because they serve a function in the early life of the group. Thus, when the group is forming, it might be important that people are polite and supportive, conditions that become the status quo and later limit the extent to which members can critically evaluate ideas.

Other norms may reflect the larger culture of the organization within which a team is imbedded. Unfortunately, this chapter has tended to describe teams as if they are in isolation, but that is rarely the case. Most often they are tied into larger systems that have their own norms and patterns of behavior. If the organization prizes individuals who appear invulnerable, the team will likely develop a similar norm and no one will ever admit to being uncertain or confused.

The larger organization also influences how power is distributed in a group. Members come to a group with accoutrements from the larger organization. They are not just Jane Jones, but Director of Marketing or "the person who has the ear of the V.P." These larger organizational roles influence the resources they will bring and the influence they will have. And even if a team has moved beyond being a federation, members will still serve as representatives to the constituencies and groups they represent within the larger system.

An individual, if questioned, can often identify the norms and patterns of behavior that exist in the group, but rarely are they discussed within the group itself. However, for teams to increase in effectiveness, members must openly examine the rules and practices under which they operate. Unexamined norms are frequently dysfunctional because they don't meet the needs of the group at a particular point in its development. Another reason that norm examination is crucial is to prevent conformity. Today's fast-changing world requires innovation, and being pressured to think only one way inhibits the production of new solutions.

The problem of conformity is an especially potent dilemma with the types of groups I have been describing. I have argued for the various advantages of cohesive groups, yet it turns out that the more cohesive is the group, the more pressure on members to conform. Paradoxically, one of the best ways to prevent the conformity that restricts progress is to develop norms that support the dissenter—for example, the goal is to produce high *conformity* to a norm of *individuality*!

If a group is to become a high-performance team, establish the practice of periodically setting aside the task in order to examine how the group is operating. Like sports teams after an important event, work teams must review their performance. It does not have to be anything elaborate—just set aside 20 minutes at the end of every third meeting and ask "what are we doing that is increasing our effectiveness (so that we continue doing it)" and "what are we doing that is getting in the way?" Putting two such lists on the board and then deciding on desirable modifications are all that is required.

But if such processing is so straightforward, why is it so unusual for groups to examine how they operate? Do members fear that such self-examination will get out of hand and become a vehicle for finger pointing or worse? How slippery might the slope be (and how quick the slide) from an objective assessment to the personal attack? For example, the remark that "we tend to go down blind alleys" quickly turns into "Joe, you make irrelevant comments that totally waste the time of the group." Or does the leader discourage group examination because an admission that things aren't going well enough might be an admission of less-than-complete competence?

But to understand the value of taking such a risk, let us return to the case of the embattled executives at Integrated Software. As you remember, after the laborious and unproductive initial session, David Fletcher, the president, had called a midmorning break. When they had reassembled he said, "Those two hours were really frustrating; what's going on?" After a pause, Dale Wilber, the director of technology, tentatively spoke up and admitted, "We've been sandbagging; all of us are defending our positions. And I've been doing that too by being silent." (This comment was followed by laughter and nodding around the table.) Dale went on, "When I think about it, there are some new things that we're developing in the lab that could be pushed a little faster."

Without just pointing his finger at others, Dale named the game they were playing: the president and CFO playing "prosecuting attorneys" and the members acting like recalcitrant witnesses. Everyone had seen that process, but no one thought it legitimate to publicly point it out; now it could be dealt with. The president encouraged the group to spend the next hour talking about how they wanted to operate as a team. The members agreed to move away from their turf-protecting positions and to be concerned with the welfare of the company, and the president agreed not to come in with predetermined solutions. With those agreements made, the group came back from lunch to spend an hour and a half having a highly productive meeting. They not only identified ways to handle the monetary shortfall but also to increase collaboration across the units.

Clearly, groups usually don't turn around as quickly or neatly as this team did. Several factors accounted for the ease of their transition. Two months before, Fletcher and Wilber had attended a workshop on high-performance teams and had gained some sense of group dynamics (as I hope that you have after reading this chapter!). The president did several things that were extremely helpful: He raised the issue as a question, not as an accusation. When Dale did admit to the dynamics, David did not use the admission either to attack Dale or other members of the group. Moreover, the president encouraged the group to spend time looking at how they were operating and to agree on new rules.

What is crucial if a group is both to increase its effectiveness and to become a learning environment is to permit the conditions with which such self-appraisal can occur. Doing so requires the development of individual skills, such as being able to give feedback that addresses specific behaviors related to the job. Doing so will produce a climate that encourages movement beyond blame toward individual and team development. These aren't esoteric abilities; most managers and members can learn them.

To summarize, in laying out the themes of group cohesiveness, the problem-solving process, and team self-operation, I have provided three "lenses" to examine team effectiveness. One limitation, however, is that these themes have been treated as separate entities, thus leading to a static quality in the analysis. But groups are dynamic systems. Therefore, I want to incorporate another concept: group development. With all due apologies to Gertrude Stein, *a group is not a group is not a group* but changes as it matures. I will use this concept to illustrate the interaction among the three themes and to identify what leaders and members can do to move a group from its initial awkward state to being a high-performance team.

AN INTEGRATIVE CONCEPT: THE STAGES
OF GROUP DEVELOPMENT

Research on both task and process groups supports the notion that groups go through relatively predictable stages of development.[9] Although there are several different models of this process, the one that I find most helpful is outlined in Table 3-2.

Although the five stages given in the table are based on observation of actual organizational work teams, like any model, they are an abstraction. Not all members are at the same point in any one stage; for example, some people start to link up at the moment they walk into a room, whereas others need time to become committed. Although no stage can be successfully skipped, since each one serves a crucial function, there is no clean demarcation from one to the next. In addition, not all groups achieve Stage 5. Only a minority ever get there, and, even for those groups that do, it does not serve as a place where members live happily ever after. New tasks, new members, and new environmental conditions cause teams to regress to previous stages. In spite of the complexities, this model an be useful in understanding a group and in indicating what is needed to further develop the team.

TABLE 3-2   Stages of group development

Stage 1: Membership	Members are individually deciding how committed they want to be to the group. Interaction is polite and guarded as members size up each other.
Stage 2: Subgrouping	Members seek allies and tend to speak from subgroups; conflict is indirect, and positions aren't fully clear.
Stage 3: Conflict	Conflict emerges across subgroups. This is a difficult stage as members wonder if relationships and the group itself can survive these battles.
Stage 4: Individual differentiation	If conflict has been successfully resolved, members feel comfortable in being themselves. Low group conformity exists as members accept each other's individuality.
Stage 5: Collaboration	The team works collectively to solve problems and to support each other in implementation. A synergistic outcome results (the whole is greater than the sum of the parts).

Source: Adapted from S. L. Obert "The Development of Organizational Task Groups," Ph.D. dissertation, Case Western Reserve University, 1979.

Stage 1: Membership

When an individual joins either an ongoing group or one newly formed, the core question is, "how committed do I want to be?" That is an important question. Since most people belong to multiple groups outside as well as inside their organization, priorities must guide the allocation of time and energy; to be fully engaged in all groupings is an invitation for burnout! Second, it is extremely frustrating to become highly invested in a group that does not meet one's needs. Thus, the initial questioning and holding back that frequently occurs for new members reflect this normal testing of the question "will this group be worth my commitment?"

In making this judgment, a member is likely to consider a range of dimensions: the group's purpose or jurisdiction, the extent to which the person will have influence, and the attractiveness of other members. As they size up the leader and each other, some of the self-oriented needs discussed previously will probably be paramount ("will I be accepted by these individuals; are my objectives likely to be met by the goals of this group?").

This initial period in the group is likely to be marked by a great deal of guardedness among the members: Individuals will be hesitant to take many risks for fear of misinterpretation. There may be "position statements" made as members stake out their turf, but strong dissention is unlikely. It is difficult to know fully where people stand on issues; it isn't safe yet to be open.

Although most individuals (and groups) will move through this initial stage without any special assistance, the process can be speeded up by actions that increase the attractiveness of the group. Even though the issue of cohesion will come up again in the life of the group, increasing the group's attraction is one of the leader's major concerns in the initial stages. One way is to link members' goals with the group's purpose. Another way to increase the group's appeal is through the development of an exciting and challenging vision. And yet another can be through identifying the core issues or problems that need to be solved and indicating just how influential members will be in the decision-making process.

During this initial period, when relationships are still being formed and norms and procedures on how to influence each other have not been worked out, it would be too threatening to have members do much in-depth processing of what is going on. But what can be useful is to discuss expectations of what is wanted from the group. This can be nothing more complex than answering such questions as "what topics should be our focus, how do we want to go about making decisions, and how do we want to handle conflicts and disagreements?" It can be the time for the leader to share expectations about moving beyond a federation and having members be primarily committed to the group's success.

Stage 2: Subgrouping

The central theme in the subgrouping stage is finding allies. As all who have attended a cocktail party know, one often feels most alone in a crowd of strangers. It can feel difficult to fully express one's opinion in the presence of doubtful support and acceptance. Another reason that feeling connected is important is as a precondition to move successfully into the next stage. For members to take the risk of raising conflict, they need to know that they won't be isolated. One of our worst fears is of a group turning on us without our having any support (as happened to Piggy in William Golding's *Lord of the Flies*).

Again, this linking-up process is one that will occur naturally over time as members start to identify like-minded partners. The process can be hastened by pointing out similarities in problems or objectives (for example, "Mary, both you and Joe have been struggling with getting more responsiveness from Data Processing").

The good news is that finding allies increases members' sense of comfort, as well as increasing the attractiveness of the group, but there can be bad news. There is a tendency to overvalue within the subgroup and overreject outside. People tend to perceive greater agreement with their partners than does exist. Discussions start to lose some of their complexity if cross-subgroup polarization develops.

Although it is possible for groups in these first two stages to work productively, the individual forces at work can make the process cumbersome. Insofar as members worry about acceptance, it can be difficult to hear an objective assessment of their ideas without feeling personally evaluated ("love me, love my ideas"). If others are concerned with influence, then letting go of their position also can carry personal threat. And because issues of influence and status are in flux, there can be a great deal of jockeying for position.

Since these self-oriented needs haven't been resolved, there can be the feeling of two levels of work: personal and task, and of their being intertwined in a way that feels confusing and cumbersome. People argue a certain position on the task level, but doing so is actually only a surrogate maneuver in their search for influence. Others resist accepting another's ideas not because they are flawed but more because of fearing the loss of autonomy. All of this can be very frustrating; as one discouraged group member stated, "it's like wading through molasses."

This discouraging assessment does not deny that effective problem solving can occur, but the group must hold to the rigor of the problem-solving process (more than is necessary in Stage 4 or 5). For example, if people more likely overstate their positions (and underconsider others), then having members objectively list the pros and cons of each option increases the probability that evaluation will be on the relevant criteria. However, as the group begins to experience success in making decisions, the members will experience greater attractiveness within the group and thereby more willingness to work together.

As member commitment increases, as alliances and relationships develop, and as group norms are established regarding how influence will occur, members will begin to feel ready for some deeper processing. Although still anxiety-arousing, members now are willing to assess how they have been operating as a team and to examine ways they could improve. Again, it may be nothing more complex than to discuss at the end of every third meeting the following two questions, in what manner do we operate productively, and what inhibits our effectiveness? The former is important both to acknowledge progress and to be aware of what behaviors to continue. The second not only can identify the specific actions needed to improve the group but can further promote a climate that favors self-exploration and learning.

Stage 3: Conflict

This third stage seeks the answer to the question "can we fight and survive?" (a question every marriage has to answer!). On the individual level, it speaks to the question "can I have influence?" On the group level, conflict will develop as members begin to feel acceptance and support from their allies and as the group begins to deal with more and more important issues. Disagreements are not only inevitable in groups (after all, *reasonable people differ*) but are desirable. If in our fast-changing world old solutions don't fit new problems, then, in the search for new solutions, there will arise differences about which directions to take. Members must be able to raise and resolve these differences; otherwise the outcome of any problem-solving process will be seriously impaired.

Stage 3 is a turning point in the group's growth—making the difference between whether the group develops into a true high-performance team or gets stuck between Stages 2 and 3. To move fully into and through conflict requires not only that members feel comfortable raising differences and disagreements but that they also have the skills to search for integrative solutions. Unfortunately, many people have been taught to avoid and smooth over conflict. So at the first sign of dissent, the leader rushes in to pour oil on troubled waters. The group then gets the message that disagreements are to be avoided, which only drives conflict underground. Not having experienced the successful handling of disagreements, the group can't get past Stage 3.

Where does the avoidance come from? It can come from socialization. Many of us who were raised in a good, middle-class world have been taught to avoid conflict ("if you can't say something nice, don't say anything at all"). Our aversion can come from fear that task disagreement will degenerate: the all-too-easy slide down the slope from task conflict ("I don't believe that your proposal will succeed") to relational/work-style conflict ("and you keep raising these ideas that only feather your nest") to personal conflict ("if you weren't so insecure, you wouldn't need to turf build").

There can be the concern that conflict will derail successful problem solving. If disagreements turn into win-lose battles, in which the goal or triumph becomes more important than the quality of outcome, we lose the advantage that groups bring. It is difficult to achieve the desired outcome when members are more interested in scoring points and undermining their opponents and when agreement is seen as losing face. Being pushed into a corner is hardly a prescription for successful work.

I am not denying that there is reality behind these fears. Conflict does get out of hand at times, and groups can become polarized, as winning becomes the most important objective—conditions that might especially occur if individuals are feeling that their only way to have influence is through fighting. Furthermore, if it has not been legitimate until now to openly confront task disagreements (and especially not to express any negative feelings about how others have been operating), there can be the danger of a sudden explosion—during which comments are made that so deeply wound as to never be forgiven or forgotten.

What has to be considered, however, is the cost of *not* directly dealing with conflict. As mentioned, suppressing it doesn't remove it: Suppression only guarantees that conflict will play itself out in indirect ways, which are much more difficult to deal with. Additionally, if the goal is to avoid at all costs the possibility of personal conflict, does the group back way off and suppress any differences? Group problem solving then becomes a charade in which polite acceptance is given to a solution that members are only minimally committed to implement.

But individuals and groups can learn to raise and resolve differences in ways that increase the richness of the solution. Moreover, interpersonal issues can be dealt with in ways that are not only nondestructive but allow members to grow in competence. How this is specifically done is beyond the scope of this chapter, but the following paragraphs give general clues.

First, it is important that the leader values differences and disagreements and encourages their productive expression. As discussed previously, leaders who value task conflict have groups that produce more creative solutions. They can set norms that encourage the raising of divergent issues and can support members who do so ("Bob, I think you hold a different opinion; it's important that we get all points of view"). Second, if there is concern that members are overinvesting in their own positions, an emphasis on the larger purpose can be helpful in preventing polarization. Third, without denying feelings, a push for evidence can increase the objectivity of the discussion ("we clearly feel strongly about this issue and that's good, but can we list what we know about the merits and problems with these options?"). Finally, without reverting to a mediocre compromise, it is possible to pick out the best points of each argument and build an integrative solution.

Many managers who would agree to the value of task disagreement draw the line at interpersonal conflict as being beyond the pale. I believe that that is wrong; instead the distinction should be drawn between interpersonal and personal conflict. The former, because it deals with how people work together, is relevant to the job. The latter is not. The distinction I make is between an individual's behavior and his or her personality. Thus saying, "you don't come through on promises" is relevant to people working together effectively, but saying, "you are a blowhard and liar" is not.

The distinction can be a difficult one to keep, especially in the heat of battle, but it is a necessary one. Again, people can learn how to give behavior-specific feedback: It can be helpful, when the discussion seems to verge on personal attack to ask for specifics ("when was the last time this happened?" or, "can you give an example of the problem?"). As Sergeant Friday in "Dragnet" said, "The facts, Ma'am. Just the facts," and there are facts about how people are and are not dealing well with each other.

It is during Stage 3 that it is most useful to have the group examine how its members are working together. After an especially conflictful interaction (after some of the tension has decreased), it can be of value to stop the task work and have the group look at how it is handling conflict. This can also be a time to examine group norms about how differences are expressed and resolved.

Stage 4: Individual Differentiation

If members experience success in raising and successfully resolving differences, then they are able to move on to Stage 4. However, if not successful, the movement will be difficult since individual differences can be felt as threatening to the cohesion of the group ("what if people act in different ways and there is no way to influence them?"). But when members know that they can raise and resolve difficulties in their work relationships, can influence each other on task outcomes, and can confront those who do not fulfill their commitments, all members will be more willing to allow autonomy. Meetings are now held to solve problems, not to keep a careful eye on colleagues.

The core issue in the fourth stage is, "can I be myself and still be valued in this group?" This speaks to the personal need of identity: "I don't have to act in a certain group-mandated way but am valued for myself." This support for individuality decreases the chance for conformity. Coordination and control are achieved not because members are forced into a pasteboard adherence but from a coordination that comes from commitment to group goals, norms, and procedures.

Processing at this point can serve several functions. One is to maintain the level of group efficiency so that regression does not occur. Thus, periodically to stop and say, "how are we doing?" can be beneficial preventive medicine. But this can also be a time when it is useful to help members examine the roles they have played. Over time, different individuals take on responsibility for certain functions. Some are the ones who initiate ideas; others focus on making sure evaluation is thorough; still others provide support for particular members.

Although most such roles are necessary for effective group functioning, there can be the danger that people limit themselves within these role definitions. Thus, it can be useful for the group to examine the various functions that members play and see if the full range of individual resources is being used.

Groups that achieve the fourth stage (and only a minority do) tend to be very high performance teams. The group has developed appropriate norms and modes of operation, trust is higher because (most of the) interpersonal difficulties have been resolved (and new ones are caught early), individuals are granted a high degree of autonomy, and a fuller range of individual skills can be utilized. However, the group has still not achieved its full potential. Stage 4 tends to be only as strong as the sum of the members' abilities, since the emphasis is on their acting as discrete individuals (even though in support of agreed goals).

Stage 5: Collaboration

The issue in the final stage is, "can we achieve synergy through integration of the various attributes of the members so that the whole is greater than the sum of the parts?" This greater productivity arises from several sources. First, there is likely to be much greater support given to each other, and people push themselves harder with such backing. Second, of equal importance is that members can compensate for each others' deficiences in skills or knowledge. Third, the problem-solving process tends to be much more creative as new and integrative solutions are sought.

How can a team move from the fourth to the final stage? The primary force is through stressing the centrality of the group. Stage 4 is as far as a team can go if it operates under a federation model, because the individual goals are equally important to the group goals. The centrality of the group tends to involve both its goals and the members', since relations are much closer and personal than was true in the previous stage. This emphasis on the group does not have to be at the cost of high conformity by individuals. That is the benefit of the previous stage in emphasizing the value of individual differences. But now there is an integration, not a suppression, of differences; collaboration occurs with no significant loss of individuality.

Group processing continues in this stage but its emphasis is more on member learning. Since self-oriented needs have been taken care of—members feel accepted; they know that they have influence in meeting their goals and can express their individuality—then feedback from peers is heard as support for personal development, not as loss of status or as personal attack.

As I said at the beginning of this section, reaching Stage 5 is not nirvana. It takes constant work to remain at that point. New tasks (and new members) and changes in the external environment are forces that reiterate questions of commitment. Thus, constant effort is needed to sustain the progress made; like the Queen of Hearts in *Alice in Wonderland*, the group has to run very fast to stay where it is. However, the structure and processes are now in place such that the group has the possibility of dealing with the new challenges.

SUMMARY

In this chapter I have described the benefits of a team that works well, have discussed some of the inhibiting factors, and have presented a model of group development that can help leaders and members build a highly effective group. One remaining question is, "how much time does this take?" Granted, it can't be done overnight, but it can be done within a matter of months—three to five for the adventurous and a bit longer for the cautious.

It is not an easy process, but the difficulty lies less with needing esoteric skills and more with the willingness to take risks, especially the risks of self-examination (as a group and as individuals). The leader, as well as members, must be open to such exploration. As I have attempted to describe in the discussion of the developmental stages, to be a *performing* group requires that it also be a *learning* group. Thus, one does not have to make a choice between *work* and *development* but must have both. My observation is that the payoffs are usually worth the effort; the benefits are in terms of productivity, personal development, and the satisfaction of working with (not against) colleagues to achieve mutual goals.

NOTES

1. For a seminal study on individual and group decision making, see L. K. Michaelsen, W. E. Watson, and R. H. Black, "A Realistic Test of Individual vs. Group Consensus Decision-Making," *Journal of Applied Psychology* 74, no. 5 (1989): pp. 834–839.

2. Of equal importance in increasing the attractiveness of the group around a task-relevant dimension is the vision for the group. (See Peter B. Vaill's chapter, "Visionary Leadership," in this book, for a full discussion of that dimension.)

3. The two decision-making styles (consultative and joint) are part of a larger array of options that include *autonomous*, in which the leader makes the decision alone, and *delegative*, in which the problem is assigned to an individual or subgroup. These four decision-making styles were adapted from V. H. Vroom and P. Yetton, *Leadership and Decision-Making* (Pittsburgh: University of Pittsburgh Press, 1973). Vroom and Yetton found that most managers use all four decision-making styles. The central issue, however, concerns which style is used with the core problems. Autocratic leaders tend to use an autonomous style, most "participative" leaders use consultative style, but empowering leaders use joint style. A more detailed discussion of when one might use each of these styles can be found in D. L. Bradford and A. R. Cohen, *Managing for Excellence* (New York: John Wiley & Sons, 1984), Chapter 6.

4. An interesting study compared the creativity of the first and second solutions. In this research, groups were given a complex problem to solve. When they had reached a decision, the researcher thanked them and asked them to come up with a second solution. The second solution tended to be more creative than the first! See N. R. F. Maier and L. R. Hoffman, "Quality of First and Second Solutions in Group Problem Solving," *Journal of Applied Psychology* 44 (1960): pp. 278–283.

5. I. L. Janis, *Victims of Groupthink*, 2nd ed. (Boston: Houghton Mifflin, 1982). *Groupthink* is a process by which various aspects of critical problem solving are limited and distorted. When carried to its extreme form, each individual can think that he or she is the lone dissenter and goes along because everybody else wants the decision, even though, in fact, the majority are opposed. A humorous account of such "pluralistic ignorance" is found in Jerry B. Harvey, "The Abilene Paradox: The Management of Agreement," *Organization Dynamics* vol. 3, no. 1 (Summer 1974): pp. 63–80.

6. N. R. F. Maier and L. R. Hoffman, "Acceptance and Quality of Solutions as Related to Leaders' Attitudes Toward Disagreement in Group Problem Solving," *Journal of Applied Behavioral Science* 1 (1965): pp. 373–386.

7. A mode of leadership that contrasts with this traditional "heroic" mode is developed in *Managing for Excellence* by Bradford and Cohen. The "Post-heroic" leader is one who relies less on personally having the answer and more on developing a team in which the answers can be collectively developed.

8. These four dimensions were developed by Schein and are described in E. H. Schein, *Process Consultation* (Reading, MA: Addison-Wesley, 1969).

9. For reviews of work on stages of group development, see B. W. Tuckman, "Developmental Sequence in Small Groups," *Psychological Bulletin* 63 (1965): pp. 384–399, and J. Moosbruker, "Using a Stage Theory Model to Understand and Manage Transitions in Group Dynamics," *Training Theory and Practice* (NTL Institute), (1987), pp. 83–92.

I want to acknowledge the very helpful comments made on earlier drafts of this chapter by Allan R. Cohen and Craig Lundberg.

MANAGING INDIVIDUAL BEHAVIOR: 4 BRINGING OUT THE BEST IN PEOPLE

Stephen L. Fink

Effective managers learn to view organizational life from a number of different perspectives: From a broad perspective, they need to understand the overall system and to think in long-range terms. From a narrower perspective, they should know how groups function and how to build effective teamwork. However, when it comes right down to getting something done, the individual must do it, and the most competent managers understand just how to bring out the best in the people who work for them. Although this chapter focuses on the individual employee, never lose sight of the fact that the behavior of individuals occurs within the larger contexts of the group and the organization.

In today's organizations, increasing attention is being given to employee empowerment. Organizational leaders recognize that the days of coercive leadership and worker compliance belong to the past and that more effective models built on employee involvement and commitment are better suited to modern complex organizations. In this chapter we explore some ways to understand people as individuals who seek to meet needs, attain personal goals, live rewarding lives, make a difference, and find an overall sense of satisfaction with their work and personal lives. That understanding enables managers to empower their employees and to achieve the kinds of results that benefit everyone.

Let me begin with a case example, which will then be expanded throughout the chapter. A group of managers was presented with the following scenario.

> Lucy works in the financial department of a large insurance company. She usually arrives at work around 9:30 A.M. and often leaves work between 4:00

and 4:15 P.M. However, the normal working hours in the department are 9:00 to 5:00. Furthermore, every few weeks Lucy calls in to say that she has to miss work that day or sometimes just for the morning. How would you evaluate Lucy's level of commitment to her job? What action do you think her supervisor should take?

Most of the managers in the group felt that Lucy was not really committed to her job, that she should be warned that her behavior would have to change, and that if no change occurred that she should be fired.

The same group of managers was then presented with another scenario.

Ruth works in the same department as does Lucy. Ruth is a single parent whose husband died a year ago. She has two young children, one of whom is in day care and the other in first grade. Ruth usually takes work home with her and puts in extra hours on weekends, catching up on her unfinished work from the week. How would you evaluate Ruth's level of commitment to her job? What, if anything, should her supervisor do?

Most of the managers, in this instance, responded that Ruth was very committed to her job, perhaps a bit too committed, and that the supervisor should try to reduce her workload before she burned out.

It was then explained that Lucy and Ruth were one and the same person. She was an individual who was struggling to integrate her work life with her personal circumstances. Understanding her behavior on the job required more complete information than that offered in the first scenario. Unfortunately, however, we often fall into the trap of making judgments about people based on limited information—without fully understanding the world from their perspectives.

In an era of changing work patterns, changing composition in the work force, and especially an increasing diversity of backgrounds among the individuals who make up that work force, it is incumbent on managers to look carefully and open-mindedly into the unique situations of their subordinates. They can no longer rely on broad generalizations about employee needs, beliefs, and values.

Although broad concepts like Maslow's hierarchy of needs or Herzberg's two-factor theory of motivation still have their place in our thinking about human behavior, the ethnic, gender, and cultural mix of employees pushes managers toward understanding behavior more directly through the eyes of the individual. Each employee brings to the workplace his or her own set of needs, beliefs, values, cultural heritage, and whatever else defines that person's internal "system." To really understand the individual's behavior, one needs to look at all these elements and how they take shape in that person in any given situation.

This chapter looks at the various elements that make up the individual, including the person's needs, goals, values, beliefs, and abilities, but especially the person's self-concept. Furthermore, it examines these in terms of the issues that managers face in this decade: bringing out the highest levels of performance, satisfaction, and development. However, the chapter repeatedly emphasizes the importance of context, that is, the fact that a person's behavior is always determined by a combination of factors, some internal (in the person) and some external (in the situation).

THE WORLD FROM INSIDE

In the absence of complete information, people have a tendency to fill in the gaps with attributions based on their own experiences and on some very limited stereotypes they might have about people. Effective leadership requires reducing, if not eliminating, blind spots; it requires basing judgments about people, especially our employees, on information that enables us literally to see the world from the other person's perspective. Through one's own eyes, every action taken, every emotion felt, and every belief held makes absolute sense—even when to others they make no sense at all. People develop self-concepts based on everything they have experienced. Since each person is the only one who has had a particular set of experiences, the behavior of each set can best be understood by knowing how a particular situation is seen through that person's eyes.

Let us return to Lucy. (We can drop the name *Ruth* now.) As her manager, you now realize that you indeed have an excellent worker, one that ought to be encouraged and rewarded for her commitment and performance. However, you really do not know just what inspires her superior performance. Maybe she is like most employees and wants to advance in the company, make more money, receive recognition, and develop greater knowledge in her job. That would not be an unreasonable assumption, and the chances are that in many cases like Lucy's you would be correct. However, Lucy is a unique individual, with her own special needs and beliefs, her own potential for learning and growth, and—perhaps most important of all—her unique self-concept. To fully appreciate Lucy and to make the best possible decisions on her behalf, as well as in the best interests of the company, you ought to find out just what Lucy's world is like from her perspective rather than from yours alone.

The following simple proposition governs all this:

The best way to understand why someone behaves in a certain way is to find out how that individual sees himself or herself in a given situation.

This view forces us to look at both the person and the context. Whereas it definitely does help to have general concepts that fit most people, it is important to get inside the world of the other person to understand fully how such general concepts get played out.

Now what are some of the things you want to know about Lucy and her job? Obviously you would not need or wish to know everything about her, since not everything is relevant to Lucy's work situation. The next section of the chapter presents a framework for understanding her, beginning with a fairly broad concept that emphasizes the total context in which Lucy works and then proceeding to a more microscopic perspective that emphasizes Lucy's more personal ways of understanding and coping. As Lucy's story unfolds, you will be introduced to others in her world, including her boss and co-workers. Each enters the picture in relation to a particular issue that is important in a manager's world.

The issues that come into focus include the following: dealing with interpersonal differences, including cultural ones; understanding and managing employee stress and performance deterioration; developing high levels of employee commitment; observing different selves in different roles; incorporating the new ways to manage; handling difficult employees; and studying matters related to ethics and values, including the problem of sexual harassment in the workplace.

A FRAMEWORK FOR UNDERSTANDING BEHAVIOR AT WORK

From a manager's perspective, the most desirable outcomes in the work setting include high levels of productivity, high levels of employee satisfaction and morale, and continuous learning and improvement on the job. Although no magic formula exists for achieving these outcomes, there is a relatively simple way to organize one's thinking. Borrowing from a conceptual model that was created for understanding group behavior, one useful way to understand individual behavior is to look at the following facets.

a. What is required of that person in the job
b. What that person brings to the job
c. The organizational context and resources provided
d. What emerges as a consequence of combining a, b, and c

It is d, the actual behavior on the job, that leads to the organization's desired levels of performance, satisfaction, and development. Remember, however, that the failure to achieve any of the outcomes can be related to any one or combination of factors in a, b, or c. Consequently it is essential to understand each element in the model and how they combine if a manager wants to maximize the outcomes. First, I go over each of the factors and then discuss how they combine to produce the desired outcomes.

Job Requirements

We begin by determining what is required of the worker: the skills or expertise involved, prior experience or training necessary, the kind of temperament that fits the work, the personality factors that may be involved, and so forth. In some cases the work is clearly defined and the job requirements are easy to specify; in other cases—and it seems increasingly so nowadays—the requirements are not clear and make it difficult to develop an exact picture.

In Lucy's case the requirements of the job are fairly clear-cut. The tasks require a knowledge of accounting and some basics in financial management; some experience in processing insurance accounts for large businesses; a very sharp eye for details and possible errors in the accounts; a great deal of patience in wading through endless facts and figures; the ability to deal effectively with co-workers and with those in other units of the company, especially in policy production; and a strong commitment to ensuring that the work is completed accurately and in a timely way.

What the Person Brings to the Job

In some respects, matching someone to a job like Lucy's seems straightforward. Yet considering the scenarios presented at the beginning of the chapter, it is easy to see that Lucy (a.k.a. Ruth) turned out to be an especially valuable employee, one that many managers would give their eyeteeth to find. What makes her so special is her self-concept. She views herself as a highly competent, quality-minded, responsible person who lives up to her commitments and never lets anyone else down. These are qualities that go beyond the job requirements; they correspond to her very core values, traits that are not easily identified in advance of hiring someone, even with the use of references.

Some managers claim that finding the right people for the jobs is the hardest and yet the most important task. Many claim that once they have succeeded in that task, the rest is a piece of cake. That may be an exaggeration, but there is certainly enough truth in the idea to warrant a great deal of attention.

Lucy brings to the situation, then, all the skills and knowledge to do the job, the temperament and personality that helps her get along with others, and a self-concept that generates a high level of commitment to her job and the company. As the managers who misjudged Lucy discovered, it is easy to attribute one's own views to another person without ever testing to see if the views match. By encouraging employees to express their ideas and beliefs, by inquiring about the reasoning behind their actions, and by testing assumptions about what employees think and feel, it is possible to develop a fairly accurate picture of their self-concepts. The more in touch one is with the world as seen by the other person, the better one can facilitate that person's performance and learning.

The Work Context: Work Setting, Technology, Rewards, and Culture

People conduct their work activities within an organizational context. That context can bring out the best or the worst in people, when it comes to job performance. Furthermore, even when an employee's performance in and of itself is excellent, factors in the environment can reduce or cancel out the positive outcomes: A Roger Clemens can pitch a brilliant game and lose because the team failed to produce enough runs. A terrific salesperson can close a deal, only to have someone else along the line mess up the details of delivery. And apart from the behavior of other people, a number of other factors have powerful effects on the outcomes of an individual's efforts, including the physical work setting, the technology provided, the kinds of rewards offered, and the overall culture of the organization.

Work Setting

In recent years work environments have received increasing attention as important influences on work behavior. As tasks become more complex and interdependent it becomes increasingly necessary to redesign work spaces to encourage frequent interpersonal contact. Lucy's manager might need to find ways to give her easy access to other people, many in other departments, whose work she affects and is affected by. The physical location of her work area could be a significant factor in her performance. In addition, it may be critical to evaluate an employee's work space for noise level, privacy, and so forth. Lucy would certainly find it difficult to do her job amid chaos or bustling activity. Some organizations have been highly innovative in their designs of work environments. Steelcase Corporate Development Center, for example, has areas that promote a high level of employee interaction; but these are balanced by working areas that are secluded and quiet for activities that require concentration and few interruptions.

Technology

Since organizations are becoming dependent on the latest advances in technology, a manager needs to know which technology best fits the situation and how to ensure that the employee is well matched to that technology. Lucy, for example, would operate best with the latest in computer networking, since she needs to have access to and be able to provide information to many different individuals and departments in the system. The old file folders that went from one set of hands to another would not help Lucy perform at her best, nor would she find the task very satisfying.

Rewards

The manager is the one who most directly affects the rewards, opportunities, and development of the employee; the manager is the one who can determine whether or not the employee's expectations are met. Here again one can rely to some extent on general concepts, but one must make every effort to understand just what rewards are meaningful to a particular individual and what unique expectations that individual might have. Although most people value financial rewards, there are other more significant incentives. Lucy, for example, as a single mother, might find flextime to be an attractive part of a work environment. In general, finding ways to help employees integrate and balance their work lives with their personal lives has proved to be a major benefit. Given the increasing diversity in work force composition, managers may need to become more imaginative about alternative work patterns in order to reward employees more effectively than with money alone.

An important part of dispensing rewards is recognizing that they link to performance through employees' expectations. To the extent that an employee expects to receive a given reward for his or her effort and that reward has a perceived value to that employee, he or she will perform at the level necessary to achieve that reward. Keep in mind that this principle applies to what are called extrinsic rewards, such as pay, promotion, special benefits, and recognition from others (especially the boss). They are the rewards that management dispenses following satisfactory performance. If the expectation is not met, then chances are that future performance will fall off. It isn't that the reward is no longer important, it's just that the employee has lost some confidence that his or her efforts will produce it.

A basic principle here is that a manager must understand each employee's expectations about the rewards that the manager controls and that any violation of those expectations, whether intended or not, will affect the employee's subsequent performance.

It is also significant that many important rewards derive from the work itself—called intrinsic rewards. The challenge of solving a vexing problem, the excitement of designing a new piece of equipment, or the simple joy of mastering a new skill are examples of intrinsic rewards. They are controlled mostly by the individual worker, but the freedom and opportunities to exercise that control are afforded by the manager. To the extent that work is intrinsically rewarding, performance will be self-sustaining, that is, not dependent on the actions of others, including the manager.

Finally, a manager needs to recognize that the perceived value of a reward, especially financial, depends on the employee's own perspective on its equity. A given amount of money might seem appropriate from a manager's standpoint but might appear too low to the employee who knows that others, whom the employee judges to be no more deserving, are receiving more. The problem has been especially troublesome in recent years as organizations have had to deal with serious gender inequities. Unfortunately, inequities of that sort are not easily corrected. What seems from an outsider's perspective to be a minor inequity might very well be judged as significant by the individual involved. Apart from any substantive difference, the symbolic meaning can be important. It can represent, from the employees' vantage point, a message from the top about their perceived worth to the organization and particularly to their own boss.

It is tempting for management to try to keep all salary information carefully guarded in order to avoid the kind of scenarios I briefly described in the preceding paragraph. For some organizations, doing so might work, but for many the informal system seems to have a way of uncovering that kind of information, and often it gets distorted as it moves along the grapevine. Making all wage and salary information public is an alternative, but that also has its downside and is usually resisted by those in power. There is no simple answer, but organizational leaders need to recognize both the long- and short-range implications of any such policies, especially since they have a major impact on the organization's culture, which is discussed next.

Culture

A great deal has been written recently about organizational culture, which refers to the overall values, customs, norms, and patterns of behavior that uniquely characterize a given organization. It is related to the general atmosphere of the place. We have learned that organizational culture has very powerful effects on people's behavior, feelings, and attitudes—effects that until recently were not well understood or fully appreciated by organizational leaders and managers.

If, for example, the culture of the organization is characterized by competition, one-upmanship, secrecy, and political maneuvering, then individuals will tend to behave in ways that are self-serving rather than in the best interests of the group or the system. We don't really know what kind of culture exists in Lucy's company. If she is someone who likes competition, sees herself as smarter than most of her co-workers, and good at getting what she wants, then she would be successful in that kind of setting. On the other hand, if Lucy values collaboration and teamwork, sees herself as open and honest with others, and places the interests of the company above her own personal gain, then the above setting would probably not be the right one for her. Clearly there is no one kind of organizational culture that fits all people. The employees that thrive in a given setting over the long run are those whose self-concepts are congruent with the culture.

The overall message, then, is that when you hire someone for a job you are also bringing them into a larger context than is defined by just the tasks to be performed. The work setting may or may not have the right ingredients for that individual. It is not always possible to know enough about the person to be sure how well he or she might fit, but a few simple questions can give you a picture of that person's self-concept that will help you to predict the likelihood that the fit is a good one.

In general, once you know the requirements of the job to be performed and you have the right person for that job, then your role as a manager is to make sure that the situation has all the right ingredients to help the employee maintain the highest levels of performance, satisfaction, and development. Before you make the hiring decision, it is important to consider how well the individual fits the organization as a whole, and, after you hire that person—assuming the match is a good one—you need to attend to that person's orientation and integration into the system. (See Chapter 8, "Designing Effective Organizations," by Phyllis F. and Leonard A. Schlesinger, for more on corporate culture.)

Behavior on the Job

Good managers are like good scientists: If they combine all the right elements, the consequences are reasonably predictable. However, even with scientists who have a high degree of control over the events they are studying, there is always some degree of uncertainty. The typical manager does not have a high degree of control over events and, no matter how good he or she is at putting together all the right ingredients, is always faced with unpredictability. Consequently, he or she must learn to manage situations as they unfold. As often as not, there are pleasant surprises and not just disappointments.

Lucy happened to be one of those pleasant surprises to her boss, who never expected the level of commitment that Lucy showed. In fact, because of her personal situation, her boss had anticipated frequent absences and delays in the completion of her work. Had he known Lucy's concept of herself at the outset, his expectations would have been more consistent with her actual behavior. Consider the number of times that the Lucys of this world get shortchanged on opportunities because of expectations that have nothing to do with the individuals themselves and more to do with stereotyped generalizations.

All we ever see on the job is the actual behavior and expressed attitudes of people. When these behaviors and attitudes are not what they ought to be, from a manager's point of view, the next logical step is to figure out why. It is often tempting simply to conclude that the employee is not right for the job and to go look for a replacement. When the problem repeats, hopefully we realize that our previous solution was not right. Or maybe we repeat our actions again—until the light finally goes on. As the owner of the New York Yankees, George Steinbrenner hired Billy Martin as manager five times and fired Billy Martin five times. In each instance it was because the team was doing poorly. If one's role model is Steinbrenner, then one has a lifetime formula for solving performance problems—badly.

Effective managers try to diagnose the situation and identify possible causes of problems before reaching conclusions about what to do. Even though it is often the case that poor performance results from inadequacies in the performer, it is just as often the case that the situation is creating such obstacles that even the best performer (like a Lucy) could not do the job well. The value in using the kind of framework suggested here is that it provides a map for exploring many avenues for solving performance problems. And many of the contributing factors can more easily and inexpensively be changed than replacing an employee.

The greatest challenge to a manager is to develop ways of combining the first three factors (job, person, and context) to make the task of managing the fourth factor (employee performance) easier. It's like directing a play: With the right script in the hands of the right actors with the right props, the performance takes care of itself. And this notion is the key to creating a work environment that fosters employee commitment rather than compliance. In the next section we explore some ways to do this.

Marrying the Technical and Human Requirements

The tasks that Lucy had to perform in her job were outlined. They essentially constitute the technical requirements of the work. Also discussed were Lucy's attributes and how they related to the job requirements. Evidently, Lucy and the job are well matched. What I did not discuss, however, was *how* Lucy's manager might have gone about creating the match. Most managers would simply assign Lucy to the job, explain what is required, and then expect Lucy to follow preestablished procedures. Such practices have been the norm for a long time and have resulted in satisfactory performance. In short, the technical requirements are met and the work gets done. But what happens with the human requirements—Lucy's needs, personal beliefs, creative ideas, and her own development? They could easily be overlooked, especially since Lucy does believe in doing her best, no matter what.

In the past twenty or more years, a great deal of research has been conducted on work design and work redesign. One of the most important principles is the notion that people who are empowered to design and manage their work in ways that fit their own preferred styles (provided that the task requirements are met) do better work for sustained periods of time and maintain higher levels of commitment than people who are not empowered in this way. Although this principle makes obvious sense, for a variety of reasons many managers simply do not accept it, or at least do not act on it.

Much of today's increasing trend toward self-managing work teams is explicitly tied to this principle. The approach is one that empowers work groups to operate without external supervision—to rely on their own internal resources for leadership, planning, controlling quality, managing member relations, and so forth. The heart of the activity is self-management, which permits and encourages employees to put their personal identities into the work. (See also Chapter 10, "Self-Managing Teams," by Harvey Kolodny and Torbjorn Stjernberg, in this volume.)

Someone like Lucy needs little if any supervision. Give her the task and the resources to carry it out, and then get out of the way. This does not mean that the manager's job ends. Getting out of the way means letting Lucy manage herself; it does not mean that the manager no longer has a role to perform. At some time Lucy will require additional resources, specialized education, exceptions to policies, opportunities to attend conferences, and help in obtaining access to important people in the system. The manager's role needs to be more a facilitator or coach than a controller, more a mentor than a boss, and someone who can maintain a sense of the larger context in which the individual is operating.

It is especially important for a manager to pay constant attention to the human aspects of the work: challenge, variety in the work, a sense of the whole process, doing something that has meaning, and something that makes one feel valued by the organization. When these elements are embedded in the work, the employee is likely to identify with the work, as well as with the people and organization.

Knowing all this in a general sense is only the first step. To understand precisely how it translates into the special world of the individual employee is the critical next step. For Lucy, what exactly constitutes variety, what makes the job challenging, what aspects of her job constitute the whole, what has meaning for her, and what would make her feel valued? The answers to these questions can come only from inside Lucy and not from her boss. The importance of letting the employees themselves design or redesign the ways in which they conduct their work lies in the proposition stated earlier: They will do better work over the long run, and they will be more committed to the organization. They will find the ways to generate the variety, challenge, wholeness, meaning, and sense of being valued that will make the marriage work.

These approaches foster employee commitment, which in turn tends to improve employee performance. Although managers readily perceive the direct link between performance and extrinsic rewards, they do not always recognize the less-direct link between actions that engender commitment and, thereby, improve performance.

Creating Interpersonal Matches: Appreciative Understanding

Lucy often works closely with Fred. Although they generally work well together, they are very different in personality and in their self-concepts. Lucy is systematic and focused, works according to a plan, is good at managing detail, remains calm and thoughtful in a crisis, enjoys interacting with others, and has a great deal of self-confidence. Fred, on the other hand, tends to be spontaneous, flits back and forth on tasks, never plans his work in advance, likes the big picture and not the details, loses control in a crisis, sometimes enjoys working with others but more often gets lost in his own thoughts, and does not make decisions easily. Fred sees himself as the creative member of the pair and sees Lucy as the concrete implementer of ideas. Lucy agrees.

The differences between Lucy and Fred could easily be sources of conflict. In fact, until they got to know each other well enough to understand their differences, they did experience many conflicts. Lucy would try to get Fred to be more organized and often complained that he never stuck to what he was doing. Fred complained that Lucy never did anything creative or spontaneous and paid too much attention to detail. Eventually they both came to appreciate their complementarity, the fact that together they represented a balanced and more rounded approach to the work. Lucy learned to trust Fred's hunches in problem solving, and Fred learned to defer to Lucy for planning and organizing.

They both have the same boss, Larry, and the differences between Lucy and Fred make life very interesting for him. Larry happens to see the world in much the same way as Lucy, which is what made him hire her in the first place. Fred was already in the department when Larry came on board, and right from the start Larry struggled to understand Fred. He experienced the same frustrations as Lucy did, but it wasn't until she had learned to appreciate Fred that Larry began to do the same. Initially Larry had hoped that when he assigned Lucy to work with Fred she would be able to change him. The eventual outcome, as noted, was much better. And Larry became a better manager for it. He learned, as most effective managers need to learn, that the diverse personalities of his employees are an asset to be cultivated. Furthermore, he learned that trying to re-create oneself in one's subordinates is not only a waste of time, but is actually counter to what generates a strong work force.

It is this kind of mutual appreciative understanding that fosters effective working relationships and, at the same time, brings out the best in each individual employee, as well as in the manager. In the case of Fred and Lucy, the barriers were not too difficult to surmount; even in Larry's relationship with Fred, the same could be said. But what happens when the employee's psychological world is radically different from that of the manager and others in the workplace? Such is the case when cultural differences create the barriers, namely, differences in language, values, and fundamental belief systems about the meaning of work and life in general. Organizations today are increasingly multinational and multicultural; it behooves us to discover or construct bridges across the cultures that enable people from very different backgrounds to communicate with and really understand each other. We look at some of the ways a manager can do so in the next section.

A World of Differences, Differences in Worlds

Hector recently joined Larry's department. He grew up in Venezuela, moved to the United States at 18 to attend college, where he majored in business. He was hired by Larry to work with Lucy and Fred as a financial assistant.

Hector has all the necessary background to do the job, is highly motivated, and is eager to please his boss. Larry assumed that, because Hector had been a straight-A student and was pleased to join the company, Hector would take initiative. Additionally Larry assumed that, once having learned the job itself, Hector would require little supervision or direction. Lucy and Fred also expected Hector to manage himself for the most part and not wait to be told what to do. The style of supervision in Larry's group is to give very general assignments and let the employee pretty much manage the details as he or she chooses.

After a couple of weeks it became evident that things were not working out as Larry had expected. Lucy and Fred complained that Hector, while very competent and easy to relate to, was too dependent on others for direction. At meetings Hector never offered his own suggestions but seemed to be overly concerned about pleasing everyone else by agreeing with whatever was said, especially when Larry or Fred spoke and not so much when Lucy spoke. After awhile Fred began to get annoyed with Hector's behavior and Lucy began to feel put off by Hector's male bias. Larry needed to do something to solve the problems. Since he did not want to fire Hector, he began by just talking with him to see if he could understand the situation from Hector's viewpoint.

When he called Hector into his office, it was obvious that the young man was very nervous. Hector knew something was wrong and felt embarrassed that things had reached that point. He was afraid that he might get fired. Larry tried at first to get Hector to express his feelings about the job and the people, but Hector was so tense that he could not speak freely or comfortably about those things. So Larry tried a different approach: He asked Hector about his family and about life in Venezuela. The young man opened up in ways that Larry had not seen before. It became evident that Hector missed his family and was feeling out of place at the company. What also came out was that close relationships were very important to him. By pleasing people he had hoped to create such relationships. It hadn't worked and he was feeling more lonely than ever. One of the most interesting insights for Larry concerned the way in which Hector recreated family relationships in the work setting. He seemed to look to Larry as a father or uncle, to Fred as an older brother, and to Lucy as a sister. Unfortunately, since women in his country had lower status, Lucy was seen as less important.

It took some weeks for Larry to help Hector drop some of his expectations and take greater initiative. It also took some discussions with Lucy and Fred to help them understand Hector and what it might take to improve things. What was most important to Larry was what he learned about understanding a person whose background was so different. By getting into Hector's world he was able to make sense of Hector's behavior. Hector's image of the work situation was built on a family metaphor, and he behaved accordingly. Larry realized that the act of joining Hector in his world made Hector feel understood, and it allowed him to express himself in his own ways. Without fully understanding Hector in terms of his own world, Larry could easily have judged him by inappropriate standards and could have labeled him as a "difficult employee," who required some kind of corrective action. (For more on finding ways to get mutual benefit from people with differing perspectives, see Chapter 11, "Managing Diversity," by R. Roosevelt Thomas, Jr.)

Bridging the Gap with Metaphors

Most people have metaphors for life and for work. As a manager you might think of your organization as a playing field where teams and individuals compete, or as a battlefield where warring factions try to destroy each other, or as a large ocean where people try to navigate their ships through both calm and treacherous waters, or as a grand farm where many different crops are grown. Each of these metaphors has different implications for a manager. In one you are a coach, in another a general, in the next a ship captain, and in the last a cultivator of growing things.

Your concept of yourself as a manager translates into effective behavior when it is compatible with the self-concepts of your colleagues and subordinates. The coach expects assertive, competitive behavior from the team members. Unless those individuals believe that they are competent competitors, the expected behavior will not be forthcoming. In each of the metaphors just suggested, the expectations of the leaders derive from their self-concepts and the outcomes that they achieve depend chiefly on how they match the self-concepts of the followers.

Think about your own view of an organization and your role in it as a manager. Do you know how your metaphor matches those of your employees? If not, you might explore it with them. The process can prove to be enlightening and might lead to some improvements in your employees' performance and attitudes. You are probably already communicating your metaphor to others, and they are reacting to it. For example, do you tend to use terms like "troops" and "chain of command"? How about such phrases as "planting the idea" or "giving them a chance to grow"? You could probably think of many images that you and others use in your everyday conversations that convey a working metaphor. Sometimes one can discover one's own metaphors simply by listening to oneself more closely.

Furthermore, it might be important for you to consider possible changes in your organizational metaphor as things around you change. It may be no longer appropriate for today's business world, or it may be too limited for the stage of growth of your department or company. For instance, a family metaphor seems to work well in a small entrepreneurial business but may prove dysfunctional when the company grows beyond a certain size. In addition, as you hire people it could be valuable to know how they see themselves as members of the organization. Hector brought with him a family image, while those around him, including his boss, worked from a different image. It is possible that Larry—had he known what he now knows about Hector— might not have hired him in the first place, or preferably he would have done better at helping Hector enter the work setting.

Watching for Signs of Stress

Until Larry was able to help Hector out of his difficult situation, Hector had been experiencing increasing stress. The longer the problem went on, the more tension people were feeling and the worse Hector's behavior became. It is typical of people to deal with stress by falling back on familiar behavior that worked in the past. Even when it does not work in a particular situation, the behavior often persists for lack of any perceived alternative. The loop gets sealed by the reactions of others that increase the tension that elicit even more of the same behavior. Fortunately Larry picked up the signs of Hector's stress, took an action that broke the loop, and steered the process in a more constructive direction.

In this section we look at some of the sources of employee stress and how to manage the situation in order to reduce that stress. As you read this section, keep in mind that stress can be contagious. It is not uncommon for one person to generate stress in others, even when that person feels little or no stress. Remember Typhoid Mary? She managed to spread typhoid to hundreds of others and never got the disease herself. It is the same with stress: Many feel it and spread it around, and many spread it around without feeling it. In Hector's case, he both felt it and spread it. When a manager is the stress carrier, it does not take much imagination to predict the effect on employees.

Sources of Stress

Nowadays it seems that everything is a potential source of stress. Even when things are going well, we worry about when they will turn sour. So much of people's lives is governed by factors over which they have no control; it's a wonder that most people are not nervous wrecks most of the time. A manager must attend to the sources of stress that are controllable. After looking at sources of stress, I discuss the various signs or symptoms that a manager needs to be aware of, keeping in mind that whether or not a situation is stressful always depends on the person experiencing that situation. What is stressful for Fred may not be for Lucy; certainly what was stressful for Hector was a reflection of his unique needs and self-concept in relation to the situation.

I discuss three sources of stress: job ambiguity, unfinished work (especially from job overload), and poorly defined role expectations. There are certainly many others that deserve attention, but limitations of space force me to restrict the number covered.

Job Ambiguity

Some people have a much higher tolerance for ambiguity than do others. In fact, many individuals like the challenge of creating their own structure out of what others might perceive to be chaos. For employees who prefer situations of relative certainty, in which they are provided with all the necessary information to perform their jobs, ambiguity tends to shake their confidence and becomes a source of stress. If the situation persists too long, their work will deteriorate. Most employees require enough information to reduce the uncertainty to a comfortable level. Since that level varies from one person to the next, it is important to assess exactly what the individual needs and at what point too much information is being provided.

Lucy likes to have all the information she can get, because she is at her best when she can make decisions based on real data. Fred is more intuitive and is comfortable with less information; he is more willing to make leaps of faith than is Lucy. In fact, whenever Larry overloads Fred with more information than Fred wants, Fred often stops listening. That drives both Lucy and Larry crazy, but they have learned to read the signs and know when to back off. Hector, as you remember, showed signs of stress in the form of repeated dysfunctional behavior because the situation for him was highly ambiguous and full of uncertainty until Larry intervened.

Since there is so much variation among people with respect to their tolerance or even preference for ambiguity and since there is so much variation among work environments in this same regard, it would follow that part of a manager's job is to look for the right fit between the person's tolerance level and the situational level of ambiguity. To some extent it is possible to predict that a given work situation will be inherently ambiguous and to recruit people best suited to it. However, most work situations vary over time, with periods of relative certainty and periods of virtual chaos. How often one hears about all the fire fighting that organizations live with. Therefore, the best a manager can do is make every effort to support his or her employees through the periods of stress as they express the need for that support. Larry did so with Hector, and he learned that for the next time around, with future Hectors, he could take a more preventive approach.

Unfinished Work

It seems to be a very natural human tendency to seek closure in whatever we do. There is a famous story about a great composer who heard a musical phrase stopped before it was completed: He felt compelled to go to the piano and complete the phrase. Unfinished work creates a tension, a sense of uneasiness that often intrudes on other things. How many times have you left work unfinished at the office only to find it constantly popping up in your thoughts? Have you ever actually returned to your office to finish the job because you couldn't stand the tension? Some people do just that. It helps them sleep more easily because the unfinished business no longer disturbs their peace of mind.

Probably the main contributor to unfinished work is job overload. Often managers pile on work assignments without fully knowing an employee's workload, especially in today's leaner, flatter organizations. Equally often the employee colludes in the process by accepting the additional work, possibly out of a fear of saying no to the boss, but also out of a belief that the extra load can still be managed without much strain. However, if the pattern continues for too long, some of the jobs simply do not get done. Eventually an accumulation of unfinished work will generate a level of stress that can result in poor performance. All too often people try to push themselves to put in the extra time, take work home, or do whatever it takes to catch up—only to find that the quality of the work suffers and that they do not catch up anyway. As a manager you need to be on the lookout for this behavior. Up to a point it reflects the employee's commitment to the job, but beyond that point it might reflect a fear of failure or humiliation in the eyes of others, especially the boss. Since it is unlikely that the employee himself or herself will bring the problem to the attention of the boss, it is up to the latter to broach the subject and to find ways of reducing the load, helping the employee find closure on work activities.

Poorly Defined Role Expectations

The problem of unfinished work often results from a manager's failure to define the role expectations with the employee. Unclear or misunderstood expectations held by the employee will usually result in some degree of stress and often eventually result in a very high level. Similarly, expectations that are unrealistic in the eyes of the individual can exert unnecessary pressure on that individual to perform at a level beyond what is reasonable. The situation then becomes unstable and requires a renegotiation between the manager and the employee.

One of the factors that contributed to Hector's stress was his tendency to fill in the ambiguities of the situation, described earlier, with expectations that did not match those of Larry or the others. Hector assumed that his role was to act only on the directions given by his manager, that he was not to take initiative. Once he and Larry renegotiated what was expected of Hector, then the situation stabilized and Hector was able to fulfill the more clearly defined expectations.

Too often an employee tends to avoid going to his or her boss to discuss and redefine role expectations, since such action can be perceived as an act of weakness. Unfortunately the problem does not go away, it gets worse, and the level of stress makes constructive discussion extremely difficult. Tension and anger impede listening, and the parties cast blame rather than try to solve the problem; the result is often an extreme action such as the firing of an employee. Whereas the emergence of such a scenario seems unnecessary and one wonders why it was not nipped in the bud, the fact is that many people avoid unpleasant situations until they explode in front of them. In Hector's case, it took Larry's initiative to turn things around, since Hector was too insecure to do so. And that is typical, because often when a power differential exists between two people, the person in the position of greater power is the one who must initiate contact between the parties. The person in power—the manager—must be sensitive to the signs or symptoms of the problem, which are discussed next. (Chapter 5, "Power, Politics, and Influence," by Anne Donnellon, addresses the possibilities of taking initiative from lower-power positions.)

Symptoms of Stress

It should be noted at the outset that I am describing some behaviors that are a normal part of everyone's repertoire. It is only when they persist and when a number of them occur at the same time that one needs to take action. For example, an employee coming in late or missing work once in awhile is probably within normal limits. When it becomes chronic or when combined with long three-martini lunches and emotional outbursts at work, then it might very well be a sign of stress. Furthermore, it is important to judge the behavior in the context of an individual's normal style. Loud, intense expressions from someone who is very reserved and quiet represent something very different from the same behavior in someone who is loud and intense. Conversely, the talkative extrovert who suddenly or gradually withdraws from social interaction is likely to be showing signs of stress. In short, it is not the behavior itself but the behavior in the context of the individual's normal pattern that needs to be evaluated.

Also important is the realization that the same behavior in one organizational context might not produce the kind of stress that it would in another. Had Hector been working in a Latin American insurance company his dependency on taking orders might not have resulted in the same outcome as it did in the U.S. company. The role expectations might have been more congruent with his concept of himself as an employee.

The symptoms of stress that a manager should watch for can be very overt, as in emotional outbursts or repeated lateness, or they can be very subtle, as is the case with headaches, stomach upset, exhaustion, inability to sleep, and the like—symptoms that are usually known only to the person under stress. But careful attention to an employee's general behavior pattern can enable a manager to perceive even those signs. In the final analysis, it is the quality of work that suffers, and that is quite overt.

The following list gives rules of thumb that you can apply to yourself or suggest to your subordinates as ways of reducing or preventing undue stress.

1. Cultivate an awareness of the signs of stress.
2. Get to know your level of tolerance for ambiguity and go after needed information to keep it tolerable.

3. Establish priorities and focus only on those tasks that really matter, when faced with too many.

4. Take breaks from tasks frequently enough so that you can maintain concentration.

5. Assess the level of involvement that is actually required of you in a task, and delegate or share as much as possible.

6. Review and renegotiate role expectations frequently enough to prevent or minimize unfinished business.

You can undoubtedly think of many other ways, but the important thing to remember is that the longer one lets a stressful situation continue, the more difficult it becomes to confront directly and effectively. That is a lesson that many people seem to have to learn many times over.

When Performance Deteriorates

Most enlightened organizations have some form of employee assistance program (EAP). With all the stresses at work and in people's lives, it can be expected that a certain percentage of employees, including the best, will suffer from some kind of emotional problem. Too often, by the time managers and co-workers become aware of a problem, it has reached a serious stage and may show up in the form of substance abuse and psychological dysfunction. And when it reaches that stage, job performance will certainly suffer.

Few managers are trained to deal with such situations, and most will insist that it is not part of their job, that an employee's problems are not the manager's business. They might even be willing to fire a valuable employee rather than deal directly with such a situation. And often they do.

Successful EAPs do not simply remove the problem from the manager's area of responsibility; instead they educate the manager in how to spot the warning signs early on and how to confront the employee both candidly and supportively, with the objective of getting the individual to seek help before it is too late. Individuals have a remarkable capacity to deny problems, especially addictions, and they have just as hard a time denying poor job performance when it is well documented. Even though they may rationalize at first, they must eventually acknowledge the realities of their poor performance. Often that, and that alone, is enough to push them into some effort to change the situation. The ability and willingness of a manager to deal with normally competent employees who have hit a bad period in their lives and whose performance is suffering can not only save the company an investment but even save a valuable life in the bargain.

The next section discusses ways to build commitment in employees. However, on the topic of stress it is worth pointing out that some organizational experts suggest that employees may experience too high a level of commitment to their jobs, resulting in a high level of stress. To the extent that one develops perfectionist standards for one's own performance and pressures oneself to meet the standards, high stress and eventual burnout are likely to occur. That explains the importance for managers to be vigilant for signs of stress, even in those employees considered the best of the bunch, because it is this group whose commitment is valued by the employer and whose signs of stress might get overshadowed by their superior performance. Unfortunately it is only when the pressures become too great and the performance begins to deteriorate that many managers recognize the signs of stress that have been there all along. Then they may need to rely on an EAP for help.

Building Employee Commitment

Committed employees are those who identify with their work, with their co-workers, and with their organization. They are the ones a manager can trust to get a job done, to figure out ways of solving problems for themselves, to pay attention to how their work relates to that of others and collaborate when necessary, and to act always in the best interests of the organization as a whole, not placing personal priorities above group or organizational priorities. Although a newly hired individual will probably not show commitment in all three areas (work, co-worker, and organization), an employer can recruit and hire people who at least identify with the work. Commitment in the other two areas takes some time to build, and there are specific ways a manager can accomplish this.

Commitment to the Work

People who are committed to the work itself usually find it intrinsically rewarding, become so absorbed that they lose track of time, take great pride in the quality of their work, think about it even when not on the job, and make constant efforts to improve. They are the employees who do not watch the clock or sit around waiting to be told what to do next. Monetary rewards are important but are secondary to the rewards derived just from doing the work.

Lucy is an excellent example of an employee strongly committed to the work and, as will be discussed a little later, to the organization. Although she was forced to juggle difficult priorities around work and family, she did so in ways that met and exceeded the requirements of her job. And don't forget how easy it is for a manager to fall into the trap of misjudging an employee's commitment level based on very limited information. Lucy's working hours alone were a poor index of her commitment. Larry, fortunately, understood Lucy's situation and gave her the freedom to manage her own working hours: He knew a valuable employee when he had one and, as an enlightened manager, he did not let himself get trapped by some set of standardized rules or policies. Let us look at some other ways a manager can foster strong employee commitment.

Earlier in the chapter I discussed how such efforts as a job redesign that enables employees to shape the work to their own style tend to generate commitment. What such efforts do is create employee ownership of the tasks and thus identification with the work. Rather than repeat the points made earlier, in the following I suggest a few more things a manager can do to foster an employee's identification with his or her work.

1. Take a chance on trusting employees to manage themselves even when you are not sure of them. Progress will often be made, and, even when it is not, you will have lost little and learned a great deal.

2. Let your employees do things their own way even when it is not the way you yourself would do it.

3. Let your employees make mistakes, but require that they learn from the mistakes and not repeat them. Remember, preventing others from making mistakes removes opportunities for important learning.

4. Let go of the tendency to control the behavior of your subordinates, even if doing so gives you some anxiety. And don't hang around biting your nails; it only generates tension in others.

5. Develop yourself as a role model—make sure your own behavior reflects commitment to your job.

6. Make your expectations clear, but always remain open to renegotiating them as circumstances change.

Commitment to Co-workers

Employees who are committed to their co-workers tend to be aware of how others are doing; are ready to help them out when necessary, sometimes putting the needs of the other person above their own; do not just mind their own business; make an effort to bring new co-workers on board; and often perceive co-workers as members of the work family. These behaviors and attitudes are easily identified by an observant manager. But more importantly, these behaviors and attitudes can be modeled, supported, and encouraged by the manager.

Because most work is not conducted in isolation, it is important for the individual to recognize task interdependencies. Such recognition is basic to teamwork and serves to enhance the individual's performance and development. Self-directed work teams are effective only to the extent that the team members honor the interdependencies and give higher priority to the total effort than to personal objectives.

An essential part of building strong co-worker and team commitment is the ability of the group members to understand each other's individual strengths, each person's special contribution to the work, and each person's self-concept. The social bonding that makes a group cohesive must be built around member differentiation that is task-relevant, not around conformity pressures that violate the unique personalities of members. Since the manager usually has the strongest influence on group norms, he or she is in the best position to establish or change the norms in ways that maintain both group cohesion and member differentiation.

When Hector joined the group, he felt insecure and looked to others for cues on proper behavior. Because of the cultural differences, Larry, Fred, and Lucy could easily have pressured Hector into becoming more North American, which would have destroyed his true sense of self and, probably, his commitment to the group. He might have ended up complying with expectations that were incongruent with his self-concept—resulting in little, if any, identification with the group or the organization. As it turned out, under Larry's leadership Hector found his place as a member of the team, felt affirmed in his sense of self, and developed a strong identification with his co-workers and the organization.

The following are guidelines for building an employee's commitment to his or her co-workers.

1. Have individuals share their assumptions and expectations about their roles with relevant others: This helps to reinforce an awareness of job interdependencies.

2. Map the job interconnections so that all members of the group can see the whole picture and how they each fit in: Team members become sensitive to the ways in which their own actions will affect others before the fact.

3. Have individuals sort out, discuss, and negotiate any conflicting expectations suggested by the mapping process: This can save a great deal of time and aggravation later on.

One important benefit of this process is the prevention of false assumptions and attributions made about others when those others do something that adversely affects one's own situation. Although the effect is real, the intent may not be. Everyone has blind spots; they can be minimized by engaging in the steps suggested.

Finally, it is important to remember that it takes time to build co-worker commitment. Rarely will one find a newly hired employee instantly committed to his or her co-workers, even under the best of circumstances. How quickly the commitment level grows depends on the emergent relationships and the extent to which the employee experiences satisfaction and growth from task interdependencies and social bonding. Many organizations have developed employee-orientation programs that focus both on the tasks and on the ways in which the new hire's job interconnects with other jobs. Such actions taken early on set the stage for the kind of social bonding that creates cohesive work teams.

Commitment to the Organization

Employees who identify with their organization pay continuing attention to how the organization is doing overall, take pride in its success, become defensive when it is criticized from outside, and experience that their personal goals parallel organizational goals. They are willing to give the highest priority to behavior that serves the best interests of the system as a whole.

For a long time managers tended to define commitment in these terms and to pay less attention to the other two categories. With an increasing reliance on teamwork and the recognition that employees today are capable of managing their own work, more organizational leaders are empowering their employees to take full responsibility for planning, organizing, and controlling the work, often in the context of structured or natural work teams. Interestingly enough, upper-level managers, though highly rated in their work and organizational commitment, are weak in their co-worker commitment—having reached their positions by competition and not collaboration with their colleagues. What they encourage in their subordinates may not be well demonstrated in their own behavior.

By allowing Lucy to manage herself without the typical bureaucratic constraints, Larry built on her existing identification with her work and fostered identification with the company. In a similar way, Larry helped Hector to develop a strong identification with his co-workers as well as with the company. Now I summarize the kinds of actions that a manager can take to foster employee commitment to the organization.

1. Develop and share a clear vision of what the organization or the unit can be and how it can get there. (See Chapter 2, "Visionary Leadership," by Peter B. Vaill, for more on this.)

2. Encourage employee participation in decision making.

3. Help employees to understand how their work contributes to the shared vision, relative to both the unit and the organization.

4. Develop career paths through which employees can attain their personal goals by contributing to organizational goals.

Since an employee's level of commitment relative to each area (work, co-worker, and organization) can be different, a manager must understand the different profiles that are generated by the various combinations of highs and lows. For example, an employee who is committed to the work but not to co-workers or the organization represents a very different situation from one who is committed only to co-workers. Both are committed, but in very different ways. The various profiles of this kind have important implications for individual performance, teamwork, willingness to put forth extra effort for the sake of the company, and so forth.

Some of my own research indicates that upper-level management tends to have a profile that reflects a high commitment to the work and to the organization and a low commitment to co-workers. In contrast, employees in the lower ranks tend to demonstrate a low level of commitment to the work and organization and higher levels of commitment to their co-workers. One can see immediately what kinds of interventions could be appropriate in each of these cases. While the managers would benefit from efforts at team building, the workers would benefit from efforts at work redesign and from being shown how their jobs contribute to the larger picture: the goals of the organization.

In general, then, a manager who wishes to build employee commitment needs to begin by diagnosing the existing levels of commitment relative to the work, co-workers, and organization as a whole. If it happens to be high in all three areas, which is rare, then his or her job becomes one of making sure that it does not deteriorate from lack of attention. Any variation from this more-or-less ideal profile might require some type of intervention; for example, a sales force composed of individuals who identify with their work as salespeople, but who are indifferent to the company for which they work, very often pose a turnover problem. Some action is needed to strengthen their commitment to the company. On the other hand, a salesperson who is hired for only a few months needs to be committed only to the work itself; turnover is irrelevant.

Different Roles, Different Pulls, Different Selves

One day Lucy, Fred, and Hector were having lunch together and found themselves talking about Larry. Fred said, "have you ever noticed how different Larry is when he's not around here?" Lucy asked for clarification. Fred continued, "well, I've always noticed that when we're driving somewhere together or run into each other in town, he's easier to talk to, more open, even pretty funny at times." Lucy laughed: "That's no surprise. Do you have any idea what it's like for Larry to be reporting to J.G.? Everything has to be by the book, always under control, never messy. The Larry you see in his office is not the same Larry you see in the supermarket." Hector looked puzzled and said, "I always thought that a person is the same wherever he happens to be. You mean Larry is a different person with me than with you?" Lucy replied, "Hector, you of all people should realize that people are not the same in every situation. Remember how differently you behaved in meetings as compared with how you behaved outside? You get sucked into certain behavior by the situation you're in. When Larry comes through the front door he becomes Larry-the-manager and not Larry-the-drinking buddy. But he's still Larry. And we're no different. I know I don't feel free to behave the same way around you guys as I do with my friends. It's not a matter of trust so much, but just a difference in what seems appropriate."

The fact is that people have a number of selves, depending on the role and the situation—an idea that should not be new to anyone. Yet people often draw conclusions about one individual's general character from that person's behavior in just one or two situations. Then they're surprised when the person behaves very differently in a situation in which they are seen for the first time. Does this mean that the person is a chameleon or cannot be trusted to be genuine? With some people that implication might fit, but in most it would not be valid. Although the very core of one's personality— beliefs and values—tends to remain relatively stable from one situation to the next, a person's behavior and feelings at any given time are shaped by situational pulls, or influences, including others' expectations and perceived constraints.

To be effective in a job over the long run, employees should learn how different situations pull different behaviors and attitudes from them. When the behaviors and attitudes match both their core values and the demands of the situation, they will tend to be both productive and satisfied. When the match is poor, they will struggle to find a way to resolve the resulting tension. Since most people have to move from one situation to another and repeatedly face the task of affirming their self-concepts and meeting the requirements of the work and of others, it is not surprising that they appear to be different people at different times in different settings. The best way for a manager to understand that variation from the outside is to try and view it from the inside.

Making Yourself Look Good

One interesting aspect of someone's contextual self-concept is that he or she may describe the same situation to different people in ways that would make one wonder if it really was the same situation. Have you ever been in a life-threatening accident, which you then related to another person? If that person was your mother, what would you say? If it was your best friend, would

you describe it any differently? Chances are that your report to the other person would be strongly affected by how you want that other person to see you. You might tell your mother that it was really only a minor event and you were never in any danger. With your friend you might emphasize the dangers and your quick thinking that saved the day. Are you not telling the truth to your mother or your best friend? What is the truth in this case? Probably both stories are true, but each is passed through a different filter to serve different purposes. And this is usually not a conscious process but more a reflection of how people tend to shift into different selves as circumstances seem to demand.

From a manager's perspective it is important to understand that the behavior of a subordinate in the manager's office reflects only one *self-concept*, and often it is not the one that is most relevant to performance on the job: An otherwise assertive self-directed employee might seem passive and dependent in front of the boss. Remember Hector's behavior before Larry understood what was going on? It's easy to see the implications of this notion for performance appraisal. Clearly a wide range of behavior in a wide range of contexts may be necessary to generate a really thorough and valid picture.

When Things Change, Do People Change?

Barbara, the secretary in Larry's office, had held the job for 15 years. She started with Larry's predecessor, and, when Larry took over, both he and she agreed that there was no reason to make a change. Things worked out well for both, and the other people in the department seemed to be happy with Barbara. Several years ago the company computerized all of its claims files. Every employee in the claims department ended up with a desktop terminal. Almost immediately all the financial operations followed suit. In addition, the company got rid of all the typewriters, and it distributed word processors to all the secretaries. Although most took to the change quite readily, a few were resistant to giving up doing their work in the usual way. Barbara was among those who did not like the change. She held on to her typewriter and refused to unpack the word processor. Every effort on Larry's or other people's part to get Barbara to make the change fell on deaf ears. She insisted that she could turn out the work as fast as anyone and that she did not need to learn a whole new technique. "Besides," she said, "I'm too old and not smart enough to learn this stuff." Barbara was 45 at the time.

Larry was wise. He recognized that any increased pressure on Barbara to change only made things worse. He did not want to lose her, but he could not afford for her to be totally out-of-sync with the rest of the organization for too long a period. He decided to trust that after a time Barbara herself would choose to make the change, once she recognized how her behavior was affecting others and not helping the company. She happened to be committed to the company, so that the dissonance she experienced in going against the grain would be enough for her to make the right choice. Of course the downside risk was that she might decide to leave the job. Larry took the chance.

The word processor remained in its carton week after week, gathering dust. No one commented, but Barbara could not close her eyes to the fact that she had to make a choice and make it soon. She had been comfortable doing things the same way for so many years; she was afraid that she would make a fool of herself when she tried to master a whole new way of working. Her concept of herself as a skilled, competent secretary was on the line. She knew that if she did not make the change, she would eventually become obsolete and could get fired. That possibility was a threat to her, but for a long time the level of the threat of losing her job was not as strong as the threat of making a fool of herself. So the situation dragged on for months.

Larry began to lose patience with Barbara. She was slowing things down for everyone. He began to think that he had made a mistake and that the time had come for more direct action. Although he did not want to threaten her with dismissal, he felt that she needed some kind of push to get past her fear of the word processor. He could have presented her with an ultimatum, but he decided that a better course of action would be to emphasize that word processing was the technology that the office was committed to and that her failure to learn it was hampering everyone's work. He reassured Barbara that she was valued by everyone and that no one had any doubt about her ability to master the new technique. Larry stopped short of indicating that Barbara could lose her job if the situation continued; he decided to leave that as a last resort.

On Saturday morning Barbara went to her office while nobody was around. She unpacked the box and managed to figure out how to set up the word processor. It took her a long time, but she was not about to ask for help. She looked over the manual and began to play with the machine. Within minutes she realized that it was still a typewriter, but one on which she could correct mistakes without any mess. She spent the next hour just typing and then realized that there was a lot more she needed to learn before she could feel the same confidence she enjoyed before. However, the most important thing Barbara discovered was that she did not have to damage her self-concept of competence just because she had to endure a short period of low competence. A month later Barbara behaved as though the whole thing had never happened, as though she had been eager to make the change all along.

Was Larry smart or just lucky? Maybe a little of both. But at least he was sensitive enough to know that people resist change when the change threatens their self-concepts. And he recognized that the best way to change behavior, when that change represents a perceived threat, is not by increasing the threat from outside but by allowing the individual to take control of the process from inside.

Barbara, like many employees, had established a comfort zone at work; she was being asked to leave that comfort zone and venture into the arena of new learning. Not having been in that arena for a long time, she was frightened by it. However, her own desire to remain a valued contributor at work provided enough of an impetus to take the risk of leaving the comfort zone. Not only did she end up not damaging her self-concept, but she actually strengthened it in two ways. For one thing she became an even better secretary for the department; but perhaps even more importantly she discovered that she is capable of taking a risk and learning new skills.

Any perceived threat to one's self-concept is going to be resisted. It is important for a manager to keep this in mind whenever changes in work patterns are being introduced into the organization. What a manager might perceive from his or her vantage point to be a simple rearrangement of tasks or physical location might very well be seen as a threat by those who must make the change. The threat, as in Barbara's case, might be directly to the person's self-concept, or it might be related to familiar and comfortable behavioral and social patterns that have provided a sense of security for the person's self-concept. Whichever is the case, it is essential to understand the situation from the employee's own standpoint and then to provide the necessary information and support that will encourage the person to make the change—more from commitment than from compliance. Had Larry been forced to resort to an ultimatum, Barbara might have complied and things might have worked out well over the long run anyway. In many cases a manager does need to exercise strong pressure, which an employee could perceive as a threat. Keep in mind that even though understanding can go a long way, it is the final result that really counts. But also keep in mind that the final result includes a variety of effects on the members of the organization, all of which in turn affect the credibility and influence of the manager.

The Impact of Current Trends

Larry's department provided financial support services to all the other departments in the company: sales, claims, underwriting, policy production, and loss prevention. Historically these departments operated independently and relied on the managers to provide the necessary integration of functions and services. With recent pressures to improve customer service, particularly in the business lines, the company began to experiment with a team-centered matrix structure in which a given customer would be assigned to a cross-functional team of employees from each relevant function, including people from the finance department. Larry had to assign his people to the different customer teams and make sure that everyone was scheduling time out of the office to work with a team.

Since Larry had been instrumental in developing this new approach, he was eager to see it succeed and tended to shut out any expressed doubts or objections. He failed to realize that this change represented a whole new way of doing business and, consequently, a whole new way for employees to see their roles. Fred took to it like a duck to water, but Lucy was not at all happy. She feared losing control over her work and having to make constant changes in her plans and work style. She was not used to working in a group context and was unsure about working with people who did not understand the nature of her work. Fred, on the other hand, loved the idea of trying out new approaches to the business and felt perfectly comfortable in entering a group of strangers and seeing what happened. He thought the variety would keep him from getting stale and would keep him on his toes.

The other members of the department fell along the entire gamut from "it's about time we did this" to "this is the dumbest idea since pet rocks." Since the choice was not theirs, everyone ended up as a member of a cross-functional team and, to the surprise of some, actually found the situation even better than they could have imagined. Among the major benefits, finance department members could view things from a much broader perspective, and decisions were made with the best interests of the customer in mind. Such shifts in mindset were especially important for a department that normally has little direct contact with customers and usually too little interaction with workers in other areas. Lucy struggled for awhile, but because her commitment to the company had been strong, she eventually became a champion of the new structure and helped many of her subordinates adapt to the change.

As organizations move more in the direction of employee participation and team-centered management, many employees will struggle with change. Those whose attitude is "just let me come in at 8:00, do my job, and leave at 5:00—don't force me to get involved in things that others should be doing" will pose a serious problem for management. On the one hand, one can talk about the importance of giving people a choice and not forcing them into a different mold, but when their choice damages the efforts of others and of the whole system, then letting the behavior go unchecked is worse. Usually, given enough time, information, and support, people end up making the change. Barbara was a good example of this. However, every organization seems to have its share of individuals who simply dig in their heels and go about their business as though nothing is changing.

Some important rules of thumb for a manager to follow when introducing a change that might be perceived as threatening from an employee's perspective are (1) to give that employee as much information as possible; (2) to expect that there will be some degree of resistance to the change; and (3) insofar as possible, to allow the individual to make the change at his or her own pace. (For more on introducing change, see Chapter 12, "Managing Change," by Todd D. Jick.)

Managing Difficult Employees

Although the idea of a "difficult employee" can be very complex—since there are many ways to define it and many possible causes for the behavior, no matter how it is defined—we will consider the problem in a simple way. For purposes of discussion I will define the difficult employee as one who does not live up to the expectations attached to the job, including cooperation with others. These expectations are considered from three perspectives: that of the employee, that of the manager of the employee, and that of the employee's own peers.

From the employee's standpoint the behavior that others might consider inappropriate or dysfunctional makes absolute sense and serves some valued purpose. Hector was a difficult employee in the sense that his early behavior posed a problem to Larry and the others. His situation was easily corrected because Hector wanted to be accepted and do good work. Had that not been the case and had Hector been motivated in some perverse way to make life difficult for his boss, the outcome would have been very different. Similarly, had Lucy's pattern of coming in late and leaving early represented an attitude of defiance, then Larry would have had to take some drastic action. And remember how easily a group of experienced managers attributed the wrong motives to Lucy's behavior. The trick is to draw the so-called difficult employee into examining his or her behavior and its impact on others and then see if change is forthcoming. If that fails, then a manager needs to take significant action in the best interests of everyone.

Firing an employee is not easy or pleasant, but allowing a dysfunctional situation to go on too long can be worse and can undermine a manager's credibility. However, how one manages the process is just as important as the action itself, since it sends a broader message about how one handles difficult situations.

In a way, Barbara's refusal to use word processing made her a difficult, uncooperative employee. Many managers would have increased the pressure on her to change and would have threatened to fire her. Fortunately for Barbara, Larry handled the situation in a compassionate way and recognized the long-term value in keeping Barbara. He took the risk that she would come around of her own accord. Furthermore, Barbara herself recognized the fact that she was being "difficult" and that she was not living up to her own expectations as a valued employee. It was the discrepancy between her ideal self and her own behavior that generated enough tension in her to make the change. And finally, since Barbara was not living up to the expectations of her peers—who were way ahead of her in word processing—she experienced an additional impetus for change.

Whereas the reader can probably list many examples of difficult employees and can contrive a variety of worst-case scenarios, the most important thing to know is that all behavior has multiple causes and produces multiple consequences, some intended and some not intended. Often the difficult employee is not aware of the consequences of his or her behavior and is especially blind to those that create problems for others. Direct and timely feedback may not always resolve the problem, but it is clearly a good place to start. A manager's failure to provide effective feedback contributes to the very behavior that the manager deems difficult.

Furthermore, part of a manager's job is to influence the behavior of employees in a direction that contributes to the goals of the unit. Although the manager is always in a position to exercise the formal influence associated with a position of authority, there are usually many other options that can serve the purpose better. In fact, trying to correct inappropriate behavior through the use of the usual extrinsic rewards or punishments can have limited value over the long run, because it tends to reinforce an employee's dependency on the manager. Other, more intrinsic currencies—such as visibility, inclusion, challenging opportunities, assignment to important tasks, and special education—can offer an appeal that is long-lasting. Here again, one must identify exactly what the relevant currencies are for the individual. In most cases, the right match of currency and individual will move a situation in the right direction.

Managers should look at their styles of influence. Some have a natural tendency to include and to trust their subordinates in decisions, some are especially persuasive, and others have the capacity to capture employees' imagination by articulating exciting possibilities for the future. And there are managers who can do all of the above. If the so-called difficult or uncooperative employee is really seeking opportunities for inclusion in the decisions affecting him or her, but the manager either does not understand this or does not have the influencing skills best suited to meeting that employee's needs, then the employee is likely to get blamed for the problem. Hector needed to be included as a "member of the family"; attempts to convince him to behave differently had little effect. Was Hector the culprit? Barbara's currency was the respect of her peers; again all the logical arguments or pressure from the boss would have been wasted. Letting the currency of peer respect do its job turned out to be Larry's smartest move.

Next I turn to the ways in which managers themselves create difficult employees, usually without realizing it.

What Ye Sow, So Shall Ye Reap

W. Edwards Deming developed a demonstration of a worker's plight in a situation where performance improvement was demanded but simultaneously made impossible—by the very management who had designed the work. The exercise is called *The Bead Factory*. In the bead factory the worker is required to scoop 50 beads from a box containing a mixture of white and red beads. There are many more white ones than red ones, with the red beads signifying defects. The worker's task is to minimize the number of red beads in each scoopful. Five or six workers take turns, and each gets repeated opportunities to improve performance. A supervisor records the results and keeps up the pressure for quality improvement. Despite the fact that there is no real way to improve performance, that the number of red and white beads in a scoop occurs in random fashion, each worker believes that he or she has control over the work and, given enough practice, can do better. The supervisor also behaves as though that were true. By the end of the exercise, the workers feel the discouragement and helplessness often reported by employees who are expected to demonstrate improved performance over time but who have no control over key factors that affect that performance. Instead of recognizing that the problem is in the technology itself, which only management can change, the manager will tend to perceive the employee as the problem.

The important message here is that the label *difficult employee* might easily show a displacement of management's failure to establish the appropriate setting, technology, or reward system for the job. In order for employees to be held truly accountable for their performance, they must be empowered to exercise their own control over it. The irony is that many managers refuse to give employees that control yet hold them accountable anyway. Then they wonder why an employee's performance is not up to expectations.

The Valuable but Difficult Employee

One of Lucy's most technically competent people was Warren, who had a very strong education in accounting and financial management, as well as a brilliant track record in his job as a financial analyst for the company. When Lucy had him promoted to a first-line managerial position in which he was in charge of a number of major business accounts, things began to go down hill. Not only did many of Warren's subordinates complain that he was demoralizing the group and treating them with little respect, but some of the people from the accounts he was serving found Warren unpleasant and irritating. As soon as she learned what was going on, Lucy took immediate steps to correct the situation. She met with Warren and told him what she had been hearing, especially from the customers. Warren was completely dumbfounded. He promised to try to be more aware of his behavior, but things did not change. At a second meeting with Lucy, Warren appeared to be just as surprised, which really puzzled Lucy. It became clear to her that the situation was going to be more difficult to change than she had thought.

Lucy decided to consult Larry in order to get a third perspective. She told Larry that the situation had reached a point where the company could lose valuable accounts and she could not leave Warren in the position of accounts manager much longer. Larry asked Lucy why she had made Warren a manager. She explained that Warren had earned it through his superior performance. Larry asked whether Warren himself wanted the promotion; Lucy acknowledged that she had not asked him and simply assumed that he would. Larry said no more.

Lucy once again met with Warren and asked him the same question Larry raised. Warren stated that he really never wanted to be a manager, that he loved the analytical work, and that managing people made him nervous and gave him a sense of incompetence. Financial analysis made him feel as if he was contributing in the best way he knew. Lucy became aware that Warren's self-concept got affirmed in his job as an analyst and disaffirmed as a manager. The promotion meant little to him, since he saw his career path as a technical one and not a managerial one.

The choices for Lucy were not simple. On the one hand, she could have Warren return to his former job as an analyst. On the other hand she felt that such a move might not, in the long run, be in Warren's best interests: He did have talent and a great deal of expertise that could be shared with others more readily if he remained in a managerial position. Furthermore, she believed that it was part of her job to stretch her employees in new directions and to help them grow. The fact that Warren was uncomfortable in dealing with people did not mean that he could not or should not learn the skills that would make him interpersonally competent. What Lucy finally decided to do was to share her dilemma with Warren and let him know that, if he did return to his former job, the door was open for him to change his mind. She also emphasized the fact that she would accept this choice, but that over the long run she would like to see him build his managerial skills and would provide him the necessary support.

It is not uncommon for managers who seek to move up the ranks to assume that everyone else has a similar career path. However, in an age when technological advances create constant challenges in the work itself, for many people career advancement may be more related to mastering the increasing complexities of new technology rather than managing bigger and bigger pieces of the system. Again, it is important to understand the choice through the eyes of the employee, without preconceived expectations based on one's own preference. However, it is also important for a manager to see beyond the short-run decision of an employee, to recognize the individual's possible fear of mastering new and unfamiliar skills, and to foster that individual's growth and development. (See also Chapter 7, "Managing Yourself," by Douglas T. Hall.)

In summary, the task of managing the so-called difficult employee requires a thorough analysis of the circumstances to determine the extent to which the problematic behavior is related to situational factors that elicit the behavior, a lack of feedback to the employee regarding impact of the behavior, or the way in which the behavior represents some valued aspect of the person's self-concept. Elements of each are probably involved, often forming a vicious circle. However, a careful analysis will suggest ways to break it. When all reasonable attempts fail, a manager is wise to remove the employee from the situation altogether. That may mean firing the employee, but there are other alternatives—including finding a better match between the individual and the job, a match that considers the individual's self-concept, and giving the employee a strong voice in the decision. What appears to be a puzzling choice from one person's perspective makes absolute sense from another's, such as a decision to reject advancement in the organization's ranks in favor of staying with the more technical aspects of the work.

Beliefs, Values, and Ethics: Christine's Dilemma

Lucy was sent to a training session that was attended by financial analysts from a number of different insurance companies. There she met Christine, who worked for a competing firm, and they became friends very quickly. At lunch on the third day, Lucy noticed that Christine was filling out a reimbursement form into which she was entering figures that seemed inflated. For lunches that had cost $10 to $15, Christine was entering close to $20. She was adding the costs of taxis that Lucy knew Chris had not taken. She asked Chris about this. Chris readily explained that her company had very strict per diem limits, some of which were unrealistic, on specific items. Therefore, if a dinner cost more than the allowed amount, she would add the difference to a lunch or to taxi costs.

At first Lucy thought that there was a natural logic to Christine's practice, but she also felt that it raised ethical issues. What Chris was doing violated company policy and was therefore unethical. It also violated one of Lucy's basic values: honesty. She raised the issue with Chris, risking a defensive reaction, which was exactly what she got. Chris insisted that there was nothing wrong with what she was doing, since the company's policy was the problem in the first place. Besides, she insisted, everyone else in her department did exactly the same thing. When Lucy suggested that a better alternative was to change the policy, Chris insisted that it had been tried, and to no avail. The discussion that followed revealed an even more complicated situation than Lucy ever expected.

Christine told Lucy that in her opinion the whole company had serious problems with ethical behavior. She described an instance when her boss asked her to delete some figures from a monthly report because they made the department look bad. When challenged, he made it clear that she must follow orders. Fearing the loss of her job, Chris deleted the figures. She knew the act was not right, but she rationalized it. Lucy was upset about what she was hearing and felt disappointed in Christine, who sensed Lucy's disapproval. She asked Lucy what she would have done in the same circumstances. Lucy acknowledged that she really could not answer the question honestly, since she had never faced such a dilemma. She said that she realized how easy it is to take a clear ethical stand when the choice is hypothetical and that the realities of having to choose between conflicting values or needs was a different matter altogether. As a single mother, Lucy knew that she could not afford to jeopardize the security of her family, but she also knew that doing something blatantly dishonest was equally unacceptable.

People often struggle with situations in which their different needs or goals conflict. They compromise between goals, or they sacrifice one for the sake of another. They put off receiving immediate gratification for the sake of a long-run gain. However, most hold on closely to certain basic beliefs and values that form the core of their character. They are usually developed at early ages and do not change much throughout our lives. These values include honesty, honoring friendships, protecting our loved ones, and so forth. Situations that threaten these values are resisted; efforts on the part of others to violate them are resisted. Moreover, one tends to avoid persons perceived as holding beliefs or values that run counter to one's own. If they cannot be avoided, there will likely be conflict.

Although Lucy and Christine did not actually have a value conflict, Christine's behavior conflicted with certain values that both women hold. Unfortunately for Chris, she also experienced an internal conflict in which her survival and security were at odds with her desire to be an honest person. The best she could do after the fact was to rationalize her behavior in a way that allowed her to live with herself. There was enough reality to her fear about losing her job to support her rationalization that she was just following orders.

Lucy did not judge Christine harshly, but many people might. Again, from an external perspective it is not always easy to understand another's behavior, but it seems that many people find it easy to judge that behavior by their own standards. There is no question that Christine did something dishonest and should bear full responsibility for her actions. However, organizational leaders and managers need to examine their complicity in creating the conditions that foster unethical behavior. Christine's boss was even more culpable than Christine in requiring her to delete information from the report. Not only was he a party to a dishonest act, but he was placing another person in jeopardy at the same time. And that person could easily become a scapegoat, should the situation be revealed in the future.

Most organizations espouse high standards of behavior yet fall into unethical practices when threatened, especially when the threat may be to their survival. B. F. Goodrich in the late 1960s, Ford Motor Company in the 1970s, and Morton Thiokol in the 1980s are examples of companies that were discovered to have engaged in major coverups to protect themselves. In fact, some of the executives at Goodrich justified their behavior in the name of protecting the security of their employees, fearing that full exposure to what they had done (namely, falsifying data on the testing of brake linings for Air Force planes) might damage the company irreparably. In Ford's case the situation was even more cynical: It was discovered that behind the falsification of data was the judgment that it would be cheaper for the company to pay the damages in law suits related to the explosion of the Pinto gas tank than it would be for the company to change the location of the tank on all its Pinto cars.

Among the most powerful factors in the culture of an organization are its core values. In organizations today that are striving for total quality, a clear articulation of core values has been found to be essential. The customers and clients served by most organizations expect the highest levels of quality, not just in the products and services provided, but also in the public behavior and image of the organizations. The employees of a company, who are the internal customers, should expect no less. Companies that are committed to the highest standards of behavior for their employees, including a commitment to honesty in all practices, will not create the kind of dilemma faced by Christine or those faced by the employees at Goodrich, Ford, or Thiokol. A manager should examine an employee's apparently unethical action before judging it, in order to see how the situation itself, especially as a result of organizational pressures, might be contributing to the action.

Larry's Moment of Truth

Larry had an excellent reputation as a competent and compassionate manager of his people. His employees felt free to come to him with problems or to ask for help, did not hesitate to let him know when they were upset or unhappy about something he did, and felt a strong commitment to him as a leader. One of the ways Larry earned all this respect was through frequent meetings in which he both gave and asked for feedback and encouraged the others to do the same. The meetings were convened away from the office, where people felt freer to be direct and open with each other. Larry had learned a long time ago that letting interpersonal problems fester only made it harder to confront them, often leading to explosive interactions. At first the meetings seemed forced and unnatural, but over time everyone participated and benefited from them.

The focus of the feedback was usually task-related, so the learning that took place generally resulted in better working relationships and improved performance. However, it was not unusual for some of the feedback to be quite personal, which made some people uncomfortable. But after the first time that happened, the group established the rule that any feedback of a personal nature must be clearly relevant to the work setting.

During one of these sessions Lucy decided to raise a very difficult matter. She had observed for several months that Larry seemed to have developed the habit of putting his arm around some of the female employees and showing other signs of affection. At first Lucy simply wrote this behavior off as harmless, since she knew that Larry was happily married and that he was just a naturally warm and affectionate person. However, she did notice that some of the female employees seemed bothered by Larry's behavior. They didn't say anything to him, but their discomfort was obvious to Lucy. Not wanting to make any unwarranted assumptions, Lucy checked out her observations with these women; they acknowledged that she was right. Consequently, she decided to confront Larry.

Larry at first seemed stunned. Then he asked Lucy to describe in detail what she had observed. He sat silently for a few moments and then, shaking his head, said, "I can't believe they were upset; I intended nothing by it. I hope they didn't think I was hitting on them."

Lucy replied, "I think they were confused by your actions and didn't know what to assume. Remember, Larry, it isn't a question of your intent, but a matter of the effect. And the effect amounted to harassment." Larry jumped. "Harassment? I don't consider that harassment. It was harmless." Lucy was quick to reply, "it doesn't matter that you don't consider it harassment, if the women feel harassed, if your gestures are not welcome, then the law defines it as harassment. And that isn't harmless by any standard."

By this time the entire group was tense. It was the first time that anyone had given Larry threatening feedback. It was a real test of Larry's own philosophy. Although he still seemed to be in a state of shock, Larry began to calm down. "I think I owe them an apology. The last thing I want is for people to think I'm some kind of letch. Besides, I don't want anyone's behavior, especially mine, to set the wrong tone here. I wish I could feel free to be openly affectionate with people, even at work, but I guess I better be a lot more careful." Lucy jumped in. "Larry, you don't have to censor your behavior with people who really know you, but be careful about possible misinterpretations by those who don't."

Larry finally looked at Lucy and smiled. "You have guts. I don't know if I ever could have confronted my boss with that kind of behavior. I could have blindly gone along, making the situation worse and never knowing the damaging effects I was having. I appreciate what you did. How about a hug?" Lucy laughed, "Stuff it, boss!"

What Larry needed to learn went beyond any specific incident and even beyond the issue of sexual harassment. He needed to recognize the importance of the *pattern* of his behavior, plus the fact that this pattern tended to foster an atmosphere that was deleterious to the objectives of his own department. It raised questions about his character and created uncertainties about his motivation. When employees are faced with these kinds of ambiguities, they tend to pull away from the source of tension, which can only reduce their level of commitment. As long as Larry was blind to this effect, the situation was destined to get worse. He was fortunate to have Lucy around, since it was her intervention that made it possible for him to change his behavior.

With respect to the specific issue of sexual harassment, even the law recognizes the significance of behavior patterns and the role of a manager in fostering an atmosphere conducive to harassment. Any action in relation to another person that is considered by that person to be unwelcome, whatever the intent, may constitute a form of harassment. This is not a pleasant notion to contemplate, but nevertheless it is a fact to be recognized. For many people who have grown up in families where affection was expressed openly and who have been inclined to bring such behavior into their work relationships, the idea of having to contain such behavior, or at least to be much more cautious and selective about it, seems unnatural. However, one needs to recognize the fact that there are many managers who abuse their power and whose intentions are less than honorable, which makes all managers potentially suspect. The smartest rule of thumb is simply to know your audience.

Sharing Your Power Brings Out the Best in Your Employees

Larry was willing to make himself vulnerable. Too few managers, including many good ones, are willing to open themselves up to workplace feedback. They got to where they are by being cautious, competitive, and self-protective. They make the assumption that by holding on to power they actually increase their influence when, in fact, the opposite is usually true. Furthermore, to the extent that a manager's power remains unshared with his or her employees, the net result is performance on their part that is far below what could have been attained. Sharing one's power, though hard to accept for some, is the best means to increase one's influence. In general, a manager's willingness to shift from a controlling mode to a facilitating one will result in employee commitment, high performance, and continuous improvement. What more could a manager want?

SUMMARY

1. The best way for a manager to understand an employee's behavior is to view that behavior from the employee's perspective.

2. An employee's behavior results from a combination of factors, including what that employee brings to the situation and what the situation requires of the employee.

3. The factors that affect the situation include the setting, the technology, the reward system, and the organizational culture.

4. It is the job of the manager to understand interpersonal differences, including cultural ones; to find ways of creating good interpersonal matches; and to help employees learn how to bridge their differences.

5. All employees are subject to stress at one time or another; it is the job of the manager to understand both the sources and the symptoms of stress, and to learn how to cope with them in order to prevent serious performance deterioration.

6. The most desirable state of affairs for a manager is to have employees that are committed to their work, to their co-workers, and to the organization.

7. People have different selves in different situations, depending on the roles they are required to play; consequently, how they appear to others in one situation may be very different from how they appear in another, even though they always retain their core self-concepts.

8. Employees respond differently to changes, even those changes that are designed to improve their productivity. Some even resist opportunities for participation and self-management. Most, when given the opportunity, embrace it.

9. Most managers struggle with "difficult" employees, But again, once understood from the perspective of that so-called difficult employee, the behavior just might make sense and might be related as much to the situation as it is to the employee. The most valuable employees can sometimes be among the most difficult to manage.

10. Beliefs and values are powerful determinants of behavior. They form the core of an individual and shape the ethical standards by which that individual behaves. The problem of sexual harassment in the workplace is just one example of ethical standards gone awry.

CONCLUSION

We now say goodbye to Larry and his crew. Each was a unique individual with special assets, and each posed a particular dilemma for Larry to learn to manage. In combination they represented a special group of talented people who learned to understand and work well with each other, making Larry look good as a manager. Let us hope that reading this chapter will also help you to look good. But, more important, let us hope that it will help you to be an effective manager of each individual, and of yourself.

FOR FURTHER READING

This list includes only those books that provide a basic introduction to or an overview of the key areas covered in the chapter. It is not intended to be comprehensive. However, many of the books have extensive references, for those readers who wish to pursue topics in greater depth. Included in the list are some old classics in the field and some recent publications.

Block, P. *The Empowered Manager.* San Francisco: Jossey-Bass, 1987. Provides some excellent insights and suggestions on ways to empower people in the workplace.

Bradford, D., and Cohen, A. *Managing for Excellence.* New York: John Wiley & Sons, 1984. Presents the concept of the developmental manager, with a strong emphasis on how managers can foster the growth and development of their subordinates.

Cohen, A., and Bradford, D. *Influence Without Authority.* New York: John Wiley & Sons, 1990. Shows how people can be influenced via those things, which the authors call *currencies,* that are important to them. Emphasizes the fact that even without formal authority, most people have a variety of ways to exercise influence through these currencies.

Dertouzos, M. L., Lester, R. K., and Solow, R. M. *Made in America.* Cambridge, MA: The MIT Press, 1989. Offers an outstanding overview of the changing face of the American workplace. Has excellent chapter on human resources.

Fink, S. *High Commitment Workplaces.* Westport, CT: Quorum Books, 1992. Looks at commitment in three dimensions: the work itself, one's co-workers, and the organization. Provides a diagnostic framework that generates commitment profiles for helping a manager to understand employee performance.

Hackman, J., and Oldham, G. *Work Redesign.* Reading, MA: Addison-Wesley, 1980. A comprehensive look at everything known about work redesign and its impact on employee performance.

Helgesen, S. *The Female Advantage*. New York: Doubleday, 1990. Offers powerful and practical insights into women in the workforce and what special value they represent.

Herzberg, F., Mausner, B., and Snyderman, B. *The Motivation to Work*. New York: John Wiley & Sons, 1959. The classic introduction to Herzberg's two-factor theory of motivation, which had a major impact both theoretically and practically.

Homans, G. *The Human Group*. New York: Harcourt, Brace & Jovanovich, 1950. Although its focus is on the group, the Homans model was used as a framework for part of this chapter.

Maslow, A. H. *Motivation and Personality*. New York: Harper & Row, 1970. One of the major contributions to understanding human motivation in general, as well as in the workplace specifically.

Morgan, G. *Images of Organization*. Newbury Park, CA: Sage, 1986. For someone interested in the use of metaphor as a way to understand behavior in organizations, this is a must.

Rogers, C. *On Becoming a Person*. Boston: Houghton Mifflin, 1961. A key book in self-concept theory. Especially useful for self-understanding as well as for interpersonal insights.

Steele, F., and Jenks, R. S. *The Feel of the Workplace*. Reading, MA: Addison-Wesley, 1977. A well-articulated analysis of organizational climate and culture. Especially useful for understanding the impact of norms on the behavior of individuals.

Vroom, V. *Work and Motivation*. New York: John Wiley & Sons, 1964. Looks at motivation in terms of expectations. Provides an excellent model for understanding an individual's behavior in a given situation.

Weisbord, M. *Productive Workplaces*. San Francisco: Jossey-Bass, 1989. Using an historical perspective, the author offers excellent insights into managing in the future. Effective in getting the reader to examine and revise many basic assumptions about how to bring out the highest levels of productivity in people.

POWER, POLITICS, AND INFLUENCE: THE SAVVY AND 5 SUBSTANCE OF ACTION IN ORGANIZATIONS

Anne Donnellon

> Power is America's last dirty word. It is easier to talk about money—and much easier to talk about sex—than it is to talk about power.[1]

> Position, title, and authority are no longer adequate tools, not in a world where subordinates are encouraged to think for themselves and where managers have to work synergistically with other departments and even other companies. Success depends increasingly on tapping into sources of good ideas, on figuring out whose collaboration is needed to act on those ideas, on working with both to produce results. In short, the new managerial work implies very different ways of obtaining and using power.[2]

Power is still a dirty word in the United States, and anyone who pays attention to political campaigns and government-appointment processes will find it difficult to believe that politics has a natural and desirable role to play in organizations. But in this increasingly complex and interdependent world, the achievement of important organizational goals requires not only power; it also depends on those debates and jousts over goals, strategies, and tactics that we call "politics." Furthermore, as Rosabeth Moss Kanter implies in the above excerpts, having the ability to analyze situations marked by differences of opinion and interest, and the ability to form alliances among interdependent parties, are now essential for effective performance, as well as career success. These career considerations are some of the reasons why it is valuable to understand power, politics, and influence. Another compelling reason has a more negative motivation.

Much of the discomfort that people feel about the subject of organizational power and influence stems from a fear of its misuse or abuse. At its most dysfunctional, organizational power is an end in itself. In fact, when we refer to an organization or office as a "very political place," we are describing

113

an environment in which political activity is devoted to the acquisition of power, thus consuming the time and energy that should be directed toward the accomplishment of organizational objectives. The most effective way to guard against the personal and professional dangers of such an environment is to become so familiar with the dynamics that you can easily recognize and prevent or counter the detrimental effects.

Thus the aim of this chapter is to explain power, politics, and influence in the workplace and to help you develop skills for dealing with these issues effectively and responsibly. To do so, we will consider the sources of power, power dynamics, a variety of influence strategies and the situational factors that affect their success, some interesting paradoxes of power, and the ethics of power. The chapter concludes with a guide for analyzing power situations and exercising influence.

WHAT IS POWER?

To understand power in organizational terms, it is useful to recognize that in physical terms, it is the ability to produce change.[3] Power is the capacity that lights dark rooms, heats cool homes, and puts our computers into a state of readiness. Among people in organizations, power is the ability to produce change by mobilizing one or more people to take action. Influence is the exercise of that ability.

Politics has been defined as "the study of who gets what, when, and how."[4] This definition fits a range of situations, from legitimate organizational processes like budgeting and promotion decisions, to clearly undesirable activities such as bureaucratic infighting, to questionable individual behaviors such as flattering superiors and blatant self-promotion. Indeed, a critical feature of political savvy and skill is the ability to distinguish appropriate political activity from the inappropriate.

According to his biographer, Robert Caro, Lyndon Baines Johnson had an extraordinary political sense that was evident on Capitol Hill even before his first election to the U.S. Congress.[5] While working as an aide to a Texas representative, he applied his understanding of "who gets what, when, and how" to the challenge of developing a social club for legislative aides into a well-known and highly regarded forum for congressional debate. The "Little Congress" also became a platform for the development and exercise of his own power. He used a variety of influence tactics—including the use of parliamentary and club rules, creating opportunities for politicians to speak on the issues and for journalists to get advance notice of developments, padding the votes to get himself elected speaker of the Little Congress, and using that position and its opportunities to make himself known to powerful people in Washington.

Johnson's takeover and transformation of the Little Congress created numerous benefits. Under his direction, the club became a vehicle for the development of legislative expertise among congressional aides. It provided lawmakers and journalists opportunities to make and break the news. Because the debates among the legislative aides often reflected the members' positions, Johnson's Little Congress also allowed important policy debates to be rehearsed and modified. Last but not least—because it gave Lyndon Johnson visibility, position, and therefore, resources to dispense—it also made him very influential subsequently in formulating progressive social policy. Nevertheless, although he was effective personally and organizationally, many claimed that he had stolen the election and never trusted him afterward.

Now that the terminology is defined, this chapter proceeds to a business case that illustrates many of the concepts in the model of power and influence.

THE CASE OF JULIA DOBBINS

Julia Dobbins had been the manager of systems engineering for APEX, Inc., a medium-sized software manufacturer, for the five years since her graduation from the Penn State MBA program. (See Figure 5-1 for an organizational chart of the company.) Dobbins's first-rate performance in that position made her a logical choice to lead the team (the "Government Team") being assembled to develop and market financial management systems for the federal government. She knew that her presentation at the upcoming management

FIGURE 5-1 Partial organizational chart for APEX, Inc.

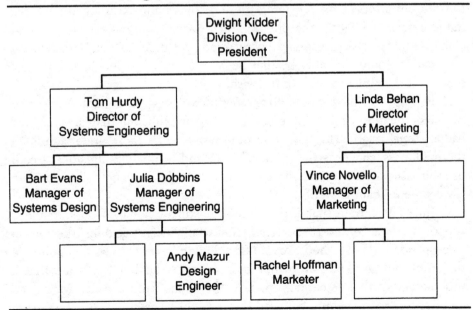

retreat could be critical to the decision of whether to give her the high-profile assignment. Her analysis would have to be perfect and her recommendations thorough to counter the inevitable criticism from Bart Evans, manager of systems design. However, until Julia had resolved the heated dispute between her engineers and the marketing representatives, she could not give full attention to the presentation.

Lately, conflict seemed to flare up regularly between the systems engineers who were designing new software products and the marketing representatives who translated customer needs into product specifications. Customers were becoming more price-conscious and demanding higher performance in their software. Although APEX enjoyed a dominant position in the market, the recent entry of new competitors had resulted in a shift of strategic emphasis from technological innovation to meeting customers' needs. For the system engineers, who reported to Julia, the shift meant that their jobs were no longer as innovative and challenging. Furthermore, because recent cost-control measures had led to some layoffs, the engineers had more work to do in less time.

Julia understood the frustration and resentment they felt when the marketing reps kept insisting on adding new features without altering product delivery dates. When Andy Mazur, her top designer, complained about the pressure tactics from marketer Rachel Hoffman, the situation was serious. But Dobbins also knew that the engineers were having a hard time adjusting to their new, subordinate role in the organization. Eventually they would have to learn how to cooperate with marketing. In the meantime, she wondered if she should intervene directly with Vince Novello, the marketing manager, to work out a means for resolving these disputes once and for all. She hesitated before picking up the phone: Vince was not the easiest person to get along with. He always seemed overworked and defensive. His response to this matter would probably be that he would order his people to cooperate more and that Julia should do likewise.

Perhaps she should take up the matter with Linda Behan, Vince's boss. As two of the most senior women in the company, Julia felt that she and Linda had a special relationship. "Linda would probably be more understanding of the engineers' concerns than Vince," Julia said to herself. "Besides, I could use this issue as an opportunity to ask her if she knows who will become the Government Team leader."

Julia felt certain that Linda and Tom Hurdy, her own boss, would be supporting her. However, she was less sure of Dwight Kidder, the division vice-president. He seemed to avoid her, though he was always pleasant when they met and she knew from her bonuses over the last few years that he was pleased with her contribution to the organization. Andy Mazur had told her that many people believed that Dwight favored Bart for the position because they played golf together. Although Julia found the rumor hard to believe, she was troubled by the fact that she had also heard it from someone outside the company. Don Calvert, Julia's neighbor and also one of APEX's big government clients, told her that Dwight had introduced Bart to him at the golf course as the newest star at APEX and as someone he would soon be seeing frequently.

Even more disturbing to Julia than the prospect of her losing the team leader appointment was the idea of Bart's getting it. Not only was he arrogant and uncooperative, but his superficial understanding of the technical dimensions of the work and his tendency to make unrealistic work projections could create significant problems for the clients, the company, and the employees. Surely, Tom understood all this and would exercise his authority to get the most competent person named team leader. Julia would just have to be certain to show her competence in her presentation to the top management at the retreat. But, first, what should she do about the conflict between Andy and Rachel?

Analyzing Power Dynamics

Julia Dobbins has two major power and influence problems at the moment. One is how to get cooperation rather than conflict from the systems engineers and from the marketers, who report to Vince. The other is how to influence the decision to make her the team leader. Although one appears to be a personal problem of career management, both situations have important implications for organizational performance. From Julia's perspective, she seeks the position both because she wants the increased responsibility and recognition and because she genuinely feels she has the critical competencies necessary to do the job well.

To solve these problems, Julia needs savvy and substantive understanding of how the organization works. She needs to start by thinking, rather than acting. She needs to determine what factors have caused these situations to occur, to develop and evaluate some alternative strategies for action, and finally to choose and implement appropriate actions.

Analyzing organizational problems is like peeling an onion: There are always many more layers than you would suspect; the more you peel, the closer you get to the heart of the matter; but all of the layers make up the onion. The onion of power problems (see Figure 5-2) starts with the outer layer of some other person one needs to influence. The typical first question we ask ourselves is, "how can I get that person to do what I want done?" But as explained in the following pages, one must go deeper to ask, "what am I trying to accomplish, and what do I have to offer the other in exchange for what I want?" Often, to answer the latter question, one must go still deeper

FIGURE 5-2   The layers of the power onion

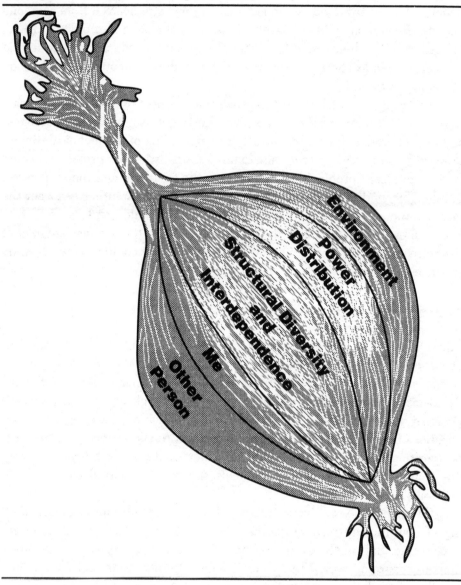

to consider how structural factors may shape or constrain the behavior of the other person and oneself. Structural factors also reflect and affect how power is distributed within the organization. For example, the size of a department and the number of levels of management may affect a particular manager's power and so might the specific assignment of responsibilities. Deciding on a course of action should also involve consideration of what environmental forces may be affecting both the power distribution and the structural factors.

One final caveat about taking action in political situations is indicated by the onion metaphor: When onions are not peeled properly, they can make you cry! The following sections provide instruction in the proper peeling of the onion of power.

Structural Factors in Power Dynamics

Essentially, three structural factors affect power dynamics in organizations: diversity, interdependence, and resource scarcity. *Diversity* refers to differences among people's values, stakes, goals, assumptions, and perceptions.[6] When organizational members differ along these lines, members will likely act in ways that benefit themselves or that support their values, interests, or perceptions. For example, the conflicts that erupt between Julia Dobbins's system engineers and the marketing representatives probably derive from a diversity of perception as to what is "a good design"—a technologically sophisticated one or one that meets the expressed needs of the client. If the marketers receive a bonus for meeting promised delivery dates but the engineers are not eligible for bonuses, the difference in their stakes may also fuel the conflict. The conflict is political activity, as is the common behind-the-scenes effort that some marketers might employ to get a change in the engineering personnel assigned to their project.

Diversity alone is not a sufficient condition for triggering power dynamics or political activity. When people are able to act independently, diversity does not generate power dynamics. Power is a function of interdependence.[7] When person A is dependent on another (person B), person B has power over person A. If, as in most work organizations, person B depends on person A for something in exchange, they are interdependent to some degree. When person A is more dependent on person B than vice versa and the two differ in terms of interests, values, or goals, there is the potential for person B to exercise her power to achieve the outcome that she desires.

Most often, the dependencies and interdependencies within an organization are determined by organizational structure and the nature and design of the work done. In the Dobbins case, the essential work of manufacturing computer software involves learning what the market wants and needs, designing and writing the software, and distribution of the software to the market. The people responsible for distributing the software to wholesalers or clients are clearly more dependent on those who develop and write the software than vice versa. If the company's competitive strategy is to innovate, then everyone is dependent on the designers. On the other hand, if the strategy is to meet customer needs, the marketers will be the most critical to the organization, thus making them one of the most powerful groups in the organization.

When resources are scarce, the potential for power dynamics is high because people and groups within the organization will be exercising their power to get what they want and need. Events like budget time, performance appraisal, organizational restructuring, and office moves lend themselves to political activity because they are occasions of resource distribution. To recognize the potential for power dynamics, one must be able to think of resources broadly. As such examples of resource distribution indicate, resources include people, information, physical space, money in the form of budgetary control, and money in the form of salary increases.

Being able to anticipate power plays or political activity and to recognize how power is distributed in the organization gives one a distinct advantage in the exercise of influence. It enables you to understand how structural features of the organization are shaping others' attitudes and driving their behaviors or, at least, compounding their own personal inclinations. One other significant external factor helps explain some of the political activity in organizations—changes in the environment. The environment of an organization comprises customers, competitors, suppliers, government, and society.

Changes in these factors can alter the interdependencies among people and departments of the organization and can affect diversity as well as resource availability. APEX, Inc., for example, experienced a change in the competitiveness of its environment. As more competitors entered the market, its top managers felt that it could no longer afford to compete on the basis of technological innovation. It needed to meet customer demands, if it was to retain its market dominance. Thus the change in the environment led to a change in the degree and direction of dependence between engineers and marketers. Although the case does not mention it, this strategic shift was probably also accompanied by a redistribution of budget for personnel and the political activity that is part of such allocation.

But what does this all mean to Julia Dobbins and how can she use this understanding to solve her two power and influence problems? The organizational chart of Figure 5-1 shows that systems engineering and marketing are differentiated just below the level of the division vice-president, which means that the people who report to him, Tom Hardy and Linda Behan, have different responsibilities and goals. The people who report to each of them also differ from others at the same level in the other department. Julia should therefore understand that some part of the conflict between the engineers and the marketers is due to the structure rather than wholly due to the personalities involved. She may find that calling this fact to the attention of the people who report to her would help defuse some of the negative emotion and facilitate a greater willingness to explore structural solutions to the structural problem.

Julia should also recognize that the interdependencies and therefore the power distribution have shifted. The marketing personnel as a group are now more powerful than the engineers, and that could have several implications for Julia: First, it may mean that Linda, as director of marketing, will be more influential than her own boss in determining who will get the team leader position. This is particularly likely for the new team, because their task involves high customer contact in order to get those large, customized government projects.

Second, it implies that Julia should approach Vince as if he has more power than she has. To start, she needs implicitly to negotiate a new relationship with him, because their old ways of relating were based on her having more power. She will need to demonstrate her recognition of his power, her dependency on him, and their interdependence. Julia should keep in mind that if Vince acts defensively, his stance may be a vestige of his prior, less-powerful position. That is, he may not yet realize how things have changed, how power dynamics have shifted. If so, he may not accurately interpret her signals about dependency. Julia may need to be more explicit about their new roles and may need to allow some time for Vince to adjust. These complexities and uncertainties make it necessary for Julia to proceed very carefully and sensitively if she chooses to gain his influence in working with her to resolve the conflicts.

Third, Julia should recognize that the changing power distribution between her staff and marketing may not be fully recognized or accepted by the engineers. By virtue of their technical expertise and the company's history and identity as a technology-driven company, the systems engineers have reason to consider themselves to be critical resources. Despite meetings, memoranda, and mission statements announcing the new customer-driven strategy, they may still feel and act superior to the marketers. This behavior may in turn be causing the marketers to act in a negative and demanding manner, either to assert *their* greater power or, more importantly, to get the new goals of the company met.

Finally, Julia should consider the possibility that the two problems, engineering-marketing relations and the leadership of the Government Team, are connected. The new project team's mission is to develop and market financial systems for government clients; the team will be cross-functional, consisting of marketers and engineers, among others. Therefore, one of the likely requirements for the team leader is the ability to generate cooperation between the marketers and engineers. Resolving the current dispute productively may be an important demonstration of that skill. As a member of the engineering department, Dobbins may need to demonstrate her own personal grasp of marketing perspectives in order to gain support of her candidacy for team leader.

Before taking action to influence the necessary people in the two instances, Julia needs to consider who they are. Clearly, her performance and success could depend on influencing numerous people in (and even outside) the organization, including Kidder, Hurdy, Behan, Novello, Mazur, Hoffman, and Calvert (see Figure 5-3). Then she needs to consider what sources of power she has and how she might best use them.

SOURCES OF POWER AND HOW THEY ARE ACQUIRED

Power, the ability to mobilize others to action, has many forms and derives from many sources. Even though they often converge and are easier to distinguish in abstraction than in reality, this section identifies and explains six different sources of power: position, resources, information, expertise, performance, and personal attraction. (Figure 5-4 lists these sources of power.)

Probably the first source of organizational power that comes to mind is *position*. A person's or group's formal position in an organization provides a set of responsibilities, a set of people with whom to interact in the execution of those responsibilities, and a certain amount of authority to act and to direct the actions of others. Position typically provides people with other sources of power, such as *resources* and *information*. For example, the positions of manager and supervisor typically give people the resources of promotions, raises, excused absences, and work assignments that they can use to get their subordinates to act in accordance with their wishes.

FIGURE 5-3   Dobbins's targets of influence

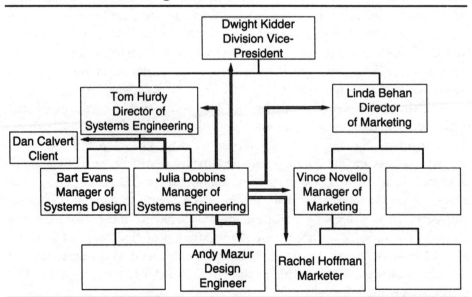

FIGURE 5-4   Sources of power

Position
- criticality
- relevance
- visibility
- flexibility

Resources

Information

Expertise

Performance

Personal Attraction

Positions other than managerial also provide their incumbents with resources and information. For example, buyers often possess extremely valuable information about the materials that other people require and the timing of their availability. They may also have the discretion to choose one source over another—a discretion that they can use to help or hinder the employee who will be using the supplies. People who manage facilities may have authority to decide on the allocation and use of space. Secretaries to important and influential executives may control their calendars and be able to give or deny access or information. Even people in temporary or part-time positions like task-force members or secretaries to committees can provide information and access to others with more information and resources.

Positions can also have certain characteristics that increase the potential for the people in them to influence others. These include criticality, relevance, visibility, and flexibility.[8] The more of these characteristics a position has, the more power it provides to the person who holds it.

Criticality is the extent to which others are dependent on you. Just how critical a position is depends on how often it is needed, by how many people, how many other positions like it exist in the company, and how important a role it plays in the work flow. For example, the person responsible for operating and maintaining the computer system has a critical position in an insurance claims office, especially if there are few others who have the same expertise and the computer regularly stops functioning.

Relevance in a position is determined by its relationship to the organization's top priorities. In the Dobbins case, the marketing department became the set of positions most relevant to the company's mission of focusing more on customer needs. Design engineering was still critical to the task of manufacturing software but that function had become less relevant.

Visibility is the degree to which the performance in the position is seen by powerful people in the organization. "Jobs that straddle the boundaries of organizational units or between the organization and its environment tend to have more noticeable activities."[9] Assignments to special task forces or committees also provide enhanced visibility. The position as executive secretary to the president may not be relevant or critical to the organization, but it is highly visible and so confers a certain degree of power to the person who occupies it. Leading the new project team at APEX is attractive to Julia Dobbins because of its visibility. Since the team will have members from each function, the team performance will be seen across the company and the team leader is likely to have reason to interact with heads of each function. Furthermore, the leader of the effort is likely to become well known among major clients, which would also enhance Dobbins's internal visibility.

Flexibility is the amount of discretion a position offers its incumbent. Having the flexibility to innovate and take initiative enables a person to enhance the criticality, relevance, and visibility of the position. Another desirable feature of the new team leader position at APEX is that because it is a first cross-functional team, there will probably be considerable flexibility in it.

Several sources of power are more individual than positional, though one's position can enhance or constrain the potential to develop and use some of these power sources. These include *expertise, performance,* and *personal attraction.*[10]

Expertise is the specialized knowledge that a person obtains from higher education or specialized work experience. It is a particularly significant source of power in organizations that rely on knowledge in their core business. Both design engineers and marketers have expertise power at APEX. However, expertise in areas peripheral to the core can also be a source of power; at budget time, financial analysts are very powerful people in most organizations. Expertise is often the largest source of power for new professional employees. Lacking resources, information, a track record of performance, and a network of relationships within the company, they must rely on the expertise that they possess to develop those other sources of power.

A track record of high performance can be an important source of power for experienced professionals. Companies are dependent on their high-performance employees, and that dependency gives the employees some-power to influence their own future, as well as other aspects of the organization. Strong performance enhances one's reputation with peers, which makes possible new working relationships and access to other sources of power.

Personal attraction as a source of power is much broader than one's physical appearance, although it includes that individual feature. It also includes personality and friendly behavior. Researchers have identified several behaviors and traits that enhance a person's "likability," including honesty, acceptance, supportiveness, admirability, similarity of values and interests, and willingness to endure costs for the relationship.[11] People who are judged likable are seen as more effective speakers,[12] are given the benefit of the doubt in performance appraisals,[13] and bosses are likelier to use reward rather than coercion to influence them.[14]

Physical appearance operates as a source of power in ways similar to agreeable behavior and personality. People tend to assume that attractive people have other attractive qualities, like power. Studies show that attractive people are also believed to be more virtuous, efficacious, and intelligent. In school settings, a self-fulfilling prophecy has been discovered: Because teachers expect the attractive to be more intelligent and good, they spend more time with those students and, consequently, the students do perform better than others. At work, attractive subordinates get more favorable performance appraisals.

A person's attractiveness can, of course, be shaped as much by clothing and style as by his or her physical features. The *Dress for Success* book of several years ago translated that idea into a prescription that gained wide popularity.[15] The savvy person, however, will recognize that there is a danger in focusing too much on personal appearance as a source of power. Those who seem too conscious of their dress and appearance tend to be viewed as less serious about their work. As a result, their opinions and accomplishments are often discounted.

TYPES OF POWER

Implicitly, the discussion of the preceding section identifies two different types of power: formal, which is based on one's organizational position, and informal, which is usually based on personal characteristics. As mentioned, formal power is so pervasive in modern organizations that even people who know better act occasionally as if formal power were the only, or at least the most significant, source of power. However, it has been increasingly observed that formal power is not only failing to mobilize action in organizations—it is impeding effective action.

To understand these dynamics, we need one other distinction in the types of power: legitimate power and illegitimate. The legitimacy of a person's power is determined by two criteria: whether the person in power is perceived to have appropriate qualifications for having the power and whether the process by which the power was acquired is perceived as legitimate. For example, when women are promoted to formal positions of power partially in response to affirmative action policies, the legitimacy of their authority is often questioned or denied by those who believe that women are not suited to such work and that affirmative action is an unfair policy.

Cohen and his associates suggest four types of power that can be recognized by combining these two distinctions: formal-legitimate, informal-legitimate, formal-illegitimate, and informal-illegitimate.[16] They also offer a useful figure for understanding the differences among them (see Figure 5-5). *Formal-legitimate* power is that which is organizationally assigned and considered appropriate. When people say, "he's the boss, he must know what he's doing," they are recognizing the boss's power as formal and appropriate, based perhaps on knowledge, expertise, or seniority.

Informal-legitimate power is not assigned but is considered appropriate. When people say, "that's not what I think, but you're the expert. I'll do it that way," they are acknowledging the legitimate influence of someone who has superior expertise. If he or she is a colleague or someone who has no formally assigned power over them, this influence is informal-legitimate.

The case of a woman in a supervisory position whose power is questioned by her subordinates—if looked at from their perspective—is an example of *formal-illegitimate* power. As far as the subordinates are concerned, she has been assigned formal power based on a process (affirmative action considerations) that they find inappropriate. The fourth type of power, *informal-illegitimate*, is not assigned by the organization and is not considered appropriate by those over whom it is used. One example is a colleague who is considered incompetent but who has influence over the boss's decision making.

The initial sections of this chapter have examined where power comes from, how it is acquired, and what forms it can take. Covered next is influence, that is, the exercise of power. Several influence strategies and the situational constraints that determine their effectiveness are discussed.

FIGURE 5-5   Examples of influence types

	Formal (Assigned)	*Informal (Not Assigned)*
Legitimate (Accepted as Proper)	Boss gives work-related orders to subordinate: "Stop making widgets and begin making frammisses."	Respected colleague helps you solve a problem by showing you the proper order to make calculations.
	Teacher assigns an analytical paper, based on concepts in the text.	Basketball benchwarmer notices flaw in opponent's defense and convinces coach to alter offense.
Illegitimate (Not Accepted as Proper)	Boss makes strong hints about subordinate's family life: "Send your son to a private school."	Co-worker threatens to beat you up if you continue to produce so much.
	Student is put in charge of class discussion by instructor.	Fellow students ridicule you for asking questions in class, despite instructor's request for questions.

Source: Allan Cohen, Stephen L. Fink, Herman Gadon, Robin D. Willits, *Effective Behavior in Organization*, 5th ed. (Homewood, IL: Irwin, 1992.)

INFLUENCE STRATEGIES
AND SITUATIONAL CONSTRAINTS

Researchers have identified a wide variety of strategies people use to influence others, but there are essentially three: threat, exchange, and appeal. (Figure 5-6 lists these strategies and examples.) Influencing by threat occurs when person A tries to get person B to comply with his or her wishes by indicating that there will be negative consequences for person B if he or she does not comply. Influencing by exchange occurs when person A gets person B to comply with his or her wishes by offering something that person B wants or needs. Influencing by appeal occurs when person A gets person B to comply by referring to values, emotions, or facts that support person A's

FIGURE 5-6   Influence strategies and examples

Threat

Implicit	"If you can't get this report done by tomorrow, I'll be very disappointed."
Explicit	"If you can't get this report done by tomorrow, you'll need to work on the weekend to finish it."

Exchange

Bargaining	"If you'll stay late today, you can leave early tomorrow."
Settling a Debt	"Please take this call, you owe me."
Creating a Surplus	"I've got some free time today, would you like help?"

Appeal to Values

"Being customer-driven means finding a way to collaborate with each other and solve this problem."
"We must promote more women and blacks to demonstrate our commitment to a diverse workforce."

Appeal to Emotion

Fear	"If you don't accept these wage reductions, we'll have to move our operations offshore and you'll lose your jobs."
Hope	"If we can meet this sales goal, we'll all be eligible for the travel award."
Pride	"You need to close that deal to prove that women can handle tough clients."

Appeal to Reason

"The client has always insisted on a low-key approach; your design ignores her preferences and risks losing her business."
"Choosing strategy A will lock us into an annual ROI of 2% for the next three years, whereas strategy B costs less and produces an ROI of 5% by year two."

point of view. One example of influencing by appeal to emotion was the 1988 Bush campaign advertisement linking Dukakis and Willie Horton, in which fear and racism were used to persuade people to vote against Dukakis.

Influencing by threat sounds sinister, yet it is the basic strategy built into organizational structures and work relationships. Many, if not most, people are influenced to do what their superior demands, commands, requests, or prefers *because* of the explicit or implicit threat that they will otherwise experience either more of what they dislike or less of what they like—more grunt work or less of a raise. Thus the "power" that people so often feel that they require or lack is the potential, typically based on formal authority, to make good on such threats.

Exchange is probably the most common and effective strategy for influencing people in work organizations. It is frequently used because it works well up, down, and across the organization and because it can be used with many different "currencies."

> The metaphor of currencies can help you determine what you might offer a potential ally in exchange for cooperation. Because they represent resources that can be exchanged, currencies are the basis for acquiring influence.... All too often people in organizations think too narrowly about the needs of potential allies.[17]

Arguing that "you are more powerful than you think," in their book entitled *Influence Without Authority,* Cohen and Bradford have identified five types of currencies that people have or seek in work settings: inspiration-related, task-related, position-related, relationship-related, and person-related. Examples of each type of currency are presented in Figure 5-7. As this figure makes clear, a manager like Julia Dobbins could influence the engineers who report to her through an exchange of vision, resource, and challenge currencies for their currencies of assistance, rapid response, task support, and comfort. She might also try to influence her peer, Vince Novello, to collaborate with her in influencing their people to work through their differences by exchanging task-, position-, and person-related currencies of task support, recognition, gratitude, self-concept, understanding, and ownership.

The influence strategy of appeal to values, emotions, or reason is similar to Cohen and Bradford's inspiration-related currencies. Explicit appeals link the desired action with the values or emotions of the person being influenced. For example, if Julia wants to get Linda's support for her promotion to team leader, she might assume that Linda would share her values about the need for more women in leadership positions and would appeal to that. Or given the company's difficult competitive situation, she might make an appeal for the job with Dwight Kidder using facts about her prior performance or client contacts. Dobbins might try to influence him implicitly to see Bart Evans

FIGURE 5-7   Currencies frequently valued in organizations

Inspiration-Related Currencies

Vision	Being involved in a task that has larger significance for unit, organization, customers, or society
Excellence	Having a chance to do important things really well
Moral/Ethical Correctness	Doing what is "right" by a higher standard than efficiency

Task-Related Currencies

New Resources	Obtaining money, budget increases, personnel, space, and so forth
Challenge/Learning	Doing tasks that increase skills and abilities
Assistance	Getting help with existing projects or unwanted tasks
Task Support	Receiving overt or subtle backing or actual assistance with implementation
Rapid Response	Quicker response time
Information	Access to organizational as well as technical knowledge

Position-Related Currencies

Recognition	Acknowledgment of effort, accomplishment, or abilities
Visibility	The chance to be known by higher-ups or significant others in the organization
Reputation	Being seen as competent and committed
Insiderness/Importance	A sense of centrality or of "belonging"
Contacts	Opportunities for linking with others

Relationship-Related Currencies

Understanding	Having concerns and issues listened to
Acceptance/Inclusion	Closeness and friendship
Personal Support	Personal and emotional backing

Personal-Related Currencies

Gratitude	Appreciation or expression of indebtedness
Ownership/Involvement	Ownership of and influence over important tasks
Self-Concept	Affirmation of one's values, self-esteem, and identity
Comfort	Avoidance of hassles

Allan R. Cohen and David L. Bradford, "Influence without Authority." Copyright ©1990 by Allan R. Cohen and David L. Bradford. Reprinted by permission of John Wiley & Sons, Inc.

as a risk by appealing to Kidder's well-known embarrassment over an earlier contract that had been badly bid and lost through Bart's negligence.

As the last example suggests, influence by appeal to emotion is often accomplished implicitly and sometimes unintentionally. Most charismatic leaders are said to rely heavily on this strategy to influence their followers.

Hitler preyed on the hopes of Germans that they could overcome their economic depression and linked those hopes with their fears and resentments of Jews and Jewish financial concerns. Mandela appealed to South Africans' fears of a vengeful black majority. Gandhi appealed to Indians' hopes of self-government.

Each of these strategies works well only in certain situations. Understanding the situational factors that determine the effectiveness of a particular strategy is thus critical to successful influencing. To extend the onion metaphor a bit, this is akin to knowing that, though cooked onions are the only kind that can be peeled with the certainty of avoiding tears, there are some ways to limit eye watering, if you need uncooked, peeled onions. For example, "research" shows that holding raw onions under water while peeling reduces their potential to make eyes water. But if you need to cut the onions after peeling, chilling may be the best solution.

The situational factors that affect influence include the following:

1. The balance of power between influencer and influencee
2. The degrees of dependency and interdependency
3. What outcomes are desired (compliance or commitment)
4. How much time is available
5. Whether or not important values are shared by the parties
6. How emotional the situation is
7. The nature of the relationship between the parties
8. The availability of substitutes for your contribution.

Figure 5-8 shows which strategy fits a certain situation and how the situation can constrain or determine the effectiveness of the chosen strategy. You can use it as a guide to select a strategy or to test whether, given the features of the situation, the strategy you select will be effective.

The x's of Figure 5-8 indicate that the strategy will work under those conditions. The words *Must, Never, Best,* and so on indicate if a given situational feature must be present for the strategy to work—or if that feature guarantees that the strategy will never work effectively—and where it is possible, which strategy is best under those circumstances.

Let us begin with the threat strategy and read down that column to identify the situational factors that fit this influence strategy. First, we observe that to successfully utilize threat, a person *must* have greater power than the other person. The reverse is also true—one should *never* threaten when he or she has less power than the other, *unless the other person does not know that you have less power.* This exception to the rule of power and threat is itself a rule of power that is applicable more broadly. Generally stated, it is that the perception of power gives power. There is, of course, some risk

FIGURE 5-8 Situational constraints and influence strategies

Situational Constraints	Threat	Exchange	Appeal to Values	Appeal to Emotion	Appeal to Reason
You have more power than others.	Must	x			
You have less power.	Never	x			
Other is more dependent on you than vice versa.		x			
You are more dependent on other than vice versa.		x			
There is some degree of mutual interdependence.		Must	x		
Other's compliance is sufficient.	x				
Other's commitment is required.	Never	x	Best	x	x
Time is limited.	x	Sometimes	x	x	x
Time is unlimited.		Usually			
Situation elicits strong emotion.	x			Must	Never
Situation elicits fear.	x			x	
Situation invokes values.			x		
Values are shared.		x	Must		
Relationship is competitive.		Best	Maybe		
Other respects you.	x	x	x	x	x
Other trusts you.		Typically	x		Must
Other admires/loves you.	x	x	x	x	x
There are few substitute sources for your contribution.	x	x			

entailed in having one's power derived from perceptions, as the Wizard of Oz discovered.

Threat can also be used when the outcome you seek is compliance; however, if commitment is necessary, threat will not be effective for producing that emotional reaction. Threat also works when time is limited, assuming that the requisite situational conditions have been met—that is, conditions of greater power and no requirement for commitment. Threat also works when the situation elicits strong emotion like fear and when the other person respects you (because of the greater power). You can also threaten when there are no substitutes for what you do or contribute to the enterprise, because you can threaten to leave and feel certain that you will not be allowed to do so.

Exchange, as mentioned, works under numerous and varied circumstances. Although it can be effective regardless of the power balance or dependencies between two people, there must be at least some degree of mutual interdependence for it to work. When compliance is not sufficient and the commitment of the other person is necessary, exchange is an appropriate strategy. Depending on the currencies exchanged, the amount of time available for negotiating may determine how effective the exchange is. When time is unlimited, exchange can be very effective in finding a win-win solution. Exchange can also work well when values are shared, though shared values may make the giving unnecessary.

Depending on the currency exchanged, the relationship between two people may or may not be a critical situational constraint. If the exchange is not simultaneous, then trust will be critical. If the relationship is competitive, a simultaneous exchange is probably the best form of influence. When the other person respects, admires, or even loves the influencer, an exchange can generally proceed smoothly, with a display of reciprocal feeling on the part of the influencer.

Figure 5-9 provides a format for analyzing the potential for exchange among two people. First, you need to identify what currencies you have and what you need (plot them on the horizontal dimension). Next, you need to consider what the other person needs and what he or she has to give (plot them on the vertical dimension, so that his or her needs are in the same place as your "haves"). Overlaying these two lists should allow you to identify some possible exchanges as well as other alternatives to exchange.

Where one person's "needs" match the other's "haves," there is the potential for trade, and mapping "haves" and "needs" helps make explicit what could be exchanged. Where both need similar currencies, there is the potential for cooperation to gain them, as well as the potential for competition. Where there is a similarity in what both parties have, there is the potential

FIGURE 5-9 A matrix for exchange analysis

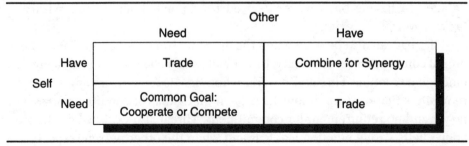

for combining the resources to achieve ends that both parties seek. In the latter two instances, appeals will probably be the most effective influence strategy.

Appeals to values can only work if the parties do in fact share the same values and attach relatively similar priorities to them. If those values are strong, this strategy can motivate cooperation in situations where there is some mutual interdependence, limited time, and even a competitive relationship. The appeal to values works best when there is a requirement for commitment. At APEX, where engineers and marketers were highly interdependent and working under a tight deadline on a task that demanded commitment rather than compliance, an appeal to the company values of cooperation and customer service from someone who was admired, trusted, and respected by all may have facilitated the necessary cooperation.

For an appeal to emotion to be effective, the situation must elicit strong emotion. For example, during times of war or other intensely competitive periods, appeals to emotions of fear, pride, and hope can be very effective in influencing people. Mary Kay Ashe, founder and still-active board member of Mary Kay Cosmetics, Inc., is known for her appeals to the emotional needs for belonging and self-esteem of women who, in the sixties and seventies worked primarily in the home.

The appeal to reason can be effective in a situation that requires commitment. Although such appeals generally require a certain amount of time for discussion, influence through reason can occur when time is limited, if there is significant trust in the relationship. For any appeal to reason to be effective, there must be a basic belief that the person using this approach is trustworthy. Appeals to reason are not effective in highly emotional situations because they do not address the feelings that are shaping the moment. When fact or reason is the likeliest basis for influence but the situation is emotional, the influencer is best advised to postpone the attempt to persuade or to shift focus in order to address the emotion and, in that way, remove it as a barrier to reason.

PARADOXES OF POWER

Power is a complex phenomenon. It is difficult to comprehend partially because it is dynamic. Since power is based on dependency, exercising the power may fulfill the dependency and alter the relationship. Power is also hard to understand because it is paradoxical; that is, it involves some apparent contradictions.

The first paradox of power is specific to its organizational context. Whereas most people think of power as a rampant and negative force in organizations, powerlessness is actually more pervasive and more threatening to organizational well-being.[18,19] People prefer working for a powerful boss, one who has access to information and resources, and whose success is likely to create credit and opportunities for his or her people. Kanter has pointed out the following.

> [P]owerlessness often creates ineffective, desultory management and petty, dictatorial, rules-minded managerial styles. Accountability without power— responsibility for results without the resources to get them—creates frustration and failure. People who see themselves as weak and powerless and find their subordinates resisting or discounting them tend to use more punishing forms of influence.[20]

Looking at Kanter's list of the ways that organizational factors contribute to power and powerlessness (Figure 5-10), one gets a sense of why powerlessness is so pervasive, especially in large organizations. Most organizations are designed to operate with maximum predictability and reliability. There are numerous rules and routines established for ensuring that. Flexibility and task variety are not very common in most jobs; this continues to be the case despite large-scale efforts like General Electric's Work-Out process and numerous other experiments aimed at creating flexibility and employee empowerment. Despite such initiatives, corporations' basic orientation toward control and predictability lead employees to feel quite restricted and therefore more likely to retain whatever degree of autonomy or power they may have. That instinct, of course, can lead to the organizational politics, parochialism, and bureaucratic infighting that impede organizational performance.

The second paradox of organizational power is that the excessive use of power can actually reduce a manager's ability to influence. Research has shown that influence strategies of threat and manipulation can produce resistance and resentment on the part of those being influenced.[20]

The third paradox pertains to changes in the power holder with the use of power and influence. The frequent use of power leads to a distortion in the power holder's self-perception and the power holder's perception of the person being influenced: The power holder tends to exaggerate his or her self-worth and contribution to outcomes and to diminish the contribution and worth of others.[21] Over time, this tendency toward self-aggrandizement and denigration can easily lead to the abuse of power, because the power holder comes to think that he or she is the only person capable of understanding and doing what needs to be done. Then, as the second paradox indicates, the excessive use of power produces its own resistance, which ultimately makes it self-defeating.

That leads to the fourth paradox of power in organizations: The more one shares power, the more one has. Managers who share power with their subordinates create both increased commitment and enhanced skill in decision making, which contribute to improved group performance. As the per-

FIGURE 5-10   Ways that organizational factors contribute to power or powerlessness

Factors	Generates Power When Factor Is	Generates Powerlessness When Factor Is
Rules inherent in job	Few	Many
Predecessors in the job	Few	Many
Established routines	Few	Many
Task variety	High	Low
Rewards for reliability/predictability	Few	Many
Rewards for unusual performance/innovation	Many	Few
Flexibility around use of people	High	Low
Approvals needed for nonroutine decisions	Few	Many
Physical location	Central	Distant
Publicity about job activities	High	Low
Relation of tasks to current problem areas	Central	Peripheral
Focus of tasks	Outside work unit	Inside work unit
Interpersonal contact in the job	High	Low
Contact with senior officials	High	Low
Participation in programs, conferences, meetings	High	Low
Participation in problem-solving task forces	High	Low
Advancement prospects of subordinates	High	Low

Source: Reprinted by permission of *Harvard Business Review.* An exhibit from "Power Failures in Management Circuits," by Rosabeth Moss Kanter, 57 (July/August 1979). Copyright ©1979 by the President and Fellows of Harvard College; all rights reserved.

formance improves, generally the credit given to the manager increases and, with the credit, more of the resources and information that constitute one's base of power.

These paradoxes help one recognize that learning about power and influence is a mixed blessing. The lessons provide insight and skill that can enhance your own human capital, but learning them too well may prove dangerous. One of the most effective antidotes to the potential toxins of power is clear thinking about the ethics of power.

THE ETHICS OF POWER

As discussed in the beginning of this chapter, power is the most troublesome to people and organizations when it becomes an end in itself rather than merely a means to other ends. The challenging aspect of organizational power is that it is quite easy to delude yourself about your motivations when what is "good for the organization" is also good for your career. Forcing yourself to ask where the greatest gain is may help keep you honest about your motivations. For example, if Julia Dobbins forces herself to answer this question, she might have to acknowledge that she wants the team leader job as much — if not more — for her own gratification as for the good of the organization. This motivation is in itself neither unusual or inappropriate — there should be congruence between organizational goals and individual goals. The point of this exercise is for you to recognize your own interests so that you can more accurately consider whether there is an appropriate match between the ends that you really seek and the means you choose for pursuing them.

Another helpful exercise is to consider what you think is the difference between influence and manipulation. To get at this question, you can ask yourself the following set of questions about exactly where you draw the line in terms of action, regardless of what you label it.

1. Is it when you influence someone to do what he would not otherwise do?
2. Is it when you intentionally influence someone to do what she would not otherwise do?
3. Is it when you intentionally deceive someone in order to influence him?
4. Is it when you intentionally deceive someone to influence her to do something that is not in her best interests?
5. Is it when you intentionally deceive someone to influence him to do something that is not in his best interests but your gain is great?

The last question is perhaps the hardest to answer, because often actions that serve the organization's interest also serve the interests of some managers. Therefore, it is quite easy to ignore pangs of conscience over the ethics of influence by telling ourselves that "although I may have violated some of my personal ethical standards in a particular situation, I did so *in the interest of the organization and ultimately in the interest of everyone who is associated with that organization.*" The overlap allows us to ignore the question of whether we hurt someone for our own self-interest.

Other antidotes to the misuse or abuse of power include sharing power, avoiding positions that have few or no checks on your power, and creating a context in which others can disagree with you without fear of retribution.[10]

A GUIDE FOR EXERCISING INFLUENCE

Several authorities on power and influence have proposed questions to guide the analysis of power dynamics in organizations[6,19] and the effective exercise of influence.[22] Several other questions have been suggested in this chapter. The idea is to use your own influence problem or situation as a case, to analyze it, and to design an effective action plan with the following set of twelve questions as your guide.

1. What are my objectives?
2. Whose cooperation do I need to accomplish my objectives?
3. Whose support do I need to get the objectives implemented?
4. Who will be affected by my plan?
   a. In terms of power and status?
   b. In terms of performance evaluation and rewards?
   c. In terms of how they do their work?
5. Whose resistance could prove fatal to the successful implementation of the plan?
6. Who are the friends and allies of these influential people?
7. What are the goals, stakes, assumptions, perceptions, and feelings of those influential people?
8. What are my sources of power?
9. What currencies do I have that any of these people might want?
10. What are the situational factors that will constrain the effectiveness of my influence strategy?
    a. What are the interdependencies among us?
    b. What is the distribution of power among us?
    c. How much time is available for me to exercise influence?
    d. To what extent do we share the same values?
    e. How emotional is the situation around this issue?
    f. What is the nature of my relationship with these people?
11. Which influence strategy is likely to be the most effective, given the situational factors?
12. When, where, and how should I employ my influence strategy?

Julia Dobbins's situation provides an opportunity for demonstrating the power of these questions to generate a thorough analysis and to design an effective influence strategy. Let us examine her case once again from this perspective.

1. What are my objectives?

Julia has two major objectives. The first is to influence the engineers and the marketers to collaborate, and the second is to influence those making the team leader selection to give her the position.

2. Whose cooperation do I need to accomplish my objectives?

To achieve her first objective, Julia needs the cooperation of Vince Novello, of the marketers reporting to him, and of the engineers who report to her. It is not entirely clear whose cooperation she needs to accomplish her second objective. The answer may be someone outside the organization, a client like her neighbor Don Calvert. It is clearer whose support she needs.

3. Whose support do I need to get the objectives implemented?

To accomplish her second objective, Dobbins needs the support of her boss (Tom Hurdy), the director of marketing (Linda Behan), and possibly Vince Novello. To accomplish the objective of getting marketers and engineers to collaborate, she may require the support of Hurdy and Behan to persuade Novello that it's worth some time and money to train those employees in cross-functional teaming or in collaborative approaches to problem solving.

4. Who will be affected by my plan?

At this stage, Julia does not yet have an explicit plan for achieving either of her objectives. However, with the framing of her first objective, she has already decided to deal with the engineering-marketing conflicts as a long-term problem. All that she can say with certainty now is that the two warring camps will be affected in some way. In terms of her second objective, if she is named the Government Team leader, her presumed rival (Bart Evans) will be affected negatively. Hurdy may also be affected if her job responsibilities change. In fact, she should be sure that she has someone in mind to take over some of the critical functions she would have to stop fulfilling, if she wants to elicit Hurdy's support for her. Otherwise, he may be inclined to want to keep her in her current position.

a. In terms of power and status?

In terms of power and status, the objective of getting engineers and marketers to collaborate does not have much effect. Depending on how it is accomplished, the shifting status of both groups may become more explicit. If Dobbins gets the team leader position, her own power and status will increase owing to the increased relevance and visibility of that team's work and to the flexibility that she would have as the first leader of a new cross-functional team. The status of her boss may be enhanced if she is promoted but continues to report to him, because this new project team's work is so relevant to the company's strategic goals. She may be able to influence him to support her selection by helping him see this; however, that strategy could backfire and make it appear that she feels she is leaving him in the dust.

b. In terms of performance evaluation and rewards?

The collaboration of engineers and marketers would not necessarily affect anyone's performance evaluation and rewards. However, if Dobbins believed it would significantly improve the two groups' performance, she might persuade Novello to join in the planning with the expectation that the two managers would get credit for the improvements.

The creation of the new cross-functional team might in itself, regardless of who is team leader, lead to changes in the organization's performance-evaluation-and-reward system. The changes could occur if the team is so successful that functional managers come to be seen as contributing less to the company's performance than the team. However, such changes would occur over the long term and are not specifically related to the naming of Dobbins as team leader, so she probably doesn't need to concern herself with them.

c. In terms of how they do their work?

The collaboration plan might make engineering and marketing jobs less independent and therefore less attractive. The engineers were already feeling frustrated with their work load and the reduced technological challenge in the new marketing orientation. Dobbins would clearly have to talk about, and design, this collaboration so that it would add challenge with increasing work. That would not be easy, since collaboration would mean meetings and meetings take time. In addition, Novello seemed overworked, and the effort to create a climate and procedures for collaboration might be an extra burden he would not need.

The same sort of challenge would be faced by the cross-functional Government Team. Perhaps if Dobbins is successful in creating collaborative procedures or conflict-management strategies for her engineers and the marketers, she could use that experience as team leader.

5. Whose resistance could prove fatal to the successful implementation of the plan?

Novello's resistance to the collaboration idea could prove fatal to the collaboration. He would therefore have to be Dobbins's primary target of influence. With regard to the team leader promotion, the resistance of three people could prevent Dobbins from getting it: Hurdy, Behan, and Kidder (the division VP). Dobbins's influence strategy will therefore need to consider all three of those people. Hurdy, as her boss, is probably the easiest to influence because she has frequent contact with him and they are mutually interdependent. Dobbins believes that Behan will be sympathetic to her interest because they share the experience of being women managers. Kidder is the least accessible to her and will likely be harder to influence directly. Dobbins should consider the possibility of influencing him only indirectly through the other two or should at least seek their advice on how to influence Kidder.

6. Who are the friends and allies of these influential people?

This question does not seem relevant to the first objective; however, given that Dobbins has decided to focus on getting Novello's cooperation, she should consider it with regard to him. If on learning that they share a mutual friend in the company, she might consider asking this person to arrange a casual lunch during which she and Novello get to know each other in different ways. Or perhaps Evans is a friend to Novello, and her rivalry with him may make cooperation from Novello hard to obtain.

7. What are the goals, stakes, assumptions, perceptions, and feelings of those influential people?

With regard to the collaboration, Dobbins has a good sense of how the engineers feel but she does not know how the marketers experience their work and the conflict. She needs to get that information before proceeding very far with a design for collaboration. Nor does she know much about Novello: Getting better acquainted with him might be useful in terms of both objectives.

It would also be helpful to know more about how Linda Behan sees the new team and current needs for collaboration in ongoing projects. However, given that Novello tends to be defensive, Dobbins should probably assume that he would take her conversing with his boss as an end run around him or something more sinister. Therefore, her plans for learning more about Behan's point of view must ensure that she does not give Novello cause for concern. One low-cost approach might be to talk to him first and ask about Linda's point of view. He might just propose that Julia go ask her directly.

One assumption that Dobbins has made about Behan is that their both being women means that they have had similar work experiences and that, as a result, they share similar values and agendas. Dobbins should test the assumption before she acts on it.

Dobbins also needs to learn more about the way her own boss envisions the future with the cross-functional team. In such a conversation, she might learn whether he feels concern about changing status, rewards, and the like. Moreover, she could test and solicit his support of her candidacy.

8. What are my sources of power?

Dobbins's sources of power are relative to her two objectives. In terms of influencing Novello to join with her in fostering collaboration among their subordinates, she cannot draw on many of her general sources. Her position has no formal power over him, nor it is more relevant, flexible, or visible than his own. As a technical manager, Dobbins is probably more critical to the organization than Novello, since marketers are a more available resource than technical managers. Her performance in this critical role gives her some power in both influence situations. The engineers are likely to acknowledge her formal-legitimate power to propose an approach that will resolve the ongoing conflicts. Novello may, on the basis of her reputed high performance as a manager and her expertise, accord her informal-legitimate influence. Because Dobbins lacks positional power over Novello, she may have to draw on resources and information to influence him.

Dobbins's sources of power specific to the promotion are her performance and expertise. Since her targets are her boss and his colleague, she cannot use formal position to influence those higher up in the hierarchy. She might try to point out the relevance of her current position to the team leader role and to the organization's goals. Or she might try to enhance her personal attractiveness, specifically her amiability, to demonstrate that she has the interpersonal skills requisite in the leader of a client-focused team.

9. What currencies do I have that any of these people might want?

To influence Novello, Dobbins has several currencies that might prove attractive to him. She could offer the money left in her training budget to create team-training seminars for engineers and marketers. She could offer quicker response time as the trade-off in collaboration. She might highlight the potential of their joint effort to give Novello and the marketers greater recognition, visibility, and reputation. Their early underdog status may make them still particularly eager for those. She could give him understanding, acceptance, gratitude, and some ownership in the project.

To get support from her boss for the promotion, she could offer any of the position-related, relationship-related, or personal-related currencies, depending on which he seemed most eager to get. For example, she knows he feels underappreciated by Kidder, so she might influence his support by stressing his efforts and accomplishments in developing her. To Linda, she may need to offer primarily task-related currencies, unless she has gotten confirmation that Linda does sympathize with her as a woman executive.

10. What are the situational factors that will constrain the effectiveness of my influence strategy?

a. What are the interdependencies among us?

Dobbins and her engineers are interdependent; they require her resources and support. She requires their commitment to her and to doing their job well in order to get them to cooperate in the new initiative with marketing. She and Novello are interdependent, though it is not clear that he understands that. To accomplish her career objective, she is dependent on Hurdy, Behan, and Kidder. They are dependent on her excellent performance in her current job. If she plans to ask her neighbor for help in the promotion process by casually pointing out her high performance and excellent credentials during his next golf game with the vice-president, she will be dependent on him, though the reverse would not be true.

b. What is the distribution of power among us?

The power distribution now is that Dobbins is still slightly higher than Novello based on her higher performance, greater criticality, and higher personal attractiveness. With her engineers, she has significant formal and informal power based on her expertise in design engineering. Dobbins does not know the distribution of power between herself, Behan, Hurdy, and Evans with regard to influencing Kidder about the team leader position. The decision may depend on currencies she does not have or that she doesn't know count. She knows only what her own power base and currencies are vis-à-vis Behan and Hurdy. If she can collect more information on the currencies Kidder values, she might improve her chances.

c. *How much time is available for me to exercise influence?*

The collaboration is a long-term project, so Dobbins has time to influence Novello, the engineers and marketers, and anyone else whose support might be needed. The time to influence the leader selection process seems more immediate. Dobbins should start to collect the information she needs and to influence those she already knows well.

d. *To what extent do we share the same values?*

We have already acknowledged that Dobbins lacks this insight and needs to get information on Novello, Hurdy, Behan, and Kidder. With Behan, she may want to test her assumption about the similarity of views about women managers, in addition to learning about her views on the new team.

e. *How emotional is the situation around this issue?*

The collaboration issue needn't be emotional. Dobbins can reduce the impact of emotion on her efforts by waiting to take up the idea until all past conflicts have not only been resolved but have been dealt with emotionally. The issue of the team leader may become emotional if the company's performance slides in the near term. But that is unlikely. Therefore, neither issue has emotional overtones to it.

f. *What is the nature of my relationship with these people?*

Dobbins believes that she has a good relationship with each of these people. However, some of her past conversations with Novello have not always been warm and happy. Before trying to influence him, she should test his sense of their relationship and work on improving it.

11. Which influence strategy is likely to be the most effective, given the situational factors?

Several factors in the collaboration situation suggest that exchange is likeliest to work well here. Dobbins and Novello are colleagues, with roughly equal power and some interdependence. Novello's commitment would be critical to getting and sustaining the marketers' cooperation. There is sufficient time to influence him through an exchange. As managers, they share a concern for the company's competitive position, and they have a reasonably trusting and respectful relationship.

To influence her superiors to give her the team leader position, Dobbins may need to use a variety of strategies. If she wants to influence her neighbor to recommend her, she should probably use an exchange strategy. She has no formal power over him, so she cannot threaten. As a client relationship, it is essentially an exchange relationship to begin with. Neither values nor emotion characterize the situation, ruling out appeals to those. She could use the appeal to reason, but, given that he will be seeking something in return, that approach will likely lead to an exchange anyway.

With Hurdy, her boss, Dobbins might use appeals to values or reason. His commitment would be required, and they do have the positive relationship required for either type of appeal. They share similar values with regard to the company, thought Dobbins does not know how Hurdy evaluates the team concept. Therefore, she might consider trying an appeal to reason first, and if it doesn't work, try an exchange. Exchange, of course, always costs something, so it less costly for her to try an appeal first.

As has already been mentioned, Dobbins has been assuming that she and Behan shared similar values concerning women in management. This assumption could lead her to try to influence Behan with an appeal to that value. If she is wrong about Behan, this approach could create such distance between them that it would rule out the possibility of influence for some time. Therefore, Dobbins should develop an influence plan with some contingencies built into it. If she tests her assumption and finds she is correct, an appeal to that value may be sufficient. However, it is also likely that Behan, as a competent and successful manager may hold that value but find it insufficient to warrant her support. Therefore, it is advisable for Dobbins to adopt an exchange strategy to influence Behan.

12. When, where, and how should I employ my influence strategy?

Answering these questions is tricky, because the myriad details of personal histories, relationships, organizational culture, and personal style all converge to make the best answer a very specific one that takes account of all these factors. The best advice is to consider each of them very carefully and try to identify a time, a place, and a sequenced approach that allows you to produce with accuracy the message you want to convey and that *allows the other person to give you easily what you seek.*

As you attempt to use these questions as a guide to analysis and action planning in your own situation, you may find yourself wanting to return to earlier answers and change them. That is a good sign: It means that the questions are helping you to refine and develop your understanding of the situation and to design a strategy that fits it.

CONCLUSION

The primary argument of this chapter is that power, politics, and influence are the savvy and the substance of action in organizations. Savvy is knowing in a very practical way *how to get things done;* it is understanding or being able to guess how things work—below the surface, behind the curtain, inside the onion. Substantively, action in organizations amounts to acquiring and using resources, creating and sustaining the cooperation of others in coordinated effort, making and implementing decisions. To perform those activities, a person needs to know who has power, how to influence people, and where and how political activity might enhance or threaten the achievement of one's goals.

Because power, politics, and influence are central to organizational action, they are important considerations in the daily performance of your job as well as in the management of your career. Using the concepts in this chapter, you can prepare for political situations, by assessing the power dynamics in your organization and by determining and developing your own power base. An exchange analysis will have to wait until you are considering a specific problem and person as a focus of your influence. Lastly, it bears remembering that the Cohen and Bradford comment that "you are more powerful than you think" is both an encouragement and a challenge. Effective organizations need powerful and influential people.

NOTES

1. Rosabeth Moss Kanter, "Power Failure in Management Circuits," *Harvard Business Review* 57 (July-August 1979): p. 65.

2. Rosabeth Moss Kanter, "The New Managerial Work," *Harvard Business Review* 89 (November-December 1989): p. 88.

3. William Torbert, *The Power of Balance* (Newbury Park, CA: Sage Publications, 1991).

4. Harold D. Lasswell, *Politics: Who Gets What, When, How* (New York: McGraw-Hill, 1936).

5. Robert Caro, *The Path to Power: The Years of Lyndon Johnson* (New York: Alfred A Knopf, 1982).

6. John Kotter, *Power and Influence* (New York: Free Press, 1985).

7.   Richard M. Emerson, "Power-Dependence Relations," *American Sociological Review* 27 (1962): pp. 31–41.

8.   Rosabeth Moss Kanter, *Men and Women of the Corporation* (New York: Basic Books, 1977).

9.   Ibid.

10.   David Whetten and Kim Cameron, *Developing Management Skills* (Glenview, IL: Scott, Foresman, 1984).

11.   David Whetten and Kim Cameron, *Developing Management Skills*, pp. 261–262.

12.   D. Bramel, "Interpersonal Attraction, Hostility, and Perception," in J. Mills (ed.), *Experimental Social Psychology* (New York: Macmillan, 1969).

13.   S. Jones, "Self and Interpersonal Evaluations," *Psychological Bulletin* 79 (1973): pp. 185–199.

14.   B. R. Schlenker and J. T. Tedeschi, "Interpersonal Attraction and the Use of Reward and Coercive Power," *Human Relations* 25 (1972): pp. 427–439.

15.   John Molloy, *Dress for Success* (New York: P. H. Wyden, 1975).

16.   Allan R. Cohen, Stephen L. Fink, Herman Gadon, and Robin D. Willits, *Effective Behavior in Organizations*, 5th ed. (Homewood, IL: Irwin, 1992).

17.   Allan R. Cohen and David L. Bradford, *Influence Without Authority* (New York: John Wiley & Sons, 1990), p.73.

18.   Rosabeth Moss Kanter, "Power Failure in Management Circuits," pp. 65–75.

19.   Jeffrey Pfeffer, *Managing with Power* (Boston: Harvard Business School Press, 1992).

20.   Rosabeth Moss Kanter, "Power Failure in Management Circuits," pp. 65–66.

21.   D. Kipnis, *The Powerholders* (Chicago: University of Chicago Press, 1976).

22.   Allan Cohen and David Bradford, "Influence Without Authority: The Use of Alliances, Reciprocity and Exchange to Accomplish Work," *Organizational Dynamics* 17 (Winter 1989): pp. 5–17.

FOR FURTHER READING

Cohen, Allan R., and Bradford, David L. *Influence Without Authority*. New York: John Wiley & Sons, 1989. An engaging and helpful treatment about how to influence people at work. Cohen and Bradford show how to cut through interpersonal and interdepartmental barriers and motivate people, over whom you have no authority, in order to lend you their support and share their valuable time and resources.

Pfeffer, Jeffrey. *Managing with Power: Politics and Influence in Organizations*. Cambridge, MA: Harvard Business School Press, 1992. Deals with the topics of power and politics at a more organizational level than does Cohen and Bradford's *Influence Without Authority*. Pfeffer shows that an effective use of power is an essential component of strong leadership.

6 NEGOTIATING STRATEGICALLY

Roy J. Lewicki

For many people, their first image of the process of "negotiation" is large, multiparty deliberations: contract talks between labor and management, international trade or arms limitation negotiations, or major corporate acquisitions and divestitures. The second image may be one of more personal negotiations, which are often difficult and conflict-laden: buying a used car or a new house or trying to get a better salary from the boss. Yet negotiation is much more pervasive than these examples show. Negotiations are an integral part of our everyday personal and professional lives. Each day, we are involved in one or more of the following situations.

1. We arrive at a four-way stop sign at the same time as three other vehicles; somehow, we need to decide who is going to go through the intersection, in what order.
2. We need to share a scarce resource—a laser printer, a copy machine, or the skills of a key technician—with several co-workers.
3. We must coordinate with others to divide up the chores of daily living—who will clean the kitchen, who will walk and feed the dog, who will pay the bills, who will do the laundry.
4. We need to influence someone to change her mind—for example, agreeing to accept our report three days after the due date, to waive the fine on our overdue library book, or to give us a pay raise.

The list is endless, actually. All of these situations are negotiations. And we can learn to negotiate better. Effectiveness in negotiation is not simply

The author would like to thank Blair Shepard for his intellectual contribution to the development of these ideas and Allan Cohen for his comments on earlier drafts of this chapter.

a matter of having a certain kind of personality; it is definitely a matter of understanding how negotiation works and how to make the process work better for you. The purpose of this chapter is to provide a road map for managing negotiations effectively; it explains the key principles of negotiation and applies them to all of the different situations in which we negotiate daily.

THE ELEMENTS OF NEGOTIATION

What are the key elements for an understanding of the negotiation process? If one examines a number of definitions of *negotiation*, the following five elements can be identified.

1. Negotiation is primarily a *two-party* or *inter*personal process—two individuals, two groups, two organizations. Negotiation also can be viewed as an *intra*personal process—a debate inside us about whether we are going to spend our Sunday playing tennis or washing the car. Negotiation can also be a group process, as when a planning team, project group, or task force works together to agree on a strategy or a policy document—or when a group of friends tries to decide where to go for dinner. But negotiation is mostly one-on-one, as are most of the examples I discuss.

2. The parties have a *conflict of interest.* They do not agree on something. It may be a conflict of preferences, a conflict of priorities, or—most commonly—a conflict over resources: a disagreement over who is to receive what size, amount, or allocation.

3. Negotiation is largely a *voluntary activity.* Most negotiators, in most situations, are seldom *forced* to negotiate; rather, we *choose* to negotiate because we believe that the process will help improve our outcomes. We can always simply take what is offered to us, without challenging the offer or asking for more. Negotiations are voluntary in the sense that we can always "take it or leave it," but we negotiate in order to improve our outcomes through a process of dialogue and discussion.

4. Negotiations involve the management of two kinds of entities: *the tangibles and the intangibles.* The tangibles are the substantive issues to be resolved through the negotiation: They are the "issues" that are at stake in a conflict of interest. For example, in making a purchase, the tangibles might include the price to be paid, the interest rate at which money is borrowed, the number of items bought, when and how they get delivered, and the specific wording of a written contract. Through negotiation, the parties attempt to resolve their conflicts of interest on the tangibles.

   However, in addition to the tangibles, which are the pragmatic and visible stakes, negotiation involves intangibles, which are the less visible, psychological stakes. Most of the attention in planning, preparation, and actual negotiation is given to the tangibles—achieving the desired price or preferred delivery terms. Given less attention, but sometimes more important, are the psychological goals, or objectives. Intangible goals may include winning, "doing better than the opponent," "maintaining a precedent" (for example, being unwilling to even discuss an issue that the opponent wants to negotiate), "standing by our principles," "looking tough and strong," or "being fair to all sides." Intangibles can sometimes be translated into tangibles; for example, "being fair to all sides" can be translated into a statement like "in my view, this would be a price, interest rate, and delivery terms that I think would be fair to everyone." But other intangibles are not directly translatable into specific tangibles; in such cases the definitions of what it will take to satisfy them and when they are satisfied are very personal and private. When negotiations break down and when parties fail to agree, it is often because the parties are unable to identify the key intangibles that must be satisfied or because they have set undefined (and unattainable) goals for the intangibles at stake. Sound planning in negotiation requires two key processes: First, the parties must identify all of the tangibles and intangibles at stake in the negotiation, and, second, they must remain mindful of what is required to effectively satisfy the intangibles.

5. Finally, when we enter a situation that we call *"negotiation,"* we fundamentally expect a process of *give and take*. When parties anticipate negotiation, they expect to start with asking prices, opening bids, or initial positions; such openers are *not* the same as where they would like to end the negotiation. In other words, formulating an initial demand is done with the expectation that each side will do so, that they will be some distance apart in those initial positions, and that they will then "bargain" with each other to move toward some common ground. The process of modifying one's own initial position and persuading the other to do so until a common point or target is achieved is the *heart* of bargaining. It may take only one or two modifications of one's position in a three-minute period, or it may take thirty or forty modifications over a six-month period. But ultimately the parties expect to move toward each other, in some form of anticipated but not exactly predictable dance, until they agree to a common price, a common set of terms, a unified contract language, and a personal satisfaction that their fundamental goals were achieved.

POWER FACTORS IN NEGOTIATION

Having defined the key elements in the process of negotiation, I now discuss several important factors that contribute to a negotiator's "power." There are many ways that a negotiator can achieve power during negotiation. A *power factor* is an element that can significantly either enhance or diminish a negotiator's ability to achieve the objectives. These factors affect all negotiations. If a negotiator has one or more of the power factors on his side, he will be in a considerably better negotiating position relative to the opponent and to achieving objectives; if the negotiator knows that the power factor is largely benefiting the other side, then he will be at some negotiating disadvantage. I discuss the following six key factors that operate in this manner.

1. The nature and type of information available.
2. The presence of constituencies and the support they provide.
3. Time and deadlines.
4. Legitimacy factors that derive from an organizational context.
5. Alternatives to dealing with an opponent or arriving at the proposed agreement.
6. Personal qualities of a negotiator's style and personality.

1. Information

At the heart of its process, negotiation is an exchange of information; this information is marshaled and organized to persuade the other person to see it our way. We have an objective we want to achieve—for example, to negotiate for a bigger budget for our department or to persuade a friend to go to the restaurant we like. In order to be effective in this effort, we need *information,* which we can assemble to argue persuasively for the case we want to make and which we can use to challenge, contradict, or negate another's arguments. If we are trying to negotiate for a bigger budget, then we must tell our manager why we need more money, what it will be used for, and why it is important to our department. If we are trying to persuade a friend to try our favorite restaurant, then we need information on why that restaurant is great and why she should try it! Information is the dominant currency of negotiation. It is not sufficient just to state (or to demand) that we want something. Negotiation is supposed to be a rational process: We must be able to state why we want it and use our arguments to persuade. Therefore, effective negotiators anticipate what information they will need in any given situation and do appropriate homework in order to be thoroughly prepared. The better the preparation, organization, and use of information, the more likely one will have a persuasive case.

To the reader, this may all seem self-evident. But when one looks at negotiation "failures," in which one or both negotiators fail to get what they want, it is clear that one of the most common causes of failure is inadequate information planning! Many negotiators, particularly inexperienced ones, prefer to wing it rather than to prepare adequately. Although the exact nature of information planning—what specific information will be needed—changes from one negotiation to the next, the following information preparation is usually necessary for success.

a. A definition of my objectives: What do I want to achieve? What are my goals? How specific can I be about this?

b. A definition of the information needed to argue for my objectives: How can I construct a persuasive case to support my goals? What facts or figures do I need? Where can I get this information? How do I assemble it to be persuasive and clear?

c. A definition of the information needed to challenge the other negotiator's arguments: Can I anticipate what they are going to want? And if I can anticipate it, how would I argue for it? How can I challenge the arguments they will make? What facts and figures will help me challenge them effectively?

d. After I make my arguments, what are they going to argue in return? What can I do to rebut their arguments or their efforts to undermine my position?

e. How do I define my "opening request" and my "limits?" Negotiators need to know where to begin negotiation, that is, what to ask for initially, and where to end negotiation, that is, at what point to walk away or refuse to settle rather than agreeing to a poor deal. If we are negotiating a budget increase, we need to know what our objective is, what we can "reasonably" ask for, and how far we can be pushed before saying that the deal is unacceptable. If we prepare our information well, we can make intelligent decisions about what level of request will be seen as reasonable, given that we will probably make concessions, and still achieve the objective.

f. Finally, good preparation suggests that negotiators get as much information as they can about their opponent—not only the opponent's goals, but also his style and reputation. In any interaction, particularly a competitive one, the more we learn about an opponent, the better we can predict how he will behave. Is that person honest or dishonest, trustworthy or untrustworthy, competitive or cooperative? What kind of a strategy will he prepare? What does he expect of us? And what strategy might work against that particular opponent?

In summary, the first element of negotiator power is achieved by observing the famous motto of the Boy Scouts: "Be prepared." Better preparation, through anticipating the information needed to effectively argue one's position or challenging the opponent's arguments, is central to enhancing one's strength. In contrast, negotiators who are poorly prepared, by not having the critical information or not having thought out the six points just identified, are much more likely to be at a major disadvantage in a negotiation against a well-prepared opponent!

FIGURE 6-1   Two negotiators

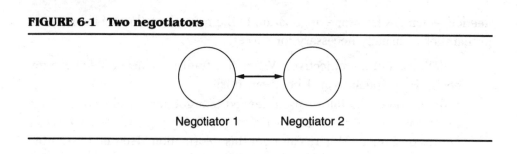

Negotiator 1   Negotiator 2

2. Constituencies and Organizational Support/Authority

In some negotiations, there are only two negotiators. (See Figure 6-1.) If my friend and I are trying to decide where to go to dinner—she wants Italian, I want Mexican—then where we eventually go to dinner will be completely resolved between the two of us. No one else is involved in the decision, and so no other party can influence the negotiation in any way.

Whereas some personal negotiations involve only two parties, many business negotiations involve more than two. In those situations, I am no longer just negotiating for myself. The goals and objectives I set are not *just* for me; they are set together with other people who will benefit if I achieve them or will lose if I do not. When I negotiate for a budget increase, I am trying to help the others in my department. When I negotiate with a customer, I am trying to get a better deal for my organization. In such situations, my department or my organization is my *constituency* (see Figure 6-2). A constituency is a group that we belong to and whose interests we advocate or protect.

Constituencies play two important roles in negotiation. First, they help us define our objectives. They tell us what is acceptable or unacceptable in terms of the opening bid, goal, and bottom line. Then they send us off

FIGURE 6-2   Two negotiators with constituencies

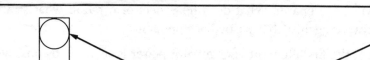
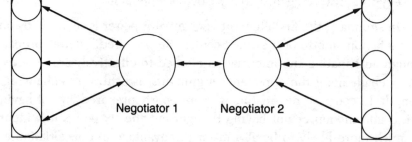

Negotiator 1   Negotiator 2

into negotiation, expecting that we can achieve exactly what they told us to achieve. Second, constituencies evaluate us after we come back from negotiation. They judge us on the basis of our achievements and either reward or punish us accordingly. If we come back and report that we have achieved everything, we get a positive evaluation—a pat on the back, a round of applause, the approval from our peers, and perhaps even a raise. But if we come back and report that we did not achieve everything we were sent out to do, we get a negative evaluation: a look of disappointment, the criticism of our negotiating effectiveness, and—in the most extreme situations—we are even relieved of our responsibilities to represent the group in future negotiations. With some incredulity on their behalf, our constituency tells us that they are disappointed, that they can't understand why we couldn't achieve the simple task they sent us to accomplish, and that we probably are not very experienced or sophisticated at our task.

Experienced negotiators, who understand these dynamics well, report that their experience has led them to the following conclusions about the role of constituencies:

- Constituencies are almost always "unreasonable." Since the constituency has little or no *direct* experience with the opponent, who also wants to achieve his or her own objectives in negotiation, constituencies come to believe that the goals they have set for the negotiator should be fairly easy to achieve. Constituencies *always* seem to want more than what the negotiator believes is possible. As a result, they are not sympathetic to the returning negotiator who tries to explain that the objectives were much more difficult than earlier planning and preparation suggested. Constituencies always appear to expect more than can really be delivered in negotiation; moreover, when objectives are not met, they blame their negotiator.

- Because constituencies are frequently isolated from the negotiations, their "unreasonable" expectations become more firm. Since they have usually not heard the opponent's arguments first hand, they see little reason to modify their own initial demands. As a result, many negotiators find that it is more difficult to convince their constituencies about what goals are really achievable (given what the other side wants) than it is to convince their opponents on the very nature of the goals. When my colleagues and I have asked hundreds of executives, who is more difficult to negotiate with—your opponent or your constituency?, the answer is clear: the constituency! Therefore, constituencies must be carefully "managed" by negotiators. They must be constantly educated about what is possible and realistic in negotiation, so that their aspirations are not permitted to get out of control.

- Constituents control their negotiators in two ways. First, they give positive evaluations and rewards for good performance and negative evaluations and punishments for bad performance. Most negotiators want to secure a positive evaluation and avoid a negative evaluation. To be told by one's constituency a negotiator did poorly, and particularly to criticize the negotiator in public, is a threat to his self-image and "face."[2] Negotiators desperately want to save face—maintain a strong, positive image with their constituency—and to avoid looking weak and foolish. Thus, constituencies manipulate a negotiator by how they judge the negotiator's performance; their efforts are designed to get the negotiator to pursue their objectives vigorously, in order to obtain the desired positive evaluation.

  Second, constituents control a negotiator by controlling his authority: his ability to agree to a deal on his own, rather than to return to the constituency for "permission." Typically, it is done by telling a negotiator that she cannot agree to any deal without constituent review and approval of the proposed deal or that her authority is limited to such agreements that are below a certain dollar amount, for instance. Although negotiators who can make deals on their own authority typically are seen as having more power (as defined here), unlimited authority is not necessarily an advantage for a negotiator. *All negotiators* can be subject to extreme pressures to agree by their opponent; a negotiator who must check with her constituency always has a "safety valve" that protects her from succumbing to unreasonable pressures. Thus, it is not surprising that, when asked who makes the worst deals for their companies, many executives acknowledge that it is the president or CEO, because there are no limits to the president's authority to agree to almost anything while in negotiation. Paradoxically, then, controlled and limited authority is actually more powerful than unlimited authority.

In summary, when a negotiator has a constituency, and when that constituency sets reasonable goals for him and thoroughly backs him through the deliberations, that negotiator has a lot of power. When a negotiator's constituency does not support him and when it either severely constrains his authority or gives him unlimited authority, his power declines significantly.

3. Time Pressures and Deadlines

Time pressures make up the third factor of power in negotiation. Negotiation is fundamentally a time-drive activity. Like the well-known proverb "work fills the time available," negotiation tends to follow the same principle—it fills the time available. This means that most concessions tend to come toward the end of a negotiation time period.[3] If an hour was allotted to the negotiation, and the parties believe that there is some important reason to settle before the end of the time period, then most of the concessions occur in the last ten minutes. If a day was allotted, then most concessions come late in the afternoon. Anyone who has observed the behavior of management and labor during contract talks will note that, although the parties may have begun negotiation several months before the end of the contract, it is not uncommon for marathon bargaining to commence in the week preceding the actual expiration date and for the union to be organizing its walkout and the management preparing for a work stoppage, as negotiations are completed.

Why does this phenomenon occur? There are many reasons: The parties fail to create an agenda, lose track of the time, argue their points too long, get sidetracked on minor points, and so on. But the most important reason is that the deadline creates an appropriate rationale for making concessions. Each side can present their arguments and point of view forever; if there is no deadline, the parties will frequently carry on—stalling, hesitating, and delaying in an effort to wear each other out. But when there is a deadline, the parties can use it as a reason for making a concession. "It's not that I'm changing my mind or agreeing with your arguments"—goes the famous line. "But, in the interest of time, I'm going to modify my position." Furthermore, delaying can be effective for persuading your constituency that you "held out as long as possible" before making a key concession.

When both sides have the same deadline or neither has a deadline, deadline power is equalized. But when one side has a deadline and the other does not, the party without the deadline has the advantage. The reason is that the party with the deadline feels the pressure to make some movement toward settlement, whereas the one without the deadline feels no such pressure; as a result, the latter can stall and put undue time pressure on the former. The negotiator who has to catch the plane leaving in an hour, be at another appointment, meet a deadline for funding, or even go to the rest room is under more pressure. Examples abound. The reader may remember the flurry of activity in January 1981 to solve the Iranian hostage crisis as President Jimmy Carter left office, because the Iranians presumably preferred to deal with President Carter than with the newer and reputedly tougher President Reagan.

While negotiators are at a disadvantage when they have a deadline and the opponent does not, this disadvantage may be offset by creating a deadline for the opponent. Such deadlines may be created by offering particularly attractive options and alternatives that are only available for a short period of time. Retailers have long known that a sale—a temporary decrease in the price—is a good way to move merchandise off the shelf. Similarly, many companies now make job offers to new recruits that are only valid for several weeks, thereby enticing candidates to make a quick decision, before the company offers the jobs to others.

In summary, time is not a power factor when deadline pressures are equally strong or weak on both sides; it is a power factor when one side has a deadline and the other does not. The side without the deadline—or with a longer fuse—has more power in negotiation, since they can delay a negotiation and put undue pressure on the opponent, regardless of the issues or other factors in the negotiation.

4. Legitimacy

The fourth factor of power is legitimacy, which is defined as the formal authority, the quasi-legal system of rules, policies, procedures, and practices that dictate how issues and problems will be handled or resolved. Legitimacy therefore limits the range of what is negotiable. A newly minted MBA wants to work for the Solid Company, but Solid is offering a salary considerably less than what others are paying. So she tries to negotiate the starting salary with Solid. The personnel officer says, "I'm sorry. We don't negotiate starting salary. Our company policy states that all new personnel in this job classification must start at the same pay level." There is no negotiation; you can't easily negotiate with a company policy that has precluded negotiation!

Bureaucracies of all forms—governmental, business, and educational— are loaded with regulations that limit or preclude negotiation over things like pay, schedules, benefits, or job assignments. In general, the organizations see the policies as highly functional, which explains why they make so many of them! Policies and rules allow organizations to treat all employees "fairly" (that is, equally) and save time by not requiring independent negotiations for every employee who wants to do something a bit differently. At the societal level, governments argue a comparable case for regulating the economic, social, and political behavior of organizations in order to ensure societal fairness. But for the most part, such rules and regulations are made to protect the interests of the rule makers and to limit the choices, options, and negotiation activity of those whose behavior is regulated. It is a power strategy, invoked by the rule makers, to limit the flexibility of those who it seeks to control. The impact is a net decrease in power for the individual negotiator.

In this context, power is both real and illusory. Most negotiators are so used to being controlled that they seldom question the controls, their source, or their flexibility. They are asked to sign a lease or a sales contract; if they inquire about certain language or clauses, they are told "it can't be changed," "our lawyers wouldn't approve it," or "that would be against company policy." Challenges to these policies are usually tedious, time-consuming, and frustration-producing—largely in an effort to discourage any further challenges. We come to learn that to challenge the "system" requires significant effort, time, and often personal risk; so instead we take what little we are given and bypass efforts at further negotiation. The system teaches us that negotiation is significantly less valued than compliance: That is legitimacy power in full use. If the policies and procedures back our preferred position and we are one of the rule makers, we have a great deal of power; if we are up against the policies and procedures, attempting to argue for a waiver, exception, or variation to meet our individual needs, we are likely committing ourselves to a very expensive, time-consuming, and perhaps personally risky venture. However, investing the effort may prove to be fruitful if we have some of the other power factors on our side.

5. Options to the Agreement

The fifth factor is the power of having alternatives to the proposed agreement. People frequently negotiate as though the specific outcome they hope to derive is the *only* outcome in the world that is possible; as a result, they commit themselves fully to the process, doing whatever it takes to obtain a deal. That is highly unproductive negotiation behavior, for several reasons. First, in the emotional heat of negotiation, we become overcommitted to getting a deal (*any deal*), just to feel the sense of psychological success from completing the negotiation. Moreover, we become very committed to the outcome we are pursuing, to the point where we are willing to pursue it at all costs. Psychologists call this process of overcommitment *entrapment*. In entrapping situations, we behave as though we are addicted to the desired outcome. We do so because we are emotionally involved; because we cannot back down from commitments, which are often publicly made, without believing that we will look weak and foolish; and because we have invested so much time, money, and energy already that we cannot afford to back down.[4] Whether it is putting more money on the roulette wheel to recover our gambling losses or committing more troops and missiles to a war we can't or shouldn't try to win, entrapment is an expensive and dangerous psychological process.

Good options (to the potential agreement under discussion) give us power because they release us from these dynamics. We no longer have to pursue a negotiation to achieve a settlement "at any cost." First, if we have a good option, then we need not pursue the negotiation with any sense of desperation; if the deal falls through, we always have the alternative to fall back on. Second, good options act as an alternative "bottom line" or as "limits" (see the foregoing discussion of information power). If I have a good option, then I should pursue the current negotiation only if it will give me a *better* option, in some way. If I am economically rational, then at some point I can afford to walk away and take the option. Noted authors Roger Fisher and

William Ury call it the *best alternative to a negotiated agreement* (BATNA).[5] BATNAs serve as the viable options that permit us to walk away from unattractive deals. They also permit us to tell our opponents how to shape their offers, because the deal under discussion must be better than our BATNA for us to find it attractive. Good BATNAs, therefore, provide us with powerful tools for persuading our opponents that a deal must meet our needs.

6. Personal Power

The previous five factors of power—information, organizational accountability, time, legitimacy, and options—are sources of power that negotiators derive from the issues themselves, and from the social structure or context of the negotiation. But negotiators also have certain personal qualities that can make them more powerful. They include the following.

a. *Persuasiveness.* Good negotiators can not only put together the right information, but they can argue their point of view eloquently and can structure arguments in a way that makes them convincing. Although I mentioned having good information earlier, the power of persuasiveness is derived by how effectively that information builds a case for what is wanted. The things that make communicators effective, in the media, politics, and elsewhere, also contribute to good negotiation. Strong logical reasoning, good communication skills (eye contact, clear voice), and a strong *personal* commitment to the objectives contribute to powerful persuasiveness.

b. *Tenacity.* Good negotiators are tenacious. Initially, at least, they don't take no for an answer. Executives often agree that their children are excellent negotiators because they are so persistent in trying to get what they want. A negotiator must be careful not to be an annoying "pest," but he also must be careful not to fold up in defeat, simply because the first reply to his request was no. Tenacity helps good negotiators discover that there are many *maybes, possibles,* or *depends* behind an early no.

c. *Integrity and character.* Finally, effective negotiators have excellent reputations for being trustworthy, honest, and principled. If our character is questionable, then so are our motivations, and people will refuse to negotiate with us because they are afraid of being tricked and deceived or because they are unsure that we will fulfill our commitments. In contrast, if we have a reputation for high integrity, people will want to negotiate with us because they know that we have told the truth, that the deal is fair, and that we will follow through. We will not require a pack of attorneys to interpret our agreements or to spend a year in expensive litigation fighting over interpretation. This type of reputation will give us significant power in negotiation.

TABLE 6-1 Power factors in negotiation

Negotiators are more powerful when

- They have the information they need, they are well prepared
- They have the full endorsement of their organization or constituency
- They do not need to complete a deal under some deadline
- They have the power of an organization's rules, policies, and procedures to back them
- They have good options to completing this agreement
- They have strong reputations for being persuasive, tenacious, and having personal integrity

Negotiators are less powerful when

- One or more of the above factors is operating against them
- One or more of the above factors resides on their opponent's side

---

In this section I have described six significant factors of power in negotiation: information, organizational support, time, legitimacy, options, and personal power. I have shown how each operates and how each can either enhance or diminish the effectiveness of a negotiator (see Table 6-1). Negotiators who feel powerless need to examine how each factor is operating in an upcoming negotiation and to explore ways to either enhance his or her own power or defuse that of the opponent. In the next section I turn to the key process of choosing a negotiation strategy.

HOW TO CHOOSE A NEGOTIATION STRATEGY

Much of the literature on negotiation has focused on polar-opposite pairs of strategies variously called competitive versus cooperative, distributive versus integrative, win-lose versus win-win.[6] These strategies are explored in detail later in this chapter. But what has received less attention are the two critical questions that drive the choice between these particular strategies and two other strategies that have received much less attention in negotiation research.

Savage, Blair, and Sorenson have done the best job of stating the two questions that need to drive strategic choice.[7]

> Before selecting a strategy for negotiation, a manager should consider his or her interests and the interests of the organization. These interests will shape the answers to two basic questions: (1) is the substantive outcome very important to the manager? and (2) is the relationship outcome very important to the manager? (p. 40)

These are the two critical questions, and they must be treated independently. First, how important is the outcome on the substance of the negotiation (the issues) to the negotiator? This is not a casual question. Some outcomes are very important; others are only somewhat important; and others, in the grand scheme of things, are not very important at all. Although all outcomes may look "very important" at the time, one must decide how high a priority the issues in the negotiation really are. Second, one must also decide on the importance of the relationship between the negotiators. Every negotiation has relationship outcomes as well as substantive outcomes; that is, how we negotiate now has an impact on the quality of our relationship in the future. Relationships are measured by such factors as (1) the degree of interdependence between us (how much are we dependent on the behaviors of the other to achieve our own outcomes?), (2) the time span of the relationship (have we been working together for a long time; do we anticipate working together for a long time in the future?), (3) the level of friendship we feel toward the other party, and (4) the regularity and ease of communication with the other side. Conflict between people raises tension and anger, creates distrust and miscommunication, decreases the ability to work together, and harms the ability to repair the relationships in the future. So we must decide in the present not only what kind of a substantive outcome we want to achieve, but what kind of a relationship outcome we want. If we want or need a high-quality relationship with this opponent in the future, we should negotiate very differently than if the relationship is unimportant.

Based on a yes or no answer to these two questions, Savage, Blair, and Sorenson have outlined four major strategies for negotiation. These are shown in Figure 6-3. The four strategies are as follows.

1. Trusting Collaboration (C1)

The strategy to pursue when both the substantive outcome and the relationship are important is that of trusting collaboration, most commonly described as integrative or win-win. The negotiator wishes to achieve a good substantive outcome and also ensure that the relationship will sustain open communication, trust, and a willingness of the parties to sustain ongoing negotiations (for example, to get both a good raise from your boss and the opportunity to work with her in the future). Parties frequently treat negotiation situations as "problems to be solved" rather than confrontational disputes. Unfortunately, to effectively achieve the outcome while maintaining the relationship, parties must often make notable sacrifices on the substantive issues in order to effectively preserve and protect the relationship. Whether it is a relationship between spouses in a marriage, colleagues in a workplace, or suppliers and customers in a production process, trusting collaboration is the desired strategy. As you will see, however, trusting collaboration is much easier to read about and describe than it is to actually produce.

FIGURE 6-3   Four strategies for negotiation

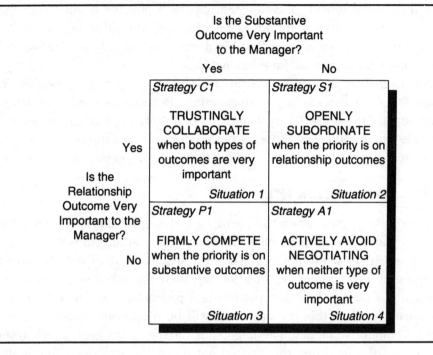

Is the Substantive
Outcome Very Important
to the Manager?

	Yes	No
Yes — Is the Relationship Outcome Very Important to the Manager?	*Strategy C1* TRUSTINGLY COLLABORATE when both types of outcomes are very important *Situation 1*	*Strategy S1* OPENLY SUBORDINATE when the priority is on relationship outcomes *Situation 2*
No	*Strategy P1* FIRMLY COMPETE when the priority is on substantive outcomes *Situation 3*	*Strategy A1* ACTIVELY AVOID NEGOTIATING when neither type of outcome is very important *Situation 4*

2. Open Subordination (S1)

The strategy to pursue when the parties are strongly concerned about the relationship but the substantive issue is less important is that of open subordination. In this strategy, we resist aggressive negotiation on the substantive issues in order to keep the other side "happy," that is, to give them what they want on the issues and to preserve or enhance the relationship. Other names for this strategy include *accommodation* or even *ingratiation*. It is a strategy that has received considerably less attention in the traditional negotiation literature, although psychologists have written about it in other contexts.[8] Why would a negotiator choose this strategy? Several reasons can be offered.

First, it is usable when the negotiator truly does not care about the substantive issue, but wants something else from the opponent: If I want a good recommendation from my boss for a promotion, I may decide to put in more time and effort on his high-priority projects in order to gain his approval.

Second, it is usable when the negotiator is willing to trade off the possible substantive outcomes in the present negotiation for a possible better advantage in a future negotiation: I may not challenge my boss now on his demands for me to work overtime, expecting that, if I put in that time, I will be in a better position to ask for a longer vacation at the end of the year.

Finally, it is usable when the negotiator truly cares about the relationship and does not want to increase tensions by a possible conflict over the current substantive issues: By not negotiating over the substantive issues, I can minimize the possibility of hostility, keep communication friendly, and increase mutual support in the relationship.

Subordination is a difficult strategy for some negotiators, because it appears to be condescending or demeaning. But experienced negotiators will agree that there are times when it is definitely appropriate to let the other side win and thereby preserve the relationship and the opportunity to return later when the stakes are considerably more important and desirable.

3. Firm Competition (P1)

The strategy to pursue when the parties are strongly concerned about the substantive outcome but not concerned about the relationship is that of firm competition. It is usually pursued when the negotiator does not care about developing or maintaining any relationship with the other side, when the relationship is already less than positive and productive, or when the negotiator clearly expects that the opponent will be dishonest, mistrustful, and will use competitive tactics. The negotiator pursues a strategy of "whatever it takes" in order to obtain the desired outcome. This definition frequently leads to the use of tactics that are aggressive, demanding, and perhaps even manipulative or dishonest.

Because negotiations often take place in a conflictful atmosphere, the very dynamics of conflict can lead us to expect the other side to approach negotiation with a competitive strategy; as a result, we adopt a competitive stance, not from an offensive but from a "defensive" posture, attempting to protect ourselves from the other's competitive behavior or to preempt the opponent. Our competitive posture generally leads the opponent to behave competitively, whether or not they originally intended to, and produces behaviors that serve to justify initial expectations. Such a decline into mutual competition is very common among inexperienced and unsophisticated negotiators and usually leads to highly unproductive outcomes for both sides. Defeating and changing the cycle of competitive escalation requires negotiators to signal clearly their preferred intentions to each other prior to negotiation as well as to communicate very clearly at the beginning of a negotiation about the strategy one would like to pursue, vehicles for achieving the strategy, and consequences for the other if the negotiator deviates from the strategy.

4. Active Avoidance (A1)

The fourth strategy that a negotiator should pursue when neither the substantive outcome nor the relationship is important is known as active avoidance. Thus, in some situations, the negotiator may determine that little can be gained from negotiation on the substantive issues and that the relationship is sufficiently unimportant to exert energy working on it as well. Whereas active avoidance—refusing to negotiate—is the most aggressive form of avoidance, other forms of avoidance are pleasant, well mannered, and socially acceptable, such as simply not showing up, not raising any strong concerns or objections, or focusing one's attention on pursuits that are likely to be more productive.

In this chapter I focus primarily on the collaborative (C1) and competitive (P1) strategies. Even though there are some important negotiation strategies and tactics that do occur in the context of the subordinative and avoidance strategies, these two approaches are used considerably less than the other two, because there is less engagement with the other and less actual give and take (see the earlier definitions). I now turn your attention to a fuller description of the two primary strategies, considering first the competitive strategy and then the collaborative strategy.

COMPETITIVE NEGOTIATION STRATEGY AND TACTICS

As indicated, a competitive strategy is pursued when the negotiator is strongly concerned about the outcome but not about the relationship with the other party. It is pursued when one is willing to do anything necessary to achieve specific objectives. The competitive strategy (also called distributive bargaining, "hard" bargaining, or win-lose bargaining) is usually pursued when the following conditions are present.

1. The negotiator has short-term goals, that is, to secure the best possible settlement now, without concern for what happens in the future.
2. The negotiator believes that the goals of the two negotiators are fundamentally incompatible; that is, the more the other side gets, the less I get (and hence I must get as much as I can to make sure the other side doesn't get it).
3. The negotiator places most of the emphasis on the tangibles: achievement of the best price, rate, terms, or the other substantive objectives. This predisposition fits with the previous one, in that competitive negotiation is presumed to be both necessary and desirable when the issues at stake are largely economic and finite.
4. The negotiator believes that the other side is likely to be competitive, which legitimizes or even necessitates that the negotiator select a competitive strategy to protect the self or even to preempt the other side's anticipated competition with tough, competitive tactics.

Finally, the competitive strategy is used by negotiators who have little or no training or experience in negotiation. When told to "negotiate," they will likely assume some or all of the characteristics of a classic competitive negotiator.

The following paragraphs define key elements of a typical competitive strategy. Such a strategy requires the definition of some "points" in the bargaining range. The first point is a *target point,* which identifies where the negotiator would prefer to end the negotiation; another name for a target point is a *negotiation goal.* For example, if the objective is to buy a used car to drive to work, the target point, or goal, is the amount of money the individual would optimally like to spend. Let's assume that it is $3000—enough to buy a small and reasonable used car. This amount may have been determined in a variety of ways: by examining one's savings and budget and then estimating how much one can afford, by evaluating what kind of car is needed and then selecting from those available for $3000, or simply by learning that a good friend paid that for her used car. Although better planning of the target point leads to a greater willingness to stick to it during negotiation, any good rationale can lead to setting a reasonable target point.

The second point is a *resistance point,* or bottom line. The resistance point is the limiting point beyond which a negotiator won't go. In the same example, the negotiator may have decided that under no circumstances will he spend more than $3500 for a car. This is his resistance point. The advantage of a resistance point, particularly one set in advance, is that it ensures that the negotiator will not get drawn into a deal he later finds unsatisfactory. In spite of the wisdom of doing so, naive negotiators very seldom define their resistance points in advance. As a result, some drop out prematurely—not having made enough concessions to get together. Or if they are up against a successful, high-pressure opponent, they end up spending more than intended.

A third point, related to the resistance point, is the existence of a BATNA (best alternative to a negotiated agreement), or of *options.* I mentioned these earlier in the discussion of power. The difference between a BATNA and a resistance point is that a BATNA is an alternative settlement, which can be pursued if the one currently being negotiated is not obtained, and a resistance point is a point at which we will drop out of the negotiation even if no other viable option or BATNA exists. BATNAs can serve as resistance points because they offer an alternative solution that we can pursue if the current negotiations are not going well. In fact, one very successful strategy is to cultivate a good BATNA and to insist that our opponent must either meet or exceed the value of our BATNA to close the deal. Thus, if we know of another good car that we can definitely buy for $3200, we should insist that our opponent be willing to sell the car for less than $3200 or we will automatically select our BATNA.

FIGURE 6-4   Definition of bargaining range (buyer's perspective)

```
- - - - - |- - - - - - - - - - - - - - |- - - - - - |- - - - - - - - |- - - - - - - - - - - - - - -
```

$2500		$3000	$3200	$3500
Opening		Target	BATNA	Resistance
Bid		Point		Point

The final predetermined point is an *opening bid,* which is the negotiator's starting position: the first offer or request. By starting with a bid and then making concessions, the negotiator expects to move from the point of opening toward the target. The opening bid is the hardest point to define, because it depends less on what we want or can afford and depends more on the context in which we are negotiating. Let us assume that the used car negotiator has decided on an opening bid of $2500; the discussion of opening bids will resume later.

These four points—the target point, resistance point, BATNA, and opening bid—constitute the negotiator's *bargaining range.* Visualizing the bargaining range allows us to discuss the essence of competitive negotiation (see Figure 6-4). The bargaining range spans from the opening bid, where a negotiator "starts" with the first offer, to the resistance point, beyond which the negotiator will not go. Let us expand on the impact of visualizing negotiation in the following ways.

First, a bargaining range can be assumed to exist also for our opponent. If our opponent is rational, and is out to maximize her outcomes as well, then the opponent will also have a bargaining range. I have represented this range in Figure 6-5. Note that the seller's bargaining range includes an "asking price" (opening bid) of $3500, a target point of $3200 (point where the seller would like to sell the car), a BATNA of $2900 (another buyer who has expressed interest in the car at that price but has not yet completed the sale) and a resistance point of $2600 (the lowest price that the seller will take for the car).

Given this full information, one can see that the bargaining ranges overlap; that is, there are a number of settlements that will meet the needs of

FIGURE 6-5   Definition of bargaining range (seller's perspective)

Resistance			Target	Asking
Point	BATNA		Point	Price
$2600	$2900		$3200	$3500

```
- - - - - - - - |- - - - - - - - - - |- - - - - - - - - - - |- - - - - - - - |- - - - - - - - - - -
```

FIGURE 6-6 Definition of bargaining range (both perspectives)

Resistance Point $2600	BATNA $2900	Target Point $3200	Asking Price $3500

```
- - - - - - - -|- - - - - - - - - -|- - - - - - - - - - -|- - - - - - - -|- - - - - - - - - - - - - - - -
- - - - - -|- - - - - - - - - - - - -|- - - - - - - - -|- - - - - - - -|- - - - - - - - - - - - - - - -
```

$2500 Opening Bid	$3000 Target Point	$3200 BATNA	$3500 Resistance Point

both sides (Figure 6-6). This area of overlap is called the *zone of agreement*. Any settlement between the resistance points of the two parties (from $2600 for the seller to $3500 for the buyer) is acceptable to both sides; any point between the target points of the two parties ($3000 for the buyer to $3200 for the seller) will be a very desirable settlement for both sides. Thus, it should be relatively easy for the parties in this negotiation to find a mutually acceptable price. When there is considerably less overlap between the resistance points or target points (for instance, if the buyer's resistance point is $3500 and the seller's resistance point is $3400), the parties will have a more difficult time finding a price that both can accept, and settlement will be far less easy to achieve.

It is easy to comprehend the zone of agreement when full information is available: when we know our own opening, target, and resistance points, and those of our opponent. But in most negotiations, *we start off by knowing only our points*. We may not even know the opening of our opponent. For example, if the car is on a dealer's lot with a price sticker in the window, one can assume that the price is dealer's opening bid; but if the sticker reads merely For Sale or Great Value or if we are being asked to bid on the car sight unseen, we have no information other than our own planning. As a result, it is clear that *the more information we can get about the other's opening, target, or resistance points, the more intelligently we can plan our own range*. On the other hand, it is clear that we ought to plan our own target and resistance points in advance, so that we are confident in our planning, but also in order to understand that we may have to modify these judgments once we gain information about the other.

Gaining information about an opponent's opening, target, and resistance points is an *essential part* of strategy development and execution. For example, in setting one's opening bid, the rule of thumb is that one should make an opening that allows the negotiator some room for concessions yet obtains a settlement that is equal to, if not better than, one's target point. Thus our buyer would like to spend $3000 for a car, and is willing to spend as much as $3500 for the right car, but certainly would not protest if he could buy it for $2800! To do so, the buyer needs to know how little he can offer without offending the seller. Unfortunately, there are no rules of thumb for that; they vary considerably from negotiation to negotiation and industry to industry. When buying a piece of furniture at a yard sale, it may be customary to offer 50 percent of the seller's asking price; when buying a house, it may be customary to offer 90 percent. If there is an active "market" for any set of goods or services (such as automobiles, houses, starting salaries for employment, or consulting fees) the market has probably also defined a generally acceptable opening range.

It is *important* for a negotiator to know this range before beginning to negotiate, if at all possible. Significant violation of the range can cause major problems: An outrageously high or low opening bid will cause one to lose credibility, but an opening bid that is too modest can lead to a quick settlement that probably suboptimizes the deal you could have made if your opening had been more reasonable from your perspective. To learn more about the commonly accepted range in any market, ask people who have negotiated for similar things, read books and articles on the subject, or get advice from an expert.

General Strategies

Focus only on this deal

Ignore whether the parties have a past relationship or whether you have any interest in developing or maintaining a future relationship. Instead, treat the current negotiation as a single isolated transaction, in which your objective is to get the best deal you possibly can. Note, however, that inside organizations, even very large ones, you can't be sure that the person you think you will never encounter again won't resurface at another point in your career and remember your behavior!

Get as much information from your opponent as possible

Generally a "reactive" strategy is the best one for competition. In other words, be in a position to learn what the other side wants, and react to that, rather than being "proactive" in the disclosure of information about your wants, desires, and preferences. In order to be effectively reactive, you must first learn as much as you can about how the other side views the negotiation—what they want, information about the product they are selling, how little they will take, how badly they want to sell, and so on. Such information can be gained by asking your opponent a lot of probing questions, by talking to other parties, and by doing research prior to negotiation. Interview them first: Get them to talk about themselves, what they want, why they want it, and how far they are willing to go to achieve it. Admittedly, there may also be times in competitive negotiation when you want to take a proactive rather than a reactive stance, that is, when *you* want to define clearly the price, terms, and conditions of sale (a take-it-or-leave-it position). However, negotiators would seldom want to do so, unless they already know a fair amount about the marketplace and their opponent's desperation level and believe they can defend their unwavering position effectively. The less information you have about the opponent or the marketplace, the more you need to pursue a reactive strategy and secure information first.

Set your opening as high, or low, as possible

Your information and research will help you define the limits beyond which you would lose credibility. If your opponent is very anxious to sell the car, for example, and there are many used cars on the market, you might try a lower opening price than if your opponent is under no pressure to sell and there are very few good used cars available.

Stick to your preplanned target and resistance points

Once you learn about the opponent's initial opening, you may be prone to buy into their reasoning. The less confident you feel in your preparation, the more convincing they may sound. In addition, during the course of negotiation, they will undoubtedly tell you that your goals and objectives are unreasonable, impractical, and impossible to achieve (even if *they* don't believe that to be true!). Finally, once both sides quote their opening bids, there is a great tendency for both sides to assume that they will settle somewhere around the midpoint between those opening bids. Negotiations between inexperienced negotiators frequently consists of no more than each side tentatively stating their opening bid and then both quickly moving to a settlement at the approximate midpoint between the bids. I strongly urge you to resist all of such pressures—direct and implied—to compromise at the midpoint and settle quickly! Stick to your earlier planning of target point and resistance point or BATNA, unless it is very clear to you that your planning was based on incomplete or erroneous assumptions that must now be reexamined.

Let your concessions be as few and small as possible

Another mistake made by inexperienced negotiators is that they give too much away and give it away too quickly. That often happens because inexperienced negotiators are uncomfortable with conflict or do not understand what they are doing; as a result, they want to end the negotiation quickly by making a number of concessions toward an agreement. Don't give away a dollar if they will accept a dime! You should argue as strongly and convincingly as you can, for as long as you can, on your opening bid. If they are demanding that you be flexible or give something away to help achieve agreement, make small concessions (such as $50 at a time). Moreover, take your time. Make concessions slowly. Remember that time is a power factor; *persistence and patience* are distinct virtues in competitive negotiation. The longer you take, the more likely the opponent may give more than you or may give it away quickly in order to wrap up the deal. Finally, make concessions one at a time and in a disciplined manner. Concede only *if* they do, only *when* they do, and only *as much* (or less) as they do.

Never disclose your real target point or bottom line

Whereas learning as much as you can about your opponent's information, target, and bottom line will help you implement your own strategy, you should disclose as little as possible about your own information, target, and bottom line. The more information you can gain about your opponent while not disclosing information about yourself—other than to position yourself so as to get the best deal possible—the better off you will be. I am not advocating any intentional forms of deception here (more will be said about that in the ethics section at the end of the chapter), but I am suggesting that you voluntarily disclose as little as possible about your target point, resistance point, and any weaknesses in your information or position. If you are asked direct questions, answer them in a way to give away minimal information. You might add some possible put-off lines such as "you aren't even close" or "you're on the right track, but you need to do more."

Get them to concede as much as they will while you concede as little as you can

The sum total of advice from the previous points is that you should try to give away as little as you can from your opening bid, while getting them to give away as much as they will without walking away from the deal. Admittedly, at the margin, finding this point cannot be described as a science; consistently being able to find that point may be an art form that comes only from a great deal of negotiating experience and learning how to read the more subtle meanings in people's words, nonverbal behavior, and emotional cues. The objective is most straightforwardly achieved by learning as much about your opponent while disclosing as little about yourself as possible and by getting them to concede a great deal as you concede only a little.

Competitive Negotiation Tactics

A great number of tactics are typically associated with the implementation of a competitive strategy.[9] Many tactics involve some level of dishonesty or deception. I am not specifically advocating the use of such tactics as a part of your competitive negotiation strategy, but I will describe the most common ones. It is useful to know these tactics if only to identify them easily and know how to counteract them.

Lowball and extreme offers

These are outrageously low or high opening offers, designed to undermine the opponent's confidence in his or her modest opening bid. For example, if the buyer makes an outrageously low opening bid (a lowball) for the car (such as $1500), he may effectively communicate to the other side that, in his view, the car isn't worth very much money. If the seller is desperate to sell the car, has had no other offers, or did a very poor job of preparation in deciding on the opening sale price, then the outrageous offer may work to some degree. In addition, since we said that both parties look to the midpoint once opening bid and counter have been set, even an outrageous opening can succeed in dropping the apparent midpoint where settlement might occur.

Emotional strategies

These strategies include temper tantrums; feigning ignorance, confusion, or lack of preparation; or otherwise behaving "irrationally." Negotiation is expected to be a rational give-and-take. If you are seen as irrational, you may temporarily gain the upper hand because people do not know how "to reason" with you effectively. Just as it is difficult to reason with a two year old who is throwing a temper tantrum over a bag of cookies in the supermarket, it is also difficult to reason with a thirty-five year old who is behaving the same way. We do not like it, but they often get what they want, because people give in to them just to keep them quiet and make them go away.

Delays and wasting time

In the discussion of power, I have identified time pressures as a key factor. If the other negotiator has a deadline (and we know it) and we believe the other negotiator wants a deal badly and will not walk away empty-handed, then we can add pressure by delaying settlement. It may pressure him or her to give more away in order to ensure a settlement before the deadline.

Signaling commitment to one's own strategy

These tactics involve silence, taking an inflexible position, refusing to concede, and even refusing to negotiate. Often they are no more than displays of toughness, obstinacy, unyielding commitment to one's position, or even refusal to talk further about something until the other side gives in. They may also indicate that one is so committed that one is willing to endure a disaster if neither side yields—much like the teenage game of chicken with automobiles on a deserted road or like a nuclear arms race. In playing this strategy, each side hopes that the other will never call the bluff, that is, ultimately test the other with head-on collision or nuclear holocaust, just to see if the commitment was serious. So with every threat of unyielding commitment goes an associated risk that the commitment may be tested. One must clearly calculate these costs before one decides to engage in this strategy.

Consistently pushing for concessions

Like the persistent child who wants the cookies in the supermarket, competitive negotiators are always pushing, asking for just one more concession. One classic tactic is the "nibble," in which a negotiator consistently pushes for little concessions on every single issue, over and over again, until the opponent strongly balks. The nibble is particularly effective when the opponent thinks that the entire package deal has been agreed to and all negotiations are finished, only to have you make one more "minor" demand on another issue. At some point, the opponent becomes outraged and refuses to concede more; the trick is to pursue the strategy until just *before* that point is reached.

Using your constituency as a competitive weapon

If you have a constituency in the negotiations, they can help you implement several other competitive tactics, such as the tactic of "limited authority," which is played by stating that you would like to give your opponent a major concession, but the people to whom you report will not let you. When you buy the automobile from a car dealer and he says that "he would love to sell it to you for $2800 but his boss won't let him," that is limited authority at work. Another tool provided by having a constituency is to send in more than one negotiator. Sometimes it is done just to confuse the opponent; one does not know which individual can really make the decisions for the organization. Another purpose is to use the ploy of "good guy-bad guy," by providing two negotiators—one who is easy to deal with and one who is inflexible and unpleasant. This tactic allows the good guy to secure major concessions from the opponent, because the opponent fears the bad guy and would rather make concessions than be forced to deal with him.

Problems with the Competitive Negotiation Strategy

The previous sections give only a sample of the tactics commonly used in the service of a competitive negotiation strategy. Do these threats work? Yes, sometimes they do. Like any strategy, the more predictable, the less likely that it will be effective, because it can be anticipated and counteracted. Surprise is of the essence. And does this strategy cause problems of its own? I answer with an emphatic yes. Many who experience this strategy, and the associated tactics, will find the strategy problematic and even personally offensive. And it is, in many contexts! Although the strategy may be effective under the conditions specified earlier—short-term goals, no future relationship, perceived incompatible goals, an emphasis on the tangibles, and a belief that the other person is going to be competitive—it is not likely to be effective when the opposite conditions are true. Using the strategy is also more likely to prompt one's opponent to be very competitive, making the opponent more contentious and less agreeable.

By contrast, *collaborative* negotiation is more likely to be effective when the negotiating parties exhibit the following characteristics.

- The negotiators have long-term goals, that is, to secure a settlement that will permit them to work together effectively in the future or even enhance the quality of that future working relationship.

- The negotiators believe that their goals are fundamentally compatible; that is, both sides can achieve their goals without significantly inhibiting each other.

- The negotiators place strong emphasis on the intangibles, that is, their reputations, their pride, their principles, the quality of their relationship, and their sense of fairness. Therefore, they promote a climate of trust, cooperation, openness, and the ability to communicate and problem solve effectively.

These are the conditions that usually prevail when we consistently negotiate with others inside the same organization or when we negotiate with long-standing customers, clients, suppliers, or professional service people on a long-term basis.

As Table 6-2 shows, the differences between the competitive and collaborative strategies lie not only in the preliminary assumptions but also carry over into a radically different set of strategies and tactics. The collaborative negotiation strategy is characterized by the following general assumptions.

An orientation to satisfying mutual needs

The goal of the negotiating parties is to identify each other's real needs and to design a solution that meets the needs of *both* sides. Whereas competitive negotiation is driven by a desire only to satisfy one's own positions, collaborative negotiation focuses on mutual need satisfaction. (More will be said about the difference between positions and needs in the description of the collaborative negotiation process.)

**TABLE 6-2 Comparison of assumptions, strategies, and tactics:
competitive versus collaborative negotiation**

Assumptions	Competitive Negotiation	Collaborative Negotiation
Goal perspective	Short term perceived as incompatible emphasis on tangibles only	Long term Perceived as compatible Emphasis on tangibles and intangibles
Perceptions	Mistrust, suspicion, defensiveness	Trust, honesty, openness

Orientation
  to issues
	Extreme demands and
	  positions
		Satisfy mutual needs

Orientation
  to relationship
	Ignore and exploit
	  relationship
		Build trust; preserve and
		  enhance relationship

Orientation to rationality	Emotional, irrational	Rational, reasonable

Orientation
  to concession
  making
	Keep concessions few and
	  small
		Concede as necessary;
		  work toward mutual
		  agreement

Orientation to authority	Limited or no authority	Controlled authority

Orientation
  to time
	Ignore deadlines; use time
	  as tactic
		Follow deadlines; use time
		  for problem solving

A desire to build trust and a working relationship

Rather than to ignore or even exploit the relationship (a key factor in competitive negotiation), collaborative negotiation seeks to build and strengthen it. The process assumes that the parties have worked together in the past, will need to work together in the future, and that their strategy and tactics will sustain or enhance this relationship.

A desire to maintain the negotiation on a plane of rationality and reasonableness

Whereas competitive negotiation attempts to use tactics of irrationality and emotionality as ways to surprise, distract, or anger the opponent, collaborative negotiation consistently searches for and invokes standards of what is "right," "reasonable," and "fair" as criteria for a good solution.

A willingness to make concessions

Competitive negotiators should make very few concessions (while getting the other side to make more of them), and the concessions that they do make should be very small. In contrast, collaborative negotiators should be willing to make concessions when necessary in the service of designing an optimal solution that meets the needs of all parties.

The use of controlled authority to make agreements

Whereas competitive negotiators frequently use their constituencies as tactical weapons (such as limited authority or good guy-bad guy), collaborative negotiators use their constituency to support them in finding a good agreement. However, that does not necessarily imply *unlimited* authority to make agreements. If a negotiator has a constituency, he or she should always be able to check with them, using them as a sounding board for proposed solutions. As stated earlier, negotiators with unlimited authority—who do not have "to check" with anybody before signing an agreement—are more likely to sign those that even they find unsatisfactory, once they have reflected on the nature of the deal.

Observing deadlines

Finally, whereas competitive negotiators frequently use time and deadlines as a tactical weapon, collaborative negotiators are strongly encouraged to respect deadlines and use them as a way to help achieve an agreement. Neither side should want to put undue time pressure on the other; if more time is needed to work out a quality solution, they should find a way to renegotiate their deadline so that the best outcome can be effectively achieved.

COLLABORATIVE NEGOTIATION STRATEGY AND TACTICS

Having defined the primary differences between the competitive and collaborative strategies, I will now describe the major features of the latter. Collaborative negotiation has also been called integrative negotiation, win-win negotiation, cooperative negotiation, or principled negotiation.[10] These various approaches can be summarized into two primary approaches to the collaborative process, approaches that presume that collaborative negotiation is very much like joint problem solving and Fisher and Ury's "principled negotiation" model. The principled negotiation model has received a great deal of attention and acclaim for its pragmatic usefulness to negotiators but has actually been the subject of much less research. In my summary, I will draw heavily on the Fisher and Ury principles, while also integrating ideas and concepts developed from the study of effective problem solving. The *key concepts* of effective principled negotiation and problem solving are as follows.[11]

Each party should be committed to understanding the other negotiator's real needs and objectives. Since negotiators want different things and have different values, priorities, and preferences, each must initially understand how the other side "sees the world." In contrast to competitive negotiation, in which each side's point of view is defined and defended vigorously, the first commitment in collaborative negotiation should be to give equal time and treatment to a description of one's own goals, and to hearing and understanding the other's goals. Admittedly, it is difficult to complete this process well when one believes that the other side's needs, objectives, or position is wrong, flawed, erroneous, or improper, but without a commitment to try before evaluating it or judging it, collaborative negotiation cannot proceed.

Each party should be committed to a free flow of information. To understand the other's real needs and perspectives, the parties must be committed to exchange accurate information rather than to hide, protect, or distort it. This commitment will require two parts: first, a process of "interviewing" each other—asking questions that draw the other side out and listening carefully to the responses—and second, a simultaneous commitment voluntarily to share information. To design an effective solution that meets their mutual needs, each must be committed to help the other side learn how it views the problem, the issues, the goals, and the priorities.

Each party must be committed to arrive at the best solution to the problem, one that meets the needs of both sides. This may require that the parties spend some time in redefining their own preferences and priorities. Before negotiation, each party has usually considered only its needs and goals; however, collaborative negotiation should be focused on satisfying mutual needs and goals. As a result, the parties may not only need to learn about each other's perspective, but they may have to redefine those individual perspectives into a commonly accepted statement. This process of "reframing" the joint, or common, goal is often easier to describe than to do, since it requires us to be temporarily less committed to the goals and objectives we want so dearly while we search for a new way to state them that integrates the needs of others. It also requires the parties to downplay the differences between them while emphasizing the similarities. Although differences will have to be addressed eventually, efforts to maximize the similarities will enhance the belief that the parties have a great deal in common and that a mutually acceptable solution will not be so difficult.

Given that both sides have made a pledge to pursue the preceding commitments, key points in the strategy of collaborative negotiation are as follows.[12]

Separate the People from the Problem

When negotiating parties have opposing goals or are in conflict, they are highly prone to distortions in perception. One's own ideas, perspectives, goals, needs, and values become "right," "proper," "necessary," and "absolute," and the other's ideas, perspectives, needs, and values become "wrong," "unnecessary," or "improper." Moreover, our likes and dislikes for people generalize to our perceptions of the value and worth of their goals and objectives. Effective collaborative negotiation requires that we be able to depersonalize the process, so that we can effectively communicate with the other party to achieve an adequate sharing of perspectives and point of view. In the words of Fisher and Ury, we need to be "nice to the people but tough on the problem"—to treat people with respect and courtesy but also to take a tough-minded approach to solving the problem and ensuring that everyone's goals and objectives will be addressed and integrated.

Focus on Needs and Interests, Not Positions

The second key principle is to focus on needs and interests, not positions. In our collective commitment to understanding, we must distinguish the difference between positions and interests. Negotiators commonly state their preferences as positions—a clear, firm, definitive statement of what they want, much as I described in the competitive negotiation section. In contrast, their interests are the underlying needs, values, or concerns that they seek to actually meet. The difference between a position and an interest is best expressed as the difference between *what* we want and *why* we want it. In their traditional opening statements, negotiators define their positions: a statement of demands, positions, target point for settlement. It is this mutual statement of positions that often makes an upcoming negotiation look so confrontational, conflict-laden, and win-lose in nature. At best, it looks as though the parties can arrive only at a middle ground, doing no better than a compromise. However, by getting at interests, the parties may learn that their underlying needs, values, or interests are not really in conflict and that it is possible to find a mutually acceptable solution with ease.

As an example, suppose that an employee wants more job responsibility, which he thinks can be gained by asking to be considered for a position that recently opened up. The boss says that she can't give him the position, because her budget is so tight that she has to leave the position unfilled in the coming year. On the other hand, the boss is worrying that not filling the position will overload her with tasks that she won't be able to accomplish. If the employee never shares the critical information (that he really wants more responsibility, not the specific job opening) and the boss never shares the critical information (that she really can delegate a lot of additional responsibility, but not through filling the open position), neither will really understand the other's interests. Only by learning each other's interests can they discover that their needs are not mutually exclusive. Interests may be learned by asking the other party questions about their position, to learn "why they want what they say they want." Asking ourselves these same questions is important, since many negotiators are often not in touch with their own interests, which will be important to know if they intend to share those interests with others.

Inventing Options for Mutual Gain

Once each side learns of the other's interests, they can be used as the key parameters that will need to be addressed in the solution. Negotiators should create a common statement that identifies all of their interests, since it will be the statement of the problem that needs to be solved. The next step is to identify possible alternative ways of solving the problem and addressing some or all of the interests. The following list gives ways of inventing options.[13]

1. *Brainstorm.* Particularly when the negotiation is over a problem to be solved (and the negotiating parties differ in their preferred solutions), one technique for inventing options is to brainstorm. Parties are encouraged to list as many possible solution alternatives as they can, without discussing, evaluating, or judging the quality of any of them. A listing of brainstormed options may be done on a blackboard, flip chart, or overhead projector screen. Parties are urged to be spontaneous, even impractical, and not to censor their own ideas or evaluate others' ideas in any way. Once a complete list is brainstormed, the parties can return to evaluate the practicality or suitability of each item on the list.

2. *"Expand the pie."* A second alternative, particularly when the negotiation is over the distribution of limited resources, is to expand the pie, that is, to figure out how to secure more resources so that, should the parties have to divide up resources, they can be divided in a way that will ensure more than 50 percent for each side. Brainstorming can focus on how to enhance the resource pool so that there is more for everyone to share. For instance, two departments were squabbling about how to use limited budget funds to store important raw materials; by pooling their funds, they found that they could not only buy the raw materials at discount price, but could rent a large nearby warehouse that adequately met their mutual storage needs as well.

3. *Nonspecific compensation.* A third alternative for inventing options is to create a way for one party to receive something that is not necessarily part of the negotiating package but is sufficient to address their needs and interests and permit the other side to achieve theirs. Take the ex-

ample of a married couple's negotiating on the place for their summer vacation. If the husband agrees to abandon his preferred locations altogether and agrees to let the wife choose where to go, in exchange for his being allowed to buy a new portable computer, this solution is an example of nonspecific compensation.

4. *Logrolling.* A fourth alternative for inventing options is particularly easy when there are multiple issues in the negotiation; solutions are then achieved by beginning to "package" or "trade off" preferred solutions on the multiple issues. Successful logrolling requires the parties to identify all of the issues (or agenda items) at stake, identify which ones are of highest priority to each party, and then construct an agreement so that the parties achieve their preferred solution on their top-priority issues. In the vacation example, if the wife's first priority is to go to the beach to read books and get a suntan and the husband's first priority is to play golf, then picking a seaside resort with a good golf course will meet the interests of both sides.

5. *Bridging.* Finally, the parties may in fact be able to invent solution options that meet the needs of all sides simultaneously. In the same vacation example, the longer the husband and wife talk, the more they really understand what each wants out of a vacation. The husband wants to rest, do some sightseeing, and play golf. The wife wants to rest, read novels, and be someplace near a major beach resort. If the couple finds a location that offers all of these activities simultaneously, they will have effectively found a "bridging" option.

Insist on Using Objective Criteria

Another key element in the collaboration strategy is to make good choices among the options by finding ways to shrink the pool of options. First, the parties can reduce the list of options by assigning some type of preference ratings to each option, such as a ranking system, putting priority weights on options, and the like. Second, the options should be evaluated on the basis of some form of "objective criteria" that would classify which solutions are of the highest quality, which ones are the most fair, which ones are the lowest cost, and so on. These criteria will vary from situation to situation, from problem to problem, and from one pair of negotiators to the next. If the parties can agree on which criteria should be used to evaluate solutions and how these criteria will be applied, they have come a long way toward agreement. If the selection of alternatives is expected to be highly controversial or problematic, this argues even more strongly for developing and putting into place the criteria to judge solutions before one actually discusses and evaluates the solution options themselves.

Create a Clear Agreement

Finally, it is strongly recommended that in a collaborative negotiation the parties attempt to write down the exact language of the solution and a plan for its implementation. It is usually when the parties attempt to draft the exact language and plan that hidden misunderstandings, ambiguities, and unclarities rise to the surface. It is at this stage of the negotiation that some experts recommend a "one text procedure."[14] In this procedure, one negotiator attempts to write down the exact language and wording of the agreement. The agreement is then passed back and forth between the parties until all parties agree to all language, terms, conditions, implementation plans, and so on. A similar outcome can be achieved if the parties conduct the collaborative negotiation process in a room that has a flip chart, blackboard, or computer screen around which all can gather. The process of writing down and recording their ongoing work begins to surface possible ambiguities, clarifies them for all, and reduces the likelihood that problems will arise as the parties carry out the agreement.

CONVERTING COMPETITIVE NEGOTIATORS INTO COLLABORATIVE ONES

After reading the section on collaborative negotiation, many readers will comment, "well, that's the way I like to negotiate. But how do I convert my opponent, who wants to negotiate competitively, to negotiate collaboratively as well?" This is a common concern. Many negotiators are aware that when a collaborative negotiator squares off against a competitive one, the negotiations are far more likely to turn competitive than collaborative. So what can collaborative negotiators do to tame and convert a competitive opponent? Fisher and Ury suggest three different approaches for three types of problematic opponents.[15] The following subsections explain.

1. What If The Opponent is More Powerful?

The first form of difficult opponent is one who has more power—more resources, more control, more authority, more weapons, or more time to negotiate. The best strategy is to protect yourself from the other side's power by not unnecessarily exposing your vulnerabilities and by not giving away things unnecessarily. Second, it is important to cultivate a good BATNA—a best alternative to the negotiated agreement. By selecting a good BATNA, you have a good alternative available that will permit you to escape the power of the other negotiator. And by announcing this BATNA to your opponent, you may effectively reshape the opponent's negotiating position. Particularly if your opponent does not have a good BATNA and really needs you to be involved in a deal, a powerful BATNA may well be the effective leverage to defuse the opponent's power, allow the opportunity for you to build powerful alliances with other people, and push your opponent toward a more collaborative process.

2. What If They Won't Play the Game?

The second form of difficult opponent is one who won't play the collaborative negotiation game; they simply take a tough, competitive stance and lock themselves into it. To deal with this type of opponent, Fisher and Ury advocate a form of "negotiation jujitsu," in which the negotiator should attempt to use questions, inquiry, and careful listening to "get behind" the opponent's position and identify interests. Rather than attacking the opponent's position (and defending one's own position), you should use open questions ("why," "how," "explain that to me in more detail") in order to understand the interests that lie behind that position. A recent book by Ury significantly elaborates on this strategy by proposing ways to gain some perspective on the opponent's strategy, effectively listen to the opponent to discern interests, propose approaches to recast or reframe the issues from position statements to broader interests, and create options by which the interests of both sides can be addressed.[16]

A second strategic alternative for dealing with an opponent who won't play the game is to go outside the boundaries of the negotiation relationship and *take the dispute to a third party*. If a viable third party (or some form of an organizational system for resolving conflicts) is available, this route can be taken by one or both parties whenever negotiations fail. When taking a dispute to a third party, the most important thing to understand is *how* that third party will help resolve the dispute. The following three paragraphs describe the types of third parties that are often available.

Arbitrators and inquisitors

Arbitrators are third parties who listen to all of the parties in conflict and then make the decision. Arbitrators ask each side to make a complete presentation of the issues in dispute; they then review the facts, arguments, and evidence presented, consider it against their own knowledge and expertise about the issues, and tell the parties what the resolution should be. The resolution may or may not be binding, depending on whether the parties have so agreed. Inquisitors act in very much the same way, except that they may conduct an independent investigation to gain additional viewpoints and perspectives before "handing down" their decision. Research has shown that when asked to serve as a third party to resolve others' disputes, most managers act like arbitrators or inquisitors.[17] The advantage of taking a dispute to an arbitrator or inquisitor, therefore, is that they are likely to solve the problem for you; the disadvantages are that you may not like their decision and that you may lose control over the process and the outcome once that party becomes involved.

Mediators

A mediator is a third party who helps the parties negotiate more effectively but does not resolve the dispute for them. Mediators also ask both sides to make a presentation of views and perspectives on the key issues. But rather than make a decision and tell the parties how to settle the dispute, the mediator assumes that the parties' failure to resolve stems from conflict dynamics that are making the negotiation highly competitive and laden with ineffective communication. So the mediator's efforts are designed to control the pace of communication between the parties, manage emotion, listen effectively to identify interests, and help the parties invent mutually acceptable options for settlement. The advantage of taking a dispute to a mediator is that the parties maintain a lot more control over the actual outcomes; the disadvantages are that mediation may be more time-consuming than arbitration and may not achieve a resolution if the parties are truly polarized—there is no overlap in their bargaining ranges.

Ombudsmen, fact finders, and referees

The third form of third party is an ombudsman, fact finder, or referee. These types of third parties do not resolve the dispute for the parties, nor do they directly facilitate negotiation. Rather, their role is to keep the dispute-resolution process on a level playing field—keeping the process fair. These roles are more common when a party is attempting to negotiate with "the system," that is, filing some form of complaint or grievance with an organization. These third parties ensure that there are appropriate channels with which to file the concerns, that individuals understand how to use the channels, and that concerns are given a fair hearing. These neutrals may also conduct independent investigations of the situation to ensure that all relevant information and perspectives are presented and heard.[18] Negotiators should use these forms of third parties when one wishes simply to make sure that the negotiation process is fair, when the other side has more power and may abuse that power by precluding effective negotiation, or when one is negotiating against the rules and practices of a large organization or system. However, like mediation, the disadvantage of using such neutrals is that the specific outcomes may not be the ones originally desired.

What If They Use Dirty Tricks?

The third form of difficult opponent is the negotiator who uses dirty tricks—tactics of deception, intimidation, and inappropriate pressure, some of which I described earlier in this chapter. The first and most effective way to deal with this opponent is to *identify* that these tactics are being used: Being able *to identify* a dirty trick is the first step to being able to defuse it. The second step is to be willing to raise, as a negotiable issue, the rules and procedures that the parties will follow in negotiation. If you can openly talk about the rules that both sides will follow in negotiation—what is acceptable and unacceptable conduct—these tactics may be effectively eliminated by mutual agreement. Finally, should dirty tricks occur, the negotiator can indicate that he or she is aware of what is going on and warn the opponent about the consequences of continuing to use the tactic. By identifying the tactic, suggesting that it may be inappropriate, and offering to move toward a more collaborative process, negotiators can steer away from dirty tricks rather than escalate the conflict through their mutual use.

Negotiator Ethics

Any discussion of dirty tricks in negotiation inevitably leads to a discussion of negotiator ethics. It is a very important subject and one that I can scarcely do justice to in a few pages. But a responsible review of negotiation strategy and tactics must address the issue. I briefly discuss three facets: why unethical conduct occurs, what types of unethical behavior a negotiator might experience, and why ethical standards need to be a part of the process.

Why unethical conduct occurs

There are probably many reasons for unethical behavior. At the risk of simplification, the most common factors that motivate unethical conduct are explored in the following.

Competition. It should be obvious from the previous discussion that the very nature of competition pushes people toward behaviors that will bring them to the competitive edge, even when that edge moves beyond the boundaries of the rules. Competition is at the very heart of Western society, whether we are looking at the world of business, the world of sports, or our personal world of achieving occupational and career success. In all of these contexts, the rules for "appropriate" and "inappropriate" behavior need to be set, to be made clear to all parties, and to be explicitly endorsed by all parties—everybody agrees to play by those rules. When the rules are less clear, as they sometimes are in negotiation, parties may be more likely to violate them because they can claim ignorance of the standards for appropriate conduct. Negotiation is particularly vulnerable to such vagueness because it is generally expected that negotiators will engage in a certain amount of "legitimate dishonesty" in their efforts to secure a better deal. Thus negotiators are expected to exaggerate about their goals, periodically "bluff" about their intentions, and not tell "the whole truth" by disclosing their bottom line. For new negotiators, the difficult part is determining the dividing line between "legitimate" and "illegitimate" dishonesty!

Ego gratification and greed. In an environment in which parties are motivated toward self-gratification, serving their own ego needs, and "looking good" to an important audience (that is, looking successful, powerful, rich, and accomplished), ethical standards may often be violated. We bend the rules to get ahead. We deny wrongdoing and cover up mistakes that we made, refusing to take responsibility for them or to correct them. We're more concerned with the social approval and recognition we get from peers than the rules we broke to get there. Although sociologists may claim that the "me generation" is gone, its vestiges live on in our search for ego gratification at the expense of the rules.

Restoration of justice. A third motivator for unethical conduct may be that the negotiator believes he has already been unfairly treated and needs to get "revenge." By that logic, the other has already gained unfair competitive and tactical advantage and our negotiator needs to take "drastic action" to regain some power and control. Lying and cheating in negotiation are often motivated by the claim that "the other side already did it"; even though logic dictates that two wrongs don't make a right, the emotional satisfaction derived from a clear-cut act of revenge often wins out.

Short-term perspective. A common criticism of Western businesspeople, and negotiators, is that they share a very myopic, short-term focus in their actions. The focus on being successful in the short term—whether it is in business profitability or negotiation—leads them to ignore and abuse long-term relationships. This chapter has pointed out that competitive tactics are more appropriate for short-term, single-iteration negotiations, but that the same tactics, if used in long-term relationships, will tend to disrupt and destroy those relationships. Yet the myopic, short-term focus of many negotiators frequently leads them to competitive and even unethical tactics in order to secure a temporary advantage.

Common types of unethical conduct

What are the types of unethical conduct that most frequently occur in negotiation? The following actions have been identified.[19] Note that in moderation many of these would not be judged unethical, but in the extreme all would probably raise significant concern.

Selective disclosure and exaggeration. A negotiator highlights the positive side of the case and ignores the negatives (or vice versa, depending on the side she is on). If you actually spent the summer putting pepperoni and onions on pizzas but listed "culinary artist" on your resume, you would be exaggerating. Or if you are recommending a colleague for a job and only tell about his positive features while not telling that he is unreliable, you are not disclosing everything you know.

Misrepresentation. When a negotiator is intentionally dishonest about the preferred settlement point or the resistance point, the negotiator is engaging in misrepresentation. If you are selling a used computer and the buyer asks what the minimum is that you will accept and you say "$1000" when you really would take $800, you are misrepresenting.

Falsification. The giving of clearly incorrect information is falsification. The buyer of the computer asks you if it will run the latest financial software package; you know it won't (which explains why you are selling it), but say that it will to sell the machine. Another form of falsification is seen in negotiation when buyers and sellers state that they have another buyer (or seller) ready to make a deal as a way to get their opponent to settle more quickly.

False intentions: Threats and promises. Statements of false intentions, often called *bluffs,* are similar to falsification in that your statements are erroneous but they describe what you intend to do if the other acts or does not act in a particular way. To continue the computer example, if you state that you will throw in some computer paper and a printer stand free—but don't intend to do so—that would be a false promise. Similarly, if you threaten to walk away and take your business elsewhere if they don't complete the deal with you—but you don't intend to do so—that would be a false threat.

Deception. Several of the preceding behaviors are similar to deception in that one constructs a logic that leads the other negotiator to make conclusions that aren't true. In selling the computer, you might show her a picture of a computer that is "like" the one you are selling, but not the exact machine. Many forms of advertising and promotion are frequently accused of deception when they lead the buyer to assume things that are actually untrue: If I smoke that brand of cigarettes, drink that brand of beer, or join that diet program, I'll look as good or have as much fun as those people in the ad seem to be having! In its most severe forms, deception can turn into fraud when negotiators and their organizations "certify" facts, events, and performance that are simply not true.

Inflicting direct and intentional harm. The most severe violation of ethics would probably be to inflict direct, intentional harm. This category might include a variety of severe actions: spying on the opponent and theft of their files to learn their confidential information, maligning them in the eyes of others by spreading lies and rumors, or disruption of their operation to keep them from competing effectively. Although not common to many negotiations, these actions are also not unheard of in very competitive deliberations.

Applying ethical principles to negotiation

Dealing with dirty tricks in an opponent has been explicitly discussed in the preceding section. This section is explicitly devoted to helping you understand their unethical behavior in greater detail. But even more importantly, *negotiators must understand their own ethical standards and limits.* The following factors must enter into the ethical reasoning.

- As pointed out, competitive motivations, personal ambitions, and the tendency to view things in the short term can all push a negotiator toward some of the behaviors identified. A negotiator must understand that such pressures can affect everyone, even the most honorable among us. Competition, greed, and the opportunity to gain tactical advantage—particularly when we forget that what we do now can come back to haunt us in the future—color and distort our vision in many ways!

- Second, negotiators must define their own limits a priori. That is, negotiators must develop a personal creed, a set of principles that clarifies what they will and will not do! This personal code is usually shaped by one's personal standards of honesty and integrity, religious and philosophical training, and often by the hard consequences of either acting unethically or having others act unethically toward oneself.

- Finally, negotiators must recognize, however, that defining ethical boundaries in conflict and negotiation is not absolute. For example, one cannot vow to always "tell the truth, the whole truth, and nothing but the truth." As stated earlier, a certain amount of "legitimate dishonesty" is generally considered appropriate in negotiation. This is not as oxymoronic as it appears; and it is problematic because there are no codes of ethics that help negotiators define what is appropriate (negotiator codes of ethics for attorneys and some other professions, such as purchasing agents, are exceptions). Most negotiators seem to agree that mild exaggeration and selective disclosure (emphasizing the positives of your product over the negatives and not telling your bottom line) are accepted within the ethical bounds of negotiation but that the other forms of ethical violation identified earlier may be inappropriate and less acceptable.[20] So if the negotiator completely told the truth, others would see him or her as a genuine sucker, because he or she would tell everything, disclose the bottom line, and get deals far worse than the average. The ethical challenge in negotiation is to keep from being a sucker by disclosing and giving away too much and to keep from being a shark by bending the truth and the rules in a way that gains tactical advantage but destroys the fabric of trust and the relationship between the parties.

SUMMARY

This chapter has focused on the key aspects of negotiation in business relationships. The following essential components must be taken into account in planning for and executing any negotiation.

- The tangible and intangible outcomes at stake, and their relative value to the negotiating parties.
- The role of key power factors in the situation, including the preparation and use of information; the roles played by constituencies, deadlines, and organizational legitimacy; and the BATNAs or options open to all parties.
- The importance of the particular substantive outcomes to the parties.
- The importance of the relationship between the parties, in terms of the history that the parties bring to the negotiation and the type of relationship they wish to have in the future.

As indicated, these four factors will have a strong impact on the type of strategy that negotiators select, the planning they employ, and the tactical execution they use. Effective negotiators understand how these factors contribute to strong settlements and endeavor to control them in their strategic planning and execution. Good luck in your own personal and professional negotiations!

FOR FURTHER READING

Brown, B. "The Effects of Need to Maintain Face on Interpersonal Bargaining." *Journal of Experimental Social Psychology* 4 (1968): pp. 107–122. A research article that documents the power of face-saving behavior—looking strong to a valued audience or constituency—in negotiation.

Cohen, H. *You Can Negotiate Anything.* Secaucus, NJ: Lyle Stuart, 1980. A well-known management book on negotiation strategy, primarily emphasizing win-lose dynamics.

Fisher, R. and Ury, W. *Getting to Yes.* Boston, MA: Houghton Mifflin, 1981. The ground-breaking book that describes the strategy and tactics of principled, win-win negotiation.

Gray, B. *Collaborating.* San Francisco: Jossey-Bass, 1989. This book describes strategies of collaboration and applications of the strategy to different contexts and problems.

Jones, E. E. and Wortman, C. *Ingratiation: An Attributional Approach*. Morristown, NJ: General Learning Press, 1973. Describes a theory of ingratiation.

Karrass, C. *Give and Take*. New York: Thomas Y. Crowell, 1974. A well-known management book on the tactics of distributive negotiation.

Lewicki, R. and Litterer, J. *Negotiation*. Homewood, IL: Richard D. Irwin, 1985. A comprehensive textbook on the negotiation process, strategy and tactics, ethics, and mechanisms for resolving disputes.

Lewicki, R., Litterer, J., Minton, J., and Saunders, D. *Negotiation*. 2nd ed. Homewood, IL: Richard D. Irwin, 1993. A revised edition of our 1985 title.

Lewicki, R. J. and Spencer, G. "Lies and Dirty Tricks." Paper presented to the International Association of Conflict Management, Vancouver, Canada, 1990. This paper describes a number of commonly used "dishonest" tactics in negotiation and how they are perceived by negotiators.

Lewicki, R. J. and Spencer, G. "Ethical Relativism and Negotiating Tactics: Factor Affecting Their Perceived Ethicality." Paper presented to the Academy of Management, Miami, FL, 1991. A follow-up to the earlier paper, this study explores the impact of a long-term relationship, and the motives of the opponent, on the predisposition to use "dishonest" negotiating tactics.

Murnighan, K. *The Dynamics of Bargaining Games*. Englewood Cliffs, NJ: Prentice Hall, 1991. This book approaches the subject of negotiation from the perspective of a number of simple economic games, and it describes the strategy and tactics used to play each game.

Pruitt, D. *Negotiation Behavior*. New York: Academic Press, 1981. An academic-theory book on negotiation, with emphasis on integrative negotiation.

Pruitt, D. "Achieving Integrative Agreements." In M. Bazerman and R. Lewicki. *Negotiating in Organizations*. Beverly Hills, CA: Sage Publications, 1983. This chapter describes alternatives for inventing options in integrative negotiation.

Pruitt, D. and Rubin, J. *Social Conflict*. New York: Random House, 1986. This book reviews conflict dynamics, negotiation, and mechanisms for resolving conflict.

Roth, A. E., Murnighan, J. K. and Schoumaker, F. "The Deadline Effect in Bargaining: Some Experimental Evidence." *American Economic Review* 78 (1988): pp. 806–823. This research article focuses on the impact of deadlines on negotiating behavior.

Rubin, J. and Brown, B. *The Social Psychology of Bargaining and Negotiation*. New York: Academic Press, 1975. One of the earliest, most comprehensive, and authoritative reviews of conflict and negotiation research.

Salacuse, J. "Your Draft or Mine?" *Negotiation Journal*. vol. 5, no. 4 (1989): pp. 337–342. An article that describes the process of writing the draft agreement and the impact on its orientation and clarity.

Savage, G. T., Blair, J. D., and Sorenson, R. L. "Consider Both Relationships and Substance When Negotiating Strategically." *Academy of Management Executive*. vol. 3, no. 1 (1989): pp. 37–48. A key management article that reviews four types of negotiation strategy: collaborative, competitive, accommodative, and avoidance.

Sheppard, B. "Managers as Inquisitors: Some Lessons from the Law." In M. Bazerman and R. Lewicki, *Negotiating in Organizations*. Beverly Hills, CA: Sage

Publications, 1983. A research article that reports on the ways managers tend to handle disputes on the job.

Sheppard, B., Lewicki, R., and Minton, J. *Organizational Justice.* New York: Lexington Books, 1992. This book explores the nature of "fairness" in organizations—how we decide what is fair, what we do when we judge a situation to be unfair, and the ways that managers must consider fairness in their daily activities.

Thibaut, J. and Walker, L. *Procedural Justice: A Psychological Analysis.* New York: Erlbaum/Halstead, 1975. This book reports the results of a number of research studies on the importance of fair procedures in dispute resolution and the perception of justice.

Teger, A. *Too Much Invested to Quit.* Beverly Hills, CA: Sage Publications, 1980. This book summarizes research on the "escalation-of-commitment" phenomena—the conditions by which decision makers commit more resources to a previously chosen course of action, even when there are strong indications that the commitment should be abandoned.

Ury, W., Brett, J., and Goldberg, S. *Getting Disputes Resolved: Designing Systems to Cut the Costs of Conflict.* San Francisco: Jossey-Bass, 1988. A groundbreaking book on the key factors in designing an effective dispute resolution system.

Ury, W. *Getting Past No.* New York: Bantam, 1991. An excellent management book on the strategy and tactics to be used when negotiating against a competitive, distributive opponent.

Walton, R. and McKersie, R. *A Behavioral Theory of Labor Negotiations.* New York: McGraw-Hill, 1965. A landmark book on the social psychology of negotiation in labor relations, the seminal work for describing the distributive and integrative negotiation models.

NOTES

1. See J. Rubin and B. Brown, *The Social Psychology of Bargaining and Negotiation* (New York: Academic Press, 1975); H. Cohen, *You Can Negotiate Anything* (Secaucus, NJ: Lyle Stuart, 1980).

2. B. Brown, "The Effects of Need to Maintain Face on Interpersonal Bargaining," *Journal of Experimental Social Psychology* 4 (1968): pp. 107–122.

3. A. E. Roth, J. K. Murnighan, and F. Schoumaker, "The Deadline Effect in Bargaining: Some Experimental Evidence," *The American Economic Review* 78 (1988): pp. 806–823.

4. A. Teger, *Too Much Invested to Quit* (Beverly Hills, CA: Sage Publications, 1980).

5. R. Fisher and W. Ury, *Getting to Yes* (Boston: Houghton Mifflin, 1981).

6. R. Walton and R. McKersie (1965); *A Behavioral Theory of Labor Negotiations* (New York: McGraw-Hill 1965); D. Pruitt and J. Rubin, *Social Conflict* (New York: Random House, 1986); R. Fisher and W. Ury, *Getting to Yes.* (Boston: Houghton Mifflin, 1991).

7. G. T. Savage, J. D. Blair, and R. L. Sorenson, "Consider Both Relationships and Substance When Negotiating Strategically," *Academy of Management Executive* vol. 3, no. 1 (1989): pp. 37–48.

8.   For example, see E. E. Jones and C. Wortman, *Ingratiation: An Attributional Approach* (Morristown, NJ: General Learning Press, 1973).

9.   C. Karrass, *Give and Take* (New York: Thomas Y. Crowell, 1974); H. Cohen, *You Can Negotiate Anything* (Secaucus, NJ: Lyle Stuart, 1980).

10.   R. Walton and R. McKersie, *A Behavioral Theory of Labor Negotiations* (New York: McGraw-Hill, 1965); D. Pruitt, *Negotiation Behavior* (New York: Academic Press, 1981); R. Fisher and W. Ury, *Getting to Yes* (Boston: Houghton Mifflin, 1981); R. Lewicki and J. Litterer, *Negotiation* (Homewood, IL: Richard D. Irwin, 1985); R Lewicki, J. Litterer, J. Minton, and D. Saunders, *Negotiation*, 2nd ed. (Homewood, IL: Richard D. Irwin, 1993); B. Gray, *Collaboration* (San Francisco: Jossey-Bass, 1989).

11.   See especially R. Lewicki and J. Litterer, *Negotiation* (Homewood, IL: Richard D. Irwin, 1985) and R. Lewicki, J. Litterer, J. Minton, and D. Saunders, *Negotiation*, 2nd ed. (Homewood, IL: Richard D. Irwin, 1993) for a fuller treatment.

12.   As framed by R. Fisher and W. Ury, *Getting to Yes.*

13.   See D. Pruitt, "Achieving Integrative Agreements," in M. Bazerman and R. Lewicki, *Negotiating in Organizations* (Beverly Hills, CA: Sage Publications, 1983).

14.   R. Fisher and W. Ury, *Getting to Yes* (Boston: Houghton Mifflin, 1981); J. Salacuse, "Your Draft or Mine?" *Negotiation Journal* vol. 5, no. 4 (1989): pp. 337–342.

15.   R. Fisher and W. Ury, *Getting to Yes* (Boston: Houghton Mifflin, 1981); W. Ury, *Getting Past No* (New York: Bantam, 1991).

16.   W. Ury, *Getting Past No* (New York: Bantam, 1991).

17.   J. Thibaut and L. Walker, *Procedural Justice: A Psychological Analysis* (New York: Erlbaum/Halstead, 1975); B. Sheppard, "Managers as Inquisitors: Some Lessons from the Law," in M. Bazerman and R. Lewicki, *Negotiating in Organizations* (Beverly Hills, CA: Sage Publications, 1983).

18.   For an understanding of the key aspects of these systems, see B. Sheppard, R. Lewicki, and J. Minton, *Organizational Justice* (New York: Lexington Books, 1992); and W. Ury, J. Brett, and S. Goldberg, *Getting Disputes Resolved: Designing Systems to Cut the Cost of Conflict* (San Francisco: Jossey-Bass, 1988).

19.   R. Lewicki and J. Litterer, *Negotiation* (Homewood, IL: Richard D. Irwin, 1985); R. Lewicki, J. Litterer, J. Minton, and D. Saunders, *Negotiation*, 2nd ed. (Homewood, IL: Richard D. Irwin, 1993); K. Murnighan, *The Dynamics of Bargaining Games* (Englewood Cliffs, NJ: Prentice Hall, 1991).

20.   R. J. Lewicki and G. Spencer, "Lies and Dirty Tricks" (Paper presented to the International Association of Conflict Management, Vancouver, Canada, 1990); R. J. Lewicki, and G. Spencer, "Ethical Relativism and Negotiating Tactics: Factors Affecting Their Perceived Ethicality" (Paper presented to the Academy of Management, Miami, FL, 1991).

7 MANAGING YOURSELF: BUILDING A CAREER

Douglas T. Hall

"All these years of hard work and sacrifice have finally paid off!" Those were the thoughts of Allison Frank as she started her first day of work at one of the largest New York investment banking firms. She was one of only three women the firm had hired as new associates that year. The time: somewhere in the 1980s.

Allison had graduated *magna cum laude* from one of the "Sister Seven," a group of small elite private eastern colleges, formerly all-female but now some coeducational. She went on to get her MBA at the top-ranked business school in the country, graduating with a 4.0 grade-point average. Although her family was solidly middle-income, Allison was one of several children to be put through college, and it was always a financial struggle. A combination of loans, merit-based scholarships, and many jobs (full-time during the summer and part-time during the school year) managed to get her through. There was a definite feeling of relief and accomplishment to know that she had achieved her goal of a career in investment banking, with a firm that was definitely "the" place to be.

After the training program, Allison was given some of the most challenging accounts that were available to new associates. Like everyone else there, she was expected to work independently in this fiercely competitive environment. When her performance started to trail her peers', her response was the same as it had always been in the past: to dig in and work harder. She became the first to arrive in the morning and the last to leave at night, doing extra research, running more spreadsheets . . . and increasingly questioning her ability.

Work on this chapter was supported in part by the Executive Development Roundtable of the Boston University School of Management.

She had been assigned a sponsor, an older male partner, but, other than an initial lunch and an invitation to come see him any time, he initiated little contact. And Allison felt that, in the culture of the firm, any request for help would be seen as a sign of weakness. As for her peers—they were the competition, definitely not a source of support. She began to get increasingly discouraged.

Her bonuses, traditionally the main form of performance feedback from the firm, were equal to those of her peers. "So at least," she thought, "I'm not off track in the eyes of my superiors." (What Allison did not know was that the firm was careful to keep the compensation of their few women associates at the same level as most of the men, regardless of performance.)

In her third year, one of her key customers requested that he be assigned to someone else. Then another switched to a competitor. At that point, Allison Frank was unceremoniously fired. The reason given for such swift action was that, in today's turbulent, competitive investment banking environment, no firm can afford to carry someone who can't carry her weight.

How could a career as successful as Allison's become derailed so quickly? In this chapter we will examine factors in the person and in the environment that can lead to career failure, as well as those that promote success. And in particular we will consider the process of *career self-management*. What can you as an individual do to enhance your own career? In what ways do your boss and organization affect your success? And how can you have impact on your boss and your organization? In recent years, much has been written (but less is known) about career success, and in this chapter we will attempt to present the findings to you in a usable fashion.

Most of my research has dealt with issues of careers in organizations and of the relationship between careers and home and family life. After years of studying (and living) the experience of the two-career family, I have come to a conclusion: the bad news is that you cannot have everything, but the good news is that you can have what is most important to you.

So the key is how to determine what is most important to you and how to go after it.

Perhaps the bottom line in career management was expressed recently by a successful career woman/wife/mother based upon her years of career and family experience, at her twenty-fifth college reunion:

Rule 1: Don't sweat the small stuff.

Rule 2: Everything is small stuff.

Several years ago there was a picture in the newspaper of an event called "the Toronto Rat Race." It showed runners in a long distance road race through the business district in Toronto, but there was an interesting twist: all runners had to be wearing business suits and carrying brief cases. The incongruity of the picture was a nice way of capturing much of the craziness which can show up in our attempts to juggle different facets of our lives: careers, relationships, family, leisure, religion, community, and others.

Because of the turbulence and complexity in today's work environment, *self-management* and *self-empowerment* are critical factors in career success. Not only does no one else care more about your career than you, but no one else knows as well as you what would make you happy.

CAREERS AND THE CHANGING CONTRACT

What exactly do we mean by the term "career"? What is your first association with the word? Does it evoke images of advancement, upward mobility, money, power? Often careers do result in these outcomes, but a career can be described more simply as follows:

> The career is the individually perceived sequence of attitudes and behaviors associated with work-related experiences and activities over the span of the person's life.[1]

By "individually perceived" we mean that the career is whatever you make it out to be. If it seems to have order, if it seems to be advancing, if it seems to be changing, if it feels successful or stagnant—these are all *your* perceptions, and they constitute your career.

It appears to Allison that "success" meant upward mobility in a high-status organization. Her academic career was marked by high achievement in an elite college, and she felt she had "arrived" when she landed an offer with the prestigious investment banking firm. Unfortunately that linear concept of success caused her problems when she was fired, since in her eyes that event represented the ultimate failure.

"Sequence of attitudes and behaviors" means that the career consists of both your feelings about your career and your actual experiences and accomplishments. And "over the span of the person's life" means that the career is a life-long process; the total sequence of your work activities is what makes up your career. Fortunately for Allison, she is just at the beginning of her career, and if she can see the potential for longer-term learning from this early setback, her experience in this firm could be a very valuable event.

What about work in a particular organization? This is an area that represents major change in our society. The "psychological contract" between the individual and the organization is changing. (The psychological contract is the set of unwritten mutual expectations that employees and employers hold of each other.) The old contract contained an expectation that the person would spend his or her full career with the organization (lifetime employment), the motivating factor was the opportunity for advancement, and the organization would take care of people's careers. "Trust us" was the slogan.

"Just accept this move from San Francisco to that undesirable location, and you will be rewarded in time." Consistent with this notion was the view that development was a long-term process. Again, fortunately for Allison, work in that firm was, in fact, just one portion of her career. This is normal in this day and age, although Allison may not have seen this immediately, and may in fact have felt that her career had come to a crashing halt.

The former contract was also based on the idea of there being one career in the family (that of the man). So if the organization wanted to relocate the employee, there was not another career to take into consideration.

As Richard Campbell and Joseph Moses have pointed out, the contract has changed in many ways.[2] Now the time span of a career is much shorter. The organization cannot promise long-term employment; at best it can provide a good job with learning potential. Development is focused more on immediate job skills and on the person's ability to learn how to learn, as a way of dealing with corporate turbulence. Advancement is still a relevant motivator, but learning, meaning, and accomplishment are also important intrinsic rewards.

Perhaps the most important single difference in the contract regards who manages the career. Now the career is seen as mostly the *individual's responsibility*, perhaps with some of the responsibility being shared by the employer. The employer's share of the responsibility is to provide good learning opportunities, information about those opportunities, and support in obtaining them. But the employee is expected to seek that information, seize those opportunities, and utilize that support.

The key in managing the contract from both sides is to be sure that at any point in time both the employer and the individual are receiving equitable benefit from the relationship. *Any time you or your employer feel that the exchange is becoming too one-sided, it is time to initiate a discussion about it.* Do not assume that a balance will be achieved at some time in the future—there may be no future!

LIFE IN THE LEARNING ORGANIZATION

In today's turbulent environment increasingly firms need to transform themselves into *learning organizations* in order to survive.[3] A learning organization is one that has the capability to be self-reflective, to have smooth communication across functions and levels, and to be able to respond quickly to changing customer requirements. Such an organization is able to manage the interconnections among its complex components (functions, business units, hierarchical levels) through self-monitoring and self-learning. Some of the more familiar forms of learning organization are seen in the activities of Total Quality Management and sociotechnical systems.

To operate effectively in this emerging form of organization, you must have or develop analogous personal characteristics. You must be capable of self-reflection: looking at yourself, with the help of other people and feedback instruments, so that you can assess yourself accurately. You must be capable of changing your view of yourself (your self-identity) as you change or your role changes (for example, in different career stages, at different organizational levels, and in different relationships such as parenthood). You must be capable of recognizing and correcting skill and experience deficiencies.

In short, you must be capable of *learning how to learn throughout your life*. Learning is no longer confined to formal educational settings. You will have to create your own school for the rest of your life.

This same notion of the importance of learning applies to your work as a manager, as well. Increasingly, the manager's role is that of *developer*,[4] the person who enables and supports the growth of subordinates. By helping subordinates learn how to learn, the effective manager can gain great leverage for his or her activities. This is in contrast to the manager who sees himself or herself as either a conductor (orchestrating the work of diverse others) or a technician (the super expert, doing it all alone), both of which are seen as part of the old school of leadership.

SUCCESS

The bottom line for the individual in all of this is that the meaning of success has also changed for most people. No longer do people think of success only in vertical terms (for example, in terms of promotions). Increasingly, people define success in their own terms, measured against their own particular set of goals and values in life. We call this "psychological success."[5]

The good thing about defining success from the individual's point of view is that *while there is only one way to achieve vertical success (that of moving up), there is an infinite variety of ways of achieving psychological success.*

CAREER STAGES

In recent years research by groups like Daniel Levinson and Associates[6] and Marjorie Fiske Lowenthal and her colleagues[7] has shown that careers and lives tend to evolve in predictable stages or periods of relative stability separated by transitions or changes that move the person from one stage to the next.

These life and career stages can be summarized as follows.[8]

- *Exploration:* Searching for information about oneself and about areas of interest in which to work, a period when one is open to a wide range of alternative work futures.
- *Trial:* Trying out a type of work to test one's interest and reactions. This could take the form of a summer job, a part-time job, an internship, a project, volunteer work, or some other temporary involvement.
- *Establishment:* Choosing an area in which to work and settling in. Learning the ropes and establishing mastery of the work. Becoming seasoned.
- *Advancement:* Growth and development of one's skills and attitudes in relation to one's chosen field. This growth could take the form of promotion or increased performance and achievement within a level.
- *Maintenance:* A period of stability or plateauing, once one has achieved a high level of proficiency. Because of one's expertise, it generally takes less effort to achieve a given level of output.
- *Disengagement:* Phasing out of this field of work and reducing one's psychological involvement in it. This could be the start of a transition into another field or into retirement.

These stages are shown graphically in Figure 7-1. The necessary tasks to be accomplished in each stage are quite varied. In the exploration period, you need to have a wide range of sources of information, and you need to learn to be comfortable asking for help from others as you do your exploring. Search and self-assessment skills are critical here. In the trial period you start actual work, so technical performance skills are obviously important. But interpersonal skills are at least as important, because you can generally

FIGURE 7-1   The career success cycle

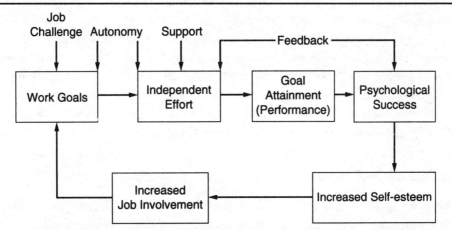

Source: Douglas T. Hall, *Careers in Organizations* (Glenview, IL: Scott, Foresman, 1976).

accomplish results in cooperation with others. Also, communication with others is a useful way to get more information about this career field.

Going back to Allison's situation, we can see that she missed a great opportunity to obtain help from the other people with whom she worked. Although it does not appear that she was offered any help, it is also true that she did nothing to solicit help and emotional support. By defining the situation as a competitive one, she shut herself off from potential help from her peers. And by buying into the "macho" culture of the firm and accepting the idea that she had to make it on her own, she deprived herself of possible mentoring, coaching, and other help from more experienced people in the firm, such as her boss, other partners, savvy administrators, and so on.

In the establishment phase, the initial job challenge is perhaps the most important factor in later career achievement. Therefore, knowing how to select (or request) a good, challenging assignment is critical. Also, managing your relationship with your boss, co-workers, and customers is another essential element in the equation. Developing mentoring relationships is very useful.

In the advancement phase, more job challenge is essential. It is also important to gain exposure and visibility, so that your successes are noticed and recognized. You should constantly ask for feedback, since most bosses do not feel comfortable offering it and you need it to improve your performance. Establishing networks is also a great way to get emotional support and to pick up performance coaching.

During the maintenance period, it is important to engage periodically in some form of exploratory behavior. If this sounds like mixing two separate stages, it is! Research has found that the most adaptive midcareer managers are those who continue to explore.[9] With all of the uncertainty of today's job environment, you need always to be aware of options in other jobs and in other organizations, and you should always be honing your skills or learning new ones in order to keep yourself marketable.

In the disengagement phase it is important to be focused on what you are *moving toward*, not just on what you are leaving. The most satisfied retired people are those who have a plan and clear interests to pursue after retirement. The ability to revise your concept of psychological success to fit a new set of activities is important here, as well. People who do not adapt in this way often experience depression after they retire.

SUCCESS FACTORS

There are certain factors in success that cut across all stages; they are always important. First in importance is *job challenge*. While challenge in the very first job is critical,[10] research at AT&T and the Center for Creative

Leadership has shown that challenge continues to be important for learning throughout the career.[11] Not only is a challenging job the setting in which you can learn important new skills, self-conception, and adaptability, but a key job also gives you exposure and visibility which will let other people become aware of you and your competence. (This success factor was definitely present in Allison's job.)

The second critical success element is *relationships*. You cannot succeed without the help of other people. The most familiar form of helping relationship is mentoring, which is a combination of task assistance and psychosocial support while you are "learning the ropes" in your career.[12] Since mentoring consists of a whole set of activities, there are actually different degrees of mentoring assistance that a mentor can provide; it is not an all-or-nothing situation. So, do not expect that any one person will do all of your mentoring for you; you will be disappointed if that is what you are seeking. Look for different people to help you in different ways, and if one special person emerges to "do it all" for you, consider it a nice surprise.

We also know that in a mentoring relationship the mentor learns at least as much as the protege, so do not feel shy about initiating contact with people who might be helpful to you. But do not lose sight of the need for you to contribute to the relationship and to help the mentor. You can provide him or her with new ideas, new methods, appreciation, recognition, and assistance in meeting his or her job objectives.

By not contributing more to others, Allison missed a golden opportunity. What never occurred to her was that among her key assets were her technical competence, her motivation, and her quick mind, all of which provided her with a great ability to help her boss and peers. (Making oneself indispensable is a great win-win career strategy!) If she had chosen to work more cooperatively and to form team relationships with them, she could have helped develop boss and peer mentoring relationships that would have been just as helpful to her as to them. And this would have established her as a key resource in the firm, adding greatly to her visibility and influence.

You (and Allison) should also be aware that *peer relationships* (peer mentoring) can be at least as helpful as mentoring by a senior person. Peers are much closer to you in age and life experience, so they may in some ways be more relevant role models than seniors and may often be able to provide more emotional support.

Other help, for example in the form of feedback, can come from subordinates, customers, colleagues in the organization, and family or personal friends. There is much stress in industry now on "360-degree feedback," or feedback from all sources in all directions. You never know where or when you might encounter good feedback and learning opportunities.

And remember Ken Blanchard's dictum: "Feedback is the breakfast of champions."

Formal training and education is the third source of learning for success in the career. Surprisingly, this factor is not as important by itself as are job challenge and relationships. But in combination with job challenge and relationships, formal education is a potent success factor. You can best utilize a seminar or conference for management development when as a result of a job assignment you have a clear need to learn. And if you can get help through a relationship (for example, from your boss) in deciding when is a good time for training and what is a good job project to take to work on in the seminar, then you are getting real leverage out of that training. So do not think of training as simply "ticket punching" for getting that next job; think of it as a means of enhancing your learning and performance in your current job—which will, of course, help you get that next job.

The final factor which is critical to success is *hardship*. This factor has been identified in research by Morgan McCall, Michael Lombardo, and Ann Morrison in which people were studied who had either arrived at the top of their organizations or had derailed along the way (been fired, plateaued, or quit).[13] Surprisingly, the arrivers were just as likely to hit failures or setbacks along the way as were the derailers. The big difference was that the arrivers were more likely to learn from their failures. They were more likely to ask others for help, for feedback, and for ideas on what to do next. The derailers were more likely to blame someone else, to avoid personal feedback, and thus to repeat their mistakes.

Therefore, you should anticipate that you will hit some setbacks along the way in your career. However, you can do your own research, perhaps with information from your mentor or helpful peers, about pitfalls that have hurt other people in your organization, and you can try to avoid those situations. And you can prepare yourself for the inevitable setbacks that will occur by having your network of supporters there, ready to help you when you stumble.

(As I write these words, we are in the midst of the Summer Olympics, and it is striking to see how some athletes can deal so gracefully with failure through help from friends, and in some cases they come right back and win medals in later events. Shannon Miller in gymnastics and Summer Sanders in swimming are examples. Other athletes are loners who have fewer resources to help them cope with failure, and they seem to leave feeling defeated.)

Obviously, there are personal qualities as well that play a role in career success. In this turbulent environment, personal flexibility, tolerance of uncertainty, and drive are all important. Resilience, the ability to bounce back from setbacks, is becoming increasingly necessary.[14] Again, these personal qualities become more important in connection with specific experiences that you might encounter in the job environment. Also, note that the three qualities just mentioned seem to be *developable;* you can work on them. In other words, effort makes a difference. The most important qualities are not inborn abilities or qualities such as height or eye color. It would be difficult to change your height. It is not so hard to work on your flexibility, reaction to uncertainty, or motivation—if you want to.

Total Quality Self-Management

One of the ways you can put forth this effort is to practice at the individual level some of the concepts of total quality management. See any job, assignment, presentation, or other experience as a "license to learn." Ask a lot of questions. Think in terms of customers. Ask yourself who your customers are. What are their requirements? What is the *total process* of which you are a part, and how might it be improved?

There is a nice irony here. The less you think of your career as linear (upward) and the more you think of it in terms of continuous learning, the more effective you will be, and the more fulfilled you will be. And the more effective and fulfilled you are, the more others will see you as successful. As a result, you will most likely be offered more and better opportunities, including promotions! So, the less you dwell on advancement, the more likely you are to get it.

It is not quite as simple as Woody Allen's dictum that "80 percent of success in life is showing up." But it is not much more than that, either. What counts is showing up and being there: Being psychologically engaged in the tasks and relationships at hand and being open to learning will carry you a long way in your career.

ALLISON'S CAREER REVISITED

Let us review Allison's experience in the light of what we have been saying about career stages. She had been extremely focused in her pursuit of investment banking. She did not do a lot of *exploring,* either of other fields or of investment banking itself. (All of her part-time jobs were chosen on the basis of convenience or pay and not for career exploration.) Nor did she do a lot of *self-exploration,* getting data about herself from vocational or personality tests or counselors which she might have compared with profiles of investment bankers in order to assess her fitness for that field.

She really had no jobs which she saw as *trial* jobs. She jumped right into full-time professional work. In fact, later in her career she will look back on this period and see that these three years have been, in fact, a trial stage in her life. But it is hard to have that perspective when you are in the trial period. *For most people, the first job after school turns out to be a trial job.*

As she was attempting to get herself established in the firm, Allison was effective in getting a challenging position. However, she was not effective in seeking and utilizing the help of others, in particular her boss and peers. She missed a great resource by seeing all peers as competitors rather than allies.

Even in the most competitive of environments, such as Olympic sports, it is not unusual to hear of some rivals being best friends and supporters. That is not to say that everyone in your peer group will help you, but it is good to seek out helping relationships and to be receptive to overtures from others. Often it turns out that friends made during this fiercely competitive stage in life end up being your closest friends throughout life. (A good example from the sports world is the friendship of Magic Johnson and Larry Bird.)

Allison also missed out by not asking for straight feedback on her performance from her boss. If her boss would not have provided it, she could have asked some other partner whom she trusted. Or, again, peers could have helped. She could even have done this after she was fired. Everyone experiences setbacks in life; the people who bounce back are those who seek help in learning from them.

And, of course, gender was probably a factor operating here, as well. As one of only three women in her class, Allison was definitely a "nontraditional," as Ann Morrison would describe her.[15] Like many firms, this one has a "glass ceiling,"[16] and the environmental supports (from peers, from bosses, and from mentors) routinely made available to men *even if they do not request assistance* were not offered to her. So even though it is true that Allison chose to be a loner, the culture of the firm colluded in reinforcing this loner status.

HOW CAREER SUCCESS CAN CAUSE PERSONAL FAILURE

One of the ironies which shows up in the research on careers and adult lives is that in our early career years we are so busy striving to achieve rewards to support a rich family life that often we are not available to enjoy them. Consider the experience of Karen Camp, an account manager responsible for an organization that spanned eight states. While on a business trip just after her son Webb's first birthday, she called home. The housekeeper had some news: Webb had just taken his first step. Said Ms. Camp, "I realized that his first year had gone by so quickly, I had been like a visitor in his life."

Another irony is that we often start on one career track that represents a good fit at the time, and then we stay with it through thick and thin, without reflecting on how good the current fit is. When we hit crises our first inclination is to work harder and do better rather than doing something different.

Consider what happened to Tom D'Agostino, a 42-year-old research manager. In the middle of a workshop on career planning, as he was writing out his career and life history, he yelled out, "My God, I just realized I let a 20-year-old choose my wife and my career!" Both Karen and Tom went on to make major career changes to bring work and home into better balance.

It is useful to stop occasionally and just ask yourself whether you are doing what you really want to do. My college chaplain was the Rev. William Sloane Coffin (a prominent 1960s figure and the inspiration for the character Rev. Sloane in "Doonesbury"). Coffin used to tell the freshman class at Yale, "Just remember, even if you win the rat race—you're still a rat!"

So You Are Not a Rat. Are You a Cormorant?

It is too easy, especially if you are competent and highly motivated, to get into that rat race, to let others—the organization, your boss, your peers—determine your path for you. Consider Dr. Ralph Siu's tale of the cormorant.

> Observe the cormorant in the fishing fleet. You know how cormorants are used for fishing [in China]. The technique involves a man in a rowboat with about half a dozen or so cormorants, each with a ring around the neck. As the bird spots a fish, it will dive into the water and unerringly come up with it. Because of the ring, the larger fish are swallowed but held in the throat. The fisherman picks up the bird and squeezes out the fish through the mouth. The bird then dives for another, and the cycle repeats itself.

> Observe the cormorant... Why is it that of all the different vertebrates the cormorant has been chosen to slave away, day and night for the fisherman? Were the bird not greedy for fish, or not efficient in catching it, or not readily trained, would society have created an industry to exploit the bird? Would the ingenious device of a ring around its neck, and the simple procedure of squeezing the bird's neck to force it to regurgitate the fish have been devised? Of course not.[17]

What does this say to us? If you are greedy, talented, and capable of learning, you are a prime candidate to be exploited to serve someone else's goals. However, in order to achieve their objectives, all of our institutions—schools, employers, professions—are designed to instill in you those qualities that make society prosper: ambition, progress, and success. Yet these qualities will gradually but surely increase your risk of becoming a cormorant.

I saw many examples of this tendency during my recent trip to Japan. Although we have many lessons to learn from Japanese business, I hope we do not try to emulate the way the Japanese manage their work/family balance. When I asked one executive when he usually gets home at night, considering his late hours at the office and after-hours drinking with colleagues, he replied proudly, "I'm usually home before midnight."

BECOMING A SELF-LEARNER

How do you keep in touch with your own personal definition of success, with psychological success? The first step is being a self-learner. Being a self-learner means more than being trainable (in the cormorant sense). It means both being able to learn on your own, from experience, and being able to self-reflect and learn about yourself.

As we said earlier, everyone hits failures at one time or another. The difference is that effective people are able to look at their mistakes, ask others for feedback and help, and thus are able to learn from them. As the saying goes, experience is the best teacher—if you can learn from it.

For most of you reading this book, college or graduate school was your last formally structured learning experience. After that, you have to be a self-learner. No matter what nice words an organization or boss might use about their concern for your development, the fact is that no one cares more about your career and your adaptation to future business needs than you do. No one else has the same stake in your future that you do. You cannot expect your employer to plan your career for you or to be sure that your career does not hurt your family and personal life.

This brings us to the second step. You will have to learn to be self-directed in your career. As one of my former deans, Henry Morgan, once reminded us, the time span of a career has changed drastically over the years. In the twelfth century, a career spanned many generations, because crafts were passed down within a family. Earlier in the twentieth century, a career lasted a lifetime.

Now, however, a career lasts five or ten years, and this period of time will not become longer. Why has this period shortened so? It is because technology advances and organizations restructure so rapidly. Research at

AT&T (a firm that has been hit especially hard by turbulent change) has found that *resilience* is now critical to success—the ability to recognize the need for change, to learn new skills, and to adapt to new areas of work as they emerge.

FINDING YOUR "PATH WITH A HEART"

All of this has nothing to do with career paths. Rather, for self-direction in the career, the final step is the ability to find your own "path with a heart," to use the words of Herbert A. Shepard, a wise management practitioner and scholar.[18] By "path with a heart" he means psychological success in terms of your own unique vision, your own central values in life. It also means finding your unique genius, your talents that you love to develop and use. As Shepard has said,

> These are the things that you can now or potentially could do with excellence, which are fulfilling in the doing of them; so fulfilling that if you also get paid to do them, it feels not like compensation, but like a gift.[19]

Shepard offered a few hints about how to look for your own genius. First, *look at your play*. Observe what you are doing when you are not required to do anything. What catches your eye when you browse through a magazine? What are the common themes?

A second source is *your own life history*. What were the times in your life when you were doing something very well and enjoying it very much?

A third valuable source is *feedback from others*. What do people who know you well (friends, coworkers, family) say about your strengths and weaknesses? What do people who knew you as a child have to say about what captured your attention and curiosity and what special promise and talents you displayed?

And, of course, various tests and career professionals can be helpful in this process, as well. Try using a variety of sources. You may find the same messages coming from different sources. Shepard advises us to employ the truth strategy from Alice in Wonderland: "What I tell you three times is true."

But what about luck in all of this? Are not most major turning points in our lives and careers shaped by luck? Not only does self-learning make you more self-directed, but also better prepared to take advantage of those chance opportunities that shape our lives so strongly. As the saying goes, luck is where preparation meets opportunity. And if we want to speculate on the source of that chance opportunity, another saying informs us that "Coincidence is God's way of remaining anonymous."

CONCLUSION

In closing, then, I encourage us all to find our own genius and our own paths with a heart. We can do this through a process of self-reflection, self-learning, and constant review of important truths about ourselves. In this way we can continually rediscover the basic threads that run through our lives, but at a deeper level. This is where we find our genius.

This lifelong learning process is the message behind the response I once received in Boothbay Harbour, Maine, from an old fisherman when I asked if he had grown up in that town. "Not yet," he smiled.

NOTES

1. Douglas T. Hall, *Careers in Organizations* (Glenview, IL: Scott, Foresman, 1976), p. 4.

2. Richard J. Campbell and Joseph L. Moses, "Careers from an organizational perspective," in *Career Development in Organizations*, ed. Douglas T. Hall and Associates (San Francisco: Jossey-Bass, 1986), pp. 274–309.

3. Peter Senge, *The Fifth Discipline* (New York: Doubleday Currency, 1990).

4. David L. Bradford and Allan R. Cohen, *Managing for Excellence* (New York: John Wiley & Sons, 1984).

5. Hall, *Careers in Organizations*, p. 29.

6. Daniel J. Levinson and Associates, *The Seasons of a Man's Life* (New York: Alfred A. Knopf, 1978).

7. Marjorie Fisk Lowenthal, Majda Thurnher, and David Chiriboga, and Associates, *Four Stages of Life* (San Francisco: Jossey-Bass, 1975).

8. Hall, *Careers in Organizations*, p. 57.

9. Robert F. Morrison, "Career Adaptivity: The Effective Adaptation of Managers to Changing Role Demands," *Journal of Applied Psychology* 67 (1977), pp. 549–558.

10. David E. Berlew and Douglas T. Hall, "The Socialization of Managers: Effects of Expectations on Performance," *Administrative Science Quarterly* 11 (1966), pp. 207–233.

11. Morgan W. McCall, Michael M. Lombardo, and Ann M. Morrison, *The Lessons of Experience: How Successful Executives Develop on the Job* (Lexington, MA: Lexington Books, 1988).

12. Kathy E. Kram, *Mentoring at Work* (Lanham, MD: University Press of America, 1988).

13. McCall et al., *The Lessons of Experience*.

14. Manuel London and Edward P. Mone, *Career Management and Survival in the Workplace: Helping Employees Make Tough Decisions, Stay Motivated, and Reduce Career Stress* (San Francisco: Jossey-Bass, 1987).

15. Ann M. Morrison, Randall P. White, Ellen Van Velsor, and the Center for Creative Leadership (1992). *Breaking the Glass Ceiling: Can Women Reach the Top of America's Largest Corporations?*, 2nd ed. (Reading, MA: Addison-Wesley).

16. Ibid.

17. Herbert A. Shepard, "On the Realization of Human Potential: A Path with a Heart," in *Working with Careers*, In *The Organizational Behavior Reader*, ed. David A. Kolb, Irwin M. Rubin, and Joyce S. Osland (1991), p. 170.

18. Ibid., p. 178.

19. Ibid., p. 180.

FOR FURTHER READING

Adler, Nancy J. *International Dimensions of Organizational Behavior.* Boston: PWS-KENT, 1991. While this short book addresses all major aspects of organizational life in international careers, it deals especially well with the career issues involved. It provides excellent coverage of ways of understanding and appreciating national and cultural differences. It describes ways of achieving "cultural synergy" when working in multicultural teams, as well as negotiation skills and how to handle cross-cultural career transitions. The book also deals with women's career issues and the management of two-career families.

Barwick, Judith M. *The Plateauing Trap: How to Avoid It in Your Career... and Your Life.* New York: AMACOM, 1986. Most career self-help books deal with the early stages of the career: how to explore, to get published, and to get ahead. This book covers the rarely discussed topic of what to do when your career has plateaued, an experience that is becoming far more widespread these days. Dr. Bardwick examines the causes of plateauing (structural, demographic, and so on), the experience of being plateaued, and steps that an individual—and the boss—can take to deal with this phenomenon.

Bolles, Richard. *What Color is Your Parachute? A Practical Guide for Job-Hunters and Career Changers.* Berkeley, CA: Ten Speed Press, 1992. This is the best career self-assessment and planning workbook available today. Revised annually and widely available in low-cost paperback form, it is extremely readable and practical. It is especially useful for people in transition, whether contemplating or experiencing a major career shift.

Hall, Douglas T., and Associates. *Career Development in Organizations.* San Francisco: Jossey-Bass, 1986. This is a discussion of the career issues facing organizations in this era of global competition, restructuring, and downsizing, combined with the movement of "baby-boomers" into peak-growth stages of their careers. The book details techniques for improving career management programs in organizations as well as methods for effective career planning by individuals.

Hall, Douglas T., and Judith Richter. "Career gridlock: Baby boomers hit the wall." *Academy of Management Executive*, IV, (1990), pp. 7–22. As the baby-boom generation hits middle age, just at the time when they might expect their career success to peak, they find that corporations are restructuring and eliminating middle management positions, limiting promotion possibilities, and increasing job insecurity. This paper describes the career values of this generation and the experiences that they and their employees are having. It discusses steps that individuals and organizations might take to maximize psychological success in the career for this large group.

Kram, Kathy E. *Mentoring at Work*. Lanham, MD: University Press of America, 1988. Dr. Kram is considered the foremost expert researcher on mentoring, and this book is an excellent summary of what is known about mentoring and other forms of what she calls developmental relationships. The book shows how mentoring aids the development not only of the protege but the mentor as well. It describes the many functions that comprise mentoring, as well as the stages that a mentoring relationships goes through. Cross-gender and cross-race mentoring are examined, as well.

McCall, Morgan W., Jr., Michael M. Lombardo, and Ann M. Morrison. *The Lessons of Experience: How Successful Executives Develop on the Job*. Lexington, MA: Lexington Books, 1988. This is an excellent summary of a long-term study done at the Center for Creative Leadership of how people learn from job assignments. What is critical in this work is the discovery of the importance of everyday work experiences in a person's career development. Career development does not necessarily require high-priced education, such as an MBA, or selection into a fast-track corporate management development program. The study compares people who have "arrived" at top jobs and those who have "derailed". The major difference is that the arrivers are better learners. The book discusses in detail how you can learn the most from your experience.

Morrison, Ann M., Randall P. White, Ellen Van Velsor, and The Center for Creative Leadership. *Breaking the Glass Ceiling: Can Women Reach the Top of America's Largest Corporations?* San Francisco: Jossey-Bass, 1992. This is an updated version of the classic report of another major Center for Creative Leadership study of factors affecting the career success of women in large corporations. The book covers derailment in women, the nature of the glass ceiling, hitting the wall, how to find alternative career paths, and constructive ideas for the future of women's careers in organizations.

PART TWO

ORGANIZATIONAL FRAMEWORKS

8 DESIGNING EFFECTIVE ORGANIZATIONS

Phyllis F. Schlesinger

Leonard A. Schlesinger

"Breaking Up IBM" is the headline *Fortune* used to describe Chairman John Akers's drastic plans to revamp and revitalize IBM in the face of dramatic changes in the marketplace and competitive environment.[1] *Prophets in the Dark* describes "how Xerox reinvented itself" through reorganizing and changing the corporate culture—that is, emphasizing employee attention to total quality and the customer.[2] General Electric Company reorganized during the 1980s by "de-layering," or eliminating entire layers of hierarchy (along with 30 percent of the company's jobs); now the corporate culture at GE is one in which decision making and initiative is everyone's responsibility.[3] Motorola Corporation's reorganization and emphasis on employee participation were factors that led to the company winning the Malcolm Baldrige National Quality Award.

Most companies have been through multiple reorganizations; however, not all are successful. To determine the best organizational design for their purposes, managers must answer many important questions. How do leaders who want to keep ahead of the competition develop the right organization to support their vision? How do they organize in order to ensure that the necessary tasks are performed, the necessary people are in place, the organization has appropriate channels of communication, and the climate of the organization is conducive to achieving the desired results? In short, how do managers design an organization to be effective in an ever-changing, competitive environment?

This chapter will present ideas and frameworks you can use to evaluate the appropriateness of particular organizational forms. First, we will present a framework we have found useful in analyzing organizations and their problems. Next, we will discuss factors that influence organizational design decisions. Once you understand the rationale behind such design decisions, we will present various types of organizational structures and will explain when the use of a particular structure is appropriate. We will conclude with a discussion of the performance of organizations, powerfully influenced by their design decisions and the culture of the organization.

There are three basic principles to keep in mind when analyzing organizations and making organizational design decisions.

1. *Organizations are complex social systems.* This means that the parts of the organization are interdependent and that changes in one part of the organization affect other parts. Each part of the organization uses information as feedback to monitor progress and to correct errors, and all parts strive to reach a balance or steady state.

2. *Organizational designs are dynamic.* While an organizational chart may remain the same, organizational design is much more than who reports to whom and where employees are located on the organizational pyramid. Organizational design is the congruence between different parts of the organization: the people in the jobs, the jobs they do, and the formal recruitment, selection, reward, and reporting structures of the organization. All of the topics discussed in this book so far influence, and are influenced by, organizational design. As a result, the organization changes as events external and internal to the organization change.

3. *There is no one best way to design an organization.* Organizational research has shown that the more we know about particular types of organizations, the less we can generalize about the optimal design for an effective organization. Generally, organizational theorists believe that no one structure, set of systems, or method of staffing is appropriate for every organization. Organizations operate in different environments with different products, strategies, constraints, and opportunities. However, organizational design does depend on some particular factors, such as environment, strategy, and technology. The ways organizations become "organized" to operate effectively depends on how organizational components fit together, how environment, strategy, and technology interact, and how they become evident in practice. A manager uses the combination of these variables to design an organization for maximum effectiveness.

A FRAMEWORK FOR ANALYZING ORGANIZATIONS AS SYSTEMS

Organizations as Systems

Managers spend considerable time designing organizations to achieve maximum effectiveness. Complex charts are constructed to depict reporting relationships and job titles, responsibilities, and authority. However, most of the dynamic interactions and relationships between people in an organization are not shown in an organizational chart. Organizations take on a life of their own, often outside that prescribed in the formal diagram or chart. For example, the person with the most effective vision for the organization or with the most ability to accomplish organizational goals in a firm may not be the person at the top of the chart! Because organizational designers try to specify and order formal processes to achieve organizational outcomes, it is important for them to understand the complex nature of the relationships between the design of the organization, the people in it, the jobs they are supposed to perform, and the environment the organization is in. To improve the quality of their design decisions, managers must first understand how the system that is their organization behaves. They can then make the most appropriate decisions as to the organizational design.

Each organization has a set of key success factors. To survive, the organization must do well in their key areas—product innovation, quality production, fastest time to market, or customer service, for example. Key success factors are influenced by the context in which the organization operates—that is, the reality in which the organization exists. Context is the competitive environment, the physical setting, the organization's history, and its political and social milieu. While these contextual factors are not usually directly influenced by the organization, they do have an effect on the organization itself. Contextual factors are usually the last place a manager concentrates his or her efforts to achieve organizational effectiveness. However, every organization must detect and adapt to changes in the context and in the key success factors because, in most instances, the organizational design must respond to these changes.

A system is any set of mutually interdependent elements, within a given set of boundaries. A change in one part causes a change in another, which in turn affects the original changed part. The elements of the system constantly adjust and readjust to reach a balance or steady state. All this occurs in a constrained environment, with minimal levels of acceptable performance. In addition, the system depends on information from the environment in order to set acceptable levels of performance.

Managers who design organizations utilize the idea of the organization as a system in the choices they make about each design element. For example, if a sales manager wants to increase sales to new customers, she may choose to give a bonus to the salesperson who has increased new customer sales the most as an incentive to other salespeople. The sales manager hopes that this change will result in more new sales. Using one element (a reward) to influence another element (sales patterns/job design) is using the concept of the organization as a system.

Such decisions may have unanticipated consequences, however. If, for example, the sales manager discovers that so much time is spent on new customers that the number of sales to existing clients drops, she will have to diagnose the reasons for the change in the system. Possibly, sales have dropped because the sales representatives do not have enough time to devote to both new and old customers and are spending time on the new customers to get the reward. Another possibility is that production time is being allocated to new orders only, and existing clients are not getting their goods on time. This causes dissatisfaction, and a drop in renewed orders. Manufacturing may be overloaded by the number of increased sales. Customer service may not be able to handle calls from an increased volume of new customers.

Through understanding the organization as a system, the sales manager can try to anticipate both the functional and dysfunctional effects of a change in one part of the organization on another. Functional and dysfunctional effects may result from the same behavior, depending on the system in which the change is made. The sales representatives and the manager see the change to emphasize new customers as functional; new sales were made, and results improved. However, the manufacturing and service departments view the change as dysfunctional; the goods could not be produced as needed, and customers were dissatisfied.

Organizational systems find ways of controlling behavior so as to maintain the balance in the system, even when that balance may be less than optimal for the organization's success. For example, an industrial chemicals manufacturing organization was marked by a belief that production employees did not want to be responsible for any decisions beyond those concerned with their job performance. A new production manager decided to give a production group increased responsibility for events on the shop floor (schedules, quality control, etc.). The group quickly set new records for production and quality. The organization as a "system" viewed the experiment as interesting; however, there was great concern in the "system" that people with little knowledge of complex manufacturing issues were given responsibilities they weren't supposed to have. Senior manufacturing management quickly brought the organization back to equilibrium by ending the experiment and reprimanding the manager. Strongly held organizational values acted to maintain the balance in the system.

The relationships between parts of organizational systems become more complex as the size of the organization increases. For example, many large organizations that previously maintained tight control over particular policies (human resource policies, pay systems, and the like) are loosening that control in order to allow subunits to be more responsive to particular market needs. Environmental changes may result in changes in the systems themselves, so the organization can maintain itself in its environment. However, too much change can be very disruptive, so there is a constant tension between initiating change and maintaining equilibrium in the system. Each organization must look for ways to adjust its "system" to meet the key factors for success.

Organizational Design Factors

Organizational design factors are the people in the jobs, the tasks they perform, and the formal organizational structure and operating systems in place. Managers spend much of their time working with design factors. They can determine the levels of hierarchy and reporting relationships, they can set the level of performance and its measurement, and they can hire people to fill roles they design. Ensuring that these combinations of variables fit together to produce the desired culture and outcomes is the preeminent design task. This chapter will focus on understanding how to achieve balance between the factors and how the factors fit each other and the demands of the environment.

Organizational Culture

Every organization has a culture that sets the rules for behavior in that organization. Culture is the important concerns, goals, and values that are shared by most people in the organization and that are likely to persist over time. In addition, at another level of abstraction, the culture is the style or behavior patterns that organizational members use to guide their actions. For example, an organization whose culture values the initiative of all its members will have a different climate than an organization in which decisions are made by senior managers and enforced by their subordinates. Most likely, the people in the first organization will feel more positive about the effects of their actions on organizational success and will have a greater sense of ownership than those in the latter organization, who may feel that they have no stake in the organizational outcomes. The combination of design factors drives behavior, which both shapes and reflects the values and patterns of the culture; however, the culture itself often determines the arrangement of design factors. For example, when an organization values attention to customer service issues, measures that emphasize (internal and external) customer service may be in place. These measures in turn drive further attention to serving the customer.

Organizational Outputs

Finally, each organization has particular outputs. Organizations produce goods and/or services. Organization members have both opportunities for growth and development, or for stagnation. They can be satisfied or dissatisfied with their work. The outputs, productivity, satisfaction, and growth and development of individual employees can be measured and used to guide design decisions.

ELEMENTS OF DESIGN

An organization is a system of variables that affect each other. Key success factors play a role in determining what an organization has to do to be effective. Contextual factors affect the nature of design factors. The mix of design factors affects the culture and organizational outcomes. Some assessment of the outcomes influences the design factors, which in turn affects the culture. Any decision to alter or change any piece of the organization will affect the other pieces, in functional or dysfunctional ways. Managers should have the ability to think of organizations in terms of these complex interdependencies in order to limit the dysfunctional effects of change on the system. Managers do not often control the existing culture or interpersonal relationships in an organization; however, they can make certain design decisions that will affect the organizational outcomes. It is this delineation of design factors that formally defines ways to get people to do what is necessary to achieve the organization's objectives. The combination of these elements determines organizational design. The tasks, people, measurement systems, reward systems, selection and development systems, and organizational structure are the crucial design elements.

Tasks

Jobs in organizations are a set of tasks assigned to an individual. These tasks either can be clearly defined, perhaps in a detailed job description, or vague. Most organizations are comprised of different jobs. Some of these jobs contain similar tasks that can either be difficult or simple, while others require a variety of activities.

People

People who fulfill specified tasks differ in their skill, interests, values, preference for variety and structure, and desire for challenge. Formal processes can be designed so that appropriate people can be hired for each task. Ensuring that the appropriate people are hired for each particular task is covered in Chapter 9, "Managing Human Resources Strategically," by Charles J. Fombrun and Drew Harris.

Measurement Systems

Measurement systems enable managers to gather, aggregate, disseminate, and evaluate information on the activities of individuals and groups. By focusing on either ongoing or past activities, measurement systems use quantitative and/or qualitative data to measure progress toward organizational objectives. Management control systems measure how the organization's resources are used to accomplish organizational goals. Performance appraisal systems measure individual employee contributions toward goal achievement.

Reward Systems

Reward systems are intended to induce people to join the organization and to perform appropriate work. Criteria are established to allocate varying types of rewards. Reward systems are sometimes tied to measurement systems so that the reward is based on some measured result. Other measures are not tied directly to performance outcomes, but to other important criteria (seniority, loyalty, cost of living, and the like). While the most common type of reward is money, other possible rewards include fringe benefits, promotions, recognition, and intrinsically satisfying jobs.

Selection and Development Systems

These systems affect behavior patterns by influencing the knowledge, skills, values, and personalities of people who work in the organization. Both selection and development processes can be simple or elaborate depending on the type of jobs or people hired.

Structure

When managers make decisions to allocate responsibilities, activities, and authority to various individuals, and coordinate these individuals horizontally and vertically, they define a structure, or organizational design. It is helpful to think of organizational design elements as building blocks that can be used to create a structure to fulfill a particular purpose. A structure is built by defining the requirements of each individual job and then grouping the individual jobs into units. These units are grouped into larger and larger units and coordinating (or integrating) mechanisms are established for these units. In this way, the structure has been built to support organizational goals and achieve the key factors for success.

Structural elements include: (1) established subunits, such as departments or divisions, (2) a management hierarchy that delineates authority, (3) rules and plans, and (4) temporary subunits, such as committees and task forces. These elements are used to influence people's behavior by clearly specifying individual job responsibilities, where and with whom members work, their authority, their reporting relationships, and how they perform their tasks. We will cover organizational forms in more detail later in the chapter, but it is important to have an overview of types of structures.[4]

Types of Organizational Structures

Figure 8-1 lists the various types of organizational structures. In *functional organizations* the structural "blocks" are grouped by the various functional areas required to achieve organizational goals (such as sales, marketing, accounting, manufacturing). Groupings can also be made based on product or service similarity. Because functional organizations offer good economies of scale, good communication among functional specialists, and good developmental opportunities for functional specialists, it is most appropriate to group by functions when the organization is in a relatively stable environment, makes a fairly stable single product (or related product line) that is technologically stable. When environmental, product, or technological change does occur, the fact that similar functions are grouped together implies that they can respond to functional changes relatively quickly.

As communication between functions becomes more and more important to the successful completion of complicated organizational tasks, *product organizations* are formed. These organizations group functional specialists in terms of their responsibilities toward a specific product or service. For example, a consumer products firm may organize by particular lines of products (such as a soap division, paper division, toothpaste division). Because the various functional representatives are together in one subunit, the organization can more easily handle the increasing environmental uncertainty, the increasing amount of information necessary to make decisions, and the increasing complexity of the tasks themselves.

Generally, organizations utilize the *matrix organizational form* when they must manage rapid exchanging of information and strong constraints on human resources. This complicated structure enables the organization to be highly responsive to environmental changes, because this structure pre-

FIGURE 8-1 Types of organizations

Functional Organizations
Product Organizations
Matrix Organizations
Divisionalized Organizations
Cluster Organizations

sumably offers organizations more flexibility in their decision making and the ability to respond quickly to rapid changes in markets, customers, technology, and information. Authority and decision-making ability rests with the unit that has the relevant information. These decisions may be made at a lower managerial level than would be the case in a more "hierarchical, bureaucratic" organization, where decisions are likely made by more senior managers.

Most organizations place a single job in a single subunit. However, matrix organizations attempt to deal with the conflicting demands of a complex environment by assigning individual jobs to two or more subunits. These organizations coordinate different functional specialties while maintaining the functional organization. For example, an employee who has job responsibilities in the engineering and marketing departments reports to two bosses, one in engineering and the other in "the international area." This dual responsibility line exists because the functional specialists are oriented to specialized (that is, functional) resources, and the product/market departments are oriented to outputs (for example, specialized product for particular markets).

Matrix organizations are not easy to manage or work in. Often, tasks or roles and responsibilities are not clear, and the individual employee must negotiate appropriate roles, controls, and responsibilities. As a result, effective matrix organizations require dual control and evaluation systems (for each subunit a person works in/with), employee acceptance of authority and leadership based on laterally shared information, and a culture that fosters conflict management and balanced power.

Divisionalized organizations provide another structure for focusing on the demands of different customers or markets. Divisions are often totally different businesses with different markets, products, and services. They are relatively autonomous business units, with most functions reporting to a general manager who has profit-and-loss responsibilities. This means that functions are duplicated across divisions, thereby reducing economies of scale. Therefore, business volume must be large enough to support the functional organization while maintaining efficient economies of scale. Usually, in large organizations with divisionalized structures, senior managers set the long-term strategic direction of the firm and make resource allocation decisions accordingly; divisions operationalize the strategy. While divisions can be run as autonomous business units, with reviews every quarter, some may be run with extensive senior corporate involvement. This corporate involvement depends on corporate culture, division performance (some corporations may leave high-performing divisions on their own), and individual divisional management.

Most organizations today resemble the four described previously. However, some writers (most notably, Peter Drucker) believe that the organization of the future will be designed by the need for and access to particular information necessary for decision making. Technological innovations have enabled today's managers to have a plethora of information available to them at will. Drucker contends that this information overload will mandate that managerial jobs be held by people who can analyze and diagnose vast amounts of widely available data. When important data is readily available to all employees, regardless of level, whole layers of management who previously served as interpreters and conveyers of information from one level of hierarchy to another will become obsolete. As a result, the organization of the future may be flatter and may employ fewer specialists. Key actors will be clustered in relevant task forces and/or groups—hence, the name *cluster organization*.[5]

Most organizations use some combination of functional, product, divisional, and matrix structures. A consumer goods manufacturing company may have five major product divisions, each with four functional departments (manufacturing, sales, engineering, and marketing) and one geographical department (international manufacturing, sales, engineering, and marketing), and a marketing department that is further divided into market-oriented units. The manufacturing functions may be organized geographically. Engineering and product research may be organized as a matrix, so that the new-product-development process includes all the necessary people. Particular new-product teams may be organized in clusters, forming and dissolving as needed. The important thing to remember is that each part of the organization must be organized so that the needs of the firm's external environment, technologies, strategies, and goals are met and are congruent with the other design factors (people and tasks) of the organization.

Distribution of Authority

Every organization has a management hierarchy that specifies reporting relationships and delineation of authority and responsibility. Most organizations are arranged hierarchically, almost like a pyramid, with power concentrated at the top of the organization. The people who report to the head of the organization, usually those in charge of the largest subunits (functions, divisions, and the like), are given less formal authority, and so on as you move down the organizational pyramid. *Centralized organizations* concentrate the authority in the hands of a few high-level people. These organizations tend to be more bureaucratic, responding to less complex environments, tasks, and activities. *Decentralized organizations* distribute authority throughout the organization, so that important decisions may be made by a variety of individuals with appropriate information and/or responsibilities, regardless of their position in the hierarchy (this presumes strategic direction/rules set by a management team). Depictions of decentralized organizations are rather flat; centralized are rather tall. *Span of control* refers to the number of people reporting to each manager. Some organizations have small spans of control (managers with two or three direct reports) and are very centralized. These structures would resemble tall triangles. Others have broader spans of control, with perhaps 10 to 15 people reporting to the manager. These decentralized organizations, with large spans of control, tend to be rather broad and flat.

THE NOTION OF FIT

The challenge to the manager designing the organization is to find the most compatible way to piece the organizational building blocks together. The unit's tasks (the technology, the environment, the objectives) must fit with the unit's employees (their characteristics, values, learning style) and with the design itself (measurements, structure, selection criteria). Organizational research[6,7] has shown that when each block demonstrates the compatible fit with the others, organizational goals are achieved effectively and efficiently and with high levels of employee satisfaction. However, it is not as easy to achieve this compatibility as it seems; many variables (organizational design, tasks, and employees) complicate the situation (see Figure 8-2). Managers may think that they have achieved the fit between these dimensions, yet one or two may be incompatible and cause unanticipated organizational problems. It is impossible to eliminate all mismatches; however, it is possible to examine key relationships and learn to avoid common mistakes!

FIGURE 8-2   The notion of fit

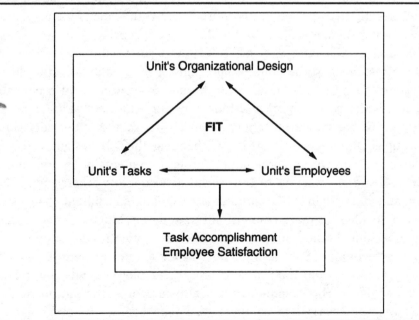

THE RELATIONSHIP BETWEEN ORGANIZATIONAL DESIGN AND PEOPLE

Structure

Compatibility must exist between the organization's (or unit's) design and its employees. The structure, measurements, reward system, and selection and development systems must all be compatible with employees' needs, abilities, and expectations. For example, a large industrial products corporation had traditionally been a market leader. Its environment had been relatively stable. Many rules and procedures had been established, because experience had proven the need for consistency and the criteria for success were so clear. However, as the environment became more competitive and customers became concerned with quality and service, management felt that it was time to encourage new ideas about competing. They recruited many independent, analytic business graduates who questioned authority and the established ways of operating the business. However, because of the many rules and procedures the organization had in place, these valued new hires quickly became disillusioned with the slow pace of decision making and the paralyzing effect of the established rules. Many left, very dissatisfied, after a year or two, leaving the organization less able to compete. Managers, attributing the problems in retention to the hires themselves rather than to the mismatch of design factors, said the new graduates "were too impatient and too demanding. They just didn't understand that we move slowly around here."

While very sophisticated techniques have been developed to assist human resource managers in matching job requirements and employee skills and abilities, these are often costly to use. As a result, many managers rely on their own judgment to match people with appropriate jobs, often with limited success. Managers may make inappropriate assumptions about the job's requirements and the abilities and skills of the people asked to do the jobs. Factory jobs that are designed to be narrow, routine, and predictable no longer fit the characteristics of today's better educated, affluent worker who has his or her own expectations about challenge and job variety. Some organizations counteract this misfit by changing the job designs to enrich or enlarge the jobs. Job enlargement combines elements of several routine jobs to increase the variety of the work (for example workers measuring, cutting, and folding fabric in a clothing factory). Job enrichment changes the job design to allow for more responsibility, autonomy, and challenge (such as cleaning personnel scheduling work themselves, budgeting for supplies).

These techniques fail when job designs are altered without the analysis necessary to understand the required tasks or employee needs, and further mismatches occur. For example, in a health-care organization, all medical records were transferred to computerized data banks. However, many of the support personnel were not familiar with or adequately trained to use the new technology. Records were lost or incorrectly entered. By the time the organization recognized that additional support and training was necessary, the damage had been done.

Often changes in the task environment lead management to redesign jobs that do not happen to fit the skills of current employees. This means retraining or replacing the existing employees. Achieving a balance between the demands of growth and the demands on employees to change is difficult. As organizations grow and add more people to perform more tasks, it becomes necessary to increase the number of organizational units, which adds levels to the hierarchy. This in turn increases individual job specialization, increases the formal rules and procedures, and restricts decision-making authority. These changes can be very demoralizing for employees who are used to being relatively autonomous and informal. Effective organizational design would try to minimize these mismatches before they occur.

Measurement Systems

The type and frequency of feedback that measurement systems provide may create compatibility problems for organizational designers. One such mismatch occurs when the newly hired college graduate, who is accustomed to frequent quantitative feedback, enters an organization that only provides feedback annually and at his or her request. Alternatively, the appraisal system can be so elaborate that managers feel uncomfortable using it. They may not have the interpersonal skills necessary to provide regular, constructive feedback to their subordinates.

Any aspect of the measurement system may be out of step with employees. For example, a work group may be concerned with meeting goals on providing product information. As they are trying to track the changes in their responsiveness to customers, they would like to chart their progress weekly. However, the computer system only measures responsiveness monthly. An organizational designer working on this system would need to make sure that the measurement system provides the information required by the team.

Reward Systems

The fit between the reward systems and employees' ideas about what they deserve as a reward is very important. Unless the reward is perceived as fair and appropriate, severe problems can result. For example, in one administrative unit rewards had traditionally been given on the basis of seniority. A new manager initiated a system based on specific customer service objectives. At the end of the first year, some short-term employees received larger rewards than those with more seniority, because the short-term employees had achieved or exceeded their targeted objectives. The employees with the most seniority did not perceive the distribution of rewards as fair. Their dissatisfaction showed in subsequent work.

The types of rewards that an individual or group finds attractive varies with the education, value, culture, age, aspirations, or life-styles of the people. Effective reward systems recognize these differences and attempt to give different people different types of rewards. These rewards may include pay, promotion, extended health benefits, challenging assignments, or job security.

It is also important for the rewards to be perceived as fair. Factors affecting the perception of equity include the general economy, the nature of different jobs, an employee's perception of his or her performance and how it relates to performance measurement and feedback and to the rewards of others in similar jobs in other companies. Some large organizations have complicated personnel systems that attempt to measure and revise the reward systems as appropriate.

Selection and Development Systems

The selection and development systems present in a company can cause organizational problems if the systems do not select the right people for the critical tasks or do not develop employees appropriately. There is often a mismatch between organizational and individual expectations about personal and professional job requirements and developmental opportunities. This sometimes occurs with recent business school graduates, who expect an opportunity to utilize their new skills and may not receive that opportunity as quickly as they deem appropriate! The organization may view them as inexperienced and naive and not give them responsibilities until they are trained. Either way, there may be a mismatch of expectations. When an individual expects to be given job responsibility quickly and little is given, the employee may quit.

Environmental conditions may also affect the tasks people are selected for in organizations. For example, familiarity with available technology may become a new task requirement for a job. If there is no training that enables people to learn the new technologies, employees may become dissatisfied.

THE RELATIONSHIP BETWEEN ORGANIZATIONAL DESIGN AND TASKS

Structure

In order to have fit between a unit's design and its tasks, there must be a fit between the various design elements and the activities of the unit itself. When a unit fits its tasks, employees know to perform particular tasks in effective and efficient ways. According to Lawrance and Lorsch, the nature of the tasks and the design depends on many factors.[8] If a unit's tasks are certain, predictable, and clear, the most effective design is the one that is formally structured—the one with clear rules, procedures, and job descriptions. Managers can identify the best ways to perform a task. These can then be written into a job description. If, on the other hand, tasks are uncertain and unpredictable, then a relatively unstructured design may be best, because formal delineations of ways to perform tasks may be impossible.

Different situations require different designs. For example, most manufacturing plants are designed so that tasks are relatively routine and predictable. Formal, often hierarchical, structures are in place so that task requirements are specified and jobs are performed appropriately. In a research lab, however, tasks are not routine and, depending on the results of an experiment, can be unpredictable. As a result, research labs are usually relatively unstructured, or informally designed.

The timing of task completion is also different depending on the situation. For example, a research unit may have two to five years to achieve particular results, while a production unit needs daily, even hourly, output. Span of control becomes important here as well. The number of people reporting to a manager can vary with the characteristics of a manager's job. The more complex the tasks, the more attention the manager has to devote to hiring, training, and reviewing subordinates. There is a greater need for a small (five to eight people) span of control. The same small span of control is important for tasks that are highly interdependent; the interdependency is relatively easy to manage if fewer people are in the group. Organizations that are "delayering" and increasing the number of direct reports a manager has in order to cut costs need to be careful to assess the effects that the enlarged span of control has on effective job performance. While on the one hand, people may feel free to make decisions and take initiative, it is difficult for a manager to maintain communication and manage the complex interdependencies between tasks with a large span of control. This situation also makes it more difficult for managers to have the type of relationships necessary to coach and develop all their subordinates.

Measurement Systems

While it appears obvious that measurement systems must focus on crucial task-related variables and provide feedback to people who control them, often the measurements used do not fit the task. For example, in one organization managers had been concerned about constantly increasing in-plant inventory. In order to keep inventories low so as to manage costs effectively, they decided to measure inventory levels and reward those purchasing employees who kept inventory as low as possible. After several years, inventory was down to "acceptable" levels. However, overall production costs were not proportionally reduced. The costs of transportation, telephone service and facsimile service were very high. Plants were missing scheduled deadlines, and customers were upset. Upon closer examination it was discovered that in their efforts to lower in-plant inventory for a particular measurement date, purchasing managers were refusing to accept shipments of needed material. Once the inventory was measured, they scrambled to "expedite" shipment of the needed material, regardless of costs incurred. Clearly, the measurement system did not cover all the important variables.

Reward Systems

The most common mismatches between tasks and the reward system occur when unimportant or inappropriate behavior is rewarded while important behavior is not, and when people are rewarded for tasks not under their control and are not rewarded for tasks under their control. For example, in an effort to boost company profitability, one company president established a reward system for marketing managers. The system was based on individual performance 25 percent and on corporate earnings 75 percent. He reasoned that marketing managers would work harder toward company goals if he rewarded them accordingly. However, he abandoned the plan after three years, because the managers protested vehemently that they had little control over corporate profits and so should not be rewarded (or punished) on that basis. Although tasks can change, rewards may not change accordingly. The purchasing managers in a previous example were rewarded on maintaining low levels of in-plant inventory. Regardless of the needs of the production unit for inventory to be present when required for manufacturing, the purchasing managers refused to allow inventories to rise beyond certain levels. As a result, manufacturing frequently missed their production schedules. There was a clear mismatch between the tasks of the unit (that is, having requisite parts available for manufacturing to use) and the reward system (that is, being rewarded for keeping in-plant inventory very low, regardless of the effect on production). Eventually, the organization recognized the dysfunctional consequences of the emphasis on low inventory and worked hard to change the measurement and reward system to fit the required task. They also developed procedures that required less in-process inventory, so that the needs of manufacturing and tasks of purchasing aligned better.

Selection and Development Systems

Organizations must have selection and development systems that enable managers to facilitate a fit between a unit's tasks and its employees. Again, mismatches occur when the task changes but the selection and development systems do not. For example, one company shifted its product line from a purely industrial focus to include a broad base of consumer products— products that required a very different type of salesperson. When the company conducted a study of the overall company morale, they found that the sales force had high turnover and very low morale. Closer examination revealed that the selection system had not changed to meet the new task requirements and that the salespeople hired were not suited to represent the new mix of products.

MANAGING THE "FIT" BETWEEN ORGANIZATIONAL DESIGN, TASKS, AND PEOPLE

As you can see, managing the relationship between these complex variables can be very difficult. It is important for managers to constantly watch and assess the changing nature of each variable and to make adjustments as necessary. It is difficult for managers who are busy performing their own tasks to spend the time analyzing the fit between the design variables. However, because of the organizational problems that can occur if variables do not mesh, it is worth spending time to anticipate the problems and to achieve the necessary balance before problems occur. By examining each of the variables—task, organizational design, and people—assessing their alignment, and analyzing the problems in detail, managers can usually make intelligent inferences about the sources and causes of organizational problems. They can then make the changes needed to fix the problems.

Designing the Complex Organization

Given how complicated it is to manage the relationships between design variables for a single organizational unit, managing the relationship in a large organization with several units involved and with one or many lines of business is a complicated process. Deciding on the tasks, people, and formal design components for an organization with many units means that designers must pay attention to these variables at many organizational levels. They must draw boundaries that fit the tasks of each of the many units. Even if you have organized each unit appropriately, there are still more questions to be addressed. Should the organization be divided by function, by product, or by geography? How can tasks be organized for effectiveness? How can managers ensure that the different parts of the organization work together to achieve the organization's overall objectives, and not just the objectives of each unit? Can the different parts of the organization work as a whole?

Interdependence

Understanding the nature of the interdependence among the parts can help us structure an organization that works together. An organization is a system; therefore, each part depends on each other part. Each functional area in an organization depends on another for information and resources. In a very simplified example, a marketing unit utilizes information from customers and from the marketplace to decide which products to sell. The marketing unit shares this information with the members of the production design unit, who design and manufacture the products to meet certain specifications. The salespeople in turn sell the product and give orders to manufacturing, so they can make the products in a timely, efficient manner. In most organizations, life is not that straightforward. Suppose that the marketplace demanded new products every six months or that manufacturing had high tolerance standards that it had difficulty meeting. The particular nature of the interdependence between units must be understood in order to choose the appropriate ways to organize and manage that interdependence.[9]

Failure to understand the nature of interdependence between units causes many organizational problems to occur. Walking the halls of any complex organization, one overhears many comments:

> "We can never get a straight answer out of manufacturing. They only tell us what we design can't be built!" (from a design engineer)

> "Why didn't they tell us the customer wanted that feature before we built it?" (from a manufacturing engineer)

> "Too bad they never told me they needed that component for the next run." (from a purchasing manager)

> "I never knew you needed that information before you put together a marketing plan." (from a sales manager)

> "Our turn-around times on new product development have gone from one year to two, yet our people still seem to think they have all the time in the world. They just won't talk to one another." (from a company president)

Even though there is no organizational design that can eliminate all these problems, there are design techniques that managers can use to minimize problems caused by lack of coordination. First, managers must understand the nature of the interdependence involved. What type of interdependence exists? How complex and intense is the interdependence? Second, managers must understand the differences that exist between the organizational units involved.

FIGURE 8-3   Types of interdependence

Pooled Interdependence

Sequential or Serial Interdependence

Reciprocal Interdependence

Types of Interdependence

There are three main types of interdependence in organizations (see Figure 8-3). *Pooled interdependence* means that each unit contributes to the success of the overall organization but is not directly involved with another unit. *Sequential* or *serial interdependence* means that one unit cannot begin its work until another unit has completed its work. For example, the production unit manufactures a product based on specific designs prepared by an engineering unit. *Reciprocal interdependence* occurs when units need to exchange information and resources on a continual basis. Developing an idea for a new consumer product is an example of reciprocal interdependence between marketing, sales, manufacturing, engineering, and administrative groups.

Most organizations exhibit all three types of interdependence at the same time; sequential and reciprocal are the most common. Obviously, in a situation of reciprocal or sequential interdependence, organizations must be able to coordinate the work of the different units. The organizational designer must understand both the nature of the interdependence and the factors that make achieving coordination between the units difficult.

Difficulties in Managing Interdependence

One difficulty encountered in trying to manage the interdependencies between organizational units occurs because of the complexity of the interdependence itself. It is difficult to manage a situation of reciprocal interdependence, in which hundreds of complex decisions are made daily. Designing a new, complex product (or marketing plan, or merger and acquisition) requires many complex decisions by many experts every day. Mechanisms must exist to coordinate the multitude of decisions required.

Integration is complicated by the differences in units themselves. As organizations grow they tend to group specialists together. This grouping purposely creates differences between organizational units. Specialization is functional in that each unit can perform specific tasks well; it can be dysfunctional, however, if the differences in personality, time frame, and design factors become paramount and make coordination difficult. When problems occur, people often fail to understand the view of the other specialist, and they blame the problems on interpersonal differences rather than organizational ones. This is not to say that interpersonal differences are not real; however, managers often fail to understand how structure may aggravate these differences. In these disagreements, company goals are often forgotten, and unit goals become paramount. Imagine the dialogue between a production manager and a salesperson:

Sales: But this is a big customer. He needs the product shipped as soon as possible. We promised him delivery on time!

Production: I can't just postpone my schedule because your customer needs shipment. Other customers do, too, and if you had outlined the specifications on time you wouldn't have had this problem.

Sales: If you had gotten back to me with comments on the specs, I would have gotten them in on time. You just can't build what I can sell.

Instead of working together to solve a customer problem, the two employees are aggravating their differences and making more problems. When this infighting spreads over entire functional areas, or divisions, necessary integration becomes more difficult.

Poor informal relationships between organizational units also cause difficulties. Organizations have long memories, and bad relationships between units perpetuate easily over time as the stories about "those bean-counters who check up on us production people" or the "wireheads in engineering who want everything to be perfect to the 0.001 cm" spread throughout a unit. These attitudes, which become the norm for many groups, make it difficult to work through differences in organizations.

Finally, integration problems increase as the organization's size and the distance between units grows. As more and more people enter into an organization, the number of interdependencies increases. As people become more and more geographically spread out, it is easy to minimize the interdependencies and to forget about different units that are more difficult to contact. Even with advances in technology that can enhance integration, such as electronic mail, fax machines, voice mail, it is difficult to manage interdependencies across distances.

A classic example of the difficulties in managing interdependencies exists in staff-line conflict within complex businesses. Each person holds responsibilities necessary to the organization, but these responsibilities sometimes conflict. The people in staff organizations act in an advisory capacity to people in line organizations who are responsible for the good or service the organization produces. Essentially, the line depends on the staff for advice that enhances their ability to do their job, get along with others, manage effectively, and so on. The staff depends on the line to take their advice and act on it, giving them recognition and credit for process improvements. Staff jobs tend to be specialized, and their work cannot always be measured objectively. Line jobs tend to be objectively measurable, because people in line positions have considerable bottom-line responsibilities. These two groups are highly interdependent (line depends on staff for advice, staff depends on line to implement), are different in orientation (staff specialist versus line generalist), and sometimes are located a great distance from each other (staff is at headquarters, line is out in the plants). Poor informal relationships may exist. Line people may accuse staff people of not being realistic; staff people may say that line people are unwilling to take risks and change.

Unless adequate mechanisms exist to coordinate the line and staff, these difficulties can cause real organizational problems. For example, in one company, senior human resource staff members were very eager to implement self-managing work teams in each plant. In fact, they had convinced the corporate manufacturing management that only plants that had "corporate-certified," self-managing work teams could receive new production orders. Corporate certification was achieved when line management presented their team organizations to a panel of staff judges for review. The human resource staff felt that the standardized reviews and guidelines for teams was crucial for their "proper implementation." However, line managers in the plants felt that the pressure to follow corporate rules was limiting the very aspects of team development that made them self-managing, and many rebelled against what they viewed as "intrusion from corporate staff who have never managed anyone." They joined together to resist the certification process. The differences in staff and line orientations resulted in many conflicts, and in the end the company dropped the idea of self-managing teams because they were "not implementable." Resentment between staff and line grew worse as a result of the decision. This organizational problem could have been prevented with proper integration between staff and line.

The more complex the interdependence between organizational units, the greater the differentiation between the units, the lower the level of trust and perceived need to cooperate; and the greater the distance employees are located from one another, the more difficult it will be to achieve and maintain the coordination necessary to enable the organization to function efficiently and effectively.

Designing Multibusiness and Multinational Organizations

Multibusiness and multinational organizations face even more complex problems. They operate in dozens of countries (with their own laws and regulations), with hundreds of products, in structures staffed by thousands of people. The organizational design issues for multibusiness and multinational companies are very similar to those described earlier; however, they are made more complicated by size, diversity of products and markets, and geographical spread. To complicate matters further, mergers and acquisitions, even when strategically appropriate, sometimes leave residual resentments that make designing and working in the "new" organization even more difficult.

In multibusiness and multinational organizations, each variable must be assessed for many more countries, people, and complicated situations. For example, a division manager in a multibusiness organization decided that acquisitions would enable the division to be more effective and profitable. He reasoned that adding new products and manufacturing facilities would enable the division to be more vertically integrated, producing elements of the products from beginning to end. He also believed that the diverse product lines of the acquired companies would enable division sales to grow. He targeted and acquired four new businesses during the first year of this strategy. In each business, he replaced the selection, reporting relationships, and measurement and reward system with the system used by the division and corporate office. One acquired business had always been proud of its reputation as a maverick in the industry. The smallest of the acquired companies, it was a small (500-person) paternalistic firm with little formal controls and procedures but with a dynamic product the division manager felt was destined to be the product of the future. The little business resented the imposition of controls and procedures. The division manager continually pushed interunit cooperation and formal controls; the firm continued to rebel and ignore directives from the division. Within six months the leader and several key members of the research team left the business to start up another company, and the new product development process was severely hampered. This in turn affected other parts of the division, which were counting on components from this company. The division missed key product introduction dates and could not gain market share for new products. The division lost money and opportunity because the manager did not assess the organizational problems that can arise from the diversity of structures in a multibusiness organization.

For multinational organizations, the situations become even more complex. They have considerable product diversity, and cultural and legal issues become very complicated. For example, economies of scale for marketing and manufacturing in a consumer goods company can be lost because product requirements can be very different from country to country. Flavorings particular to one country may be anathema in another. Legal requirements for worker participation in Europe, for example, are very different from those required in Mexico. Geographic dispersion makes communication difficult. Acceptable business practices vary from one country to another. Organizations that operate in many environments have difficulty maintaining and controlling standards of behavior in these situations. Reward and measurement systems may work at cross-purposes. For example, placing a manufacturing plant in one country instead of separate countries may, through economies of scale, increase a corporation's net income but reduce the net income of the subsidiaries waiting for parts to cross country boundaries. There are tax and compensation implications no matter what decisions are made. Designers must balance these decisions to maximize effectiveness. The factors affecting multinationals and multibusiness companies complicate the organizational design issues, but the importance of fit remains the same. (For more discussion of the complex issues involved in managing the global aspects of business, see the conclusion of this book, "Future Leaders Must Be Global Managers," by Rosabeth Moss Kanter.)

Dealing with Problems in Integration of Units

All of the design factors presented so far can be used to solve the integration problems discussed (see Figure 8-4). Utilizing the *management hierarchy* is one way to solve integration problems. Having two or more units report to the same manager links the units together and enables the manager to solve intraunit conflicts as they arise, traveling up the hierarchy until they are resolved by the appropriate person(s). However, this method of decision making is expensive because it is time-consuming and complex. Too often, organizations cannot wait to have decisions made by someone in the hierarchy, because time to market is crucial or technological change is important. They could lose money by waiting for a decision. In fact, many organizations are reducing their layers of hierarchy in order to speed decision time and enable the organization to be more responsive to market needs or employee initiatives.

FIGURE 8-4   Integrating devices

Management Hierarchy

Staff Units

Rules and Procedures

Goals and Plans

Integrating Roles

Selection and Development Systems

Formal Authority

Measurement and Reward Systems

Physical Setting

Building *staff units* is another way to integrate units. Staff can provide information for decision making in many organizational units. However, the problem with utilizing staff as an integrating device is that they are expensive (without visible, direct contribution to bottom-line profitability) and often cause conflicts instead of solving them.

The initiation of *rules and procedures* is another way of integrating and coordinating units. These rules and procedures can delineate ways people in the organization should perform their tasks. They are economical and can be fairly explicit in an organization that is relatively stable; however, they can also be dysfunctional. Rules specify the behavior that is minimally acceptable and may not inspire people to go beyond the minimum acceptable level of performance. In addition, adherence to rules must be monitored. When this monitoring is done by managers, they are seen more as police than as developers.

In addition, it is very difficult to change rules once they have been established and practiced, even if the change is warranted or one set of rules conflicts with another. For example, one organization had specific rules and procedures for their customer service representatives to follow. These procedures called for supervisors, not customer service people, to reveal shipping information. The customer service representative was not allowed to release shipping information to the customer. The organization implemented a customer service program and encouraged all customer service representatives to do whatever was necessary to provide customer service. However, the rules were contradictory, so when a customer called to inquire about delivery dates and a supervisor was unavailable, the customer service representative, obeying the rule about shipping information, refused to tell the customer when to expect the order. The customer was furious, but the procedure had been followed.

Goals and plans also can serve to integrate two units, for a limited amount of time. Setting exact timetables and procedures for new product development can serve to induce the different units of the organization to work together to accomplish the development by the target date. The units must work separately and together to accomplish the goal. The goals must be realistic, or they could be a source of problems.

Organizations also use *integrating roles* to coordinate different organizational units. These roles range from permanent tasks (such as the product manager who integrates engineering, sales and marketing, and manufacturing) to service on committees or task forces that have representation from organizational units. Often, people in integrating roles do not have formal authority over the people whose work they coordinate; this means that they must have and must use considerable interpersonal skills to achieve the necessary integration and coordination. (For more about the skills necessary for those in integrating roles, see Chapter 5, "Power, Politics, and Influence," by Anne Donnellon.) They need to be able to build and lead a team and over-come all the barriers to integration described earlier. This requirement has some real implications for selection, measurement, and evaluation criteria for people who perform these roles. Thus, *selection and development systems* can be another integrating device. The costs of salary and benefits for people who can accomplish integration can be high. However, in organizations in which the work of many functional specialists needs to be coordinated to make progress, it is an integration device well worth the cost.

The distribution of *formal authority* also can be an effective tool for integration. Distributing authority so that people who have the necessary information to make decisions also have the authority to make the decisions helps the coordination process. As described in Chapter 10 ("Self-Managing Teams," by Harvey Kolodny and Torbjorn Stjernberg), many organizations today are moving to self-managing teams. Formal authority in these organizations should be decentralized so that the people with the relevant information make the appropriate decisions (this also saves time and money that would be lost by slow product development). Organizations that rely on rules and procedures to coordinate their efforts usually have centralized authority.

Measurement and reward systems that are designed to measure the successful integration of organizational units are also common integrating devices. For example, product managers need to have accurate accounting and production information to determine profitability, sales, and costs by product line. These measures can be used to drive particular behavior; however, they can be dysfunctional as well, if the parts of the measurement and reward systems don't fit. For example, if the production people are measured on keeping costs low and the engineering people are measured by the multiple designs they can deliver, the desired integration may not occur.

The final way organizations can drive coordination is by effective use of the *physical setting*. Proximity makes communication easier, so organizations often group different units in the same area, particularly if they are working on a project together. For example, the academic officers of a small college wanted faculty from different functional areas to share information about class content, faculty research, and so forth. Individual faculty offices were moved so that each faculty member shared a common area with faculty members from other disciplines. Not long after that move, new courses that contained different elements from several disciplines were proposed!

When organizations reach a certain size, they may reorganize the boundaries between units in order to achieve more efficient integration. As we have seen, organizations generally start with functionally oriented structures. As they grow, coordination and integration across functions becomes more difficult. The need for information flow between functions increases the interdependencies. Specialization increases with size, and attitudinal differences may occur. Physical proximity tends to change, and access to people in different areas becomes more difficult. Shifting to product divisions enables the organization to manage the interdependencies easier. Grouping people around their particular product area presumably makes communication easier. It does, however, decrease the economies of scale of functional specialists and makes communication across product lines more difficult.

Integrating Multibusiness and Multinational Organizations

Organizations use many of the methods described in the previous section to coordinate the complexities of operating across countries and/or with many products and markets. Modern communication facilities, such as telephones, fax machines, electronic mail, and teleconferencing, have helped coordination immeasurably. Many organizations utilize extensive integrated information systems to share relevant information. Other coordination mechanisms include group structures, corporate staffs, selection and management assignments, area structures, and the corporate culture.

Group structures, in this sense, are product divisions that are grouped together so that the group leader manages the interdependencies of the units and works with corporate staff to make key business decisions. Such structures can significantly increase a company's ability to process relevant information and to make effective decisions.

The use of *corporate staff* as an integrating mechanism varies. As a rule, the more complex the interdependencies, the larger the corporate staff and the more centralized the decision making. When companies have businesses that are very diverse, with less interdependence between units, corporate staff tends to be smaller, and decisions are decentralized. Just as in a small organizational unit, the level of interdependencies affects the integration method used.

Effective *management assignment* can also be used to increase coordination in complex organizations. Managers can be encouraged to take overseas assignments or to work in other divisions. Of course, organizations must take great pains to develop the human resource systems necessary to support these arrangements, but giving managers assignments in different areas increases the building of relationships and the understanding of diverse organizational assignments.

Structure itself may be used to coordinate complex organizations. Product/area structures combine a geographic structure with a product management focus if geography is a key success factor, or a product management structure with a geographic focus if product management is a key success factor. If both area and product require attention, then a product/area matrix may be used. However, the problems of matrix management are magnified by the problems of diverse units and countries.

Finally, *corporate cultures* may be used to manage key interdependencies in multinational or multibusiness organizations. The clear expressions of norms, values, and operating styles by senior managers can set the tone for operations despite the culture differences present in complicated organizations.

Choosing the Appropriate Method for Integration

As we have seen, each mechanism for coordinating organizational units has its strengths and its weaknesses. The organizational designer must weigh the advantages and disadvantages and the costs and benefits of each to the organization. The organizational designer must determine a solution that costs the least while maintaining effectiveness of each unit. Effectiveness must be maintained; the organization that establishes a geographically dispersed product development team but is not willing to pay for airfare for meetings will probably not get the efficient product development they require!

In addition, the more integration is required across organizational units, the more costly the necessary integration devices. Obviously, an organization in which there is little interdependence and specialization and in which informal relationships between people are good requires less formal coordination than an organization in which there is much interdependence and specialization and in which informal relationships are poor. In order to be effective, the latter organization may be forced to use all of the previously suggested integration mechanisms in its design.

Managers who are confronted with making design decisions face a series of complex choices. How should units be organized? What kinds of integrating devices can be used? Where should the boundaries between units be drawn? Designing an organization, or trying to reorganize in order to solve a particular organizational problem, requires analysis. The designer must answer these questions and balance the elements in the whole organizational system against each other. Designing an organization is a time-consuming and continual process that has no simple rules. Using the model of organizations as systems can help the designer predict the consequences of any particular design, so that he or she can choose a design that best fits the situation. Designers should follow these four steps.

1. Identify the company's key activities, their differences, and their interdependencies. This entails examining the key success factors, the external environment, the technology, and the strategy of the organization. What are the important characteristics of the activities and interdependencies? What is crucial for future success? How will these variables

change over time? Performing this thorough analysis is time-consuming, but designing an organization without consideration of these variables may mean the new design does not fit the competitive situation of the future.

2. Examine the company's current staffing, their characteristics, and their formal and informal arrangements. Remember, behavior and interactions that may not be prescribed on the organizational chart always emerge. Because managers must work with the emergent as well as the prescribed interactions, activities, and attitudes, it is important to recognize these characteristics and to be prepared to deal with them.

3. Assess the formal structures (structure, measurements, rewards, recruitment and development) and how well they fit the company's (or group's) business. Your assessment of the degree of fit between these components will help you analyze the causes of and possible solutions to organizational problems. Remember, organizational problems can result from any misfits that may occur.

4. Finally, identify alternative arrangements that might solve the problems identified in step 3 to develop as many alternative arrangements as you can, and assess the levels of fit in your new designs. This step requires considerable analysis of the formal and informal organization that may result from your new design; it is crucial that you assess the fit before you implement any changes. While this step is very time-consuming and difficult, the decisions you make will probably enable you to choose a design that best "fits" the situation.

ORGANIZATIONAL LIFE CYCLES

The complicated design decisions outlined previously occur over various stages in an organization's development. Each stage has particular characteristics and, consequently, has ramifications for design decisions. Larry Greiner[10] has described five key dimensions of the life structure of an organization: age, size, periods of prolonged growth, periods of prolonged change, and rate of growth (or not) of the industry itself.

Organizational practices are affected by the passage of time, age, and tradition. A concept that was innovative and creative 30 years ago and that enabled the organization to gain advantage over its competitors in the past may be the very tradition that detracts from innovation today. Employee behavior becomes more institutionalized with time, and outdated attitudes become difficult to change.

As we have seen, changes in organizational size can cause many organizational problems, particularly where coordination and communication are concerned. These problems are a result of both growth and decline in size.

Organizations that have grown rapidly often add managerial layers and functions; organizations that are forced to "downsize" or "rightsize" in response to competitive changes have difficulty deciding which people, functions, and structures to keep in place.

Organizations also experience periods of prolonged growth, or *evolution*. Five to eight years may go by without a major setback or series of crises to which the organization must respond. Generally, only minor design changes are made at these times. *Revolutions,* or periods of prolonged change, occur periodically as well. These are most often linked to the fluctuations in the industry environment. During revolutionary times, practices that have worked well for the organization in the past may not be as appropriate for dealing with the situations of the future. Organizations must find new ways of managing in order to adapt to their new environments and new success factors. For some industries there may be a long time between growth and turbulent change (such as the automobile industry until the middle 1970s or the insurance industry until the late 1980s). However, in other industries (such as the computer industry) technological and market forces cause great change to occur regularly. Organizations must be ready to adapt to these changing situations.

There are five stages in the organizational life cycle (see Figure 8-5), each one characterized by particular evolutionary and revolutionary phases. These phases occur in order, and the events of the respective revolutionary and evolutionary phases are peculiar to each stage of the process.

The first stage of an organization's life is its birth—the time at which the organization creates both a product and a market for that product. This phase is characterized by great creativity and excitement, as new opportunities unfold. Leaders tend to be more technically oriented than managerially

FIGURE 8-5   Organizational life cycles and revolutionary stages

Life Cycle Stage 1—Growth through Creativity
Revolutionary Stage 1—Leadership Crisis

Life Cycle Stage 2—Growth through Direction
Revolutionary Stage 2—Autonomy Crisis

Life Cycle Stage 3—Growth through Delegation
Revolutionary Stage 3—Control Crisis

Life Cycle Stage 4—Growth through Coordination
Revolutionary Stage 4—Red-Tape Crisis

Life Cycle Stage 5—Growth through Collaboration
Revolutionary Stage 5—Next Crisis?

oriented; their business is to create the product to be sold. The group is generally small, so that communication patterns are informal and frequent, and members depend on each other to perform necessary tasks. Formal management systems may be rare; feedback comes from the marketplace itself. Most companies have legends or stories about their creation. Xerox proclaims the creation of the xerographic process[11] and Apple Computer boasts of the creation of the prototype computer in a garage.

Because this stage is essential for the development of a key product or concept, no organization can exist without it. If done well, people buy the product or service, and the organization is successful. However, success leads to problems. The organization soon requires functional specialists to direct and manage particular areas. As more and more people join the organization, structures are needed to ensure adequate communication. Financial controls may be added. The original founders may find that they are spending more and more of their time dealing with "administrivia" rather than the creating they had done previously. This brings us to the first revolutionary stage—the *leadership crisis*. Leadership changes must be made to bring the organization to the next step. There are many examples of organizations in which the initial creator was unable to change the leadership and organizational effectiveness was sacrificed. For every Mitch Kapor (the founder of Lotus Development Company) who steps aside so that the organization can move forward, there is a Steven Jobs (one of the founders of Apple Computer) who does not, with negative consequences for the organization.

The next phase is one of growth under able, directive leadership. This stage incorporates the development of the functional organization described earlier. Control, measurement, and reward systems are established. Standards are set for selection and recruitment of new employees. Communication patterns become more formal, and perhaps more difficult. Hierarchical decision making becomes the norm. Organizations generally form the functional or product-oriented structures described earlier.

Most organizations move through this phase for years, doing well, making necessary adjustments and changes, and developing into a large, complex, effective organization. However, the development of hierarchy, formal systems, and centralized decision making may lead to other organizational problems, which causes the next revolutionary stage—the *autonomy crisis*. This crisis occurs when managers lower in the hierarchy demand responsibility over decision making for their areas of responsibility. While most companies can design the hierarchies to redistribute decision-making responsibility, some struggle with the realities of decentralizing. Control systems that have measured everyone on similar criteria may not be appropriate any longer; some managers become concerned that they will lose control over the organization if decision making is decentralized or people are given more autonomy.

Organizations that have difficulty redistributing autonomy have great difficulty decentralizing during this period. Managers at low or middle levels of the hierarchy who have never been asked to make decisions before are suddenly being encouraged to make them, and this can be a scary prospect for some people. For example, one organization had a group of employees who had been encouraged to analyze a difficult cost problem. They came up with an accurate assessment of the problem and an interesting solution to it. However, they were afraid to tell upper-level management their concerns, because they did not believe they were viewed by the organization as competent to make decisions autonomously.

Once the organization has decentralized decision making, evolution and steady growth can occur once again. Greater responsibility is given to unit managers, incentive systems are designed that encourage people to perform their jobs well, senior management concentrates on long-term management issues, and communication across the organization occurs as needed. Motivation at the lower levels of the hierarchy increases as people are encouraged to make decisions for which they are responsible.

However, this steady growth period leads to the next revolutionary stage, the *control crisis*. Managers may feel they no longer are in control of key organizational variables. Communication and coordination becomes very difficult. Companies may try to regain control from managers who may not want to relinquish it. Industry variables affect this stage of development. If a business downturn occurs, the organization has difficulty getting orders. Under such crisis conditions, senior management may try to wrest control from those who had been previously charged with decision-making responsibility. Some control is appropriate; as we have seen, integration of organizational units is critical. However, in times of crisis managers tend to panic and look for a hero from central casting who can come in and solve the organization's problems. This behavior is often not what the organization requires.

Once the organization has sorted out various decisions about coordination and control from the revolution (control crisis), it can move to the evolutionary phase characterized by the development of formal systems to achieve coordination and integration. In this phase organizations implement the integration devices described earlier to coordinate the diverse units of the organization more effectively. These can be new systems, hierarchies, or integrating roles. The organization also moves to consolidate and coordinate the many activities of the organization. However, as we have seen, even the most appropriate integration devices can become dysfunctional, and a lack of confidence in the coordination/integration methods used may result in divisions between parts of the organization. This leads to the next revolution—the *red-tape crisis*. At this revolutionary stage, too many systems and programs exist for the organization to coordinate them adequately or effectively. Reports and data proliferate and often take on a life of their own. People hesitate to eliminate information, even if the information is never read or used by anyone. Procedures abound, and often rules important to one unit may be dysfunctional for another.

Solving this system overload may take years. (One organization worked for three to four years on eliminating the extraneous reports, approvals, meetings, and memos that provided no added value.) However, the time is well spent because it leads to a period of strong interpersonal collaboration—a time when people work together to confront and solve organizational problems, allied by common goals and missions. Management approaches become flexible, and managers are encouraged to practice new behaviors and attitudes. New ideas and practices are encouraged, and managers are encouraged to take appropriate risks and to be creative in solving organizational problems together. It is during the collaboration phase that the organizational culture becomes particularly important; for an adaptable culture can ultimately lead to an effective organization.

CULTURE AND PERFORMANCE

Managing the organizational design factors is but the first step to the efficient operation of an organization. Designing the appropriate tasks and structures and recruiting and selecting the appropriate people for those tasks is relatively straightforward, analytical work. However, even the design that seems to be congruent and balanced may not always work the way it looks on paper. In order to understand why this occurs, we need to understand the way organizational culture develops. At one level, organizational culture is the set of values and assumptions that are shared by the members of the organization and that persist over time even if the members change. An example could be the value placed on customer safety by Johnson and Johnson during their 1980s Tylenol crisis, when, in order to ensure that all their products were safe, they withdrew all Tylenol products from the market rather than assume even the smallest risk that customers would receive products that had been tampered with after they left the J&J plant.

The nature of these values and assumptions becomes visible in the ways people are encouraged to behave while in the organization. For example, some companies can be characterized as very friendly or as highly competitive; these behaviors are quickly learned by new organizational members. Behavior in organizations is shaped by the ways people internalize the assumptions and values that define, either explicitly or not, the culture of the organization. Individuals in organizations quickly learn (or are told directly or indirectly) "how we do things around here" and what kinds of attitudes, behaviors, assumptions about the world, and values people in the organization hold.

No one organization has the same culture as any other. In fact, cultures across one organization differ in some ways from unit to unit, although the core values and assumptions may be similar. Cultures vary on their *content* (the set of basic assumptions held by the organization and their relative priority) and on their *strength* (the intensity of the behavior that exhibits the culture).

Content of a culture is affected by the business environment and industry itself. For example, an organization in an industry characterized by rapid technological change may hold the value of cooperation and readiness to change as part of their culture's content. Content is also shaped by the formal structures, plans, and policies of the organization. An organization that states it "values all its employees and encourages their learning" may have extensive development programs that validate those assumptions. In addition, the culture is affected by the visions of the organization's leaders and the stated strategies they have implemented to achieve those visions.

A culture's strength is influenced by the number of shared assumptions people in the organization have, the extent to which those assumptions are shared, and the priority of those assumptions. Few elements of a culture are completely shared, but each organization usually has several that are seen as crucially important to the organization. For example, a major insurance company has always prided itself on the large surplus-to-asset ratio it generates annually; the size of this ratio indicates to the company that it will always be able to cover policyholder claims. Not surprisingly, organizational members are eager to avoid any actions that may put this ratio in jeopardy, for to do so would be to violate the culture. That this organization is not noted for risk-taking behavior is merely a reflection of the content and strength of the culture; to take major risks might violate a widely held company value. This is not to say that different units in the organization don't encourage risks (investments, for example), but these are balanced by other areas to ensure that the organizational values of thrift, stability, and conservatism stand firm.

The characteristics of an organization's culture emerge from the interplay of the design factors and the context or environment in which the organization finds itself. Design factors (tasks, people, and formal organizational structures and systems) interact with each other and influence people's behavior. The culture is the behavior that emerges from this interplay. For example, in a metals manufacturing organization there was a strong emphasis on self-measurement and analysis, not on formal systems of performance measurements. The structure was functionally oriented, and decision making was highly centralized. Keeping costs low, while not unimportant, was not viewed as a key success factor; the market was expanding, and the company was quite profitable. The organization was paternalistic; layoffs were unheard of. However, people who were poor performers were eventually moved to a level where they could remain with the company but with little or no contribution to organizational effectiveness. The company was known far and wide as "Mother," as a result of these beneficent human resource policies. The fact that this organization did not use serious performance measures, combined with the fact that employees were willing to take responsibilities for task accomplishment in a hierarchical organization where the manufacturing function was paramount, would lead someone analyzing the organization to conclude that in this culture self-direction was fostered, job security was important, and loyalty was particularly valued. Elements of the culture emerge from the interplay of the design factors. As a result, managers must be very careful about the design factors they put into place; once they establish particular structures and a culture emerges, it is very hard to change.

It is important to note that because organizations are systems, the culture affects the design factors. In the 1980s the metals manufacturer found itself in a rapidly changing and competitive environment. The company had to become a low-cost producer, or it would lose its position and possibly be faced with closing altogether. The organization wanted to institute many changes in the design—to move from a functional orientation to a market orientation, to develop and use performance measures, to examine employee performance, and to cut the work force as one way to reduce costs. Making the changes was extremely difficult, because the culture was so strong and its content so clear to everyone. Only the extreme sense of urgency communicated by senior managers made the changes palatable (along with the fact that many senior managers whose performance did not measure up were slated to be released!).

Given the strong interrelationships of the many variables that determine organizational performance, corporate culture has been identified by management researchers as having a key impact on economic performance over time. In addition, corporate cultures have been found to be a strong factor in the future success or failure of a firm. Cultures help (or hinder) an organization's coming to grips with the need for change. Finally, because cultures become established so easily and are so difficult to change, it is important for the organizational designer to understand culture so that the organization can be designed to be as adaptable as possible.[12]

Because culture is such a powerful force affecting organizational behavior, many corporate leaders have tried to develop a strong culture that serves to align people with the organizational values and mission statements. However, these executives may not realize that strong cultures may not promote excellent performance; they may not be amenable to adapting to changing environments or markets in order to fit the new competitive environment. The alignments that may have worked in one environment may not be as effective in another. In addition, managers in the layers of a large organization may be wedded to one set of values and beliefs and may not see the necessity for change.

John Kotter and James Heskett have found that only those cultures that value continuous and adaptive change promote effective economic performance over time.[13] Organizations that promote useful change have managers who pay close attention to changes in the environment and initiate changes in the organization's design and strategy in order to cope with these changes. These organizations value the needs of all who have a legitimate claim on the organization, from the employees to the customers to the shareholders to the community in which the organization operates. People and processes that create and manage continual change are valued, regardless of their organizational level.

Many organizations have elaborate mission statements. However articulate these visions may be, not all organizations actually act in accordance with their values. Kotter and Heskett have found that organizations that give more than lip service to mission statements, stressing the values of people, are more likely to have effective performance because managers feel energized and willing to help the firm change with the competitive environment.

Deciphering the strengths and content of a company culture is a difficult task. One must look for things that are explicit (such as signs, memos, announcements), implicit (stories, ceremonies, celebrations, and customs), or not present at all! For example, no reserved parking places for managers may indicate an egalitarian culture. One manager, moved to reduce status differences so that lower-level employees would take more initiative, publicly gave up all senior management parking places. However, privately he bemoaned losing something he had worked so hard for. One could question the commitment to "empowerment" in this organization!

Clues to an organization's culture are everywhere, if one is a good observer and listener. It is important to view the culture as members see it, as they talk about it, and as they experience it. What may seem odd and irrational to the observer may seem very normal to those within the organization itself. Observers trying to learn about an organization's culture must try to match the statements in the mission, or the elements of the design, with the actual events in the day-to-day life of a company. For example, a group of consultants worked with a company that made sweeping statements about the importance of balancing work and family life. Senior management emphasized the need to reduce unnecessary work, reports, memos, and meetings. They encouraged managers to speak out when they felt their work was duplicating existing efforts and not adding value to the company. However, although middle- or lower-level managers espoused the values of initiative and decision making, the reality was that they would continue the same amount of work or more and not speak about it to their bosses. They did not want to be viewed as uncooperative. Observing the culture in action enabled the consultants to work with the organization to put systems into place that helped a more desirable culture to develop.

Vijay Sathe[14] has long studied organizational culture and has developed three important questions to ask to determine the culture.

1. What is the background of people who shape the culture? This could be the principles of the founder or of the current management team. For example, it would be difficult to understand the strong culture of IBM, Digital Equipment Company, or Apple Computer without understanding the background and beliefs of Thomas Watson, Kenneth Olsen, or Steven Jobs and John Sculley. The attitudes and values of the prevailing leadership shape the culture's content.

2. How does the organization respond to crises or other critical events, and what do they learn from these events? For example, the metals company mentioned earlier responded to the profitability crisis it faced by implementing formal measurement systems that could be used to determine employee placement in a reorganization. The culture adapted, due to strong employee loyalty. The crisis ultimately enabled senior managers to move the organization to balance its values of job security and loyalty with a new value of performance.

3. Who in the culture is considered different, and how does the organization respond to them? The people who are slightly (or very) different push the organization's boundaries to test the limits of acceptable behavior. An organization that values creativity and individuality will probably value creativity in dress or behavior; a bank, known for conservatism, may not. However, organizations do make room for those individuals who conform to important aspects of the culture, but not to all of them. One company took great pains to impress on their new managers that they should wear jackets and ties while on the production floor. The dress code was designed to reinforce the differences between professional managers and the union employees. Not surprisingly, this relationship was quite adversarial. One manager refused to comply with the dress code. He reasoned, "the clothes will get ruined, or get stuck in the machinery." At first, he was teased, then reprimanded, and then told to get appropriate clothing. However, as the year went on, his crew had the fewest labor grievances and above-average production and quality ratings. Comments about his appearance vanished. We can specu-

late that if grievances had increased and if production and quality had decreased, he would either be wearing a tie or working somewhere else!

These questions can be used to identify individual unit cultures as well. Each unit has its own values and assumptions that may be separate and distinct from the corporate culture. All relevant cultures must be identified and assessed before action is taken on the design factors themselves. Because design factors influence culture, and vice versa, it is crucial to evaluate and anticipate any consequences from managerial action on the culture.

Culture can be used as an asset or a liability. As an asset, culture can be used to generate cooperation, communication, and commitment in an organization. As a liability, the shared values and assumptions can cause people to behave inappropriately. For example, a culture that reveres state-of-the-art engineering, and therefore reveres the engineering group, may have problems when the engineering group designs products not valued by the marketplace. In this case, no one will discuss this problem with the engineers because they are considered "the top." Cooperation between engineering and sales and marketing may be affected.

Communication patterns are affected by culture as well. Some cultures value openness and truth, no matter what the news, while others would rather bad news be kept secret, despite the consequences. For example, when one group of managers was asked to solve a critical problem, the group uncovered a severe flaw in the organization's design. The managers were so afraid of reprisals for bad news that they spent more time deciding who would deliver the news than deciding what the solutions were. Finally, one member volunteered to give the report because he was "closest to retirement" and could take the heat. This kind of behavior was not what management wanted, but old assumptions about consequences for those who tell unpleasant truths prevailed. Culture also affects decision making. If the content of a culture is strong, then employees have clear assumptions of the direction of each decision. If the culture values debate and discussion, then a better quality decision may be reached after discussions are held.

Finally, commitment to an organization is influenced by its culture, as noted by Stephen L. Fink in Chapter 4, "Managing Individual Behavior." While strong commitment is encouraged by design factors, such as salaries, benefits, and development opportunities, intangible incentives that are part of the culture can enhance someone's commitment. The culture of the organization can encourage commitment if the individual shares the values of the culture. These may include identification with the organization's goals, a willingness to help others, and valuing individual differences and creativity. At one computer company, there was a strong value that employees would work as hard as possible to build a technically superior product.

Competitively, it was important to be the first to market with new technology. In addition, the challenge to build a new computer was exciting and appealing to the group of computer designers who wanted to be on the leading edge of technology. Management encouraged the design groups to do whatever was possible to get the products designed and built. They were able to emphasize the values of the culture to help productivity.

If the existing culture is appropriately adaptable, then the values and behaviors driven by a set of cultural assumptions can be utilized by the organization to encourage adoption of new goals or behaviors. Managers can use an understanding of the organization's culture to encourage new behaviors to be adopted. For example, the value of hard work exhibited by the computer company can be tapped to meet a new competitive threat or to solve a problem with new-product-development teams.

Because culture is the manifestation of people's values, beliefs, and assumptions, it is very difficult to change. Although specific change strategies are covered in Chapter 12, "Managing Change, " by Todd D. Jick, it is crucial for any change agent to understand the culture and the ways it can be used to help, or hinder, organizational change. Managers must understand the culture, its content, and its strength. They must also understand the nature of communication, cooperation, and commitment. They must then use this understanding to assess the resistance they will encounter when trying to change a culture's content and/or strength. It is likely that it will be more difficult to change a strong culture than a weak one, because the behavior of more people must change. In addition, the amount of resistance will depend on the number of changes made to the content. Managers may encounter less resistance to a change if only one or two elements are changed.

Cultures can be changed by focusing on the actions of current organizational members, by adding people who represent the new culture, and by socializing people to new ways of behaving. We have seen how specific design factors can be put into place to encourage particular behaviors (performance measures to direct behaviors, for example). However, it is very important to have informal mechanisms (such as stories, celebrations, and symbols) to encourage behavior change. One company wanted to encourage all employees to initiate discussions of problems and to begin to generate solutions to those problems. One group solved a quality problem by redesigning the packaging of the product, and they became instant heroes. Their names appeared on plaques and in the company newspaper; their behavior was praised in management speeches and talks. These stories can help people determine the kinds of behaviors desired in a changed culture.

In a similar vein, removal of those people who cannot or will not adhere to the new values and assumptions can help change a culture as well. General Electric's change from a culture characterized as very centralized, autocratic, and bureaucratic to one characterized by employees who take initiative and move with "speed, simplicity, and self-confidence" to make important decisions on their own has been well documented.[15] Managers who had previously only been measured on financial results were encouraged to push decision making downward in the organization in order to gain commitment and coordination. Recently, one senior manager was relieved of all managerial responsibilities, although he had met all his financial targets, because he had behaved autocratically to achieve the financial goals. His reassignment, coupled with a section in the annual report devoted to outlining the new General Electric Company, sent a strong signal from corporate management about the importance of the content of the new culture.

Sathe has argued that it is appropriate to change a culture's content when the environment has changed so drastically that the organization must change the basic way it thinks and acts.[16] This may be caused by persistent performance and/or morale problems that make it clear that the ways the organization had traditionally functioned are no longer appropriate, or it may be caused by a change in the organization's mission. Deregulation and intense competition may cause a company to change the content of its culture. The change in the telephone companies as a result of deregulation is an example of this kind of change. Major technological change provides opportunities for cultural change; for example, in some organizations communication has been enhanced by the addition of complex information networks. Major market change may also lead to cultural change. Mergers and acquisitions, or the expansion to international operations, may lead to a culture change as well.

It is more difficult to determine when to change a culture's content, particularly if the culture is consistent with the behaviors required to be effective. Managers must act to make sure that the content of the culture does not become so strong that it is impossible to change. In these situations, managers must be aware of the consequences of a strong culture and be attentive to any dysfunctional effects.

Just as managers must monitor the design factors to ensure compatibility between elements, cultural characteristics must be monitored as well. Managers who learn to nudge the culture incrementally so that effective organizational processes continue while new opportunities are explored, and perhaps implemented, can be spared the difficult process of major cultural change.

Whenever possible, before undertaking a change in the culture itself, managers should ask themselves whether or not design factors could be used to change behaviors, with a new culture gradually emerging from the new design. People in organizations tend to interpret changes in terms of the existing culture. Managers should learn to use the existing culture to propel the organization into new ways of thinking and/or acting. For example, a company that places a high value on innovation may be easier to change than one that does not. Intrinsically held values that may be dormant could be tapped and utilized. One academic institution, for example, had a collegial culture that highly valued discussion and debate about academic issues. Over the years, however, departments had become more internally focused, and the collegiality diminished over time. When the college faced a decline in enrollments that threatened its long-term viability, the leadership of the college appealed to the dormant values of collegiality to encourage a change in direction.

Kotter and Heskett[17] have identified some key behaviors for managers to use to create adaptive cultures that can enhance economic performance. For new organizations, in which the culture is forming, it is crucial to have a leader who values people and processes that create useful change. In addition, the leader must have an appropriate strategy that increases his or her credibility with employees (such as product success over time). While these attitudes are necessary for the start-up of any business, to be successful over time, Kotter and Heskett contend that such attitudes must continue to be nurtured.

Kotter and Heskett also found that in mature organizations it was more difficult to build a culture that values adaptive behavior. The leaders of the organizations they studied met with great resistance, particularly if employees equated past success with the existing culture. However, when leaders began the change process by establishing a sense of crisis or need for change, and creating a new direction based on the firm's key success factors and key constituencies, change became possible. The new direction had to be continually communicated, across and around the organization, to encourage understanding and acceptance by employees. The leaders allowed employees to internalize and act on the direction, and they modeled and encouraged the modeling of new behaviors across the organization. Attempts and successes were recognized and rewarded. Failures were studied and discussed. Gradually, Kotter and Heskett found that the organizations they studied moved in new directions. However, these changes did not occur without a great deal of time and effort on the part of the leader. Because these firms were found to be better able to cope with an ambiguous, rapidly changing environment, their potential for enhanced economic performance increased.

Adaptive cultures need managers who can balance adherence to core values with flexibility in organizational designs and processes. Designs must be flexible. They must be constantly examined for fit with the environment and with each other and for remaining true to the mission and direction of the firm. Leaders in adaptive organizations must promote leadership qualities in others and encourage the establishment of cultures and processes that enable the emergence of leaders at all levels. They must challenge the organization to strive for overall effectiveness, for congruence in design, and for adaptability to meet the competitive challenges ahead. (See Figure 8-6.)

FIGURE 8-6 Summary of principles

Adaptive cultures require:

1. **Managers who can balance core values with flexible organizational designs**

2. **Organizational designs that are flexible**

3. **Designs that "fit" with the environment and the mission of the firm**

4. **Leaders who promote leadership qualities in others**

5. **The establishment of cultures and processes that enable the emergence of leaders at all levels**

CONCLUSION

Organizational leaders at any level can use the design principles presented in this chapter to design and build an organization that operates effectively and efficiently in a business environment characterized by change and uncertainty. Managing the tasks, people, and organizational structures and processes so that they are consistent with each other and with the environment is difficult, but leaders who can do so will develop the adaptive cultures necessary for long-term effectiveness. Constantly monitoring organizational structures and processes can be time-consuming, but the benefits in terms of effectiveness are more than worth the cost.

NOTES

1. David Kirkpatrick, *Fortune*, July 27, 1992, p. 3.

2. David T. Kearns and David A. Nadler, *Prophets in the Dark: How Xerox Reinvented Itself and Beat Back the Japanese* (New York: Harper Collins, 1992), p. ix.

3. Noel Tichy and Ram Charan, "Speed, Simplicity and Self-Confidence: An Interview with Jack Welch," *Harvard Business Review* 1989: pp. 113–120.

4. For a theoretical background of organizational structure see: Henry Minzberg, *Structure in Fives: Designing Effective Organizations* (Englewood Cliffs, NJ: Prentice Hall, 1993).

5. Peter F. Drucker, "The Coming of the New Organization," *Harvard Business Review* July/August 1990: pp. 42–53.

6. Jay Lorsch and John Morse, *Organizations and Their Members* (New York: Harper and Row, 1984), p. 111.

7. Kotter and Sathe (1987).

8. Paul Lawrence and Jay Lorsch, *Organization and Environment* (Boston: Harvard Business School Division of Research, 1967), p. 203.

9.   James Thompson, *Organizations in Action* (New York: McGraw-Hill, 1967).

10.   Larry Greiner, "Evolution and Revolution as Organizations Grow," *Harvard Business Review* July/August 1972: pp. 37–46.

11.   Kearns and Nadler, *Prophets in the Dark*, p. 18.

12.   John P. Kotter and James L. Heskett, *Corporate Culture and Performance* (New York: The Free Press, 1992), pp. 3–12.

13.   Ibid.

14.   Vijay Sathe, *Culture and Related Corporate Realities* (Homewood, IL: Richard D. Irwin, 1985), p. 19.

15.   Tichy and Charan, "Speed, Simplicity and Self-Confidence."

16.   Sathe, *Culture and Related Corporate Realities*.

17.   Kotter and Heskett, *Corporate Culture and Performance*, pp. 94–106.

FOR FURTHER READING

Davis, Stanley, and Lawrence, Paul. *Matrix*. Reading, MA: Addison-Wesley, 1977. A comprehensive overview of the dynamics of matrix organizations.

Drucker, Peter F. "The Coming of the New Organization," *Harvard Business Review* July/August, 1990. A noted management writer predicts future organizational designs.

Galbraith, Jay. *Organization Design*. Reading, MA: Addison-Wesley, 1977.

———. *Designing Complex Organizations*. Reading, MA: Addison-Wesley, 1977. Background to decision making on organizational design issues.

Greiner, Larry. "Evolution and Revolution as Organizations Grow," *Harvard Business Review* July/August 1972. Introduction of the concept of the organizational life cycle.

Kearns, David T., and Nadler, David A. *Prophets in the Dark: How Xerox Reinvented Itself and Beat Back the Japanese*. New York: Harper-Collins, 1992. Story of how Xerox Corporation changed its culture and organizational systems to focus on quality and customer satisfaction.

Kirkpatrick, David. "Breaking Up IBM," *Fortune*, July 27, 1992, 44–58.

Kotter, John P., and Heskett, James L. *Corporate Culture and Performance*. New York: The Free Press, 1992. Analysis of the importance of adaptive organizational cultures. Research and examples of specific companies are cited.

Kotter, John P., and Vijay Sathe. "Problems of Human Resource Management in Rapidly Growing Companies," *California Management Review*, Winter 1987, pp. 29–36.

Lawler, Edward E., III. "Substitutes for Hierarchy," *Organizational Dynamics* Summer 1988. Creative ways to build autonomy into organizational designs.

Lawrence, Paul, Kolodny, Harvey, and Davis, Stanley. "The Human Side of the Matrix," *Organizational Dynamics* Summer 1977. Discussion of the interpersonal dynamics required in matrix organizations.

Lawrence, Paul, and Lorsch, Jay. *Organization and Environment*. Boston: Harvard Business School Division of Research, 1967. Classic research on the relationship between organizations and their environments. Focused on the need to establish ways to integrate different parts of organizations.

Lorsch, Jay, and Morse, John. *Organizations and Their Members.* New York: Harper & Row, 1974. Further discussion of the relationships between organizational design factors in achieving fit.

Miles, Raymond, and Snow, Charles. "Fit, Failure, and the Hall of Fame," *California Management Review* vol. 26, no. 3, 1984. Emphasizes the importance of the notion of fit in organizational designs.

Mintzberg, Henry. *Structure in Fives: Designing Effective Organizations.* Englewood Cliffs, NJ: 1993. Organizational design theory. Detailed information about structural options.

Nadler, David, and Tushman, Michael. *Strategic Organization Design: Concepts, Tools, and Processes.* Glenview, IL: Scott, Foresman, 1988: Practitioner's guide to organizational design issues.

Sathe, Vijay. *Culture and Related Corporate Realities.* Homewood, IL: Richard D. Irwin, 1985. Discussion of the content and elements of organizational culture and its analysis.

Schlesinger, Phyllis, Sathe, Vijay, Schlesinger, Leonard, and Kotter, John. *Organization: Text, Cases, and Readings in the Management of Organizational Design and Change.* 3rd ed. Homewood, IL: Richard D. Irwin, 1992.

Thompson, James. *Organizations in Action.* New York: McGraw-Hill, 1967. Organizational design theory. Organizations and their environments.

Tichy, Noel, and Charan, Ram. "Speed, Simplicity, and Self-Confidence: An Interview with Jack Welch," *Harvard Business Review,* September–October 1989. Welch introduces the changes to be made at the General Electric Company.

Walton, Richard. "A Vision-Led Approach to Management Restructuring," *Organizational Dynamics* Spring 1986. Utilizing management vision to guide restructuring efforts.

———. "From Control to Commitment in the Workplace," *Harvard Business Review* March/April 1985. Gaining employee commitment to organizational designs that stress autonomy and individual responsibility.

Woodward, Joan. *Industrial Organization: Behavior and Control.* London: Oxford University Press, 1970. Organizational design theory.

9 MANAGING HUMAN RESOURCES STRATEGICALLY

Charles J. Fombrun

Drew Harris

In the early 1980s, managers of the Ford Motor Company embarked on a 20-year program of change. The challenge? To stop the flow of red ink and arrest market share erosion: Between 1980 and 1982, the Ford Motor Company had lost over $3 billion, while its U.S. auto market share had dropped from 23 percent to a record low of 16 percent. The dream? To remake Henry Ford's original auto pioneer into a high-quality manufacturer of world class motor vehicles.

Rapidly changing technological, economic, social, and political conditions increasingly demand that firms like Ford, GM, IBM, and other inertial companies strategically alter how they operate: that they grow simultaneously more efficient and entrepreneurial, on the one hand, while becoming more responsive, on the other hand, to institutional pressures to behave more ethically and equitably.

In the last decade, globalization has dramatically increased rivalry and goaded firms to become more *efficient*—to search for ways of reducing costs, enhancing revenues, and improving productivity. Greater efficiency relative to rivals is not only desirable but necessary: It can provide a firm with a distinct advantage by enabling lower product prices and greater marketing and distribution support. Stimulating productivity, however, requires radically different internal systems for monitoring and rewarding human contributions—an organizational challenge that Ford's managers, for instance, are struggling to meet.

252

At the same time, efficiency is difficult to maintain: It is hard to keep squeezing profits from costs for very long. So the pressure to respond to growing rivalry is also forcing managers to attend more carefully to their firms' ability to innovate. Constant technological breakthroughs compel firms to become more *entrepreneurial* in identifying and exploiting new ideas. To gain first-mover advantages, however, requires bypassing traditional hierarchical systems that have long frustrated creativity. Not surprisingly, then, managers in many of our largest firms—firms like Ford—are increasingly looking for ways to encourage *all* employees to add value.

If competition is on the rise due to a global convergence of technologies, economies, and political systems, firms are also experiencing significant institutional intrusions. No longer are governments and outside observers content with managers whose sole interests are economic efficiency, competitiveness, and innovation; they also expect and demand of them moral scrupulousness in corporate initiatives and social responsiveness to the activist concerns of ever more specialized interest groups.

So, falling by the wayside is a long-standing willingness to tolerate dubious conduct by managers; to discount externalities like environmental pollution; to downplay the risks associated with advanced technologies and hazardous by-products. More than ever, managers are called on the carpet by regulators, investors, employees, and outside observers for failing to address adequately the *ethical* underpinnings of what their firms do. And that places pressure on them to develop stronger internal systems for monitoring and encouraging ethical behavior by all employees.

Finally, individuals and groups disenfranchised by old-style conservatism and laissez-faire philosophies have also become more vocal in demanding greater *equity* in corporate schemes that distribute income, perks, and privileges. Awareness of the skewed distribution of these benefits has heightened infighting and now forces greater attention to fairness in the allocation of rewards, be they compensation, promotions, or simply recognition.

So, as contemporary managers contemplate the opportunities open to them, they find themselves more than ever before struggling to respond to contradictory demands for improvements in efficiency, entrepreneurship, equity, and ethics—the four Es of corporate performance. Response to changing environments requires of our companies not only new strategies for competing through quality and innovation but also revolutionary approaches to managing employees that can overcome the obvious limitations of bloated bureaucracies, most evident, perhaps, in the defective products, alienated employees, social injustice, and moral turpitude that now litter the corporate landscape. As Figure 9-1 suggests, these pressures require of managers that they think ever more *strategically* about their most distinctive asset: their human resources.

FIGURE 9-1 How environments affect firms

Environmental Sectors	Pressure on Firms to Improve:	
* Economic	Efficiency	
* Technological	Entrepreneurship	Strategic Human Resource Management
* Social	Equity	
* Political	Ethics	

FORD: MAKING REVOLUTIONARY CHANGES

Consider the Ford Motor Company. Although Ford pioneered many production, technological, and human resource advances in its early days, by the 1970s it had become a stagnant, inwardly focused giant. To Ford employees, entrepreneurship had come to mean infighting for corporate resources and positions rather than innovation. Efficiency meant a short-run outlook to cutting expenses at all cost—all too often encouraging unethical acts. The series of managerial decisions that led to approval of the Pinto, for instance, despite early evidence of its catastrophic potential, not only reflected an unethical posture but proved downright costly to the firm in the long run. Similarly, labor unions like the United Auto Workers opted to fight with management over how to split the company's declining revenues equitably, while all but ignoring the fact that Ford's labor costs now far exceeded those of Ford's global competitors.[1]

By defining its objectives narrowly as efficiency and equity *within* the company, by stifling creativity with bureaucracy and arbitrary cost controls, and by largely ignoring ethical concerns, Ford had lost touch with America. The company's products developed terrible reputations, as witnessed by the unflattering acronyms "Found On Road, Dead" and "Fix Or Repair Daily." Corporate fragmentation and empire-building meant that Ford's departments had grown increasingly insulated from one another. And looking good internally had become more important than making the company look good externally. Not surprisingly, perhaps, the results were disastrous.

So revolutionary change was called for. The company began (1) to involve itself more with its suppliers, customers, and competitors; (2) to make improvements that would simultaneously increase internal efficiency and entrepreneurship; and (3) to develop and meet new norms of external equity and ethics in order to regain its reputation and the confidence of consumers. To achieve these goals would require fundamental alteration of the company's historical relationships to its employees.

Internal change at Ford began under the banner of employee involvement (EI). In the engineering and managerial ranks Ford sought to break down internal walls by creating cross-functional teams that shared the rewards of team outcomes. The company increased its investment in training and development, particularly in statistics, team-building, and other skills needed to improve efficiency and entrepreneurship. Central to the change effort was the inclusion of profit sharing for all employees. By encouraging organizational identification, profit sharing reduced the tendency to parochial decision making. Ford's managers also struggled to restructure their relationship with the UAW. Over time, a more cooperative relationship developed which focused on the common goal of saving jobs by improving competitiveness.

While getting EI off the ground, plant managers and executives had to fend off constant organizational pressure to measure performance. By sheltering employees from immediate pressures for hard results, the company saw a trickle of suggestions turn into a steady stream of ideas for improving efficiency and entrepreneurship. Focusing on long-term commitments enabled alliances to develop among workers and union employees: Everyone participated in creating a new culture and climate that attached value to equitable distribution of rewards and insisted on ethical decisions. As joint efforts proved successful, the effects became self-reinforcing.

Ford has reaped many benefits from these efforts. By 1986 Ford's profits exceeded those of General Motors, the largest car maker in the world. In 1987 and 1988, Ford posted profits that were records in the auto industry. Various car models developed through Ford's system of employee involvement have won national awards for quality and excellence. Indeed, in 1992, the Taurus, built entirely under EI, competed with the Honda Accord as the best-selling car in America, and won.

These benefits came about because Ford's executives understood the power that human resource management systems have to influence behavior, whether to inhibit, encourage, or reinforce a strategic change. And herein lies the essence of strategic human resource management: to use employee-centered policies and practices to reinforce the company's strategic objectives.

WHAT IS STRATEGIC HUMAN RESOURCE MANAGEMENT?

Human resource management (HRM) has evolved from its roots in simple record-keeping into a complex mix of legally mandated and strategically driven programs, traditions, and practices.[2] Modern HRM practices involve four generic activities.

1. *Selection practices:* corporate activities that relate to the movement of people among positions through both promotion and external hiring

2. *Appraisal practices:* feedback systems that examine and measure the different kinds of corporate performance that people deliver

3. *Reward practices:* systems through which employees are recognized and compensated for doing good work

4. *Developmental practices:* various activities that are intended to improve the match between employees' skills and the demands of their jobs

One would imagine that creating consistency between these activities would make them mutually reinforcing, thereby increasing the effectiveness of each. Sadly, many firms do not manage their human resources systematically. Often policies and practices for selecting, appraising, developing, and rewarding employees either accumulate from serendipity and happenstance, or evolve from past practice, from current best practice, or simply from what is currently most fashionable in the industry. So human resource practices seldom come together in such firms: Training programs are frequently ad hoc and do not adequately address skill deficiencies in the labor force, and pay practices are idiosyncratic and more often than not based on particularistic criteria with little support from formal appraisals.

Research suggests that such practices reflect a lack of strategic vision or overarching philosophy, which tends to confuse and demoralize employees and so to impair firms' ability to compete. Well-run firms strive for consistency across their systems and practices and attempt to build greater *coherence* among their key selection, appraisal, development, and reward systems.

Coherence can take many forms. As managers pick and choose how best to handle their companies' human resources—how best to select, appraise, develop, and reward employees—over time, their particular choices shape relatively unique cultural profiles. For instance, some firms adhere to a practice of "hiring the best." Consistent with that philosophy, not only do they recruit aggressively but they are also likely to pay higher starting salaries and to fund intensive training and developmental experiences for new recruits. They anchor their human resource practices around internal promotions and so tend to develop a labor force more committed to staying with their firms. Seldom do they bring outsiders into key positions; instead, they rely principally on an internally staffed and managed labor market. Indeed, to the outside observer, they sometimes resemble closely guarded, seemingly impregnable fortresses. The case of Ford before 1980 comes to mind when thinking of this fortresslike firm, but so do other well-known names, such as IBM, AT&T, and GM.

In contrast, other firms opt for a human resource strategy of "catch as catch can:" They hire as needed, invest little in training and development, and so often appear to treat jobs and positions as revolving doors and incumbents as transients. To outsiders, these firms seem remarkably permeable, aggressively cut-throat, and having only transitional and opportunistic appeal: They are attractive as stepping-stones and training grounds, but no one expects to spend one's career there.[3] The apparel, advertising, electronics, and personal computer industries are populated by firms whose cultures are defined by the transient character of their employee populations.

Managing People Strategically

As anyone who has interacted with a personnel department knows, HRM practices have considerable operational content. They offer detailed advice on how to analyze jobs and recruit suitable candidates; how to assess job performance using rating scales; how to set up compensation programs; and how to design on-site and off-site training programs, among many others.

In changing environments, however, a particularly critical concern is how to use HRM practices more strategically in order to capitalize on the latent potential of firms' human assets. *Strategic Human Resource Management* (SHRM) involves the systematic attempt to link firms' human resource practices and cultural profiles to their competitive strategies in order to help managers secure a relative advantage over rival firms and thereby improve corporate performance. To manage human resources strategically is therefore actively to monitor the correspondence between the human resource practices and the other structural and systematic features of firms. Figure 9-2 illustrates a generic model of how firms manage people strategically.[4]

FIGURE 9-2   Strategic human resource management

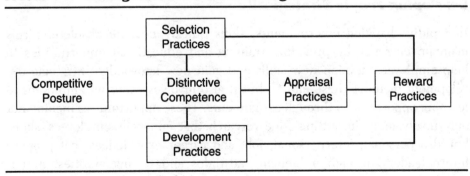

Selecting People Strategically

Most firms hire people to fill current needs. Unfortunately, highly skilled experts who perform well in the specialized jobs required for current needs are the same experts who resist long-term changes that threaten their specialties. When thinking strategically about selection, managers identify the kind of talent that will be needed to operate the firm over the long haul. Strategic recruitment must consider not only the current stock of skills, but how those skills will have to evolve to meet changing environmental conditions over long time spans.

Appraising People Strategically

A generalized fondness for measurement has made appraisal systems widely prevalent in firms. Most of them, however, dwell largely on gauging *past* results: They develop ratings of employees based on the particular contributions they have made relative to others in their department or business unit. In contrast, strategic appraisals insist on gauging potential: They assess employees in terms of their likelihood of making *future* contributions that will prove valuable to their firms.

Rewarding People Strategically

Consistent with the past orientation of appraisal systems, most reward systems are geared to short-run history: Merit raises, promotions, and other opportunities generally accrue to people who become associated with results that have noticeable impact on the bottom line, whether in terms of increased sales or profits. In contrast, rewarding people strategically calls for both monetary and symbolic incentives for employees to engage in activities and produce outcomes that signal progress towards achieving long-term objectives, even when short-run results suffer. In many settings nonmonetary recognition has proved to be a much more strategic and flexible means of motivating performance than pay.

Developing People Strategically

In rapidly changing environments, skills quickly become obsolete. Firms maintain currency by providing training and educational opportunities to help employees develop new skills and gain new knowledge. Strategic development includes these efforts, but it also involves exposing employees to learning opportunities through assignments. These opportunities include not only involvement in cutting-edge research that enhances employees' skills, but also personal, interpersonal, job, and career experiences that prepare future leaders through influencing attitudes and testing abilities. Activities such as mentoring programs build informal linkages between junior and senior colleagues and constitute a means of strategically developing future leaders and preparing succession.

Figure 9-2 also suggests that the strategic management of human assets requires choosing and implementing HRM practices that are consistent with each other and well coordinated. HRM practices that are mutually reinforcing should solidify firms' *distinctive competence*. For instance, an appraisal system that evaluates employees against long-term goals and a compensation system that rewards employees based on those appraisals both send a common message to the employees. In contrast, a human resource strategy that claims that employees are the company's most valuable resource but relies on selection practices that produce frequent layoffs broadcasts conflicting messages and is likely to baffle employees. Consistency across all human resource practices produces clarity about what is expected, what is rewarded, and what is important, and so helps firms capitalize on their distinctive competence vis-à-vis rivals in the industry.

REVISING STRATEGIC POSTURES

Savvy managers rely increasingly on their human resource systems to identify and elicit employee skills, attitudes, and behaviors that will enable them to capitalize on their firms' distinctive competence. Since human resource practices act as cues, stimuli, and reinforcements for employees, to manage strategically requires that managers understand how to improve the link between those practices and the competitive postures of their firms.

In fact, changing environments today are pressuring firms to revise their competitive strategies and to strengthen their particular distinctive competence in order to survive. Within business units, competition and technological change call for greater managerial attentiveness to the quality of goods and services provided to consumers; they also call for an ability to capitalize quickly on new ideas. In reply, managers are trying hard to magnify the features of their firms that differentiate them from rivals and to increase the speed with which they bring products to market.

In the United States, for instance, many companies have introduced programs for continuously improving product quality. But quality proves difficult to achieve in traditionally structured firms full of alienated, frustrated employees. The highly visible Malcolm Baldrige National Quality Awards, given annually since 1987 to firms and divisions most successful in improving quality, have been instrumental in spurring managers to think strategically about their human resource practices. In key business units of companies as diverse as Motorola, General Motors, Westinghouse, Globe Metallurgical, Xerox, Milliken, Federal Express, IBM, Wallace, Solectron, Marlow Industries, and Zytec—all of which won Baldrige Awards between 1987 and

1991[5]—managers have found ways to foster a sense of partnership with their employees born of treating them equitably and ethically. This in turn has led to greater efficiency and entrepreneurship, which the Baldrige Award implicitly recognizes.

In firms with diversified portfolios, managers are systematically pruning businesses in an attempt to develop synergy among related units. Where financial portfolio management techniques once dominated discussions of corporate growth, more than ever managers' conversations revolve around the far more difficult issue of how to benefit from improving relationships among their businesses. To uncover relatedness involves exploring how to build a shared cultural profile across business units that typically have evolved as historically distinct companies. The pruning of portfolios has been under way at prominent companies like General Electric and Occidental Petroleum. Throughout the financial services industry, synergistic consolidation is also evident in the high-visibility mergers of Chemical Bank with Manufacturers Hanover, NCNB with C&S/Sovran, and BankAmerica with Security Pacific.

Finally, the rapid pace of change is also forcing managers to abandon the traditional view of firms as gladiators doing combat single-handedly. Now, many recognize their firms as members of cooperative networks that themselves compete with other networks. Alliances are proliferating as managers recognize the benefits of building close cooperative relationships with suppliers to coordinate product features and delivery timetables. This is perhaps most evident as rivals pool resources to pursue risky projects in biotechnology, software design, and basic research.

Take IBM. Battered by intense competition in every segment of the computer industry, having systematically lost market share throughout the 1980s, the once-mighty computer maker announced in late 1991 that the time had come for a strategic change. The thrust of the transformation? Granting decision-making responsibility and autonomy to all major operating units in order to make them more responsive to market pressures. At the same time, whereas IBM had long been committed to a go-it-alone mentality, since 1990 the company had become involved in a growing number of joint ventures, partnerships, alliances, and consortia with other firms in the computer industry. Most heretically, IBM's Chairman John Akers warned ominously that the old paternalistic culture that virtually guaranteed lifetime employment would be incompatible with IBM's new competitive posture and would be chucked.

Figure 9-3 contrasts two types of competitive posture, the old *fortress posture*, which once typified the internal practices managers relied upon to carry out their competitive strategies, and the newer *federated posture*, which many firms now find themselves actively pursuing. As the figure suggests, each strategic thrust implies a distinct cultural profile and so a distinct

FIGURE 9-3 Corporate profiles: fortress and federated competitive postures

Fortress Posture	Federated Posture
Volume-Oriented	Quality-Oriented
Hierarchical	Egalitarian
Standardized	Customized
Specialized	Team-Oriented
Focused on Finance	Focused on Product
Portfolio-Constructing	Synergy-Creating
Doing Everything In-House	Forging Alliances
Building Walls	Breaking Down Boundaries

human resource strategy. The challenge managers face today lies not simply in matching human resource practices for selecting, appraising, developing, and rewarding employees to existing competitive postures, but in having the human resource systems of old-line fortress companies embrace the more vigorous federated posture, which is proving to be more appropriate to the rapidly changing, global corporate environment of the late twentieth century.

Changing From a Fortress to a Federated Form

Most of our large corporate entities grew up in environments that encouraged them to pursue growth through arm's-length competition. Once hired, managers were expected to devote themselves to their firms, becoming "company men" much as vassals once pledged loyalty to their feudal lords. Historical studies tell us that these firms grew first by buying rivals and consolidating production for larger markets, then by vertically integrating into sources of supply, and finally by buying businesses selling unrelated products in order to diversify the riskiness of operating in a single domain.

The net result of this growth sequence was the large leviathan companies that have become household names, firms like Dupont, General Motors, IBM, Exxon, and General Electric. They operated as *fortresses*, building ever stronger boundaries designed to insulate them from the vagaries of the environment. Growth by the absorption of rivals required strong internal systems of control, and most of those firms adopted bureaucratic practices that featured rigid supervisory hierarchies and strong internal cultures supporting lifetime employment.

As they became fortresses to outside forces their fortress mentality spread to internal activities. As in the Ford case at the beginning of this chapter, departments isolated themselves from each other, refusing to communicate and cooperate for the good of the firm. At Ford, these internal fortresses were even unofficially labeled "chimneys." Once inside the finance, marketing, engineering, or production chimney employees only looked up and moved up within the chimney; no personal gain could come from cooperating with someone from outside the chimney. And Ford was not alone in this mentality.

It is to the early administrative experiments of these behemoth firms that we owe the corpus of HRM practices that prevail today in corporate America. From them we learn how to design firms through job specialization and line assembly, payment for performance, on-the-job training, and development of employees by their promotion into supervisory positions, and on up the ladder of success. Jointly these practices constitute the essence of the fortress posture so familiar to employees of contemporary large firms.

Change, however, is clearly in the wind. The growing pressure on firms to commit themselves to the simultaneous pursuit of efficiency, entrepreneurship, equity, and ethics is challenging the effectiveness of the fortress posture. Leading firms are striving for a more flexible strategic posture, one that relies less on volume and more on quality; less on standardizing products and more on customizing them to consumers' needs; less on diversifying risk and more on building synergies; less on outright rivalry, and more on cooperative alliances with rivals.

Internally, the change in strategic posture translates into a revolution in the way employees relate to firms, a shift from the strong hierarchies prevalent in fortress firms toward a more egalitarian teamwork; away from the conventional internal careerism of fortress firms toward a view of employees as temporary participants in interfirm networks that convey skills, knowledge, and information across industries.

The result? As firms struggle to shift from their status as impermeable fortresses to a more federated strategic posture, they invite a revolutionary transformation in the way human assets are regarded and managed. At Ford they began dismantling their fortress mentality by creating new product teams that spanned the boundaries of the old chimneys. These teams were reinforced by tying compensation to team outcomes. No longer could employees in the finance chimney count on their hierarchy for reward and protection; they had to count on members of other chimneys. As Ford changed its internal view so too its employees found themselves viewing their external relationships differently.

Another example comes from Solectron, the 1991 winner of the Malcolm Baldrige National Quality Award. The company specializes in the assembly of complex printed-circuit boards, personal computers, and other subsystems for makers of computers and other electronics products. Solectron's managers attribute the 15-year-old firm's rise to its rank of second in the industry to the adoption of various features of the federated posture, in particular competing on the basis of quality and costs; establishing a strong internal culture that supports teamwork, employee involvement, and continuous process improvements; forging strong ties to upstream suppliers, which managers describe as "partners" in the pursuit of quality; and providing strong support to its downstream customers. Consequently, in addition to the Baldrige Award, Solectron has also won a total of 37 superior performance awards in the last ten years and is systematically rated by customers as being among the best contract manufacturers of electronic assemblies in the United States. Firms like Solectron epitomize an increasingly attractive competitive posture that requires a human resource strategy different from that found in more traditional fortress firms.

GENERIC HUMAN RESOURCE STRATEGIES

Firms that want to change their strategy must realign their human resource practices in order to elicit new behaviors and attitudes from their employees. These shifts crystallize through new strategies for selecting, appraising, rewarding, and developing employees. The contrast between the archetypical fortress and federated strategies demonstrates the range of choices available for managing human resources strategically.[6]

Selection Strategies

A firm's selection strategy articulates the core philosophy that permeates its human resource practices. Figure 9-4 outlines the major differences in staffing choices between the older fortress and the increasingly popular federated corporate postures.

FIGURE 9-4   Selection Strategies

Fortress Firm	Federated Firm
Internal	External
Explicit, Structured	Flexible, Informal
Long-Term	Short-Term

The typical fortress firm has long been driven by a concern with predictability and stability. It relies on formal and structured procedures for recruiting people into jobs. A fortress-type hiring plan generally involves explicit job analysis—clear task descriptions written to convey duties and processes along with the knowledge, skills, and abilities required to do the job.

Explicit descriptions facilitate job rotation and so help build the employees' commitment to the whole company. Fortress managers have tended often to involve employees in preparing their own job descriptions to further enhance understanding and plant the seed for longevity and loyalty to the firm.

Governed as they are by long-term planning, job analysis, and an internal orientation, over time fortress firms naturally tend to become internal labor markets. They tend to limit options for entry level jobs and are committed to providing training and career development opportunities to ensure higher performance. Notable fortress companies such as IBM, UPS, McDonald's, and Procter & Gamble insist that their promotion-from-within policies are the key to their publicized success in meeting environmental pressures that demand both efficiency and innovation.

Nonetheless, because they make their promotion criteria more explicit, the promotion system in fortress firms is generally less adaptable to exceptions and changing circumstances: They swap individual flexibility for gains in clarity, and although they provide many broad paths of promotion, those paths are predefined and slow-moving.

In contrast, the federated posture demands and provides greater flexibility. Jobs are defined as needs or opportunities arise. Since jobs are temporary, incumbents are transient, and employee commitment is naturally more limited. So the staffing challenge in the federated firm involves learning to manage cosmopolitan employees, people whose involvement with the job, the project, or even the firm is likely to be ephemeral.

Given the likelihood of frequent change, heavy emphasis is placed on recruiting the "right" individuals, those with uniquely appropriate and timely knowledge, skills, and abilities. Naturally, then, federated firms tend to spend little time on developing job descriptions, recognizing that such analyses quickly become obsolete. Because timeliness is of the essence, federated firms naturally favor recruiting both internally and externally at all levels. Lacking specific promotion criteria, federated firms enjoy greater flexibility in moving employees around, and quickly adapt to changing environments. A federated firm like Microsoft contends that hiring the best employee into whatever job is available later ensures they will have on hand the best for whatever unexpected questions need answering.

Finally, in both fortress and federated firms, the historic practice of screening applicants based on academic performance, references, and single interviews is giving way to more strategic procedures directly linked to the work itself. In production environments, for instance, managers rely more on work samples, aptitude tests, and simulations to get a preview of how the applicant will fit into the firm. In the service sector, in white collar positions, and in other ill-defined jobs, managers are increasingly using psychological testing, group interviews, simulations, and stress tests to derive clues about candidates' personality, creativity, and general disposition.

Developmental Strategies

Once hired, socialization programs play important functions in subsequent staffing. Through *training* activities, firms prepare employees to fulfill immediate job requirements; through *developmental* programs, they equip employees to meet future challenges. Firms differ in their mix of training and developmental practices.

Figure 9-5 suggests how training and developmental activities vary among fortress and federated strategies. The fortress posture inclines toward longer-term, developmental activities while the federated posture favors shorter-term training with developmental responsibilities left largely to the employees, who are expected to manage their own careers as they move between positions and firms.

Fortress firms establish careful procedures to immerse individuals entirely in their local cultures. During training programs and through a wide range of informal activities, core competencies and values are carefully communicated to all employees. As they become well understood and as common standards are internalized, fewer direct controls prove necessary: Employees learn that "this is the way things are done around here." Fortress firms like IBM, for instance, place a strong emphasis on structured programs to get new hires to think and behave the IBM way.

Training improves employees' skills and enables employees to learn skills that could prove relevant for other jobs in the organization. Fortress firms

FIGURE 9-5   Developmental Strategies

Fortress Firm	Federated Firm
Long-Term	Short-Term
Focused on Employee Growth	Focused on Task Accomplishment
Systematic	Spontaneous
Firm-Directed	Employee-Initiated

rely on this kind of cross-training to develop their internal promotion ladders. They tend to emphasize planned, formal development, and often stimulate employee development through programs that support formal education, executive and management development, continuing professional education, and outward-bound experiences. These activities are intended, not only to build abilities but also to encourage trust and team work.

In contrast, the fluid needs of the federated firm call for a capacity to train personnel in quick response as needs arise. Because of the flexible and transient nature of positions in the federated firm, training is done on the job and focuses on immediate needs. Development, however, is often more strategically tied to productivity improvement programs that encompass statistical methods, quality management, and other directly applicable skills.

Appraisal Strategies

Traditional appraisal programs try to fulfill three key purposes: (1) to establish a link between job characteristics and appraisal criteria; (2) to gather and combine various sources of performance data; and (3) to use appraisal results to reward and develop employees strategically.

Unfortunately, most appraisal systems fail to meet these objectives and are fundamentally flawed. First, few firms can claim to use them strategically.[7] Seldom are appraisals used systematically to reward employees, a failing that noticeably induces mistrust and anger among employees who wonder how rewards are distributed. In most firms the tension around appraisal reviews is palpable: Productive activity gives way to speculation, anticipation, and political maneuvering before the appraisal. After the appraisal, often employees are left angry, confused, and disaffected. Thus it is not surprising that performance reviews have been cited as the root cause of litigation and even murders in the work place: Clearly employees take their performance reviews to heart, and it is important that managers do them right.

Second, appraisal programs are often flawed in actually measuring employee performance. Employees rarely control most, much less all, of the variables affecting performance. In production, for instance, product design, materials, procedures, machinery, and the work environment heavily influence output. Ascribing to employees full responsibility for their performance in such settings often leads to a feeling of inequity, a sense that managers are capricious. When coupled with "performance-based pay," these appraisals tend to leave employees disaffected, discouraging performance and, in extreme cases, fostering sabotage.

Leaders in the movement to improve quality have recently suggested that appraising performance only fulfills a punitive role and should cease. In its place, they propose that firms should substitute development programs that review *system performance,* discuss the role of the employee in the system, and stimulate ideas for improving the system—a format more compatible with the awareness of interdependence fostered by federated firms.

Figure 9-6 suggests that fortress firms tend to specify in advance what outcomes are expected and then assign responsibility for those outcomes to specific individuals. In contrast, the recognition that system outcomes dominate individual efforts has led many federated firms to review employee performance in terms of the entire system in which they work. In the federated firm, the stress is placed on process: how things are done rather than how many things are done. Managers increasingly abandon traditional management by objectives (MBO) in favor of shared discussion about the collective process.

In fact, most firms employing quality improvement strategies now try to develop close coordination with suppliers and customers. Employees in these federated firms must form partnerships upstream and downstream as part of their work. Therefore, to assess the entire process, a firm might require multiple appraisers rather than the one who would assess an individual employee's performance.

Reward Strategies

Reward systems typically fulfill two key purposes: *Recognizing* past performance and *encouraging* future performance. Most reward systems are heavily biased towards monetary rewards. Increasingly, however, managers are coming to realize the value of symbolic rewards like recognition programs, lateral promotions, and nonwork assignments as powerful motivators.

Fortress firms tend to rely heavily on steady pay with many perks and benefits to motivate and bind employees. By contrast, federated firms often offer cash or cash-equivalent incentives to motivate employees and to focus on achievement of short-term (less than 12 months) goals.

Figure 9-7 shows how fortress and federated firms vary in other ways. In keeping with their internal orientation, most fortress firms try to balance compensation among equivalent employees. The traditional hierarchical

FIGURE 9-6 Appraisal Strategies

Fortress Firm	Federated Firm
Measuring Behavior	Measuring Results
Focused on the Individual	Focused on the Team
Supervisory	Participative

FIGURE 9-7 Reward Strategies

Fortress Firm	Federated Firm
Measure Behavior	Measure Results
Encourage Internal Equity	Emphasize External Equity
Give Security and Perks	Give Monetary Incentives

character of the fortress firm is typically reflected in hierarchical compensation differences between levels. The firm provides employees with a large variety of perquisites and indirect compensation that closely correspond to the hierarchy. With perks come close participation in compensation decisions and a tendency toward standardized packages. These hierarchically driven practices are largely patriarchal: They provide high employment security and few incentives that would prompt long-term changes.

By contrast, federated firms tend to vary the mix and value of key components in the total compensation package. They rely more often on flexible pay programs, cafeteria benefits plans, and a variety of other incentives to recognize and encourage performance. Since they hire as needed, federated firms tend to maintain external parity, paying what the market will bear at any point in time. Consequently, they tend to give up pay secrecy, one of the hallmarks of fortress firms.

Increasingly, fortress firms have begun offering incentive stock options (ISOs) or stock appreciation rights (SARs) to reward the entrepreneurial efforts of their employees. By providing employees with a vehicle for building personal wealth while still remaining under the corporate umbrella, fortress managers are clearly using reward systems to energize their firms' strategic transformation toward a more federated posture.

RECASTING HUMAN RESOURCE PRACTICES

Ultimately, HRM practices act to stimulate employees and to enhance corporate performance. Managers today are increasingly relying on HRM programs to stimulate their firms to higher levels of efficiency and entrepreneurship, while simultaneously ensuring a commitment to equitable and ethical behavior.

Encouraging Efficiency

Environmental pressures to enhance efficiency and competitiveness are forcing managers to find ways of improving productivity. Psychologists tell us that productivity is heavily influenced by employees' ability and effort. Employees' abilities depend on skills developed through education and training. However, the amount of effort they devote to their work hinges on their firm's compensation practices, the expectation that they can be successful and that they will be treated fairly, and a host of other factors. In changing environments, managers therefore cultivate productivity by investing more heavily in training programs and trying to create a complete environment where individuals want to contribute.

Efforts to improve employees' skills are increasingly evident as firms struggle to adapt to rapidly evolving technologies. High-tech systems are taking over in the office, the plant, and at the cash register, requiring more sophisticated skills from operators. Where typing and shorthand were once the principal skills expected of office workers, now they must show mastery of complex software packages for word processing, graphics, and spreadsheets. Where assembly lines once broke tasks into repetitive routines, reducing the skill necessary for doing the work, increasingly manufacturing environments require workers to interface with robots and computers, thus requiring more skillful and alert personnel. To prepare employees and improve productivity, managers are forced to devote more resources to tooling and retooling employees.

A popular view holds that to make firms more productive requires that managers compensate according to employees' individual contributions rather than according to seniority and loyalty.[8] To pay for performance, however, requires appraisal systems capable of distinguishing among individuals whose results often depend on other team members. Evaluation calls for subjective assessments by superiors, thereby opening the door to political bias and favoritism, and provoking anger, resentment, and cynicism among employees who feel they have been unjustly rated.

Making individual distinctions also fosters rivalry. As conflicts escalate, pitting employees, departments, and divisions against each other, firms are finding that merit pay systems discourage cooperation and dampen corporate performance—an outcome that directly contradicts the strategic objective of enhancing company-wide integration.

To counter the potentially negative consequences of merit pay but encourage productivity, many firms are inducing employees to identify with company-wide performance by creating profit-sharing plans. Senior executives have long benefitted from bonuses tied to corporate profits. In *The Share Economy,* economist Martin Weitzman proposed that we extend the opportunity to more employees. Paying employees on the basis of corporate profits, he argued, would eliminate built-in pressures that push up costs and dampen productivity.

A variety of such gain-sharing plans—the best known of which are the Scanlon Plan and the Rucker Plan—involve employees in cost-cutting and quality improvement and distribute financial gains monthly to all participating employees. One analysis of 33 such plans found that they occurred in both union and nonunion settings and in small, medium, and large firms, though predominantly in manufacturing plants. Most firms experimenting with gain sharing, in fact, consistently report productivity improvements.[9] These successes suggest that the productivity gains from profit sharing may result partly from increased involvement in decision making, partly from the financial incentive, and partly from greater perceived equity within firms.

Finally, managers concerned about improving corporate efficiency also tend to manipulate the training and reward systems to encourage employee productivity at three levels: (1) individual productivity; (2) business unit productivity; and (3) companywide productivity. To meet these objectives requires a complex training program that builds technical, administrative, and communication skills. It also requires a stratified reward system that supports individual performance through merit pay, business unit performance through profit-sharing bonuses, and corporate performance through ownership proxies such as stock options.

Stimulating Entrepreneurship

In her popular book *The Change Masters*, Harvard professor Rosabeth Kanter studied how large firms innovate.[10] Not surprisingly, she found that firms that routinely smothered innovations had segmentalist cultures, while innovative firms solved problems in an integrative fashion. With specialists in charge of projects, segmentalist firms compartmentalize ideas, reducing their probability of success. With a team orientation, employees of integrative firms share a family feeling that values individual initiatives, encourages involvement of middle managers, and equalizes power among all employees.

Kanter's subsequent book *When Giants Learn to Dance* explained in greater detail how some large firms are dismantling bureaucratic processes to become more nimble in a competitive environment. These firms explore ways to induce synergy among individuals inside business units, across divisions within portfolios, and through complementary alliances with stakeholders.

Other observers also join in championing the importance of building within firms' structures a systematic process for self-renewal. Recognizing that companies easily succumb to advanced sclerosis due to inertia induced by prior successes, managers are advised to promote human resource practices that favor innovation. A study of 100 senior electronics executives involved in product development found multiple themes to characterize innovative firms, in particular a core competency around which R&D could focus, extensive cooperation among employees, and an entrepreneurial culture. Key features of entrepreneurial cultures were the breakup of large bureaucracies into small divisions, a tolerance for failure that encouraged employees to take risks, and time to pursue outside projects.[11]

A detailed examination of one large high-tech firm found successful innovation to be heavily influenced by managers' willingness to build into their planning processes an "autonomous loop" for new venture development. Rather than completely decouple new ventures by isolating them in separate divisions, more successful entrepreneurial firms encourage employees through systems that reward not only problem solving, but also the finding of problems and the development of know-how.[12]

Since 1981, GE's maverick chairman, Jack Welch, has been systematically breaking up and decentralizing its 150 businesses in order to increase corporate responsiveness to competition and make the firm more entrepreneurial.[13] In 1989, Welch created the position of productivity czar to back him up in preaching the gospel of productivity throughout the 271,000 person firm. Similarly, General Motors's joint venture with Toyota and its launching of the Saturn plant constitute attempts to rekindle an entrepreneurial spirit at the outer periphery of its old-line bureaucracy.

Another example of a company struggling to establish and maintain a culture that prizes innovation is the NutraSweet Company, a subsidiary of G.D. Searle, itself acquired by chemical giant Monsanto in 1985. Dependent on a patent for aspartame, better known as NutraSweet, that expired in 1992, for some time the company has been actively researching innovative products (the latest in line is Simplesse, the fat substitute). One observer characterized the NutraSweet culture as "intensely focused" on the start-up's mentality of creativity and market positioning. As rivals rob the company of market share in the years ahead, NutraSweet's managers will face a dual threat: On the one hand, they ask, how can they become the low-cost producer of aspartame when their culture drives innovation? On the other hand, can they remain innovative if they become cost-conscious?[14]

Promoting Equity

Changing environments have also called managers' attention to the inequities created by the skewed distribution of bonuses, promotions, and power among employees in fortress firms. The widely publicized golden parachutes that enriched senior executives during corporate restructurings, the "greenmail" collected by maverick raiders, and the large bonuses paid to incumbent managements alienated employees and reduced productivity throughout the 1980s. Why work hard if all the gains produced by the many only go to the few?

Managers seeking to improve their firms' innovativeness and break down old cultural barriers try to generate more internal risk-taking. But when faced with risk-taking, employees often feel squeezed in a vise between large, often implicit penalties for failure and meager individual rewards for success while patents and commercialization of innovations generally mean large returns for firms. Employees view both outcomes as unfair. To address inequity, many firms seeking to encourage innovation have offered idea generators the opportunity to share in the returns from commercializing their ideas.

AT&T is a case in point. To encourage innovation, the company offers new venture participants different pay options. Under the most conservative plan, new venture employees remain at their AT&T salaries pegged to existing job grades. A more risky option, selected by most of the participants to date, freezes salaries at the level of their last job until the ventures shows a positive cash flow, at which point venture participants are eligible for a one-time bonus of up to 150 percent of their salary. The final option, favored by risk-takers, allows venture participants to invest 10 to 15 percent of their salaries in the venture, in return for payoffs of up to eight times their investment.[15]

At the new Du Pont-Merck Pharmaceutical Company, a joint venture funded by the two titans Du Pont and Merck, key researchers are given stock options for work that leads to products. Scientists advance in pay and status without having to leave the lab and take management jobs. The focus on fairness extends to the relationship between the two parent companies: Top executives of both parents sit on the board of the joint venture and match payoffs to each side's contributions.

Equity issues are also becoming more salient as firms brace for increased global competition. Large disparities in the incomes earned by managers and employees are likely to grow less tolerable in environments of slow growth. Implementing strategic change tends to be far easier in corporate environments whose managers are recognized for distributing both gains and losses equitably among groups and levels.

Endorsing Ethics

Institutional pressures are compelling managers to make their firms conform to commonly accepted ethical principles, and to incorporate them into their reward, education, and socialization programs. Impelled by cases of improper political contributions, illegal payments to foreign governments, insider trading, and espionage, U.S. companies increasingly spell out their codes of conduct explicitly. A study of 100 large firms by The Business Roundtable in 1988 suggested that "many executives believe that a culture in which ethical concern permeates the whole organization is necessary to the self-interest of the company."

As mentioned in Chapter 8 ("Designing Effective Organizations," by Phyllis F. and Leonard A. Schlesinger), during the two incidents of Tylenol poisonings, Johnson & Johnson's 40-year-old Credo—its statement of beliefs about the company's relationships to its customers, employees, shareholders, and community—was frequently credited for guiding the company's exemplary behavior. As chairman James Burke has often remarked, "The Credo is the unifying force for our corporation. It guides us in everything we do. It represents an attempt to codify what we can all agree upon since we have highly independent managers."

To communicate these values, top managers of Johnson & Johnson have held regular Credo Challenge Meetings since 1975 to explore managers' understanding of the principles it sets forth, and to explore its relevance to their businesses. In 1986, Johnson & Johnson began an annual Credo Survey to assess how well employees perceive the firm to be doing. Profiles are fed back to departments and reviewed by the executive committee.

In the wake of environmental disasters and criminal prosecution, many visionary executives have developed similar codes of conduct and sought to turn them into living documents by emphasizing those principles in all their communications to employees. Chemical Bank relies on a Corporate Values Seminar to underscore the firm's commitment to corporate social responsibility. At Norton, an Ethics Committee of its board of directors conducts an annual Ethics Review to ensure that ethical standards are adhered to domestically and abroad.

A number of companies also have set up full-fledged ethics offices: Dow Corning has had one since 1976 and Texas Instruments since 1987. Since General Dynamics staffed its ethics office with three employees in 1985, it has dealt with over 6000 contacts by employees. While these offices signal the importance of ethics throughout the firm, they sometimes also convey a mistrustful aura: Many regard them as "snitchlines," with all the pejorative connotations associated with whistleblowing. They potentially function as systems for punishing transgressions rather than systems for rewarding ethical behavior. The danger of this is that good behavior is not internalized and that employees simply become more cautious in their trespasses.

Currently under review in the U.S. Congress is a set of guidelines for sentencing corporations and other organizations like labor unions, trade associations, government agencies, and pension funds convicted of Federal criminal offenses like fraud, theft, or antitrust violations. Under the proposal, hundreds of millions of dollars in fines could be levied by judges. Fines would depend partly on how much effort the organization had made to prevent or detect illegal activities through in-house education and monitoring systems. This clearly provides added impetus for executives to build ethical cultures.

Few ethical guidelines, however, are likely to prove more beneficial than IBM's famous "sunshine test," a rule that simply requires asking of any action whether it can be fully disclosed without embarrassment. Not insider trading, influence peddling by government lobbyists, nor bribery of officials—the most common of our recent corporate scandals—would have stood up to the full light of day.

MANAGING CONTRADICTIONS

As fortress firms adopt elements of more federated postures, they face significant managerial dilemmas. Contradictions abound between stimulating efficiency and entrepreneurship, while supporting equity and ethics in firms' activities. Resolving these contradictions is a key challenge that managers face as they struggle to tap the latent pool of human talent within their firms.

Among the human resource systems, for instance, appraisals and compensation are especially tricky activities to balance. Although considerable effort has been expended in designing elaborate appraisal systems to address equity considerations, seldom do appraisal systems assess the ethical aspects of employee performance, nor do they address how ethics should be weighted against efficiency and entrepreneurship in compensating performance. The record suggests that despite the widespread publicity accorded Drexel's demise and Michael Milken's imprisonment, insider trading continues to occur throughout the financial services community. Clearly we have not yet mastered the means for maintaining balance between ethics and efficiency on Wall Street.

But the problem does not stop at Wall Street. Dow Corning has long had a formal program to reinforce the notion that highly ethical decisions are good business decisions. However, despite being in the forefront of introducing ethical considerations, the recent publicity surrounding Dow Corning's silicone breast implants suggests that the company and its managers may well have crossed the line. While no firm has come up with definitive answers, most leading-edge companies, like Johnson & Johnson, IBM, and Hewlett-Packard, contend that training in recognizing ethical questions and making them a standard part of business decision making can improve the ethical behavior of firms.

Balancing Internal and External Equity

While fortress firms emphasize internal equity in hiring, promotion, and compensation, their inward focus often leaves them at odds with the outside world. Sometimes internal pay levels lag the market, and compression results: Longtime employees are paid less than new ones. At other times, internal promotions raise pay levels higher than what the market would pay for comparable skill levels. The disparity is difficult to resolve as managers struggle to recast their firms and improve their competitiveness.

By their openness and flexibility, federated firms sometimes face great disparities in pay among employees brought in from the outside. Differences among allied firms participating in joint ventures and other alliances can create tension within participating firms, leading to dissent and unwanted turnover. Compensation compression leads to concerns for internal equity, while wage escalation threatens the firm's cost-competitiveness and efficiency.

Balancing Efficiency and Entrepreneurship

Fortress firms often stress the benefits of efficiency at the expense of entrepreneurship. Long-term planning, explicit job analysis, and structured systems try to encourage efficiency in finding employees and getting them to work quickly and productively. Fostering entrepreneurship in such a structured environment becomes difficult at best. Similarly, federated firms tend to promote entrepreneurship by hiring externally to import new ideas. However, new employees take time to train, and lost time generally means a temporary loss of efficiency.

Balancing Efficiency and Equity

In managing the selection and development activities, fortress firms work hard to maintain equity among all employees by making procedures explicit and systematic. Unfortunately, bureaucracy generally results, and the procedures become cumbersome and costly in terms of line managers' time. Fortress firms typically absorb the efficiency loss of maintaining equity because they want a long-term relationship with their employees. Federated firms, however, typically do away with these procedures and allow efficiency to overrule concerns for equity.

Balancing Efficiency and Ethics

In both fortress and federated firms, ethical considerations often stand starkly opposed to efficiency concerns. Consumers and other corporate stakeholders demand that firms pay greater attention to environment-friendly waste reduction, energy efficiency, recycling, and incineration. Although incorporating social costs into firms' decision-making practices is ethical, doing so is costly and potentially damaging to firms' competitive positions. Managers increasingly struggle with balancing the demands that they behave socially responsibly and remain competitive and profitable.

Firms that use short-term incentives to reward performance find that employees will often push and even distort the normal processing of the entire system in order to produce a short-term result. When this happens the firm almost always suffers. Some typical problems include the foregoing of maintenance, commitments by sales people that the firm cannot meet (resulting in poor customer relations), shipment of defective products, and the falsification of records.

Finally, contradictions appear when firms shutter plants and lay off low-level employees while executives take home huge incentive pay for "reducing costs." Issues like these illustrate how pervasive the contradictions are as managers struggle to maintain a competitive posture that tries to balance the four Es of corporate performance: efficiency, entrepreneurship, equity, and ethics. Choosing and maintaining effective human resource programs is clearly not a trivial issue.

CONCLUSION

As the many stakeholders of firms demand greater efficiency, equity, entrepreneurship, and ethics, managers must find better ways to balance these contradictory demands. Increasingly, fortress firms are adopting federated policies, while federated firms are adopting fortress practices to capitalize on their respective advantages and overcome fundamental weaknesses. The large modern company appears to be evolving toward a core-periphery structure in which the core retains characteristics of the familiar fortress posture and a transient periphery operation is run like a federated firm and is grafted onto the core.

New models of this sort are only now emerging. General Electric, under Jack Welch, has shifted from a traditional fortresslike posture toward a more federated posture. They have pruned their operations to a core set of businesses in which they can be either the number 1 or number 2 producer in the world. Around this core they have built a network of linked suppliers, customers, and allied firms. Because they focus outward they improve external equity against their historically strong internal equity. To establish synergy and develop managers, they move employees between divisions; this too helps balance equity within the firm.

Since the late 1980s GE has provided widespread employee stock options. Typically, over eight thousand employees a year receive options. This encourages entrepreneurship while balancing hierarchical equity. So-called Work-Out teams help improve efficiency by reducing waste and improving productivity. Outside facilitators help ensure that employees who work themselves out of jobs are treated fairly by the company either by placement elsewhere in the firm or by placement outside the firm. Chairman Jack Welch claims that these programs work; the employees feel they have been treated ethically and equitably.[16]

The new direction toward which many firms now tend therefore focuses on building a core set of competencies, which are treated with fortresslike reverence, and a surrounding federated-style set of relationships with customers, suppliers, and other outside groups. The federated periphery forces attention to issues of external equity and ethics, overcoming some of the historical parochialism of the traditional fortress posture. At the same time, continued commitment to a core competency enables the firm to place more emphasis on stability, efficiency, and long-term growth than the pure federated posture would make possible. In the core-periphery configuration, a greater degree of employee ownership obtains. Closer links to customers and suppliers increase opportunities for venturing internally and externally and thereby stimulate entrepreneurship.

Changing to a core-periphery posture requires dedicated effort. As the ongoing transformation of Ford Motor Company indicates, the struggle to combine an old-line fortress posture with a more open federated posture heavily dependent on continual quality improvement is a massive one. Ford's managers expect that a full generation of employees will pass through the company before the corporate culture can change and before the company can fully realize the fruits of its new strategy.

As companies like General Electric, Ford, and IBM struggle to adapt to rapidly changing environments, they find themselves forced to carry out wrenching revisions of thir internal HRM practices, programs, and structures. Changes in strategic posture call for new kinds of skills, new ways of motivating employees, and new psychological contracts. The challenge managers will face in coming years is to strike a balance between human resource practices that drive efficiency and entrepreneurship, and programs that ensure ethical behavior and equitable outcomes for employees.

NOTES

1. Since then those costs have been largely equalized between U.S. automakers and their European and Asian competitors. The emergence of the North America Free Trade Agreement signals a new era of concern for how to treat U.S. employees equitably as jobs migrate to low-wage Mexico.

2. James Baron, Frank Dobbin, and P. Devereaux Jennings provide an interesting and fairly detailed interpretation of the history of human resource systems in "War and Peace: The Evolution of Modern Personnel Administration in U.S. Industry," *American Journal of Sociology*, 92(2): 350–383 (1986).

3. The original contrast between internal and external labor markets was made in Peter Doeringer and Michael Piore, *Internal Labor Markets and Manpower Analysis* (Lexington, MA: D.C. Heath, 1971).

4. The model is adapted from Charles Fombrun, M. A. Devanna, and Noel Tichy, *Strategic Human Resource Management* (New York: John Wiley & Sons, 1984).

5. David Garvin describes the pros and cons of the Baldrige Award process in his article "How the Baldrige Award Really Works," *Harvard Business Review,* November–December 1991: pp. 80–95.

6. The menu of choices between competing strategies is adapted from Randall Schuler and Drew L. Harris, *Managing Quality: A Primer for Middle Managers* (Reading, MA: Addison-Wesley, 1992), pp. 109–136.

7. Edward E. Lawler provided an early and extensive review of the problems of appraisal and reward systems in "Control Systems in Organizations," *Handbook of Industrial and Organizational Psychology* ed. Marvin D. Dunnette (Chicago: Rand McNally, 1976), pp. 1247–1292. Follow-up on improved methods of appraising and rewarding can be found in Lawler's "The New Plant Approach: A Second Generation Approach," *Organizational Dynamics,* Winter 1991, pp. 5–15.

8. Cf. R. M. Kanter, "The Attack on Pay," *Harvard Business Review,* March–April 1987: pp. 60–67.

9. Lawler (1991), cited in note 7, above, reviews incentives for building a sense of ownership and involvement in firms.

10. Rosabeth Moss Kanter, *The Change Masters* (New York: Simon & Schuster, 1983).

11. See M.A. Maidique and R.H. Hayes, "The Art of High-Technology Management," *Sloan Management Review,* Winter 1984: pp. 17–31.

12. Cf. R. Burgelman (1983) "A Process Model of Internal Corporate Venturing in the Diversified Major Firm," *Administrative Science Quarterly,* 28: pp. 223–242.

13. Cf. Noel Tichy and Ram Charan, "Speed, Simplicity, Self-Confidence," *Harvard Business Review,* September–October 1989: pp. 112–120.

14. Cf. Joseph McCann, *Sweet Success: How NutraSweet Created a Billion Dollar Business* (New York: Business One/Irwin, 1990).

15. The details of this joint venture were presented in Rosabeth Moss Kanter, *When Giants Learn to Dance* (New York: Simon & Schuster, 1989), pp. 257–259.

16. See interview by Noel Tichy and Ram Charan, "Speed, Simplicity, Self-Confidence," *Harvard Business Review,* September–October 1989, pp. 112–120.

10 SELF-MANAGING TEAMS: THE NEW ORGANIZATION OF WORK

Harvey Kolodny

Torbjorn Stjernberg

INTRODUCTION

The assumptions about external stability that have dominated our work-places since the turn of the century have resulted in hierarchically structured organizations with limited ability to adapt and change. The widespread adoption of team-based organization is an indication that these assumptions are rapidly being abandoned. Team-based work arrangements are becoming the fundamental unit of design in organizations. They are replacing the boss-employee pair that has served as the traditional building block in organizations.

The extent to which team-based work organization is being accepted, in particular the self-managing teams we refer to in this chapter, is a sign that a genuine revolution is taking place in the way work is organized. These team-based arrangements are at the leading edge of change to the basic structures of contemporary work organizations, which is making organizations leaner, more flexible, and more capable of responding to the change and uncertainty of an increasingly global and turbulent environment.

Or could it be that team-based work arrangements are just another desperate attempt to find a "quick-fix" solution to the increasingly difficult competitive environment in which so many organizations currently find themselves? Are self-managing teams truly the way to organize for success in the 1990s and beyond? Or will they just flower for a while and then quickly fade, as did similar approaches, such as quality circles?

The answers to these questions are important to organizations and our futures. The change to a team-based structure is not a trivial one. It is costly in terms of the investment required in training and implementation, in designing new work arrangements, in developing new human resource support systems, and especially in the human cost of learning and sustaining new behaviors. Self-managing team structures take years to implement. Even if they are the appropriate way to organize, the price associated with waiting for assurance that they are the solution for the future may be that an organization will find itself uncompetitive and unable to survive against competitors who have adopted team arrangements early. If they are not the correct response, the investment in trying to make them work and the disruption caused by their adoption may also be high enough to cost an organization, already buffeted by tough economic times and global competition, its very viability.

Teamwork and the Disappearing Middle

Why has there been such widespread adoption of team-based organizational arrangements? Flexibility has been mentioned. Leaner structural forms have also been referred to. There are, in fact, several different factors accounting for the extensive "delayering" of the middle ranks of organizations. That decentralization gives responsibility and authority to a work force more highly educated and more capable than in the past of assuming the required responsibilities is one important factor. Intensive cost-reduction pressures that are directed more at administrative and managerial functions than ever before are another. Information technology, which makes comprehensive data and information simultaneously available at every terminal in the organization is one more reason organizations have begun to replace some middle managers and supervisors, particularly those for whom a significant portion of their duties were the collection, aggregation, analysis, and presentation of such information. Computer spreadsheets and various other software packages have largely automated many of these activities.

Under stable or not-too-rapidly-changing environmental conditions, organizations are more efficient when they can perform their core work predictably, repetitively, and with little variation. The main duty of the traditional supervisor in, say, an assembly-line operation is to take care of all contingencies and to protect the smooth flow of production. This includes keeping the demands on the workers focused on their manual work—not on planning or resolving conflicting demands. The main task of the managers and supervisors in the middle, then, is to buffer the organization's core processes from variability by absorbing any uncertainty or complexity within their areas of responsibility. For instance, a middle level manager or supervisor might deal personally with a unique request from the sales department in order to prevent it from disrupting the more standardized operations of the production floor. However, middle managers and supervisors are removed one or several steps from the work itself. With rapid rates of change, they have increasingly found themselves unable to absorb the changes and uncertainty required to protect the core processes. This inability to fulfill the buffering role has removed one of the main reasons of being for the middle ranks. Teams, in direct proximity to the work which is affected by the increasing change and uncertainty, have more capably assumed the responsibility of making the appropriate changes.

Another factor explaining the movement toward teams is the inability of organizations to develop and manage the supervisory role properly, the "man-in-the-middle" role that has been a perennial problem for organizations to manage. This has prompted many organizations to eliminate the middle entirely by allowing and encouraging people at lower levels in the organization largely to manage themselves. Increasingly, then, the middle cannot hold, and it is within this changing context that team-based organization has become so pervasive.

This chapter addresses the characteristics of one category of team-based organization: self-managing teams (SMTs). Problem-solving groups and other forms of teaming will continue to exist; however, SMTs are most likely to dominate team-based organizational arrangements in the future. This chapter examines the characteristics of SMTs and the factors that account for their success and failure, but always within the context of the organizational arrangements that contain them. It is only with pointed attention to the conditions under which SMTs are implemented—the organizational culture in which they are adopted, the design processes that create and adapt them, and the management style required to sustain them—that self-managing teams will become an effective way to organize work. Even the best-functioning teams will survive only by accident or by the extraordinary efforts of a few individuals if they are designed and developed in isolation of their organizational context. So designed and developed, they will have limited ability to sustain themselves, irrespective of how good an experience they may be for those who participate in them, and their contribution to overall organizational effectiveness will be, at best, minimal, and could even be negative.

This chapter begins with an illustration of the concept of self-managing teams by describing one small plant that is completely organized and operated by SMTs. It is an example that the chapter returns to often. This chapter then briefly examines the historical evolution of SMTs in order to build a foundation for describing their characteristics and the concepts involved. This part of the chapter also addresses the changing roles of supervision and middle management as the new boundaries of team-based organization begin to change the structure of work organizations. Teams are an enigma for unions, and the attitudes of unions towards team-based organization are addressed next. The prime focus of the chapter is on design principles for SMTs, and this issue dominates the last half of the chapter. The chapter ends with some brief mention of the skills and behavioral processes required to ensure the effectiveness of teams.

SELF-MANAGING TEAMS: AN EXAMPLE

Crown Cork and Seal Corporation's Vista plant is a relatively small sociotechnically designed plant in Mississauga, Ontario, a suburb of Toronto. It was built in 1986. The plant manufactures aluminum ecology end-units for beer and soft-drink cans (see Figure 10-1). It is a capital-intensive facility with a production process that resembles a continuous-flow operation. Each manufacturing line produces in excess of 1.2 billion units per year. The plant is currently undergoing expansion to double its production capacity. It is a small plant

FIGURE 10-1 An aluminum ecology end-unit

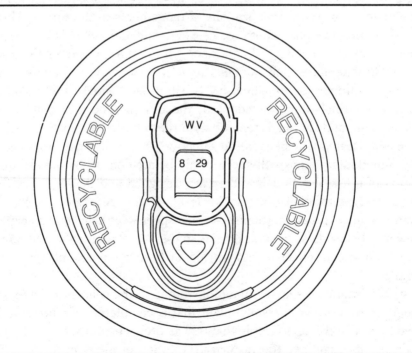

relative to many other Crown Cork and Seal facilities and others within the industry, but a very effective one, which accounts for the current commitment of its corporation to its continued growth and expansion. With four shift operations, and including support and administrative staff, the plant's present total population is approximately 60. This will grow to 90 with the completion of expansion.

Most of Crown Cork & Seal's plants are organized traditionally. The process of manufacturing cans and end-units is highly automated and the operations resemble those of a continuous-process plant. Rolls of thin aluminum sheet are inserted at the start of the process and then fed through a series of machines that punch out, cut, form, stamp, decorate, and package the cans and end units. Automatic transfer devices move the materials between operations. The work of the operators is to monitor the machine processes, watching for damages, worn and chipped tools, dents and scratches in the parts, misalignments of tools, dies, and materials, and so on. They also continuously maintain the presses, the feeding machines, and other pieces of equipment, tools, and dies, because the high rates of processing and impact cause wear on even the newest equipment.

In Crown Cork and Seal's traditional plants workers in these roles report to supervisors, who report to department managers, who in turn report to manufacturing or operations managers, who report to the plant manager, who reports to the (senior) vice-president of manufacturing. In large plants, superintendent roles are inserted between supervisors and managers. Workers' jobs are described in detail in job descriptions for each category of worker, and these descriptions change rarely. When they do change, usually after work studies by the industrial methods or industrial engineering departments or because equipment has changed, they are then negotiated between the company and the relevant union steward. Work is controlled by the supervisory hierarchy, with standards for production and maintenance monitored at several levels in the organization. Workers are expected to function within the confines of their job descriptions, meeting the quantity and quality targets expected and performing according to the formalized roles and relationships in the plant. Variations from such behaviors or performance outside the envelope of expectations are subject first to warnings from supervisors and then to disciplinary actions. Disagreements with supervision over the appropriateness or fairness of such warnings and discipline often lead to grievances filed by workers and a formal process of conflict resolution prescribed in the collective bargaining procedures and local labor laws.

Crown Cork & Seal's Vista plant is organized very differently. Four production SMTs, working four twelve hour shifts each, run the plant.

Each has 10 people (five production technicians, one electrical technician, and four operating technicians) growing to 17 with the present expansion. Each team is self-regulating and has complete responsibility, autonomy, and decision-making authority with respect to the plant's functioning. Two other teams accompany the four production SMTs: an administrative SMT (comprising the plant and operations managers, a controller, a human resources facilitator, an office administrator, and a purchasing/scheduling/shipping administrator), and a technical support SMT (with three tool and die makers, two technology instructors, and five preventive maintenance and repair technicians).

The plant is not unionized, nor are there any supervisors in the plant. In fact, two or three levels of the supervisory/managerial hierarchy are nonexistent. Traditional supervisory activities are assumed by team members. For example, production team members assume the following roles and responsibilities on a rotating basis.

- Team coordinator
- Secretary
- Work and duty scheduler
- Training coordinator
- Vacation scheduler
- Overtime coordinator
- (Continuous design team) representative
- Health and safety representative
- Continuous improvement coordinator

We will anchor our discussion of team self-management in the kind of SMT that the Vista plant's example illustrates. There are many different perspectives on the term "self-managing" and their different applications to team-based arrangements have resulted in a wide variety of teams with an equally wide range of titles; for example self-regulating, self-maintaining, self-directed, and semi-autonomous. Our viewpoint places us somewhere in the middle of a spectrum that ranges from teams that are externally managed by a supervisor, whose role is a traditional hierarchical one, to teams that are not only self-managing and without supervisors but also self-designing with respect to their structural and contextual situations. The Vista SMTs are probably closer to the latter end of the spectrum, because they are becoming self-designing. However, we will also draw examples from teams that are closer to the other end, namely, SMTs with explicit supervisory roles within their arrangements, though the roles may not be the traditional supervisory ones.

LESSONS FROM THE LONG HISTORY OF SELF-MANAGEMENT

Rural areas provide an early illustration of self-management. At harvest time, village communities cooperated to get the harvest in on time and villagers decided the order in which their local fields would be worked. That decision could be a function of a range of factors. Some of them were technical, such as how the soil was prepared and fertilized and which crops were being grown; some of them unpredictable, such as which fields ripened first; and some of them were social, such as the social standing of the villager in the community. Leadership of the harvesting teams would rotate according to which farmer's land was being worked.

The mining sector provides another historical source. In 19th century Welsh slate mining, the "schakts" were contracted out to teams of workers who designed their own organization, contracted labor for some of the tasks, and took full responsibility for production. The British coal mining research carried out by Eric Trist and Fred Emery in the 1940s provided considerable detail on the characteristics of the "semi-autonomous" work groups they observed. The groups worked in conditions subject to high levels of unpredictability; for example, the coal seams would range from the height of a coal miner to very narrow heights that forced miners onto their knees or bellies to extract the coal, and tunnel roofs could collapse even after being shored up with timbers and rocks. In their studies, Trist and Emery found that many mine managers had integrated new technology (conveyor belts, better explosives, undercutting equipment) with work groups that were organized according to the traditions of coal mining, family work groups that administered themselves with relative autonomy. Through experimentation with different *work methods* (for example, carrying on the cycle from where the last team left off), *workers* (not all of whom were multiskilled, but among whom enough skill variety existed to handle the roles likely to arise), *work groups* (who, for example, selected their own members, allocated their own tasks, and rotated tasks and shifts through their own system), and *payment approaches* (for example, common pay rates for everyone on the team with individual overtime and extra pay equally divided; incentive systems for the group; pay not necessarily equal), they developed composite social and technical subsystems of men and equipment that evolved into highly effective work organizations able to adapt to the unpredictable conditions. The results were greater productivity, lower cost, fewer accidents, and greater satisfaction with the work.

In the Swedish construction industry, the Stockholm model developed around the turn of the century. Construction firms hired teams of workers, who picked one team member as the formal boss. As the contact person and the boss, that person recruited other team members, designed and formed the team, and contracted with the site agent or the construction firm for payment. The first-level supervisors of the construction firm ensured that the team received the materials and machinery committed to them. Representatives from the union and the firm then measured and controlled production to determine the wage that was to be shared by the team.

The team and its boss functioned as subcontractors, but with almost no formal organization and no paperwork. One very successful 50-person form-setting and concrete team worked at five different sites for three different construction firms. As a general principle, each sub-team worked one man short so as to achieve a high rate of pay (20 percent above the industry average and 50 percent above ordinary industrial work averages). The team's work was coordinated by the team boss with a portable telephone and by physically rotating through the sites. He said, "I never use paper or make notes. The information I need I have under my hard hat." In reciprocal fashion, the strategy of the site agent was to contract and negotiate the work to be done informally with the self-managed team. Their productivity was almost 50 percent above the expected level.

In agriculture, in mining, and in construction, then, autonomous and semi-autonomous organization was a way to manage the uncertainties inherent in the work itself: the differentiation in how the fields would ripen, the variability in the size and characteristics of the coal seam, the range of forms and designs that the architects and the different builders and their supervisors could present to the construction crews. Teams had to contain sufficient internal variety to match the variety of their work tasks. They also needed enough autonomy within themselves to be able to adjust and reorganize their internal resources, skills, and competencies in response to shifts and variations in the work.

In the world of manufacturing a different logic prevailed. While uncertainty increasingly licked at the boundaries of the organization, the organization strove to buffer its core manufacturing units from that uncertainty by demanding that the sales department provide the firm with forecasts that allowed long production runs to be planned and by signing long-term purchasing contracts and collective agreements to stabilize the costs of materials and labor, respectively. Under such conditions, jobs could be specified with confidence that the work to which they were directed would not change. Vertical hierarchies and fractionated jobs with high degrees of specification were the methods of operating. With stable conditions assured, any coordination required for sharing equipment or material or people could be managed by the supervisory hierarchy. Furthermore, given stable conditions, any need to coordinate events or activities that might depend on prior events or activities could be satisfied by planning ahead or by standardizing the outputs from the prior event or activity as well as the inputs to the subsequent one. Hierarchy, planning, and standardization were the traditional logic of a system that worked well under stable external conditions.

That logic has since broken down, and the conditions faced by workers on the production floor increasingly resemble the uncertainties faced by the teams in agriculture, mining, and construction. The turbulence of increasingly globalized markets has blasted away at the protective buffers and worked its way inside most manufacturing organizations. The responses required and the changes needed are too quick for the traditional managerial and supervisory solution of buffering the core processes while the hierarchy deals with the exceptions. It is the core processes themselves that must be changed to respond appropriately.

The Vista plant of Crown Cork and Seal illustrates this type of response. The organization is relatively flat, with the SMTs reporting to an operations manager, who in turn reports to the plant manager. However, it is not this limited hierarchy that responds to unanticipated events. Each of the SMTs described previously deals with the issues that effect it. For instance, one weekend, when a part for one of the pieces of equipment broke down and no replacement was available, one team member called the equipment supplier to check on the availability of a replacement part. On his own initiative, he drove several hundred miles to the supplier's location to pick up the replacement part so his team could keep the line running over the weekend. He informed the operations manager about his actions on Monday.

In effect, the uncertainty of the external environment, which can no longer be buffered by the hierarchy, surfaces as part of the work itself and requires organizational arrangements that can adjust and reorganize internal resources, skills, and competencies to adapt to the shifts and variations of the task. Manufacturing organizations that have embraced SMT arrangements have done so out of necessity, out of the desperate need to achieve coordination in a context that is changing too rapidly for traditional solutions to be effective.

Within the service sector, contextual conditions similar to those in manufacturing are increasingly being experienced. Information technology is injecting a rate of response that is as disruptive to this sector as globalization and advanced manufacturing technologies have been for the production sector. Various team-based arrangements have begun to arise in the service sector as a way of responding. The impact of external uncertainty, however, has been experienced more slowly. As such, the incidence of innovations in work organization in this sector is still low, though that condition is not likely to last for much longer.

THE CONCEPT OF SELF-MANAGING TEAMS

Self-managing teams can be organized as most production is organized; that is, by specialty or function; such as "front wiring assembly team," "buffing and polishing team," or, in the case of white-collar areas, "accounts payable team." Teams organized by function are unlikely to become self-managing unless they have a *relatively holistic task;* that is, a well-bounded task that has a clear beginning and end and in which most of the relationships between task activities are contained within the boundaries of the functional unit.

Self-managing teams also usually have a *well-bounded task;* that is, a task for which there is a clear physical and/or organizational boundary. More often than not, functionally organized tasks are fractionated parts of a whole and it is difficult to organize around them so that members can experience identity with a whole task. Hence teams in these areas tend to become more problem-solving groups than self-managing teams; for example, quality circles, in which small groups of workers from the same functional unit meet to solve particular problems in their area but do not usually assume total responsibility for implementing their solutions.

However, some purely functional tasks do lend themselves to sufficient self-containment to foster self-management, particularly when the accompanying physical and organizational boundaries are reasonably contained and the teams have autonomy within those boundaries. GE Canada's Pooled Financial Services provides such an illustration. Within the pool, about 22 SMTs operate with such functional titles as accounts receivable team, ledger team, payroll team, information systems development team, analysis and reporting team, and end user team.

Most SMTs are organized to cut across traditional functional lines so that they are in the direction of the flow of production; that is, "with the grain" of the task. Organizing with the flow of the task provides a team with a relatively holistic task, that is a task that has a clearly identifiable beginning and end and specific processes between. In other words, SMTs are organized to carry out tasks that have a "natural identity." Many manufacturing plants have begun to organize their work this way in order to increase the speed of response. These natural work units are called manufacturing cells and they lend themselves well to becoming SMTs.

For example, Hawker Siddeley Canada created a "frame assembly cell" within its Orenda Division to carry out all the different operations required to weld and braze airfoil blades to a jet engine frame. The cell had responsibility for a series of sequential task such as fitting blades to the hub and the frame, tack-welding them, assembling components to the frame, applying brazing material, and brazing. The cell comprised a range of needed skills, such as sheet-metal-work, assembly, welding, brazing, and inspection. Within their area of responsibility there were opportunities for members to become multiskilled and move about the cell to handle both planned and unanticipated variations in the workload. In effect, cell members were organized to become an SMT.

The team at the Crown Cork & Seal Vista plant cited earlier is another example of an SMT with a whole task that was organized in the direction of the flow of production. In their case, the task comprised all the activities involved across the entire plant to produce aluminum ecology end units.

The basis for organizing an SMT is the particular work task or work system itself, so there is no predetermined size to a team. Small and large work systems can exist side by side in the same plant or organization and their accompanying work teams can be correspondingly small and large. It is the size and task of the work system that dictate the size of the accompanying team. For instance, a relatively self-contained manufacturing cell can have a two- or three-person team while an adjacent cell, perhaps because it is handling larger families of parts, may have six or seven persons in the accompanying work team and require several times more physical area. If they are very interdependent, several manufacturing cells might together constitute a work system and the work team would comprise all the people associated with those cells.

Other types of teams that are organized to cut across functional areas might incorporate both professional staff and plant-level workers. A frequently occurring example is that of a simultaneous or concurrent engineering team that organizes forward, in the direction of the flow of the work, incorporating production people into the engineering design of the product. Similarly, a sales-design team may begin its activities within the customer or market segment and include designers in the team so that the designers can be closely in touch with the customer's needs. Often, however, the tasks of such teams are temporally limited and, even if self-managing during their operations, are classified better as project management teams than as self-managed ones.

Northern Telecom, on the other hand, created a large cross-cutting team to evolve its next-generation switching system. The team included representatives from its Bell Canada customer organization, marketing people, design and development engineers, and members of the manufacturing organization that would ultimately build the switch, even though prototype manufacturing was unlikely to commence until some eighteen months after the team was formed.

SUPERVISORS AND TEAM LEADERS

The current popularity of the team concept has spawned a variety of terms to describe self-management phenomena. The new terminology reflects changes in the traditional roles of supervision that result in less authority and control being exercised within the supervisory ranks and more of it invested in the team. In practice this has resulted in supervisory roles with a corresponding change in titles; for example, team manager, team captain, team adviser, and team facilitator. The ultimate manifestation of this is teams with no explicit supervisors in which the supervisory activities are undertaken by the team members themselves, as in the Vista plant example cited earlier. Figure 10-2 illustrates the relative degrees of team control and supervisory control possible.

The increase in adoption of SMT arrangements has created high levels of stress and anxiety among supervisors who have always worked within traditional hierarchical arrangements. While it has been easy to speculate about changing the roles of supervisors from authoritarian and controlling ones to roles in which they carry out training and coaching functions for team members and/or act as boundary managers between the team and the rest of the organization, it has been extremely difficult to carry out this change in practice. In the transition to SMTs, this is the area with the lowest success rate. Some of the failure is due to poor implementation and poor processes of change management. Much of the failure, however, is a result of poor conceptualization of the complexities involved in changing supervisory roles.

It is not easy to visualize the organization that will evolve from successful implementation of SMTs, new work philosophy, and compatible new support systems. Too many managers and others who have been involved in the transition to SMTs have chosen to avoid trying to understand the en-

FIGURE 10-2   Team control vs. supervisory control

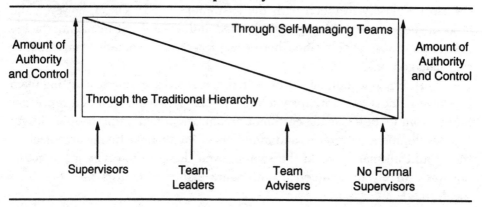

tire set of changes. Instead, they have been content to guarantee employment security for the supervisors affected by the process. They have assumed that such commitments to job protection, augmented with some choices about the kinds of jobs they would like to have in the future, were sufficient to buy off the supervisors' resistance to the proposed changes. However, it has not been sufficient. Many of those involved in the change process have been surprised at the backlash they have encountered from the supervisory ranks and the general negativism their resistance has injected into the change process, even when employment security has been assured.

It is difficult for supervisors schooled in traditional authority and control structures to unlearn behaviors they have practiced for decades, as well as to learn behaviors appropriate to team-based situations quickly, particularly when no blueprints for the required behaviors exist. One supervisor whose role was being changed was asked to work with his intended new team for a while to learn the new ways of working, but he was given very little instruction about the required new behaviors. His new role required him to be proactive and search out and anticipate problems the team might encounter. His transition was a failure because he continued to do what he had always done, which was to wait for team members to come to him for help, because in his former role he had always been the source of technical knowledge.

As the team evolves, whatever new supervisory behavior has been learned must again be adapted, which is made difficult by some uncertainty as to precisely which of the role alternatives illustrated in Figure 10-2 are appropriate to the particular team, the particular organization, and the particular supervisor. For some supervisors, the transition to new kinds of behaviors—usually at great variance from those they have practiced in the past—is not possible, and they must return to some role within a team, perhaps as a technical expert or an ordinary member.

If the change process is handled well, if the employment security issue is attended to, if supervisors are given information about the intended changes in advance of the people who report to them, if they are provided with some training about the new ways of working and the skill changes that will be required on their part, and if their future roles can be spelled out in such ways that they can visualize them *and* believe that they can succeed in them, there is a good chance of making the transition successful for most supervisors. To date, the majority of organizations have not satisfactorily attended to many of the items on this list. They have been particularly reluctant to spell out future roles for supervisors, primarily because they were themselves unclear about the composition of and duties associated with those future roles. This has left many supervisors incapable of thinking through their futures and feeling that they will not be capable of performing the new roles. Combined with skepticism about the intent of the transition and the suspicion that one of its primary objectives is the elimination of their jobs, it is not surprising that many expect that the changes will prove harmful to them.

Self-managing has sometimes been interpreted as one or another form of industrial or economic democracy (for example, worker ownership), wherein workers as owners might have more say in the management of the enterprise. This is an interesting perspective, but one that we do not have space to examine in this chapter. In the brief history of self-management described earlier, some of the examples are of this nature and illustrate the movement away from hierarchical control and towards self-management. However, there are various middle positions. The semi-autonomous teams in the coal mines, working underground and away from the deputies, tended more toward the self-managing end of the spectrum. The construction team is quite autonomous because it is an independent contractor, but in selecting a manager it has chosen to be manager-led rather than self-managed.

Complete self-management is probably only manifested in supervisor-less teams. To date, these instances have almost all arisen in "greenfield" sites; that is, in situations where both the factory or office and the workforce are completely new and there is no history of supervision to unlearn. In redesign or ongoing situations, it is difficult completely to discard supervisory roles and behaviors that have long-established patterns and it is equally difficult to change expectations that have been based on the relative role experiences of supervisors and team members.

TEAM MEMBER ROLES IN SELF-MANAGING TEAMS

The roles of team members in SMTs have several levels; for example, at their own work station, at the level of the team, or at a plant-wide or department-wide level (see Figure 10-3). The primary and secondary roles are individual roles that are usually unique to each setting's particular technology and ways of organizing work. For instance, piston head assembler, frame welder, or end-user adviser might be typical primary roles of a team member. Secondary individual roles might be maintenance-oriented or administrative; for example, keeping quality statistics for one's own machine.

Team-level roles are often generic types of administrative roles that are found in a wide range of SMTs. They have titles such as work scheduler, vacation scheduler, team meeting manager, team trainer, and team recruiter (for replacement members). Some maintenance activities that team members carry out are also general enough to be found in a range of SMT settings, such as sweeping up or monitoring frequent usage supplies. Other activities

FIGURE 10-3   Team members' roles at different organizational levels

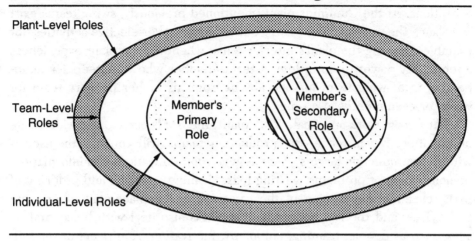

are more particular; for instance, some of the production technicians at the Vista plant also take responsibility for replacing the propane tanks on the forklifts.

There are also team-level roles that are common to most SMT arrangements, but whose similarity is more difficult to recognize because they are titled quite differently for each setting. For example, many SMTs are imbedded in organizational designs that have some form of continuous design activity to adapt the organizational arrangements to changing situations. Team members assigned to such committees have role assignments that reflect their membership in the "team norm review board" or the "concept review" team or the "social system task force." In unionized environments, every team may have a specifically identified shop steward or union representative with the additional responsibility of monitoring the relationship between the team's activities and the collective bargaining agreement.

The activities associated with team-level roles range widely in the amount of time they require. The work scheduler role is often far more onerous than a team member's primary work role, while the role of meeting manager may only occupy an hour or two a month. At the Cummins Engine plant in Jamestown, N.Y., SMT members have "horizontal" or primary roles and "vertical" or secondary roles. On the engine assembly lines, where the SMTs control their own materials, the vertical materials management role in a team typically occupies 80 percent of the team member's time, leaving her or him only 20 percent for engine assembly activities. However, vertical roles are rotated on a 12- to 18-month schedule.

Most plant-wide roles (for example, health and safety coordinator, social systems task force member, fumigation coordinator, first aid monitor) occupy only small percentages of a team member's time, but there can be significant exceptions. At the Cummins plant, mentioned previously, swing teams exist to balance the workload or to carry out nonessential or elective activities (for example, painting the plant's interior walls) whenever the plant experiences a temporary downturn in orders. A team member who volunteers for membership in a swing team may be absent from his or her primary team for weeks or even months at a time.

At Crown Cork and Seal's Vista plant, the SMTs carry out a wide range of activities. For instance, the production teams will concern themselves with daily production targets, safety issues, communications and information, demonstration of problems, writing logs, cleaning, removal and ordering of parts, cleaning and tidying of the cafeteria, and replacement of propane tanks. They and the two nonproduction SMTs also deal with behavioral issues, such as people, training, autonomy, motivation from peers or oneself, sharing skills, and ongoing leadership. SMTs in the Vista plant must also deal with problems internal to the team, such as punctuality, attendance, performance, behavior, attitude, quality of work, and acceptance of responsibility.

UNIONS AND SELF-MANAGING TEAMS

Ideologically, supervisors are the bane of union members, so SMTs that lead to a reduction in or the elimination of supervisors should be attractive to unions. However, as with everything associated with SMTs, there is a wide range of opinions and positions among unions on the subject of work teams. For example, in a formal statement on the "Reorganization of Work," the Canadian Auto Workers state, "The issue we have to address is not whether or not there are "teams"—there is nothing inherently bad about workers working together and there may even be some advantages." However, they caution their members strongly to be wary of management that advocates teams as the basis of partnerships when that same management takes other actions that are inconsistent with other union objectives for their members. Their document states, "We will not however support management attempts to use the team concept or quality circles, to manage the workplace by stress, to introduce speed up, or to encourage workers to discipline each other."

Several unions have issued position papers describing their stances on new work system designs, most of which have team-based organizational arrangements at their base. They often reflect how problematic the "team concept" is for unions, or, in the words of the position paper on workplace reorganization of the Communications and Electrical Workers of Canada, "When an employer tries to introduce concepts like Quality Circles, TEAM concept, Quality of Work Life, Multi-skilling, Multi-purpose Positions or Pay for Knowledge, to name just a few, we become downright unnerved." They note that there are good historical reasons for their concerns and go on to say, "But times are changing, and union members are increasingly looking for a new response to work reorganization—one that focuses on intelligent cooperation rather than blind obedience."

The American Federation of Grain Millers issued a statement of policy about their role in creating Labor/Management Partnerships in "New Work Systems." Among other characterizations of new work systems their description included fewer levels of management, decentralized autonomy and responsibility, and self-managing teams. They generally support the creation of such partnerships. In their statement, the Grain Millers also take the time to reply to other unions who take a position against teams because of a belief that teams are a management attempt to heighten control and that membership in teams eventually leads to inter-team competition that results in union members pitting themselves against other union members in ways that undermine the protections that the collective bargaining agreement provides. The Grain Millers' union argues that new work systems can be designed to end such competition.

The Energy and Chemical Workers Union (ECWU) have developed a two-day seminar to introduce their members to new forms of work organization, including the topic of self-managing teams. Their seminar addresses the "features a union should reject (e.g., multi-tasking) and the features to push for (e.g., upskilling) when designing teams."

The United Steelworkers and the Algoma Steel Corporation in Sault St. Marie, Ontario, developed an agreement between them to create a new company to take over the failing steel company, one that would be based on worker ownership and financial support from the union, the company, the employees, and several levels of government. Among the objectives of their "Joint Workplace Restructuring and Employee Participation Process" are the following.

- Reduction of the number of supervisors relative to that of hourly employees
- Redefinition of the roles and functions of supervisors so that they emphasize coaching and coordinating

They encourage their members to experiment with work teams when they state, "The Workplace and Redesign and Technology Task Force will design a process which will permit employees in two specific work areas in different divisions...to completely redesign their work area and further develop the concept of a Work Group." However, they also state their constraints: "The concept of Peer Review shall not be incorporated into any Work Group or Redesign Plan," and "Redesign Plans shall not include proposals which allow Work Groups to absorb the work of absent group members who are involved in training or other participatory exercises related to the process."

This particular agreement lays out some of the conditions that unions feel are prerequisites for engaging cooperatively with management in work team arrangements. These conditions include honoring the collective agreement and disallowing any discipline of a union member by a fellow member. They also seek adequate representation in the important cross-functional teams. At Shell Canada's Sarnia, Ontario, polypropylene plant, where the plant is organized by the ECWU and each shift is completely run by an SMT, every SMT has a union steward as a member and union members dominate the plant's redesign team.

Scandinavian unions are known for their exceptionally high membership—in most major companies over 90 percent of manual workers are union members. In the late 1960s and early 1970s there were several joint research programs in which the employer and employee confederations together engaged in action research to implement autonomous groups as a means to improve both productivity and the quality of work life. However, the union side found the progress of this strategy for improving quality of work life too slow. Instead they turned their attention to reforming the legislation regulating the relation between employers and unions. By the late 1970s, autonomous groups had acquired a bad reputation among many unions and employers.

In the 1980s, a renewed interest in joint developments and new forms of team-based organizations was rekindled. In 1985, the metal workers' national union formulated a policy about "The Good Work" in which autonomous groups, SMTs, and the integration of traditional blue-collar manual work with white-collar tasks such as planning, scheduling, and work rationalization, was propagated. For example, the unions have taken an active part in ABB's T 50 project to reduce throughput time by half via the introduction of new forms of work.

The current emphasis on SMTs is seen more as an opportunity than as a threat by blue-collar unions. White-collar unions have had more mixed feelings about SMTs. As an ideal for work organization, white-collar unions have been supportive of SMTs, but in many specific instances of reorganization of work their members feel that their tasks are being taken over by blue-collar workers.

Thus the general picture is that the notion of SMTs has itself become part of the unions' notion of good work organization. However there is some concern, in North American as well as in Scandinavian settings, about the effect of team-based organization on the ability of the unions to defend the workers' interests as a collective group, and on their continuing ability to attract members.

DESIGN PRINCIPLES FOR SELF-MANAGING TEAMS

Design principles for SMTs have largely evolved from a variety of experiences of team applications in a range of settings. They are also a product of some basic assumptions about work-group and self-management functioning. As principles, they must be used with discretion, particularly those that have arisen from particular situations; for example, the coal-mining teams in the United Kingdom or the work teams in the automobile assembly plants in Sweden. Whether or not they are generalizable enough to prescribe them for other situations is unclear and will only become clear when research has been undertaken across a variety of applications. Furthermore, because it is social systems that these design principles address, they must take account of local realities, with all the uniqueness of a particular situation's history, culture, experience, and so on.

We have chosen to group some of these design principles for SMTs under several categories (see Figure 10-4): (1) design principles that address "design goals" and have a *performance focus;* (2) design principles that deal with "design characteristics" and address the concepts of *whole and integrated tasks* or of *autonomy* or resemble the sociotechnical principles of *minimum critical specifications;* (3) design principles revolving around "human resource skills and support," particularly the giving of *rewards* and the development of *competencies;* and (4) those design principles associated with "continuous design" processes, namely, *continuous individual and organizational development.*

Performance Focus

- High performance is the primary source of team member satisfaction.
- Team activities should be task-oriented and not based on the feelings of team members.

In a study of SMTs in an insurance company, the team members were asked to describe the moments when they feel especially happy at work as well as such happy moments in life in general. An interesting pattern appeared. Almost all descriptions of happy moments outside work were descriptions of events *taking place* (that is, in the present tense), such as eating a pleasant dinner with some friends, listening to a concert, or gardening. The

FIGURE 10-4 Design categories for self-managing teams

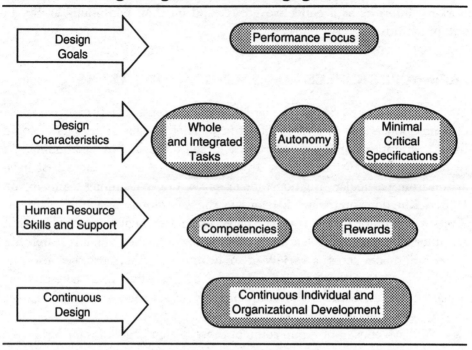

happy moments at work, in contrast, were moments when something *had taken place* (that is, in the past tense), such as having completed a difficult insurance policy. The prime source of satisfaction while at work was clearly related to performance.

SMTs have become quite common as the needs for flexibility and quick processing of information have increased. However, some managers retain reservations. The production manager at one Atlas Copco plant described one SMT, which was organized around the assembly of pneumatic drills, as a failure from the point of view of productivity. With respect to delivery times the team had lived up to the contract it had established with management. They had managed this well over the ten years of their existence. However, they had also adopted the norm that they would use any increase in productivity as a kind of time buffer rather than attempt to improve performance by cutting the cost of labor. This, of course, prevented any reduction in the size of the team. The production manager felt constrained in his ability to improve productivity within this particular team, the first in the company, because they had lost their performance focus. It was a situation he was unable to change.

At the Jamestown Engine Plant of Cummins Engine Company, the high-commitment work system had evolved over a ten-year period so that autonomy was a cornerstone of the many SMTs in the assembly and machining parts of the plant. For example, buffer areas had been inserted in the engine assembly lines to provide each assembly team with some autonomy and flexibility, from both the SMT that preceded it in the assembly process and the SMT that followed after. In this way, teams wanting to meet to manage their activities could, by working ahead of schedule, put enough completed work in the buffer so that their meeting would not disrupt the flow of work to the next team in the process. Subsequently, a just-in-time control system was installed in the plant and the buffer areas were removed because they allowed high work in-process inventories to accumulate. The seven engine-assembly SMTs viewed this as a loss of autonomy and an increase in external control. Management understood the loss, but viewed the action as necessary to increase productivity, and competitors were severely undercutting Cummins's costs.

Another example comes from SAAB Automobile. They have experimented with SMTs in their body shop since the 1970s. The primary reason for adopting SMTs at that time was to attract labor to their automobile assembly plants. Nevertheless, during the 1970s and 1980s, the SMT-organization also was seen as a success from a productivity point of view. Current top management, however, has had serious doubts about the emphasis that was placed on group autonomy rather than on the productivity that was emphasized in the old body shop organization. Today the emphasis has shifted to the need to develop productivity and quality. A new team concept has been introduced in all parts of production in order to raise productivity. In this team concept, management control, rather than self-management, has been emphasized during the transition to the new organization. The results of introducing teams and of focusing on productivity has been astonishing: a reduction from more than 100 hours worked per car to 55 in less than three years, with an improvement of quality of the same proportion.

The important issue in the longer run is not the choice between a performance or an autonomy orientation, but rather the appreciation of both as necessary components for survival, the former within the economic marketplace and the latter within the labor market. Put in terms of value, SAAB's mission is to fulfill demands from society both as a productive builder of automobiles and as a provider of human-oriented working conditions. Throughout the 1980s, SAAB was well known for providing such conditions in its body shop, based on concepts of autonomous groups. It took the economic crises of the late 1980s and early 1990s, plus the increase in unemployment, to strengthen the emphasis on performance.

While performance should be a prime source of satisfaction for team members, it is not always easy to create the conditions that make this possible. Productivity increases are often viewed by management as achievable only by cutting costs and reducing workers. From the team's point of view, such measures undermine the loyalty that team members acquire for each other as they work through the various stages of team building that are necessary for them to become effective. Management is admittedly obligated to achieve effectiveness, but it must also avoid creating conflict between a performance orientation and solidarity within the team. Building and sustaining an effective team-based organization is a precarious process and it does not take very much to undermine it and set the process back for many years. Since much of the purpose of team-based organization is performance improvement, teams must be clearly informed about the degree of slack that is possible in the organization at any given time. For instance, a performance orientation that may be achievable under a crisis situation can be considerably more difficult to attain when times are good.

Whole and Integrated Tasks

Several design principles may be grouped under the key words whole, complete, integrated. Whole tasks refer to activities that have a clear beginning and end and whose important subactivities can be contained within the boundary of the task. Within the boundaries of whole tasks, then, activities and subactivities are usually tightly coupled or integrated. The design principles in this design category have to do with conditions that are the reasons for SMTs as well as the bases for their success.

- Whole tasks should be a goal of team organization design. Variances that arise from the team task should be monitored and controlled within the team.
- Teams should be organized along the direction of the flow of production (that is, "with the grain").
- Teams should have first access to the information they require.
- An identifiable boundary, physical and organizational, should be built into the organization design.
- Team members should be within reasonable geographical proximity or be able to communicate easily.
- The size of the team is dictated by the task.

There are several reasons for the emphasis on whole tasks. One is that the entire idea of management has to do with linking information from different sources. If such information is not available, a team may fail to take into account important constraints or possibilities. The design principle implies that the boundaries should be set so as to minimize the need for intergroup communication. People have a strong need to arrange their environments so as to create simple, perceivable patterns.

Most organization is based on similarity or proximity; that is, people with similar characteristics (such as accountants, assemblers) are grouped together, or units that must work together (such as in a project team) are located near each other. Traditional organization has tended to follow the similarity design imperative, with most people in organizations grouped functionally rather than according to task accomplishment. The driving logic has been to gain efficiencies from similarly oriented groups through scale economies, an objective that was feasible as long as the external environment remained relatively stable. If it did, enough constancy of behavior and practice could be observed to allow continuous improvements to be made on carefully prescribed behaviors (for example, through job descriptions, methods, and procedures).

The hierarchy of managers and supervisors in the organization buffered the workforce from the environment's variability in order to obtain the desired constancy. The price, though, was slow responsiveness on the part of this entrenched vertical hierarchy when real change to behavior and practice was required. Such change is increasingly essential, and over the last twenty years the shift away from functional organization has been dramatic. The driving force is the need to meet or even exceed customer expectations. Instead of putting a premium on cutting costs through the scale economies of functional organization, major multinational organizations such as ABB, with 215 thousand employees worldwide, are now stressing the necessity of cutting throughput time and responding more quickly to the demands of a rapidly changing external environment that includes, particularly, their current and future customers. This is accomplished by integrating related tasks, removing informational detours, and relying on the ability of an SMT to make its own local level decisions rapidly and effectively. To support the need for speed, teams must possess all the information, resources, skills, and knowledge at their decision-making level; that is, they must have a whole and integrated task.

The goal set by ABB's regional organization in Sweden is to reduce throughput time by half by the end of 1993. Integration of tasks, organizing along the direction of the flow of production, and giving teams access to information as well as authority to make decisions based on this information, are all means to cut throughput time, to increase the organization's capacity to satisfy customers, and, ultimately, to remain competitive. The experience of many product-focused forms of organization in fabrication and assembly plants is that cycle time, one of the key components of throughput time, has been reduced by at least 80 percent and, in some cases, considerably more.

Autonomy

- The work team should have control over many of its own administrative functions (that is, be self-governing, self-regulating, or self-directing).
- Team members should participate in the selection of new members.

Integration within the team includes the team's ownership of its own administrative activities. These include tasks traditionally considered white collar, such as production planning, quality control, purchasing, training plans, and software programming for machine tools, even in a "blue-collar" environment.

Recruitment of new or replacement members is a crucial team function. If management selects the member, the team may refuse to take responsibility for integrating her or him into the team. Having the team participate in recruitment and selection increases the probability of their taking such responsibility. Some observers, however, have expressed the fear that SMTs with recruitment authority will accept only the elite. Organizations also have responsibilities to people who may not be the best producers, whether because of age, injury, family conditions, or other reasons. A personnel manager in one company with an entire department of SMTs found that while the teams tended to be negative towards some people, mainly those who did not accept the team's norms, they also tended to be positive towards accepting nonelite employees that the personnel department had to place. The important criterion was not the producing behavior of the person, but his or her willingness to accept the norms of the team.

Minimal Critical Specifications

- Team organizational arrangements should be based on minimal critical specifications.
- Individuals should be able to move about in tasks spontaneously to balance the workload.
- Mechanisms must exist for interteam coordination and workload balancing.

While engineers are taught complete specification design and most workplaces are based on this principle, SMTs operate on the sociotechnical principle of minimal critical specification that Philip Herbst proposed around twenty years ago. SMTs must evolve and change as their members grow and develop and, for example, increase their competencies through multiskilling. Specifying no more than what is critical and necessary provides room for that growth and evolution to take place. On occasion specification is needed between teams for information sharing, for scheduling, or for co-ordination, and these require some degree of standardization. Within the team, standardization is also needed and is usually arrived at through agreement on group norms. It is important to note that such norms are informally established and developed and are within the team's authority to change as required.

Giving up on maximal specification is a threat to traditional managerial control. The concern that workers will not adhere to a performance orientation unless there are detailed specifications of tasks and procedures and methods aligns with traditional management's need to control the production process. This control is given up reluctantly, even within a team concept. For instance, at SAAB Automobile, top management advocates the concepts of quality, delivery, and profitability through people (the Swedish acronym is QLE/H) and supports the concepts with standardized forms and measures through which teams may monitor their performance. The standardization and the strengthened control are seen as necessary steps toward achieving teams with a culture and a capacity for self-management.

SAAB's developmental strategy has been viewed as an attempt to learn from Japanese examples. Controlling by "installing" a common culture and common "local theory" as well as standardized tools for monitoring production, rather than specifying it all in advance, seems to be the chosen strategy for combining managerial control and minimum critical specification design.

Competencies

- Facilitation and coaching support should be available to teams as required and particularly as they evolve through different stages of team development.
- Interdependent tasks require effective interpersonal relationships and teams should receive training and coaching support to foster such relationships.
- The skills necessary to a team should be comprehensible to all and achievable by most of its members.

Traditional work organizations have been structured to minimize need for skills, for training, and for learning. In such a perspective people are replaceable parts, much like a part that is requested from material stores by its part number or a tool requested from the tool crib by its identification number. However, in the case of people, the replacing function is performed by the personnel department and the part number is a job description. The concept of direct substitutability is, however, the same.

Fred Emery has suggested that "redundancy of function" should replace this outmoded "redundancy of parts" concept that devalues human characteristics. In a redundancy of function concept, people can readily adapt to changing situations because they have the cross-training or multiple sets of skills needed to do so. In essence, the organization values people who can do more than that which is defined in their job description, in sharp contrast to traditional organizational arrangements.

Valuing multiple skills means that the work system is one that allows, and in fact encourages, people to adapt when planned changes are brought in or when unanticipated events occur. SMTs are natural structures for eliciting such behaviors when members coordinate themselves in order to adapt to changing workloads, unexpected events, or unanticipated absences, and view that activity as a normal part of their jobs.

In the early 1980s, many companies still regarded technology as a basis for achieving a competitive advantage over others. By the end of the decade that perspective had begun to change. Technology was not less important, but it had become easier to purchase, either off-the-shelf or by "reverse engineering" a competitor's product. The technological advantage was increasingly short-lived. Instead, the competence of the workforce was beginning to be viewed as a more viable basis for building competitive advantage. How individuals acquired knowledge, how the organization learned, and how both the organization and its employees learned to apply new technologies became viewed as the route to competitive superiority.

At SAAB Automobile managers have begun to view their training programs and manuals as company secrets, albeit secrets that are difficult to guard. For almost a decade, Procter and Gamble has restricted the access of outsiders to its "technician system" plants that are based on SMTs and limited the interactions concerning work organization issues that its plant management personnel may have with peers outside the plants. They view the ways in which they carry out the work in their approximately 20 greenfield sites as a competitive advantage, and they have been reluctant to reveal knowledge about them.

In one case, a setback was turned into an opportunity for competence and team development. A union official in one ABB plant described the results that transpired after a fire in the factory. Everyone, from the plant manager to newly employed operators, worked 12 hours a day, six days a week, to clean every single piece of paper in the offices and to take apart every machine and clean every single bolt. Not only was new knowledge acquired about the equipment and the paper routines, but at the same time a sense of being equals developed through joint efforts to get back into production before competitors could take over their customers. Responsibility was assumed by the person who best knew the particular equipment or the routines and procedures. Roles were switched—the managers finding themselves on many occasions instructed by their subordinates on how to disassemble and reassemble equipment.

An insurance company introduced SMTs throughout their organization. In one department they created one SMT of former team managers, which became a consulting team to the other SMTs. In technical matters, such as making a judgment on a difficult claim, any SMT member could consult the "consulting" SMT. Other former team managers became troubleshooters within a departmental staff group and the team coordinator for an SMT could turn to these people to assist his or her SMT when a problem of interpersonal relations or administrative matters arose.

Rewards

- Pay should recognize the multiple skills of team members.
- Payment is by results or some team bonus or sharing system and large pay differences between individuals should not be necessary.

The piece rate systems of the 1960s were exchanged for the salary systems of the 1970s. In the 1980s, some Western factories have combined fixed salary, part of it based on seniority and part on the tasks each person is able to perform, with a pay component dependent on the results of the team's efforts. In one Volvo factory, part of each team member's pay was dependent on individual skill and part on the overall skill-level of the group. The purpose was to provide team members with a collective incentive to create opportunities for team members to develop their competence.

The political aspect of rewards and team organization today is related to the new responsibilities assumed by the team, such as assuming tasks previously done by better-paid specialists and supervisors. This may lead to increased wages among teams and their members, though the overall wage bill for the corporation will probably decline as some of the specialist and supervisory positions are eliminated. The upward movement of this phenomenon, whereby supervisors assume the duties of middle managers, will further reduce the overall cost of wages for the corporation.

Continuous Individual and Organizational Development

- As individuals exceed team norms, avenues for leaving the team should be allowed.

- Teams require a process for continuously assessing their functioning and a means of rearranging themselves as they develop and/or the task and organizational contexts change.

In a study of the long-term effect of SMTs in Sweden, the SMTs in all ten companies studied saw major shifts in the norms of the company and in the messages sent by management about the values on which the teams were based. In the twenty-year perspective of the study, some of the structures intended to ensure a high quality of work life had fallen away, but in many companies the notion of SMTs, coupled to partly new, more performance-oriented norms, had spread. Whereas in the 1970s teams were formed to create more democratic and more humanitarian workplaces, teams in the 1990s survive and are nourished as a pragmatic solution to the problem of finding a work organization that can combine high performance with flexibility. Today the notion of self-management is discussed more often in a pragmatic rather than idealistic context.

Within SMTs, people with the ability to assume managerial tasks may have the opportunity to develop and prove their capability. The same holds for other important responsibilities within the team, such as for planning, maintenance, cost control, training, and so on. For instance, in GE Canada's Pooled Financial Services some of the white-collar SMTs were composed of both clerical people and professionals with accounting degrees. While without significant outside training the former could not aspire to become professional accountants several became quite skilled at managing their team's regular meetings and administrative activities, and more skilled than some of the professionals.

A team must be able to develop its capacity as a team and still make it easy for members to seek career-advancing positions outside the team. Six staff positions in a chemical plant that has operated with SMTs since its inception in the late 1970s were originally conceived of as requiring engineering skills. Four of them were eventually filled by employees who had begun as blue-collar team members but had developed their competence within the team until they were seen as capable managers or staff specialists.

Table 10-1 summarizes the design principles and design categories that have been referred to.

SKILLS TRAINING AND PROCESSES TO SUPPORT SELF-MANAGING TEAMS

This chapter has concentrated on the design features of self-managing teams. There are other aspects of SMTs that are also critical to their success.

TABLE 10-1   Design categories and design principles for self-managing teams

Design Category	Design Principle
Performance focus	• High performance is the primary source of team member satisfaction. • Team activities should be task-oriented and not based on the feelings of team members.
Whole and integrated tasks	• Whole tasks should be a goal of team organization design. Variances that arise from the team task should be monitored and controlled within the team. • Teams should be organized along the direction of production (that is, "with the grain"). • Teams should have first access to the information they require. • An identifiable boundary, physical and organizational, should be built into the organization design. • Team members should be within reasonable geographical proximity or be able to communicate easily. • The size of the team is dictated by the task.
Autonomy	• The work group should have control over many of its own administrative functions (that is, be self-governing, self-regulating, or self-directing). • Team members should participate in the selection of new members.
Minimal critical specifications	• Team organizational arrangements should be based on minimal critical specifications. • Individuals should be able to move about spontaneously in tasks to balance the workload. • Mechanisms must exist for interteam coordination and workload balancing.
Competencies	• Facilitation and coaching support should be available to teams as required and particularly as they evolve through different stages of team development. • Interdependent tasks require effective interpersonal relationships and teams should receive training and coaching support to foster such relationships. • The skills necessary to a team should be comprehensible to all and achievable by most of its members.
Rewards	• Pay should recognize the multiple skills of team members. • Payment is by results or some team bonus or sharing system and large pay differences between individuals should not be necessary.
Continuous individual and organizational development	• As individuals exceed team norms, avenues for leaving the team should be allowed. • Teams require a process for continuously assessing their functioning and a means of rearranging themselves as the team develops and/or the task and organizational contexts change.

Tuckman, for example, has identified a model of early developmental sequences in small groups that has been used by many teams to understand their stages of group development. His was one of several different stage theories of group evolution that have been formulated to explain the different phases that groups pass through as they evolve from their early formation to mature functioning. Stymne analyzed the interaction processes of student groups in small group tasks and developed two conceptual models to explain the degree of cooperation in groups and to differentiate according to their ability to function. One is a model of the problem-solving sequences of groups. The other is a model of the directional factors that guide the actions of groups. Concepts related to stages of development and problem-solving processes have been the basis of a large and relatively pragmatic body of literature that has developed on various aspects of team-building, such as group decision making, interpersonal communications, and conflict resolution. Although we have paid less attention to some of these issues here, they are explored in Chapter 3, "Building High-Performance Teams," by David L. Bradford, and like the design features listed in Table 10-1, they are also critical to the creation and development of effective SMTs.

Several models of work groups and SMTs, arising from different perspectives, have pointed to alternative approaches to understanding and informing team creation and evolution. Richard Hackman has developed a comprehensive social-psychological model of work groups that builds on the critical impact of group processes on several different group effectiveness criteria. His model emphasizes critical processes such as the level of effort and the amount of knowledge and skill applied to the group task as well as the appropriateness of the different performance strategies used by the group. The processes Hackman cites are situated within an organizational context that pays attention to reward, education, and information systems. These "process criteria of effectiveness" are also informed by group design parameters such as the structure of the task, the composition of the group, and the norms by which they carry out their tasks.

Larry Hirschhorn developed a strong psychodynamic model that balances empowerment with collaboration in explaining and understanding the functioning of work teams. He builds on the very strong interpersonal experiences that team members encounter as they learn to change their roles and their relationships with their supervisors and managers and with each other in their evolution toward becoming an effective team. Facilitating group processes and promoting a sense of fairness are important components of this approach.

The development activities of the SMTs in the Vista plant of Crown Cork and Seal illustrate some of these training and skill-development processes. The SMTs meet formally once or twice a month to overview and manage their team activities. Typically, once every three months, they receive team training. Once a year, with the help of a resource coordinator or facilitator, they meet for an eight-hour team-building session. The team-training topics covered are typical of those that almost every SMT must consider at different stages of its development. They include the following:

Group dynamics	Problem solving
Use of norms	Conflict resolution
Decision-making processes	Values and beliefs
Communications	Styles of behavior
Giving and receiving feedback	Distribution of duties

FEEDBACK, PLANNING, AND BUFFERS

Feedback and knowledge of results are essential if individuals and/or teams are to learn from their performance and improve upon it. In the examples cited earlier of teams in nonmanufacturing sectors, feedback was relatively easy to obtain. For instance, in rural communities whose members assembled in teams to share the work, each evening the village community could visually see how many of the fields had been harvested and how well the task had been carried out. Miners could measure their performance by the depth of their incursion into the mine face and the tons of coal they shipped out, though it was sometimes less evident how effectively they had extracted the coal itself from the coal-bearing veins. Construction crews could obtain visual feedback from the number of new walls that had risen and the amount of floor that had been laid by the end of the working day. Their trained eyes and their experience could also inform them of the quality of their efforts.

Binney and Smith, a Lindsay, Ontario, manufacturer of crayons, reorganized into a team structure, with each crayon-manufacturing team operating as an almost self-sufficient minifactory. Each team took responsibility for every step in the manufacturing process, including production scheduling, inventory and cost management, machine maintenance, and quality control. The operations director had 14 team leaders reporting to him in place of the previous five or six middle managers. Because he could no longer watch over them all, they each acquired considerably more autonomy. As one of three directors running the plant, he noted that there was one layer of management between himself and the people making the crayons, which "... means there's feedback very, very quickly from the vast majority of people. If there's a problem, I know it."

In traditional manufacturing, with its fragmented tasks, it is difficult to know at the end of a day the quantity and quality of the work achieved by the factory on that day and, particularly, how one's own work contributed to that total. However, team structures, augmented by technology, have changed that situation. In the body shop at SAAB Automobile, one of the first steps toward creating self-managed teams was to build the transfer lines so that bodies with defects could be rerouted back to the team that created the defect. This not only made it possible to take responsibility for the quality of the work done on the bodies, but it also created a system for learning how to avoid repeating the same defects in the future.

CHALLENGES FOR MANAGERS AND FOR SMTs

One reason for the widespread adoption of SMTs is that this form of organizing work combines some benefits of both the small and the large organization. Within a large organization, with its scale advantages in marketing and procurement, small teams of people can take responsibility for not only the ordinary and routine tasks, but also for solving problems and improving the work itself. This possibility of combining the values of large and small organization is both the major feature of and the greatest threat to the SMT organizational form. The demands for coordination and improvement in the larger organization may come into conflict with the principles and norms of the SMTs. In some instances, then, the very reason for organizing into SMTs can also become the reason for deserting SMT organization.

Industrial work demands continual improvement. To survive, the organization, if it is not protected from competition, must continually develop new and improved products and production processes. This improvement must take place within each team as well as in the larger systems of which the team is a part. The potential conflict this creates is between the requirement that each SMT have some control over its own destiny and the requirement that management be able to initiate efforts to rationalize the work throughout the organization.

Another way of stating this is that organizing around SMTs also means finding new roles for supervision and middle management as well as for some of the rationalization or improvement-support functions such as process and productivity improvement and industrial engineering. SMTs may take over some operative supervisory and managerial tasks and they must explicitly take over some of the rationalization responsibilities for continually developing the methods and organization of work. But middle and top management need not cease to manage. At least two tasks relating to SMTs must instead be developed and find new forms.

One task is the formulation and negotiation of the requirements for each SMT. The other is that of coordinating between teams, between departments, between factories, and so on. These two managerial tasks are accomplished by a combination of (1) standardizing the boundary conditions for each of the SMTs, and (2) creating a common culture, that is, common norms, common ways of interpreting demands, a common language, and common cognitive maps used when solving problems.

The methods for doing this include finding means for transforming competitive pressure and the demands of the end customers to information that each SMT may use as inputs and signals for its own improvement work. We have learned much from Japanese management about how this may be done by creating internal customers and by implanting the culture of not only fixing each particular problem but also trying to find and fix the source of each problem. In these processes, each SMT acquires a better understanding of its equipment, machinery, and operating procedures.

Management in team-based organizations must have procedures that are thought through, communicated, and accepted for dealing with an SMT that does not perform well or, worse, that develops norms that are not in accord with those of the organization. In Sweden in the 1970s, the concept of SMTs was "tried out" and sometimes found "not to be working here" because management was unable to deal with deviant teams. General reorganization was the approach taken to deal with the individual exception. Given our increased understanding of the processes of self-management, an examination of the particular problematic team is a more appropriate action for management. If necessary, the removal of individuals from the team or the dissolution of the team by moving its tasks to other more productive teams may be the best action to take.

This communication of culture and a common way of attacking problems can be accomplished by establishing arenas in which representatives from different teams can meet to solve common problems and to learn about each other's work. Personnel may rotate between teams, engage in careers that cut across team boundaries, or form "parallel learning structures" such as teams that are established to investigate more general issues for the organization at large. Management must provide the requirements and must provide time and occasion for the more explicit work on developmental activities. Otherwise, there is the danger that particular teams will instead focus, too narrowly, on completing only their daily operations.

SMTs have proven to be a very effective way of organizing work in a wide variety of situations. Although they are still not well defined, they are now a well-established organizational innovation. The particular form, norms, and culture may vary considerably from setting to setting. There is also still much room for innovation with respect to the organization of the management and support functions at levels of the larger systems. Developing ways of stimulating the continual development of productivity and quality by improving interteam coordination and culture are additional managerial challenges of great magnitude within team-based organizations.

CONCLUSION

Teams are becoming the basic unit of design for organizing work settings situated in turbulent, global environments. The innovative self-managing aspect of teams has intrigued those involved in organizational change processes and, as a result, considerable attention has been paid to the important process considerations of team building, interpersonal relations, stages of team development, and so on, by practitioners, consultants, and authors of numerous books and articles. This chapter has concentrated on different issues associated with SMTs: the changing roles of team supervisors and managers; the challenges that confront them as they lead their team-based arrangements into organizationally uncharted waters; the effects of uncertainty on the roles, resources, skills, and competencies of team members; decisions about team boundaries and inter-team coordination; the dilemmas and role conflicts that teams in general and self-managing teams in particular raise for unions and their members. This chapter has responded to these issues by presenting and explaining a set of design principles associated with different design categories for SMTs. These design principles, when applied in concert with the above-mentioned process considerations, should go a long way toward increasing the probability of success when self-managing team arrangements are implemented.

FOR FURTHER READING

Algoma Steel Corporation, Limited, and United Steelworkers of America. "Agreement to Negotiate New Collective Agreements with the Term 1992–1996," *Unionist*, February 1992, pp. 3–10. Summarizes an agreement between the newly formed Algoma Steel Corporation and the United Steelworkers, District 6, to reorganize the workplace under a worker-ownership plan that includes reducing the number of supervisors and applying team arrangements.

American Federation of Grain Millers. *The Grain Millers' Role in Creating Labor/Management Partnerships for New Work Systems: A Statement of Policy and Guidelines for Local Unions*. Minneapolis, MN: American Federation of Grain Millers, n.d. A well thought through attempt to provide guidance to local unions on the new work systems, including teams, that their members have been encountering, and to reply to other unions that question their approach.

Cherns, Albert B. "The Principles of Sociotechnical Systems Design." *Human Relations* 29 (8) (1976): pp. 783–92. A concise listing and a clear description of nine basic sociotechnical design principles including the minimal critical specifications referred to in this chapter.

Communication and Electrical Workers of Canada. *An Agenda for the Future: CWC's Position on Workplace Reorganization.* Presented at the 7th Annual CWC Convention, Quebec City, Quebec, May 7–11, 1990. A generally favorable attitude towards the workplace changes their members are experiencing but with cautions about the intent of the companies involved.

Cummings, Thomas G. "Designing Effective Work Groups." In *Handbook of Organizational Design,* vol. 2, edited by Paul C. Nystrom and William H. Starbuck. New York: Oxford University Press, 1981, 251–271. This article is a comprehensive review of the academic literature on work groups, with major variables identified and an overall model of groups, technologies, and supervisors proposed.

Emery, Fred and Eric Trist, "Sociotechnical Systems." In *Management Science, Models and Techniques,* edited by C. W. Churchman and M. Verhurst. New York: Pergamon, 1960. The classic article that first described the systemic nature of sociotechnical systems thinking.

Goodman, Paul S. and Associates. *Designing Effective Groups.* San Francisco: Jossey-Bass, 1986. An edited book of studies of research into work groups by some of the important academic researchers of work teams that includes a good introductory article on current thinking about groups.

Hackman, J. Richard. "The Psychology of Self-Management in Organizations." In *Psychology and Work: Productivity, Change, and Employment,* pp. 89–136, edited by M. S. Pollack and R. O. Perloff, Washington, D.C.: American Psychological Association, 1986.

Hackman, J. Richard, ed. *Groups That Work (and Those That Don't): Creating Conditions for Effective Teamwork.* San Francisco: Jossey-Bass, 1990. The editor and his colleagues, most of whom were his students at different phases of his development work on teams, have assembled 26 case studies within seven distinct types of work groups and arrived at *do* and *don't* prescriptions for effective work-group functioning.

Hirschhorn, L. *Managing in the New Team Environment.* Reading, MA: Addison-Wesley, 1991. A very readable book aimed at managers who must directly engage supervisors and team members as they change from traditional to self-managing team arrangements.

Ketchum, Lyman D., and Eric Trist. *All Teams Are Not Created Equal: How Employee Empowerment Really Works.* Newbury Park, CA: Sage Publications, 1992. A solid book by two of the acknowledged experts in the field of team-based organizational innovation that is filled with practical examples and good advice, yet is set within a conceptual understanding that will prevent the thoughtful reader from underestimating the difficulty of the change process.

Kolodny, Harvey, and Barbara Dresner. "Linking Arrangements and New Work Designs." *Organization Dynamics* 1985. Focusing on the links between teams and from teams to the larger organization, the article draws on several detailed case examples.

Kolodny, Harvey, and Torbjorn Stjernberg. "The Change Process in Innovative Work Designs: New Design and Redesign in Sweden, Canada and the USA." *Journal of Applied Behavioral Science* 22 (3) (1986): pp. 287–301. Provides an overall model of the change processes associated with the types of organizational innovations by which self-managing teams can succeed.

Orsbrun, Jack D., Linda Moran, Ed Musselwhite, and John H. Zenger. *Self-Directed Work Teams: The New American Challenge.* Homewood, IL: Business One Irwin, 1990). One of the better of the proliferating number of practical books on how to understand and establish self-managing work team arrangements.

Rice, A. K. *Productivity and Social Organization: The Ahmedabad Experiment.* London: Tavistock Publications, 1958. An early, classic study from a sociotechnical systems perspective that postulates rules for work-group design based on studies of the work groups in Indian weaving mills.

Rollin, Glaser, ed. *Classic Readings in Self-Managing Teamwork.* King of Prussia, PA: Organization Design and Development, 1992. A fine collection of many of the classic articles on work groups, including some quite recent publications.

Sandberg, Thomas. *Autonomous Work Groups.* Lund, Sweden: Liber, 1982. An excellent review of the development of autonomous work group concepts in Norway and Sweden, including much of the positioning that took place among unions, employers, and social scientists on the subject.

Stjernberg, Torbjorn, and Ake Philips. "Organizational Innovations in a Long-Term Perspective: Legitimacy and Souls-of-Fire as Critical Factors of Change and Viability." *Human Relations,* forthcoming. Based on eight studies over a period of 20 years of an insurance company, providing an illustrative and representative case of organizational innovation based on self-managing teams that is still viable after 18 years.

Stymne, Ingrid, "The Structure of Work," Doctoral Dissertation, Department of Psychology, Stockholm Univ. 1992. This study integrates several separate studies of work groups in schools into a process model of work-group functioning that examines coordination and effectiveness in small task groups.

Trist, Eric. "The Evolution of Sociotechnical Systems." In *Organization Design and Behavior,* edited by A. H. Van de Ven and William F. Joyce. New York: Wiley-Interscience; 1981. Also in Occasional Paper No. 2; Ontario Quality of Working Life Centre, Toronto, 1981. A comprehensive overview of sociotechnical systems theory and its origins, concepts, and applications, with significant attention given to the conceptual bases of work groups.

Trist, Eric, and Ken Bamforth. "The Social and Psychological Consequences of the Long Wall Methods of Coal Getting." *Human Relations* 4 (1951): pp. 3–38. A study of technology and work organization changes in the coal-mining groups of the United Kingdom and one of the best known of the original Tavistock Institute studies that became the basis of the field of sociotechnical systems design.

Tuckman, P. W. "Development Sequences in Small Groups." *Psychological Bulletin* 63 (1965): pp. 384–399. One of the best known formulations of the stages of group development under the categories of "forming, storming, norming and performing."

Wall, Toby D., Nigel J. Kemp, Paul R. Jackson, and Chris W. Clegg. "Outcomes of Autonomous Workgroups: A Long-Term Field Experiment." *Academy of Management Journal* 29 (2), pp. 280–304. A study of work teams in the confectionary industry in the United Kingdom and, as the title suggests, one of the few longitudinal studies of the subject.

MANAGING DIVERSITY: UTILIZING THE TALENTS OF THE NEW WORK FORCE

11

R. Roosevelt Thomas, Jr.

MANAGING DIVERSITY: AN EVOLVING MANAGERIAL CONCEPT

Managers have heard much about changing demographics and diversity in the last five years. Some have become concerned and have stepped up diversity activity; others have ignored the discussion and continued business as usual. Still others have bogged down in a state of confusion, not knowing what to make of all the noise. What is becoming clear, however, is that managers more and more will have to take diversity into account as they seek to ensure the viability of their organizations.

In this chapter, I will place the diversity discussion in context, present a description of a promising approach called Managing Diversity, and provide guidelines for those who desire to launch Managing Diversity.

I speak from the perspective of my experience as president of The American Institute for Managing Diversity, where for more than eight years I and other staff members have been active in fostering the evolution of the approach called Managing Diversity. We have conducted research, presented seminars, and consulted with executives in a variety of enterprises.

A word of caution is in order for the reader. Managing Diversity is truly an evolving concept. In these pages one will not find definitive, detailed instructions or discussions of how corporations have done MD. Indeed, we do not know of organizations in which MD is an institutionalized reality, but we do know of situations where the MD process has been launched. What follows below is a historical perspective and a sketch of how the future is likely to evolve as managers address the growing reality of diversity in general and employee diversity in particular. To date, MD has without a doubt been an evolutionary experience.

DISCUSSION CONTEXT

Before examining Managing Diversity in detail, establishment of a framework of definitions and historical perspective may be helpful.

Definitions

Managing Diversity (MD) is the process of creating and maintaining an environment that naturally enables all organizational participants to reach their full potential in pursuit of the enterprise's objectives.

Three words in this definition merit highlighting. One, *process* implies that MD is not a program or an initiative, but rather an ongoing way of life or way of operating. Two, *naturally* suggests that the goal is an environment that will need no special arrangements to avoid inappropriate, unnecessary barriers. Three, *all* reflects the reality that MD relates to all members of the organization, not just selected target groups.

Managing is a word misunderstood with respect to diversity. Often, individuals will ask, "Why do you have to talk about *managing diversity?* Why not talk about enabling diversity, valuing diversity, or enriching through diversity?" Typically, those raising these questions define managing as controlling, containing, or coping with, and believe that associating diversity with managing is to imply that diversity is a problem.

That is not my intent. I define managing as enabling, empowering, or influencing. Thus the fundamental question in Managing Diversity becomes the following: As a manager goes about empowering or enabling his or her work force, and as that work force becomes increasingly diverse, are there any managerial tasks that must change?

This is a question that has not been asked. Instead, managers have focused on creating diverse work forces or on including groups that have traditionally been excluded from significant roles in the workplace. Projected demographic changes suggest that creation of a diverse group of employees will become less of a challenge. The issue will be whether the enterprise has the managerial and organizational wherewithal to secure the necessary level of productivity from a diverse work force.

In the term *Managing Diversity, diversity* takes on a meaning different from how the word commonly is used. Managers tend to use *diversity* to refer to minorities, minorities and women, or simply anyone who is not a healthy white male. Instead, in *Managing Diversity, diversity*—much like the word *stew*—refers to the collective mixture.

When I say "stew," you do not think separately of meat, celery, carrots, beans, potatoes, and onions, but rather of a collective mixture of these elements and others. Similarly, diversity refers to the collective mixture called the work force and includes whoever is in a given work force, including the white male.

Accordingly, when we say "Managing Diversity" we are not referring to white males learning how to manage others, but rather *any* manager enhancing his or her ability to empower whoever is in his or her work force.

Diversity here refers not only to the dimensions of race and gender, but rather to an infinite number of dimensions, such as age, tenure with the organization, education, functional background, exempt or nonexempt status, union or nonunion membership, lifestyle, sexual orientation, and physical ability, just to name a few. The point is that individuals can vary along a vast array of dimensions.

Diversity also means more than just cultural diversity, which in everyday use refers to characteristics of individuals. Diversity is much broader and includes other kinds of diversity; for example, acquisition/merger diversity, diversity of lines of business, and functional diversity.

Increasingly, managers are recognizing that successful acquisitions and mergers depend on effective management of the organizational cultural diversity reflected in participant corporations. When Time, Inc., and Warner Communications announced their plans to merge, one question that quickly surfaced was whether the two cultures could mesh.[1,2]

In a similar vein, one manager described challenges associated with lines-of-business diversity.

> We are a mature company with a mature business line which has been our major source of revenue and profits. Over the past ten years, we have established some new lines. Managers of these new lines have complained of being shut out of decision making, of not receiving their fair share of budgetary resources, and of not being valued in general. I see this as a diversity issue.

One other attribute of diversity merits mention. We customarily assume diversity and differences to be synonymous. Thus we talk about Managing Diversity and Managing Differences as if they were one. They are not. In the context of the mixture, diversity includes similarities *and* differences. Managing Diversity, therefore, requires that managers take similarities and differences into account. Managers do not have the luxury of focusing on differences alone or similarities alone.

As we leave this discussion of definitions, I want to stress that diversity refers to the *mixture*. Consider a jar of red jelly beans and assume that you will add some green and purple jelly beans (see Figure 11-1). Everyday use of the word diversity would identify the green and purple jelly beans as representing diversity. The mixture definition says that diversity really is represented by the resultant *mixture* of red, green, and purple jelly beans (see Figure 11-2).

Most managers have not been addressing diversity, but rather what should be done about the last jelly beans added to the mixture. The good news is that we have not failed at MD, but are just now attempting it.

Why Now?

If we are just placing MD on the agenda, what are the motives?

An obvious candidate is the projected changes in work force demographics, as presented in *Workforce 2000*,[3] a report prepared by The Hudson Institute and sponsored by the Department of Labor. This report predicts that minorities, women, and immigrants will play a greater role in the workplace. Anticipating this shift, many corporations have moved to enhance their diversity efforts. As important as these projections are, they are not the primary force behind the growing interest in MD.

I believe that the principal driver is a changing attitude toward being different. In the past, people who were considered different tended to view

FIGURE 11-1

FIGURE 11-2

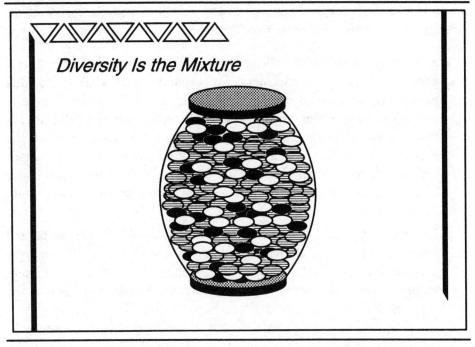

Diversity Is the Mixture

this condition as meaning they were inferior or inadequate; thus, they were eager to join corporations, to assimilate, and to be mainstreamed.

Now, increasingly, people who are considered different do not see this condition as negative and, in fact, may celebrate being different. As celebrants of their differences, they are less eager to assimilate, to be mainstreamed. They now are inclined to say, "I want to join your corporation, but I do not want to compromise who I am unnecessarily." These individuals are willing to assimilate—to fit in, to adapt—but only when absolutely necessary.

This means that the manager must deal more with unassimilated diversity: with people who differ on and below the surface, as opposed to individuals who appear different on the surface, but behave similarly as a result of assimilation. If it were not for the change in attitude about being different, individuals would be more willing to leave their differences at the door and the manager would not face the issue of unassimilated diversity.

How important is this shift in attitude? It is very important.

In seminars, we often find remnants of the old attitude. With a small number of seminar participants seated in a horseshoe we sometimes begin by going around the horseshoe and asking individuals to say how they differ from their colleagues. The inability or reluctance to come up with a difference to share stems from a lack of comfort with being different.

On the other hand, an increasing number of people in the pipeline preparing for the workplace, as well as individuals already in corporations, view difference from a different perspective.

- A group of Morehouse College students (all black males) attending a panel discussion on requirements for corporate success asked "To what extent will we have to compromise our blackness?" Twenty-five years ago, when I was a Morehouse student, my colleagues and I did not ask that question. We wanted to learn the requirements and be given the chance to meet them. African-American students today want to make certain that requirements do not unnecessarily call for the compromise of their valued blackness, even when they may disagree among themselves as to what it is.

- During an informal discussion on diversity, a white male fantasized about the advantages of knowing what different groups add to an organization. He said, "For example, wouldn't it be nice to know what white women bring to the table? Then we could more easily sell them to the corporation."

    The ranking woman in the division responded to the hypothetical inquiry in a surprising way: "If you find out what it means to be feminine, let me know. These days I don't feel too feminine."

    What was she saying? Essentially, she was expressing concern about the personal costs of her success. "I've been successful in this corporation and value my achievements, but when I look back over the past ten or fifteen years, I think that I may have given up something that I would have preferred to have kept."

    Women today are saying to all kinds of organizations that they wish to become critical players on the team, but not at the expense of compromising unnecessarily their femininity, however they define it.

- A CEO reports calling an early-morning meeting of his direct reports, only to learn that one of his key vice presidents could not attend because it was his week to drive his children to the nursery. This unavailability took the CEO aback. He said that when he had nursery-aged kids, he never had to worry about taking care of them. He was shocked that the vice president not only could not make the meeting, but also was prepared to pay the price for not attending. Now, the CEO checks with his colleagues before scheduling "call" meetings.

In sum, organizational participants are bringing their differences with them and insisting that managers take them into account, all because they are becoming more comfortable with being different. Not long ago, if an employee had a child-care, elder-care, or family illness problem, he or she was expected to take care of it outside working hours. The changing attitude toward being different has indeed been a major force behind the need to manage diversity.

This changing attitude toward being different can be traced to several factors. First, the Civil Rights Movement said to minorities that one does not have to be white to be okay. Second, the Women's Rights Movement has said to women one does not have to be male to be okay. Third, "knowledge workers" are more prevalent in today's work force and expect to have discretion in the performance of their tasks.[4] Fourth, changing family authority patterns encourage offspring to raise questions and not obey blindly. Finally, global economic developments suggest that the American way of doing business is not the only way, nor necessarily the best alternative. All of this contributes to greater comfort with being different.

The demographic changes and the growing comfort with "being different" within organizations lead to another factor driving the need to manage diversity: diversity tension. Diversity tension refers to the strain caused by an organization's or individual's encounter with something that is different. When a corporation encounters something different—whether it is other people, new lines of business, differences related to acquisitions/mergers, or differences among functions—the manager has essentially five options.

1. Deny (ignore) the differences. This alternative generates the least tension if the different element allows the denial.

2. Accept the element only if it agrees to be assimilated and to shed the difference(s) causing the tension.

3. Accept the element as long as it agrees to act *as though* it were not different. Here, assimilation is not required, but suppression of differences is necessary.

4. Accept the element, but segregate it. For example, in a firm where smoking is not allowed, smokers may be accepted if they agree to segregation and discrimination.

5. Accept the element with the understanding that changes of one's way of life will be necessary to create an environment that works equally well for the different element and others. This option generates the greatest amount of tension during the period of transition to the new way of operating but in the long run offers the most promise for sustainable progress with minimizing diversity tension and building upon differences as well as similarities. It also is the alternative increasingly being faced by managers, primarily because employees are becoming more comfortable with being different.

Questions characterize the period of diversity tension. Examples are plentiful.

- School Systems
  - What do we need to do now that our student population is no longer all white?
  - What kind of changes are required to develop a curriculum that works equally well for all members of a diverse student body?
- Volunteer Organizations
  - How do we develop a diverse group of volunteers to serve increasingly diverse constituencies?
  - How must we change our mission in light of changing demographics?
- Work Forces
  - What difference does it make if an individual is different? How does it affect his or her ability to do well in our corporation?
  - How much diversity is too much?
  - How much do we have to do to accommodate people who are different? When will we have done enough?
- Lines of Business
  - How much autonomy do we give managers in new lines of business? How far do we allow them to stray from our traditional way of doing business?
  - How do we maintain a sense of common purpose while allowing the lines autonomy?
  - How much personnel movement do we allow or encourage among the lines?
- Acquisitions and Mergers
  - Which organization's culture will be dominant in the new arrangement?
  - How do we go about institutionalizing the dominant culture?
  - How much autonomy do we allow the acquired organization?
- National Demographics
  - Given the demographic shifts, how do we assure that our traditions and values are maintained?
  - Given the demographic shifts, how must we change our culture to reflect the changing population?

The reality of diversity tension hit home in a small group meeting. This group had met several times, and at each session one member had taken a substantial amount of time to press a point of view not understood by his colleagues. Finally, one group member told the persistent presenter that he was tired of hearing and trying to understand the point of view being presented. Another member commented, "We are trying to decide how much time we should devote to understanding your perspective, and whether we should insist that you assimilate or leave." As we listened to ourselves, it became clear that we were experiencing diversity tension, although we shared a strong common interest in the topic under discussion and were alike in other significant ways.

Finally, with respect to the driving forces behind the need to manage diversity, one additional factor plays a major role: economic necessity. Diversity tension hinders organizational viability because it creates divisiveness that distracts from the participants' ability to focus on performance issues; instead, attention is siphoned off to deal with minimizing the negatives associated with the manifestation of differences. Rare is the corporation or organization that does not have to worry about economic viability. Therefore, organizations must strive to create an environment that works for all individuals and to assure continued organizational viability.

Now that we have examined definitions and the forces driving the need to manage diversity, let's complete the contextual framework with a review of traditional approaches to diversity.

TRADITIONAL APPROACHES

One can describe the historical treatments of diversity as (1) Denial, (2) Affirmative Action/assimilation, and (3) Understanding Differences.

Denial

Historically, denial of diversity and differences has played a major role in managerial thinking. Managers would tell employees who were different that their differences would not in any way affect how the organization treated them. Instead, merit and performance alone would determine how far the individual would go.

Statements reflecting the denial approach would be, "In this corporation, we are race-blind, color-blind, and gender-blind. We will not prejudge you." Or "John, when I look at you, I do not see a black man. I simply see a competent individual like myself who has done well." (This last comment was made by a white male to a black male and was intended as a compliment. It is a sign of changing times that the black male did not view it as such and thought an unspoken response, "Who wants to be like you?")

The basic assumptions of this denial approach have been the following:

- To be different is to have some kind of defect or disadvantage.
- Not to see the difference means that you are not prejudging the individual as having a weakness or limitation.

- To avoid this prejudgment constitutes a favor to the individual with the difference.
- Simply to avoid prejudment is enough to ensure the elimination of discrimination within the organization.
- The organization's culture, based on the requirements of the dominant group, would remain intact. I refer to a culture based on the needs of one group as a monoculture.

The motivation for practicing denial has tended to be legal (the law requires it), moral (personal or corporate moral prescriptions require it), or social responsibility (good corporate citizenship requires it). Regardless of the motivation, the major benefits of the approach have been that people who are different have been able to enter organjzations with the hope that they would not be prejudged, that quality interpersonal relationships have been fostered, and that blatant racism, sexism, and other discriminations have been discouraged.

One the other hand, two severe limitations exist with this approach. It requires that people who are different are willing to have their differences denied. When individuals were less inclined to celebrate being different, this requirement was not a problem. Now, this requirement makes it extremely difficult for a manager to practice denial. People just are not as willing to see their differences as negatives and to have them denied.

An additional limitation is the assumption that the major source of discrimination is within personal relationships. This premise ignores discriminatory capability unintentionally and intentionally built into organizational systems and cultures, and leaves in place conditions that do not work naturally to enable all people to reach their full potential in pursuit of the enterprise's objectives.

Affirmative Action/Assimilation

For approximately the past twenty years, Affirmative Action (AA) and assimilation have been the core of organizations' approach to employee diversity. Through Affirmative Action managers have reached out to create a diverse work force with respect to race and gender. They have aimed for a melting pot wherein new employees are supposed to lose their differences and are shaped to fit a mold that reflects existing organizational behavior norms. Hence, managers could say they had a diverse work force, for indeed they had minorities and women, but in reality the diversity was only at the surface. Assimilation through the melting pot was to ensure minimization of differences and conformity of behavior. The result has been "assimilated diversity," which in fact is diversity only of surface appearance.

Melting pot activities have included mentoring programs in which white males have modeled and taught the appropriate behavior. Another example of the melting pot is the seminar designed to help minorities and women learn how to succeed in corporations dominated by white males. Again, melting pot efforts have been aimed at minimizing, if not eliminating, differences, and at fostering acceptable white male behavior.

The above scenario describes the assimilation effort in a white-male-dominated corporation. In reality, all organizations have relied upon this approach; therefore, while specifics would change given the nature of the dominant participants of the enterprise, the dynamics would remain the same, whether the organization is a church, academic institution, country, government agency, or volunteer enterprise.

The Affirmative Action/assimilation model has been grounded on two basic assumptions.

1. The existing organizational practices deserved to be continued, and deviation from them was undesirable and detrimental.
2. The individual employee was willing to adapt.

The belief has been that this approach would be the means for creating a diverse work force and for facilitating upward mobility for minorities and women. A major benefit of this alternative has been greater inclusion of minorities and women in corporations and other organizations than before. But progress with upward mobility for minorities and women has been elusive and difficult to sustain, despite strong legal, moral, and social responsibility motives.

The limitations of this approach have been several in number.

First, in times of an economic pie that is perceived to be shrinking, it is difficult to have AA succeed without generating white male backlash and charges of preferential treatment, since AA does not include white males. Consequently, managers have had great difficulty sustaining AA progress.

Second, to the extent that employees celebrate their differences, they become resistant to adaptation except where it is absolutely necessary. The greater the resistance, the greater the difficulty in implementing AA.

Implied here is that while there always will be assimilation and the requirement to fit a mold, managers will increasingly have to focus on true requirements as parameters governing adaptation, and not on preferences, traditions, or convenience. A significant implication is that major shifts in the way of doing business may be necessary to come up with a mold that works for a diverse set of employees. In the interim, the growing tendency to celebrate differences will make implementation of AA/assimilation difficult.

Third, when success with AA is realized, the manager can never relax and pronounce AA a "done deal." A moment of relaxing leads to the threat of all progress unraveling, since AA goes against the natural inclinations built into organizational systems and culture. Relaxation allows natural organizational tendencies to reassert themselves.

Here I have assumed that, as our research has indicated, the typical organization has been built around the needs and natural inclinations of the dominant group, whatever it may be, and that these do not reflect the requirements necessary for enabling a diverse group of employees. Stated differently, managers have not built their organizations on the assumption of a diverse work force. Affirmative Action, as practiced traditionally, does not seek to change existing systems and culture, but rather complements them in order to accommodate people who are different or do not fit.

Consider this example.

A corporation's managers note that its developmental and upward-mobility systems does not sufficiently produce minority and women candidates for movement upward in the hierarchy. In an AA mode, they create a special process for minorities and women. This process generates substantial results for about two years, after which the company's executives evaluate their efforts.

In the evaluation, minorities and women acknowledge and express appreciation for the progress achieved, but complain about the AA stigma attached to the success. They argue for everyone to go up through the old system. White males similarly applaud the progress, but say they are concerned about preferential treatment. They too argue for everyone's going through the old process. Senior executives look at their success to date and conclude that they now know how to manage minorities and women, and they too argue for eliminating the special arrangements and uniting everyone under the old system.

What can be predicted as everyone once again goes up through the old system? Given that the old system has never been corrected, but rather simply complemented by the special process, it will still be unable to work for all employees. And once again, someone will conclude that the system is not working for minorities and women. If the corporation remains in the AA mode, its managers will again make special arrangements for minorities and women. And the cycle will repeat.

Fourth, AA does not have the capability of eliminating the glass ceiling, the invisible line beyond which minorities and women as groups cannot move up the managerial hierarchy. This limitation manifests itself in the disproportionate clustering of minorities and women at the bottom of organizational pyramids. I have seen this clustering in enterprises with excellent AA progress and also in enterprises with poor AA track records. Progress in eliminating the ceiling through AA tends to be temporary and grounded in special efforts. Once managers drop the special efforts, the glass ceiling of the status quo reappears.

Fifth, the "frustrating cycle of AA" undermines its implementation. The cycle begins with recognition of a problem, which might be inadequate representation, lack of upward mobility, or excessive turnover for a given group. In any event, the next phase brings forth a burst of solution activity. Typically included are efforts to enhance the quality of new recruits and also special programs to foster upward mobility and retention for target employee groups. With these solutions implemented, the manager moves to celebrate apparent progress. By "progress," I mean that programs are in place and results (better recruits, increased promotions for members of the given group, and decreased turnover rates) are beginning to appear.

Following celebration, the managers relax and await additional fruits of their labor. Regrettably, they typically are not forthcoming, largely because AA is artificial and requires continual attention and effort. The apparent progress becomes undone, the number of promotions declines, and new recruits leave or stagnate. Once again the problem is recognized and the cycle begins anew.

Most large corporations are in some phase of this cycle. The reality of the cycle and its growing costs are encouraging managers to seek ways of complementing AA.

Finally, the beneficiaries of AA often have mixed feelings about the benefits. They know AA is needed but also want to avoid the stigma attached to their achievements as "AA beneficiaries." This concern can lead to lifelong efforts "to prove" individual merit and worth.[4] These mixed feelings do not contribute to an environment conducive to implementing AA.

To some proponents of AA, the above discussion may appear to be an attack on AA. It is not. It simply is a description of AA's limitations. I too am an advocate of AA, but I am developing an appreciation for what it can and cannot do. Our challenge is to avoid asking more of AA than we should.

Understanding Differences

Understanding Differences (UD) is a derivative of the traditional AA/assimilation approach. The AA assumptions of assimilation and mono-culture hold for this option as well. Additionally, a basic assumption of UD is that conflict and poor interpersonal relationships are due to lack of understanding.

The goal, therefore, of UD is to foster awareness, acceptance and understanding of differences among individuals, with the expectation that the results would be enhanced interpersonal relationships, greater appreciation and respect of others, greater acceptance of differences, and minimization of blatant expressions of racism, sexism, and other prejudice. And indeed these expected results often do materialize.

As impressive as the results can be in terms of greater harmony, the limitations are also significant. Most critical is that UD leaves unchanged the systems and culture of the organization. The manager, therefore, can accept and understand differences, be free of racism and sexism, and have excellent interpersonal relationships, and still not know how to manage diversity—not know how to create a set of systems and a culture that will naturally enable all employees. Also, without culture and system changes, the UD manager finds it difficult to sustain gains.

A limitation shared by all three approaches is that they eliminate or minimize differences. This loss prevents the manager from realizing gains associated with diversity. One manager commented, "It's ironic. We often seek people who are different, but then work to assimilate them as soon as they join."

This irony is especially pronounced with UD, where participants often enhance their acceptance and their understanding of diversity while holding on to strong expectations of assimilation to the existing culture.

In sum, all of the traditional approaches have limitations that inhibit their utility as effective vehicles for creating an environment that works naturally for all. It is in the context of this circumstance that the concept of Managing Diversity is evolving.

MANAGING DIVERSITY: THE CONCEPT

Several attributes differentiate MD from the traditional approaches.

MD differs from Affirmative Action in significant ways. AA assumes assimilation, that the individual who is different or who does not fit will adapt. MD assumes that the manager and the organization, as well as the individual, will be willing to engage in a mutual adaptation process to produce a productive relationship between the individual and the organization.

AA focuses on recruitment, upward mobility, and retention, while MD addresses the question of utilization. Here, the assumption is that to the extent that an individual's potential is tapped, the manager has to worry less about upward mobility and retention. The emphasis on utilization suggests that it is not sufficient to meet the needs of employees, for individuals can have their needs met and still be underutilized. Employees can be satisfied and underutilized. MD is not so much a call to secure more diversity, but rather a means of better utilizing the diversity already on board.

Because of its grounding in the legal motive, AA requires achievement of the desired results as early as possible. If you are out of line legally, you wish to realign yourself as quickly as possible. MD on the other hand stresses producing the desired results as *naturally* as possible. The assumption is that the manager will be able to sustain the results longer if they flow from an environment that naturally generates them.

Finally, AA emphasizes doing something for the "disadvantaged." MD seeks to do something for the manager who needs to enhance his or her ability to enable an increasingly diverse work force. MD is not about doing something for minorities and women, eliminating discrimination, doing justice, being fair, doing good, doing the "right thing," leveling the playing field, making amends for past wrongs, or about civil rights or women's rights. It is about improving the manager's managerial capability.

Similarly, MD differs from Understanding Differences. UD works to foster acceptance and understanding of differences, while MD focuses on improving managerial capability. As noted earlier, improvement in accepting and understanding differences does not necessarily mean progress with managerial capability.

MD stresses the business (viability) motive above the legal, moral, and social motives. Given the magnitude of changes of ways of doing business associated with MD, the traditional legal, moral, and social-responsibility motives are not sufficient. Making the bottom-line case for MD represents a major challenge, simply because most managers have not viewed the traditional diversity dimensions of race and gender as business issues.

How diversity is a viability issue for a given organization depends on the nature of its operations. The following are some ways in which I have seen MD become a bottom-line factor.

- Organizations recruiting from a diverse pool of applicants and seeking to attract the best candidates can gain competitive advantage in this effort, if they create before their competitors an environment that works naturally for everyone.

- Many corporations are attempting to strengthen their competitive position. Much of what is being done for this purpose cannot be implemented fully without Managing Diversity capability. For example, Total Quality, highly committed self-managing teams, and participatory management cannot be implemented with a diverse work force without the capability to manage diversity.

- Corporations are focusing ever more on external constituencies and learning how diverse their environments are becoming. The ability to manage diversity internally enhances an organization's ability to manage external diversity.

- A corporation cannot be truly global without a Managing Diversity capability. American corporations seeking to be global will have to decide whether they will be an American company doing business internationally or a global corporation that happens to be located in America. The latter option requires an environment that will work for anyone from any part of the global work force. Such an environment cannot be created without Managing Diversity capability.

MD calls for working on the individual, interpersonal, and organizational levels. Traditionally, much effort has been devoted to helping individuals come to grips with their personal predispositions toward differences and learn to build and maintain quality interpersonal relationships across diverse groups. MD calls for the continuation of those efforts, but also recognizes the need to work on the organizational level.

Managers have ignored organizational dimensions, primarily because they have assumed that the individual employee would adjust. Under this assumption, the manager has no need to explore the possibility of change at the organizational level. With relaxation of the assimilation assumption, managers implementing MD must work organizational culture and system issues.

MD addresses the organizational dimensions of culture and systems. By culture, I mean the fundamental assumptions that drive behaviors in an organization.[5] Over the years, these assumptions have worked well and have been a source of the organization's success. They have worked so well that they are taken for granted and are not at the participants' conscious level, and yet they drive everything that happens in the organization.

These assumptions can be compared to the roots of a tree as shown in Figure 11-3. A key principle is that the roots control the branches. Nothing can be sustained naturally in the branches unless it is congruent with the roots. Herein lies the rationale for making consideration of the roots part of the MD process. Given MD's focus on creating an environment that works naturally for all, the MD manager has no choice but to seek congruence between the roots and what he or she is trying to achieve through MD.

One assumption (root) we have uncovered through research in more than one organization is expressed by the statement, "We should act as if we are family." This means that one's relationships should be analogous to those of a family. While notions of family can vary, we have found the assumption to be that of the traditional United States, father-dominated model.

Does this root hinder or facilitate Managing Diversity? It hinders it in two principal ways.

First, the concept of family is not inclusive. Only three avenues of entry into the family are available, birth, marriage, and adoption. Otherwise, it is not possible to become a member. Given these limited entry alternatives, this family concept does not facilitate inclusion.

Second, this family concept often gives rise to paternalistic climates in which managers are analogous to parents and employees are analogous to children. This hampers utilization of the empowerment model of management, since it is difficult to empower children. Given that empowerment is at

FIGURE 11-3   Culture as tree roots

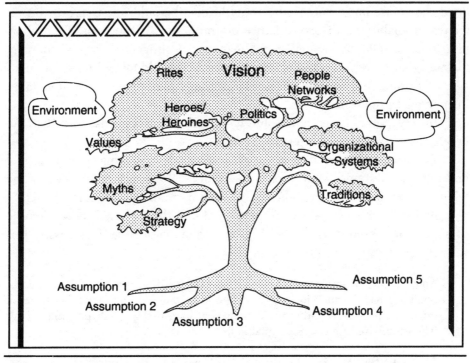

the heart of Managing Diversity, to the extent that the family root prevents use of that managerial approach, it hinders the launching of MD.

Another example of a root we have seen can be expressed in the statement, "We ought to behave in ways that are fair." In this assumption fairness is an important criterion for assessing the appropriateness of actions.

Does it facilitate or hinder MD? To the extent that this root contributes to a rationale other than the business (viability) motive for moving forward with MD, it hinders the launching process, simply because failure to see this as a bottom-line issue greatly reduces the likelihood of progress.

Given that the roots of most corporations are put in place when the work force is relatively homogeneous, now as the work force becomes more diverse, MD suggests that it is managerially prudent at least to ask whether the old roots will work under the new circumstances. Failure to check and modify old roots as necessary explains, at least in part, the frustrating AA cycle experienced by many organizations. Managers have not taken care to assure that organizational roots (assumptions) are congruent with their diversity aspirations.

Changing roots is not easy. One senior executive remarked, "I like the roots of this corporation. I came here because of the roots and have done well because of the roots. I do not want to change them."

I suggested to this manager that it was not a question of whether he liked the roots, but whether the roots he liked would allow him to be effective in enabling a diverse mixture of employees. If they would not allow him to be an effective manager, his managerial obligations to his company dictated that he develop a new set of roots that would allow him to be managerially productive with diverse organizational participants as well as meet his personal preferences.

In any event, there is absolutely no substitute for ensuring that the organization's roots are supportive of MD.

This same type of diagnostic analysis must to be made with formal and informal systems. Managers must examine these systems to determine whether they have the capability of working naturally for all participants.

Attention must be given to the formal and the informal. One example of an informal system is sponsoring. A corporate president discussed this informal process within his company:

> Above a certain level, we require more than written performance appraisals. Someone has to vouch for the candidate for promotion. Someone has to stand up for the individual and push. Without that sponsorship, we bypass individuals who otherwise might appear qualified.

MD says that there is nothing improper about the sponsoring process, as long as everyone has a chance to qualify for sponsorship. This requires a monitoring of this informal system to ensure that it is able to work for everyone. A major challenge in this regard is the unearthing of the informal and the promotion of discussion and analysis. Unfortunately, many managers act as if the informal does not exist and accept no responsibility for its functioning. This is not acceptable under MD.

Our biggest challenge with regard to formal systems is not to assume that they are acceptable merely because they work for the majority of the employees. Traditionally, as indicated earlier, if an employee does not fit with an existing system, managers place the burden of adjustment and adaptation on the individual. Managing Diversity calls for managers and organizations to share in the adjustment process.

MD requires that managers manage. Poor management is the *major* barrier to implementing MD. Research done at The American Institute for Managing Diversity suggests that managers do not manage and, indeed, have not been asked to manage.

At the heart of MD is the assumption that managers should empower or enable employees to become all they can become in pursuit of organizational objectives. Empowerment managers focus on creating and maintaining cultures, systems, and climates that foster productivity. They *do* little work; instead, they *facilitate* the work of the employees. This means that the manager of engineering and the manager of marketing do very little engineering or marketing.

In reality, we have found that managers spend more time doing work than enabling others. Furthermore, their corporations expect and accept this behavior. Even where training programs and CEO rhetoric endorse empowerment, in the trenches you will find managers doing work. Implicit in MD, then, is a call for a major shift in the role of the manager.

I have been discussing the MD concept in the context of work-force diversity. This is appropriate because that is where public concern and attention are currently focused. I emphasize, however, that the concept applies to all kinds of diversity, such as functional, lines-of-business, and acquisitions/mergers diversity. While specifics may differ, the dynamics are similar.

LAUNCHING MANAGING DIVERSITY

Over the past eight years, from the perspective of The American Institute for Managing Diversity I have observed pioneering managers launch Managing Diversity in their organizations. From these managers' efforts we can glean guidelines that can facilitate progress for those wishing to move forward with Managing Diversity.

Guideline 1: Begin with yourself. Ask yourself whether you truly understand what MD is and whether you see it as a strategic business issue, as opposed to being motivated by legal, moral, or social-responsibility concerns. Without a grasp of MD as a concept, or a sense of the rationale of strategic viability, you must gain greater understanding before moving forward. Such clarity and awareness are essential if you are to be effective as a leader of the process.

Guideline 2: Determine whether you are willing to accept the roles of advocate and agent of change. Unlike a helium balloon that ascends on its own once launched, MD requires advocates and drum majors to ensure its success. Initially, advocates will have to gain the buy-in—the acceptance and commitment of key decision makers—by making the case for MD and its potential benefits. After buy-in and commitment have been achieved, drum majors will be necessary to lead the pioneering implementation process.

Guideline 3: Develop a strategic plan. The document should at least include the following: reflections of a guiding conceptual framework, a sense of the "big picture" facing the company, an understanding of the strategic, viability rationale for moving forward, a vision of what success would be, statement about the status quo, descriptions of how to get from the status quo to the desired state, and a list of factors that will facilitate or hinder progress. This plan subsequently becomes the framework for all launching activity.

Often, strategic plans are not developed. Drawing from past experiences, change agents sometimes believe that they have only a brief opportunity to act. In these circumstances, the change leaders assume that opportunity will be so brief that strategic planning makes little sense. And indeed there is some truth in this position. Multi-year strategic plans are of little value when one expects the opportunity to last less than one year.

On the other hand, in the absence of a strategic plan, change leaders have difficulty determining how they might effectively influence key decision makers, what action options would give the greatest leverage, and what (if any) progress has been achieved. Recently, a diversity task force leader observed, "Since we have been in existence, we have put out all obvious fires. Yet we aren't certain we've done the right thing or that we indeed have made progress." These comments reflected a lack of strategic awareness and planning.

Guideline 4: Use the umbrella approach. In pursuit of full utilization of all human resources, the manager must use a four-handle umbrella as shown in Figure 11-4.

In the short run all four handles (traditional human resource systems, Affirmative Action, Understanding Differences, and Managing Diversity) must be used at the same time. In the long run, the four handles collapse into one

FIGURE 11-4 The four-handle umbrella approach

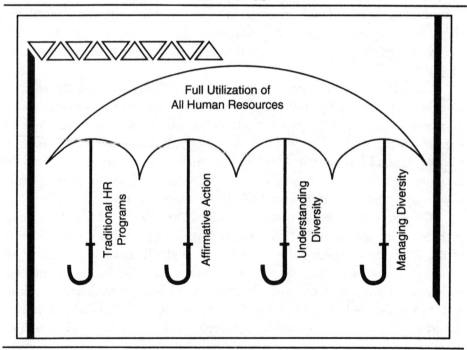

that reflects an MD capability. But in the short run, all four handles have to be utilized.

MD does not call for an either/or perspective with respect to the other approaches. This means that an organization's diversity plan should as a minimum have AA, UD, MD, and traditional human resource systems components.

Guideline 5: Develop the "strategic business" rationale for launching MD. Critical to successful implementation of MD is the understanding that MD is a strategic component of the organization's viability efforts. Without this awareness, motivation is not sufficient. Once organization participants see this as a business issue, their perspectives and attitudes become markedly different.

Change leaders, therefore, should give priority to making the "strategic viability" case for MD. Without this motive, progress will be difficult.

Guideline 6: Foster shifts of mindset. Ultimately, organizational participants will have to change their ways of thinking about diversity. If MD is to be institutionalized, participants throughout the organization will eventually have to experience mindset shifts. The required shifts will have to be in a number of directions.

- Thinking in terms of the umbrella
- Seeing diversity as including everyone
- Seeing MD as primarily for the manager's benefit
- Giving priority to the strategic business (viability) motive
- Using the doer and empowerment managerial models
- Realizing that there is no quick fix

Guideline 7: Audit and modify culture and systems as necessary. At the core of the MD process is the cultural audit. The cultural audit, a research process, brings the organization's roots to the surface and examines its systems to identify hindrances to and facilitators of the desired state. Once the analysis is complete, the necessary modifications would begin. If the natural organizational order is to be supportive of MD, there is no substitute for the auditing and modifying of culture and systems as necessary.

Guideline 8: Adopt a long-term time frame. Institutionalizing MD requires several years, perhaps, for some organizations, as many as twenty. Here we should keep in mind that we are talking about *institutionalization*. Substantial benefits can be gained early in the process long before institutionalization becomes reality.

Given this time requirement, change leaders must have the appropriate mindset. They must adopt the attitude of the long-distance runner, taking one day at a time and celebrating small victories. Without this mindset, the change agent faces the probability of not being able to handle the required time commitment.

Guideline 9: Adopt a pioneering attitude. To move forward with MD is to pioneer. The mindset of the pioneer is different from that of the individual preferring the well-trodden path. Change leaders must assist organization participants in coping with the rigors of pioneering.

FREQUENT QUESTIONS

I suspect that this chapter raises for the reader more questions than it answers. That is appropriate in the case of an evolving concept. Below are a few inquiries we at The American Institute have heard frequently.

Question: Is there any such thing as too much diversity?

Response: Yes, there is. Some people will be too diverse for a given organizational setting. The manager's job is to identify absolute job *requirements*—not preferences, conveniences or traditions—and to facilitate fulfillment of these requirements by members of the organization. Those unable to meet the *requirements* would be too diverse.

For example, an engineering manager might determine that a particular kind of engineering degree is a requirement for effectiveness, excluding from employment people who do not hold this degree. MD calls for the manager to be absolutely clear that this is a true *requirement* and not, for instance, a *convenient* way of screening out a group of individuals. Similarly, a sales manager concludes that males wearing ponytails and earrings are not acceptable to his customers and avoids hiring such individuals, or at least limits his use of these employees. MD calls on the manager to make certain that the lack of ponytails and earrings is a *true requirement*. Such questions as the following must be raised and explored.

- Would my customers, if properly prepared, be receptive to males with ponytails and earrings?
- What can I as a manager do to create an environment where males with ponytails and earrings can reach their full potential in pursuit of corporate objectives?
- Am I willing to accept my managerial responsibility to do all I can to create an environment that will work for *all* employees?

Only when the sales manager has done everything possible to create an environment that works for males with ponytails and earrings and it still appears that these traits violate *true requirements* does MD endorse the sales manager's conclusion that males with ponytails and earrings are too diverse for his or her setting.

Interestingly, we are seeing that, as managers vigorously probe requirements, they often turn out to be conveniences, traditions, or preferences.

Question: Are you saying that Managing Diversity is better than Affirmative Action or Understanding Differences?

Response: No, that is not what I am arguing. I am contending that AA, UD, and MD are different, that they represent different objectives, agendas and potentials. They can achieve different results for you.

Affirmative Action enables the manager to include and utilize people who are considered different, even when doing so is not congruent with the organization's natural way of doing business. AA deliberately and aggressively goes against the organization's natural grain in order to bring about the inclusion and utilization of selected target groups. Understanding Differences, on the other hand, facilitates greater acceptance and understanding of differences among individuals and fosters enhanced interpersonal relationships. This approach minimizes social conflict.

Managing Diversity focuses on changing the natural order (the grain) of an organization, so that the inclusion and utilization of people who are different becomes part of the way of doing business. Specifically, MD seeks to assure that the organization's culture and systems work for all employees.

The managerial challenge is to avoid misusing a given approach, to avoid asking for a potential result that is not on the approach's agenda.

Question: Can you cite corporations that are doing a good job with Managing Diversity? Also, can you give examples of the benefits gained?

Response: Because the concept of MD is in the embryonic stage, and because it is an evolving, multi-year institutionalization process, I cannot cite companies that have done MD. I can, however, discuss corporations that have started the process of institutionalizing MD. Typically, managers of these companies have been motivated by the following factors.

- a desire to maintain their firm's competitiveness
- anticipation of future changes in the external environment
- efforts to facilitate implementation of initiatives already underway, such as Total Quality
- the need to build on AA gains
- the potential benefits of better serving an increasingly diverse consumer market.

In the early stages of a MD initiative, these benefits have been evident:

- enhanced sensitivity to diverse consumer markets and to how they might be better served
- greater acceptance of Affirmative Action as a transitional approach rather than a permanent necessity

- renewed (cautiously optimistic) hope that "glass ceilings" will disappear
- enhanced enthusiasm and optimism about other initiatives (such as Total Quality, participative management, and self-managing teams, which cannot be successful without MD capability)

I must stress that these gains are preliminary and only indicative of benefits which may be realized as the institutionalization of MD becomes more of a reality.

Question: How do we secure the commitment of middle managers?

Response: I would recommend a multifaceted approach. Through educational efforts, define diversity as encompassing everyone, including *all* middle managers. Also, take care to develop and articulate the strategic, business (viability) rationale for moving forward with MD. Finally, identify and communicate the benefits for middle managers. These actions should minimize resistance from middle managers.

Question: You talk a lot about creating an environment that naturally enables everyone. Do you really believe that the creation of a diverse work force will come about naturally?

Response: Personally, I do not worry much about the creation of a diverse work force, but rather about its utilization. Indeed, utilization—not inclusion—is the principal focus of MD. If, however, for a given corporation, concern exists about the speed with which a diverse work force will come about naturally, the manager can act to accelerate the process through AA. MD's umbrella concept encourages parallel, simultaneous use of AA or UD with MD.

Question: What about the dropout rate for minorities in public school systems? Won't that make it difficult for corporations to create and manage a diverse work force? If you do not have diversity, you cannot manage it.

Response: This question refers to race and gender diversity. It is true that if you do not have race and gender diversity, you cannot manage it. But where there is little race and gender diversity, it does not follow that other kinds of diversity are also absent. It is critical to begin MD with the diversity you have. This experience will prepare you for whatever diversity will be forthcoming.

With respect to minorities and public schools, the question is whether to focus on creating a diverse work force or on utilizing a diverse work force. Our research suggests that corporations do not know how to utilize diverse, qualified workers. For corporate America, the challenge has not been lack of diversity, but rather the inability to create an environment that naturally works for everyone.

When for a given corporation and a given locale there is concern about the ability to develop qualified applicants for the workplace, the task is to work on enhancing the quality of available candidates for employment as well as the organization's to utilize the potential of all employees.

Question: Are you optimistic about the progress with institutionalizing MD in corporations?

Response: Yes, I am. Economic reality dictates that organizations can ill afford to underutilize any resource. With respect to diverse human resources, the manager can avoid underutilization through MD. More than anything else, economic uncertainty and challenges will drive the case for MD.

CONCLUSION

In this chapter I have provided definitions of diversity and Managing Diversity, examined historical approaches to diversity, discussed the major features of Managing Diversity and explored implications for launching MD. My goal has been to work through the misperceptions and confusion existing around the topic of diversity.

Clarification is essential if corporations are to remain economically viable. If managers fail to create an environment grounded in the acceptance, understanding, and managing of diversity, they risk being unable to compete effectively in a global economy. The judgement then would be that "too much diversity" contributed to their failure. This chapter suggests that the challenge is not "too much diversity" but rather that of building a house reflecting the realities of diversity. This chapter provides a framework for moving forward with construction of the "diversity" house.

NOTES

1. Paul Richter, "Clash Over Culture At Time Inc. Hearing," *The Los Angeles Times* July 12, 1989: section IV, p. 1.

2. Richard M. Clurman, *To The End Of Time: The Seduction And Conquest Of A Media Empire* (New York: Simon and Schuster, 1992), inside jacket cover.

3. William B. Johnston and Arnold H. Parker, *Workforce 2000: Work And Workers For The 21st Century* (Indianapolis: Hudson Institute, 1987).

4. R. Roosevelt Thomas Jr., *Beyond Race and Gender: Unleashing the Power of Your Total Work Force by Managing Diversity* (New York: AMACOM, 1991).

5. Edgar H. Schein, *Organizational Culture and Leadership* (San Francisco: Jossey-Bass, 1985), pp. 1–22.

12 MANAGING CHANGE

Todd D. Jick

In the real world of business, change is what will knock you off your horse a couple of times a week. In the early days of your career, maybe even more often than that. The question is: When you do get knocked off, do you just climb back on again, or do you determine to use that experience to then ride faster and harder?[1]

One of the leading proponents of corporate change, Jack Welch, Chairman of the General Electric Company, offered the above observation in the early 1980s to a group of graduating business school students. In the mid-1990s it remains applicable in all but one aspect. Change, it seems, no longer arises "a couple of times a week." We are now in an era when "business as unusual" is the way we experience doing business all week long. The pace, the volume, and the complexity of change have increased significantly during the last decade, and the forecast is for no less in the years ahead.

Some of the changes are big; some are small. Some occur rapidly, while others emerge slowly. Some are threatened, some are real. Some are planned, others are unplanned, and some are controllable, and others not. They occur in all domains: management information systems, business strategies, product lifecycles, human resource systems, leadership positions, organizational ownership and structures, technology, and so on.

Whatever the area of the business, and whatever the type, one question asked over and over again is, how are we going to implement these changes? Indeed, some say that competitive advantage today is less a matter of determining the right strategy than of implementing it faster and more smoothly than your competitors.

Let me illustrate with a story, which you may have heard in a different context. Two campers were sleeping in an isolated mountain area. Startled by the sound of a bear approaching from the next hill, one of the frightened campers jumps out of his sleeping bag and dashes in the opposite direction, barefoot and wearing pajamas. The second camper remains behind, methodically puts on his running shoes and running shorts and grabs a canteen. The first camper shouts back, "Hurry! The bear...the bear...." The second responds, "I'm OK; I don't have to outrun the bear; I only have to outrun you." (In some versions of this story, the first camper is identified as an American businessperson and the second Japanese!)

For our purposes the moral of the story is that getting out in front of competitors is not necessarily a matter of seeing threats or opportunities before your competitors do, but rather one of responding to them more effectively. It is managing the changes and responses needed by a company, which often (as in the story) is a matter of survival. For example, seeking competitive advantage is not coming to the conclusion that you must be customer-driven in order to be successful; it is implementing and creating a customer-driven organization. In the matter of technology, competitive advantage often arises from human-resource and organizational systems that have been adapted to exploit the use of the technology, rather than ownership per se of technologies.

The argument, in essence, is that a good strategy poorly implemented is useless (as would be a poor strategy beautifully implemented) and that companies today are not short of good strategies but are short of well-implemented ones.

What good companies have concluded then is that they must build up their capacity to respond and adapt to changing demands and opportunities. This requires a critical set of managerial skills, which is often described as the ability to manage change: to guide the organization to a better future through attention to (a) the process of implementation, (b) the people affected by the changes, and (c) the receptivity and learning of change agents to deal more effectively with future changes.

This chapter will address each of these areas and, in doing so, will clarify the dual challenge of managing and coping with change. As change becomes more effectively managed people will cope better with change; and, vice versa, as people cope better, change will be more easily managed.

A BRIEF HISTORY OF MANAGING CHANGE

Let's start by putting today's obsession with change in perspective. It may be difficult for some of us to remember anymore what some might fondly recall as the "good old days." Organizations operated in relatively stable environments in which predictability was a given. The rules were straightforward. The classic example was the auto industry. Carmakers produced the cars that they determined the customers needed; employees who performed had job security and lifetime employment; ownership of the firm was a constant; and a secure future was generally assumed by all. This is a stereotypic description of course but it contains a significant amount of truth: status quo and security were the constant, and change and turbulence the exception.

For many such companies impressive success was the result. They built up their capability to grow within defined boundaries and to increase managerial controls within defined boundaries. Unfortunately (or perhaps fortunately), the world changed and the formula for past success ensured present failures. If change continued to be viewed as something to be avoided, companies were doomed. Some of the most prominent in the United States—such as General Motors, Sears, and IBM—stumbled so badly that their very survival was called into question. In Europe comparable kinds of enterprises, often run or subsidized by the state and highly stable for decades, similarly faced the question of their ability to survive in the face of a global marketplace, collapsed borders, and many other significant changes in the way business operates.

What changed was an entire paradigm of doing business, and many companies were all too slow to recognize it, respond, and ride the new tiger. They had developed cultures—attitudes and behaviors reflected in reward systems, information screens, career paths, socialization practices, and so on—that treated the need to change as a necessary evil and not an opportunity to "thrive on chaos." Table 12-1 shows some key elements of the old and new paradigms for managing change. Many companies today are in the midst of this transition.

As can be seen by the items listed under New Paradigm, managing change today is a challenging endeavor. It can be rapid and continuous and can cause upheaval. Typically there is more than one change going on at a time, and there is no clear end in sight. There are bound to be failures, yet there is more risk in retreating than in pushing onward and more risk in overplanning than in underplanning and recalibrating. Moreover, many organizations want middle managers or lower-level employees to drive change, requiring an often substantial shifting of tasks and responsibilities.

This is why so many CEOs, managers, team members, and even individual contributors are keenly interested today in gaining the skills needed to manage changes more effectively. New skills are needed and more and more people are recognizing that they must stop thinking according to the Old Paradigm or, if they are new to an organization and personally more comfortable with the new approach, find ways to deepen organization-wide receptivity to change.

Managers and consultants have become increasingly savvy about the difficulties of managing change. More and more companies are investing time and money in a variety of training programs and preparatory exercises before

TABLE 12-1   Old versus new paradigms for managing change

Dimension	Old Paradigm	New Paradigm
Pace	Slow	Rapid
Scope	Incremental	Quantum
Goal	Short-term results; initiation of change	Short- and long-term results; initiation, management, and maintenance of change
Mentality	Risks and errors are to be avoided; mistakes are to be punished; change is considered difficult.	One is to show courage; there is more risk in not changing; mistakes are to be taken in stride and as learning opportunities.
Style	Gentle	Upsetting
Source of change	From the top down, and through the support of sponsors	From the middle and lower levels as well as from above, and through empowerment of others
Degree of planning	High: "Ready, ready, ready, aim, aim, aim...fire!"	Modest: "Ready, fire, aim."
Volume	One-shot	Continuous
Ethos	"If it ain't broke, don't fix it!"	"If it ain't broke, break it!"

introducing major changes. However, understanding the importance of change is one thing; actually managing change in an effective manner is quite another.

A broad study reviewing "total quality" programs in 584 U.S. companies, for example, has concluded that companies are not faring well with implementation of this specific kind of change program. The study, released by Ernst & Young and the American Quality Foundation in early 1992, found that because many quality programs are overly broad and undefined, and because they are not implemented in a consistent and focused way, they fail to achieve their intended results and do not result in long-term, meaningful change. "A lot of companies read lots of books, did lots of training, formed teams and tried to implement 9,000 new practices simultaneously," Terrence R. Ozan, a partner with Ernst & Young told the Wall Street Journal. "But you don't get results that way. It's just too much."[2]

The difficulty of the task often takes organizations by surprise. A group of executives attending a Harvard Business School program were polled about their early results with implementing change in their companies. They reported that most of their change plans had underestimated the amount of resistance they encountered, the amount of time required to shape, sell, and execute the change, the resources, support, and sponsorship required, the need to model and practice the change personally; and the impact on employees.

If they had been successful they would have reported different outcomes and experiences, such as the following.

- Visible and active support for accelerating change
- Willingness to take personal initiatives and support other people's initiatives in changing the status quo
- Risk-taking, self-confident, and empowered behavior exhibited at multiple levels in the company
- Willingness to develop and drive more change

Thus we are attempting to come a long way: from the days in which change was an aberration in the midst of stability to today when periods of stability seem largely absent. And we are attempting to come a long way in our skills at managing the new demands and opportunities for change.

THE TEN COMMANDMENTS OF MANAGING CHANGE

Basically, managing change in the decade ahead is a function of two factors: Readiness and Capability. This applies to both the organizational and individual levels. Successful change requires responsiveness to four questions.

1. Why do we have to change?
2. Why are these the right changes?
3. Is this company capable of handling the changes?
4. What will the company do to help one through the changes?

These questions essentially ask whether there is adequate motivation and incentive for and benefit in the changes (Readiness) and whether there are enough supports, enablers, and skills (Capability) to enact them. Change ultimately occurs and sticks when people are convinced that the change makes sense and that they have the skills required. Thus, managing the change process requires joint attention to both motivational and skill factors.

What follows is a detailed description of actions for managing change that have been found to contribute to effective implementation of change. They represent a summary of the thinking of academics, consultants, and managers who have participated in or observed major organizational change.

Managing change is part art and part science. Because it is an inexact and ever-changing process, there is no neat prescription for how to take an organization from one point to another. But there are a number of steps that have become well accepted as providing a foundation for change. If well implemented, these steps can give organizations a springboard from which to launch effective change.

Figure 12-1 is my own "Ten Commandments" of change, providing a useful guide to managers preparing to implement change. Although presented sequentially, with some common sense the points may often be addressed

FIGURE 12-1   The ten commandments

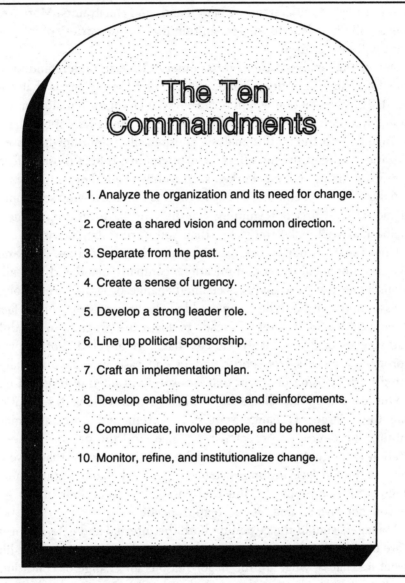

The Ten Commandments

1. Analyze the organization and its need for change.

2. Create a shared vision and common direction.

3. Separate from the past.

4. Create a sense of urgency.

5. Develop a strong leader role.

6. Line up political sponsorship.

7. Craft an implementation plan.

8. Develop enabling structures and reinforcements.

9. Communicate, involve people, and be honest.

10. Monitor, refine, and institutionalize change.

simultaneously. Commandments 1–4 are generally used to increase an organization's readiness to change, whereas Commandments 5–9 involve the building of organizational ability to change. The final commandment relates to making both stick, and starting again on new changes.

1. Analyze the Organization and Its Need for Change

Understanding an organization's strengths and weaknesses, its customers and competitors, its structures and systems, and how it operates in its environment is a critical precursor to change. This early evaluation should give managers a more systemic view of problems and opportunities and thus a more sophisticated understanding of demands and constraints. Moreover, this diagnosis will likely lead to the recognition that a wide variety of interrelated changes will be required.

Out of this analysis, then, must emerge a clear understanding of the reasons for change, the time frame, and some of the key areas that must be changed. This information will in turn lead to such important steps as crafting a vision, winning sponsorship, and preparing an implementation plan.

Ongoing and thoughtful analysis is especially important because every organization is different, and efforts to change must reflect those differences. Adopting a program that has worked successfully at another company without first analyzing the specific needs of your own is like borrowing someone else's medicine without first determining whether you have the same illness; the medicine may well make you sicker than you were to begin with.

Unfortunately, not all companies make this distinction. For example, a large, multinational telecommunications company mandated that all of its divisions adopt the same highly acclaimed change program, even though the businesses ranged from skilled, value-added electronics operations to factories producing cable. No attempt was made to adapt the program to the different business needs or divergent workforces that were affected. Not surprisingly, the program's success was spotty, and in one case may have actually contributed to the closing of a firm that was sorely in need of targeted change.

One aspect of this diagnosis is the consideration of the relationship among the degree of change required (incremental or transformational/quantum), the degree of expected resistance, and the nature of the implementation strategy. Figure 12-2 highlights this by showing that if you need major change and face major resistance, a more dictatorial implementation strategy is most appropriate. But there are other conditions under which a more collaborative strategy is more appropriate.[3]

Managers should thus examine both the internal and external pressures that are driving the change as well as the forces of resistance that are likely to obstruct it. That is, what are the major reasons for change or conditions that necessitate it, and what are the major barriers? I sometimes ask companies planning a change effort first to complete a "force field analysis" worksheet like the one shown in Figure 12-3 to identify the forces competing for and against change.

Simply put, if the forces for change are outweighed by the forces resisting it, the change goal is unlikely to be met. Each of the factors can be examined in terms of its criticality (value) as well as the likelihood that it can be increased if it is a force for change, or weakened if it is a force of resistance. This exercise serves two purposes. First, it helps companies identify the factors, whether positive or negative, likely to affect change. And second, it compels them to plan from the start what they might do to address resistance and to strengthen the forces for change.

Of course, as change has increasingly become a way of life rather than a discrete, one-shot operation, the analysis I have just described has become an ongoing process that, in a very real sense, never ends. Managers must never become complacent or assume that an organization is a static entity. Both companies and the environments in which they operate are continually changing, and those who manage change must constantly reexamine their assumptions.

Two points must be insisted upon here. The first is to be sure that the need for change is ultimately agreed upon by as many people as possible. Simply identifying a reason for changing as seen by yourself is clearly inadequate, and yet often one mistakes one's own conclusions to be obvious to anyone and everyone. The second is that in today's organizations there are often multiple reasons for changing which already exist, and it is thus often the task of the diagnosis to unify them under one "umbrella" or prioritize them, rather than to unearth reasons for changing previously unidentified.

FIGURE 12-2   A typology of change strategies and conditions for their use

	Incremental Change Strategies	Transformative Change Strategies
Collaborative Modes	Participative Evolution Use when the organization is in good condition but needs minor adjustment, or is not in good condition but time is available and key interest groups favor change.	Charismatic Transformation Use when the organization is not in good condition and though there is little time for extensive participation there is support for radical change within the organization.
Coercive Modes	Forced Evolution Use when the organization is in good condition but needs minor adjustment, or when it is not in good condition and key interest groups oppose change, but time is available.	Dictatorial Transformation Use when the organization is not in good condition, there is no time for extensive participation and no support within the organization for radical change, but radical change is vital to organizational survival and fulfillment of its basic mission.

Adapted from Dunphy, D.C. and Stare, D.A. "Transformational and Coercive Strategies for Planned Organizational Change: Beyond the OD Model," *Organizational Studies*, 9 (3), 1988, pp. 339–355.

FIGURE 12-3   Force field analysis worksheet

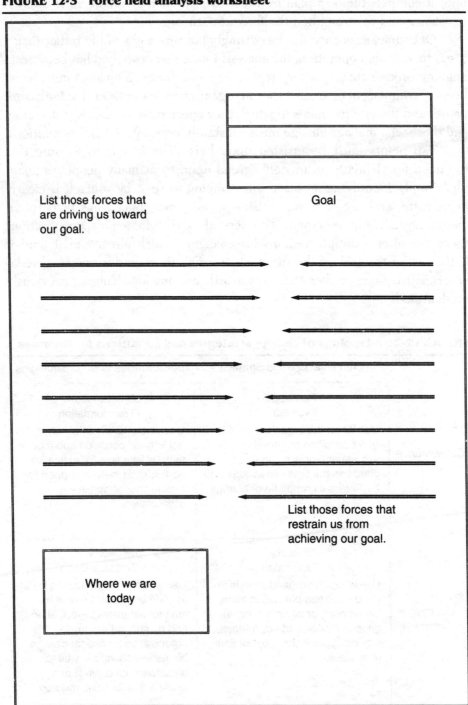

List those forces that
are driving us toward
our goal.

Goal

List those forces that
restrain us from
achieving our goal.

Where we are
today

2. Create a Shared Vision and Common Direction

Having identified some shared reasons for changing, the next question is, whereto exactly? It is generally required that there be some agreement on the desired future state. A vision is a mental image of what an organization should achieve or become. Through a slogan or a speech, a vision may motivate an organization to reach beyond its normal mode of operation and to rally behind a new way of thinking, producing, interacting, or working. A vision helps crystallize a many-faceted change effort into an understandable goal. It offers a reason for undertaking the often arduous process of change.

If the first step of diagnosis often represents the "push" factors, the vision is a way of developing the "pull" factors. The organization thus becomes motivated toward moving away from the past, but also pulled toward something more attractive in the future. (See Peter B. Vaill's "Visionary Leadership," Chapter 2 of this book, for more on utilizing vision.)

Both a vision's conception and its presentation affect how change is perceived. If, for example, a vision originates with one person and does not reflect the thinking or needs of the broader organization, it may not have much value as a motivational tool. Moreover, a vision may be more meaningful if placed in a larger context. For example, in deciding upon vision and direction a company should consider the outside environment within which it operates, including the viewpoints of both customers and competitors.

This final point is critical. Companies can become so enmeshed in trying to satisfy all the different factions within their own organizations that their visions and goals largely ignore the external marketplace. One large electronics company, for example, worked so hard to treat an acquired firm with fairness, and to unite both companies behind a vision of an equal partnership, that it failed to consider how well the new entity was serving its customers. This kind of well-intentioned but myopic approach to visioning can create a lemming-like phenomenon, with a united organization marching boldly and enthusiastically toward a waiting precipice.

Visioning, like analysis, is no longer seen as a once-a-decade exercise. A vision is not set in stone, nor does it answer all an organization's motivational or directional needs. A company may pursue multiple visions simultaneously, create different visions within different divisions, or change its vision in midcourse. Visions, like many other aspects of the change process, are most effective when regularly challenged, reexamined, and eventually recrafted in line with the organization's steady evolution.

A special challenge for managing change in today's organization is a checkered legacy with visions that have been unfulfilled, reversed, or ignored. Employees in such circumstance are cynical and difficult to reach. If this is the case, it often requires fresh leadership and bold new actions to regenerate a stale vision or create a new one. When trust is weakened, it takes much longer to rebuild it than it took to unravel it. Thus the "selling" of the vision becomes more critical, requiring visible, consistent actions by powerful players.

3. Separate from the Past

Back in the 1940s, Kurt Lewin described organizational change as a three-part process, consisting of Unfreezing, Changing, and Refreezing. Today that description is still largely apt. In order to change, an organization must first "unfreeze" its attitudes, structures, and systems so that they can be reconfigured. In other words, it must separate from the past.

How companies go about "unfreezing" can vary dramatically, however, and there are risks with each approach. Some companies spend months or even years getting their employees ready for change, creating dissatisfaction with the old ways, and promulgating a new vision for the future. These lingering introductory phases are intended to help make the change less sudden, less dramatic, and more palatable. If employees fully understand what is wrong with the old way of operating, the reasoning goes, they will more likely embrace the new order. Unfortunately, if the introduction of change is too gradual and too pleasant, an organization may never become convinced that it really needs to change, and may slip back into its old ways.

At the other extreme are organizations that have made such abrupt breaks with the past that their employees have been left bewildered and disillusioned. The classic example of this kind of uprooting, disorienting change is the Monday-morning discovery of moved desks, changed job expectations, or altered organizational charts. Such sudden and unexplained shifts create so much anxiety that employees are too busy figuring out their own losses to concentrate on the potential value of the change.

In an ideal world, both of these extremes would be avoided. Employees would understand the need to leave behind those practices and traditions that no longer work and yet would find some stability and affirmation in those that still do. For example, when Burroughs bought Sperry and became Unisys, then-CEO Michael Blumenthal sought to create a company with a new identity different from that of either predecessor. Yet, parochial loyalties to each of the merged companies was extremely strong. To help employees and managers separate from the past, an archive was created in which products, logos, and various physical artifacts were proudly collected and displayed from both originating companies. By doing so, employees reported feeling that their past was valued, and that they were then more willing to move on to the new future.

In fact, though, as the speed and complexity of change accelerates, managers are finding it ever more challenging to help employees separate from the past. A common complaint from workers today is that their workplaces are in such constant flux that there is no identifiable past to separate from.

In other words, instead of having the chance to "refreeze" a new system, as in Lewin's original equation, they are on to a new change before the old one has even set. One of the greatest challenges for managers, then, is to help employees understand the continuing need for change without denying the past, and without neglecting the tension and uncertainty that many workers may feel in a more turbulent work environment.

4. Create a Sense of Urgency

Conventional wisdom has always held that change is most likely to happen if there is a crisis or some degree of urgency. This is still true today, but there are some useful subtleties to consider; for example, how to mobilize a sense of urgency before an absolute crisis occurs.

The most effective companies are able to create the same sense of motivational urgency, but without the real hemorrhaging that often accompanies real crises and that ultimately may impede the organization's ability to make the right changes or sustain them after the crisis subsides. Thus we hear today more and more about "continuous improvement" or "kaizen" as a way to maintain a constant degree of pressure and an environment that is routinely changing.

In the past, creating a sense of urgency for change did not require much effort. Companies typically did not embark on major transformations until the need was clear. Change projects were usually targeted to solve an indisputable problem endangering a company's short-term health: Sales were falling, a new competitor had stolen the marketplace lead, or a technology was becoming obsolete. Whatever the case, the need for change was usually well understood by a large sector of the organization.

But by the 1980s many companies did not have the luxury of being able to wait until the need for change was apparent. In fact, in today's highly competitive global marketplace, by the time the need to change becomes obvious and acute, it may be too late to catch up. As a result, more and more companies are launching anticipatory change—change that is under taken in anticipation of shifts in technology or marketplace and before a crisis occurs. This approach to change is to be applauded; it indicates that strategic planners and managers are looking ahead, gauging how their organizations interact with changing environments, and evaluating long-term strategic issues rather than just responding to short-term pressures.

The disadvantage of anticipatory change, however, is that resistance may be higher than usual because many employees may see no apparent threat or justifying cause. Convincing an entire organization of the need to change is difficult enough under clear duress; it becomes much harder when a company is apparently in top form and doing things right.

Managers must therefore become masters at creating a sense of urgency based on often-intangible, long-term competitive threats rather than concrete short-term problems. Not surprisingly, some of these efforts backfire, particularly if workers are subjected to a never-ending stream of "new and improved" change programs. Employees quickly become jaded when the rationale behind change is unclear, believing that management is "crying wolf."

In order to avoid this problem, many companies are now communicating to all employees market and competitive information that in the past would have been reserved for top managers. Another technique is to visit customers on a regular basis and expand direct contact with people beyond the sales and marketing functions. The better informed their employees are, they reason, the more likely they will understand and support the need for change.

Organizations can engage in "visioning exercises" that highlight the gap between where an organization wants to be and where it currently is. Essentially, the goal is to create constructive tension whose release requires change and action. Motorola, a company with a remarkable record of continued success, has been a benchmark of how to extend a successful organization's vision in a compelling way. The creation of the "Six Sigma" goals for quality represented a significant leap which led them to win the Malcolm Baldrige National Quality Award, the nation's top award for quality in business, and set a new standard for the industry. Although they faced serious competition at the time, this sense of urgency was created without a real-time crisis.

Many managers also see tremendous power in allowing employees to be among the prime drivers of change. When workers are empowered with the ability to change their own environments, they are more likely to create their own sense of urgency and to recognize the need for and desirability of change.

5. Develop a Strong Leader Role

A change effort needs a guiding force. Indeed, many companies noted for their innovative and successful change programs have been headed by strong and charismatic leaders, such as General Electric's Jack Welch. Welch, for example, has gained a reputation for not allowing GE to become complacent, regardless of how well it performs; for instituting imaginative employee-involvement programs; and for keeping the company focused on the future.

But leaders of change come in a variety of shapes and sizes and are by no means always charismatic. They tend to respond to almost all of the other commandments in one way or another. In a recent study J. Kotter and J. Heskett examined the actions of leaders who have contributed significantly to institutionalizing new visions and new sets of business strategies.[4] Such leaders do the following.

- Restructure systems and policies
- Provide role models and communicate why new behavior is needed
- Endorse and support new activities proposed by others
- Change specific personnel or the criteria by which people are recruited and promoted
- Look for some quick but sustainable successes
- Produce positive results that reinforce new behavior and values

These actions create new behavior, and as the behavior appears to work it becomes somewhat contagious. The sheer difficulty of changing a culture and the high degree of interdependence of multiple changes seems to require both the power and the versatility of top leadership. (See also Chapter 8, by Phyllis F. and Leonard A. Schlesinger, "Designing Effective Organizations.")

In many large companies an important debate exists as to whether change should be driven by someone from inside the company or someone from the outside. Arguments and evidence from both sides seem to have some merit. Insiders have the advantage of understanding the culture, the players, and how things seemingly get done, but for many of the same reasons they are constrained, they have obligations to many inside the system and can be blinded by assumptions about how to do things. Outsiders offer fresh perspectives on change and have no obligations, but they suffer from insensitivity to or ignorance of key inside events or cultural approaches.

In their study of change leaders Kotter and Heskett found an interesting pattern. Of ten leaders studied in companies that had gone through successful transformations, four were "unconventional insiders" (leaders who had grown up in an unorthodox, typically innovative part of the company and who were mavericks), four were outsiders, and two were hybrid insider/outsiders. In other words, leaders could emerge from the inside but had to embody different qualities while still benefiting from their understanding of the local cultures. Nonetheless, the study clearly showed that a different approach or style is needed, being from either the inside or the outside, or both.

The leadership role in a change process, however, is not necessarily held by the CEO or the president or, indeed, by any one individual. While setting a company's overall strategic direction is still the special province of top management, change leaders can be found at all levels of an organization. In fact, many companies are specifically trying to avoid top-down change, because they believe that structures and systems imposed from above are less likely to be assimilated than changes that originate from lower down in the organization.

AT&T has experimented with a variety of employee team-based programs for driving change. Employee involvement has been seen as particularly important at AT&T, in part to combat the old "Ma Bell" culture left over from the pre-1984 breakup of AT&T's telephone service monopoly. At

AT&T's Dallas Works, in Mesquite, Texas, for example, a small group comprised mostly of line workers with no previous management experience was charged with launching the early phase of a long-term change program.

Specifically, this group oversaw the cleaning up, painting, and reorganization of a factory operation, incorporating worker suggestions on how to make the production process more "worker friendly" and more efficient. This "bottom-up" change leadership was intended to demonstrate not only AT&T's commitment to challenging the old bureaucracy, but also the importance of each employee's contributions to the change.

Programs like the one at AT&T depend on the willingness and ability of employees such as middle managers and line workers to assume leadership roles that may initially be unfamiliar to them. In addition, they require managers to relinquish some of the leadership responsibilities that go along with a traditional management position. Not all companies will be comfortable with this strategy, but it is an approach that many organizations feel is essential to involving an entire workforce in the process of change. (Note the issues raised in Chapter 10, "Self-Managing Teams," by Harvey Kolodny and Torbjorn Stjernberg.)

6. Line Up Political Sponsorship

How easily an organization accepts change can depend heavily on both how it is presented and on who supports it. Managers of change, or "corporate entrepreneurs" as one observer calls them, operate in a highly political environment, requiring

> campaigning, lobbying, bargaining, negotiating, caucusing, collaborating, and winning votes. That is, an idea must be sold, resources must be acquired or rearranged, and some variable numbers of other people must agree to changes in their own areas—for innovations generally cut across existing areas and have wider organizational ripples, like dropping pebbles into a pond.

> The enterprise required of innovating managers and professionals, then, is not the creative spark of genius that invents a new idea, but rather the skill with which they move outside the formal bonds of their job, maneuvering through and around the organization in sometimes risky, unique, and novel ways.[5]

This maneuvering includes building relationships with those who are opposed to the change and even winning over potential enemies. Moreover, it may require recasting change goals in order to accommodate the realities and limitations of a specific corporate environment. (For more suggestions, see Chapter 5, "Power, Politics, and Influence," by Anne Donnellon.)

7. Craft an Implementation Plan

An implementation plan is a way of transforming a vision into concrete, doable tasks. Once the visionary goal is established, the plan addresses the down-to-earth steps it will take to achieve it. This may be as detailed as a day-to-day schedule showing actions over the first few weeks of the change process and plotting specific goals on a monthly basis, or as undefined as a rough framework giving a general sense of how to operate over the next few years. Either way, the implementation plan should provide a sort of blueprint for managers to help them tackle the challenges ahead. To test whether your plan is feasible, ask yourself the following questions.[6]

1. Is the plan concise and clearly written, listing the steps to be taken?
2. Is the written plan distributed to the right personnel, in order to gain support?
3. Has the written plan had the input of an appropriate brainstorming group?
4. Have a number of influential individuals been interviewed for their input?
5. Does the style of the written plan fit the organization?
6. Is more than one method employed to make the plan visible?
7. Are there both a formal and an informal network to lend credence and support to the plan?

When Xerox started a major change program in the early 1980s, one of the things that distinguished the effort was the amount of time and resources that went into the planning of its implementation. For example, CEO David Kearns pulled 15 top managers from their regular jobs to serve on the quality-implementation team. Before the change program was launched, the team developed a 92-page document describing issues ranging from cultural changes to a five-year change schedule. The effort paid off: In 1989, Xerox's Business Products and Systems division was one of two recipients of the Malcolm Baldrige National Quality Award.

Kearns's thoughtful approach to planning and implementation was crucial to the successful realization of Xerox's change strategy. But Xerox did not go on to win the Baldrige award without substantial mid-course adjustments to the original plan. No matter how good a plan is, it must be regularly reviewed and revised in response to changes within the company and without. In fact, managers should be cautious about becoming wedded to any particular plan because they may lose the flexibility and quickness to react that are so important to the change process.

GE's Jack Welch noted two particular problems that can result from too much planning:

> First, once written, the strategic document can take on a life of its own, and it may not lend itself readily to flexibility, to the changes that will naturally occur in the five years one looks forward. And second, the document itself can become a graphics exercise. An organization can begin to focus on form rather than substance.[7]

Thus, many organizations have adopted a "ready, fire, aim" approach, which has been likened to the Cruise missile that can be calibrated while in the air and aimed to reach its target. In other words, start to take action, experiment, learn, and redirect if necessary—but don't become so locked into a plan or the planning process that you become rigid.

In addition, the methodical and meticulous approach that Xerox chose may become increasingly uncommon as the pace of change accelerates. Waiting for the perfect plan or the ideal solution can turn into one more excuse for not confronting needed change. An important part of managing change is knowing when there is time for painstaking preparation, and when it is necessary to move forward, picking up the pieces afterwards.

8. Develop Enabling Structures and Reinforcements

Launching a change effort can be a rude awakening. Some companies announce the need for change, paste slogans on the bulletin boards, and then sit back waiting for change to happen. But it takes more than an end-of-the-month incentive prize to get a company to change. Fundamentally, organizational change will not occur unless the organization believes that it has to change or already is changing. This is often signaled through changes in various systems and structures that are aligned with, and representative of, the overall change.

Such enabling structures might include changes in hiring practices, training programs, career paths, measurement and reward systems, organizational structures, task teams, and so on. They allow the organization to change by setting up structures and mechanisms that support a new way of operating, and they demonstrate the seriousness of the effort by making alterations that require employees to behave differently in order to get their jobs done or to be rewarded. The organization is accordingly "rewired" to be more tightly aligned with the desired changes. (See Chapter 9, "Managing Human Resources Strategically," by Charles A. Fombrun and Drew Harris, for more on enabling structures.)

Consider the way former Xerox CEO David Kearns described the transformation of his company in the mid-1980s.

> This is a revolution in the company and we have to overthrow the old regime. The quality transition team is the junta in place to run things on a temporary basis. The standards and measures equate to the laws of the land and of the company. The reward and recognition system is the gaining of control of the banks and economic systems. The training is capturing control of the universities. Communications is the seizing of control of the press, and the senior management behavior is putting your own people in place to reflect the revolution. All of these elements are needed to change a culture.[8]

Tactically, a company that is serious about change will use a number of substantial enabling structures to accelerate and reinforce the change. For example, here is a list of some of the steps that one midwestern manufacturing company took in the first three years of its change effort.

- Set up weekly meetings for one year attended by production, controls, and materials managers in order to improve on-time product delivery
- Restructured the management team, and sent vice presidents and middle managers to management training courses
- Launched company-wide communication, recognition, and quality program including employee suggestion boxes, prizes, and monthly meetings for managers and supervisors
- Required individual business units to complete their own strategic planning process, including mission statement, market analysis, and suggested strategies and actions
- Presented quarterly video updates summarizing progress and achievements as part of a broad-based communication strategy.
- Sent all vice presidents and middle managers to a series of off-site team-building and training sessions to give them better change-agent skills
- Began a "barrier removals" process challenging all employees to identify and remove obstacles to quality and excellence
- Established a network of committees and councils, called Building Block Councils, to focus on six key strategic areas: customer satisfaction, quality, goals, awareness, training, and recognition
- Set itself the goal of qualifying for the Malcolm Baldrige National Quality Award.

The steps that this company took are not unusual for an organization attempting a broad-based change. They ranged from the practical, such as offering management training sessions, to the motivational, such as awarding prizes. In the process, they convinced the workforce that the company was serious about change.

9. Communicate, Involve People, and Be Honest

As many companies have shifted their focus from top-down change to, at least in part, middle- or bottom-driven change, the need for communication, broad-based involvement, and honesty has become all the more crucial. The maxim here is quite simple, albeit routinely violated: communicate, communicate, and communicate, and then, just in case, communicate the same message again! Managers and workers cannot lead or embrace change unless they understand the goals of change, the motivations behind it, and what it will mean to the company. Nor will they be effective agents of change if they discover that top management lies about what change entails.

For many companies, improving communication can be as simple as openly telling employees about decisions affecting them, rather than surprising workers with actions that have not first been explained or allowing information to filter through the rumor mill. Management may balk at communicating news about layoffs, restructurings, or other actions that have negative implications, yet the anxiety brought on by uncertainty and gossip is typically far more painful and disruptive to a workforce than the hard facts. In the absence of solid information, an organization is left to imagine the worst.

Involvement can take a broad variety of forms, ranging from drawing employees into the decision-making process to forming teams to attack specific problems and to making all employees key actors in the creation of change. Many companies have attempted to use problem-solving sessions called "town meetings" to pull the entire workforce into the process of identifying necessary changes and actions.

But this form of dialogue does not happen overnight. Large organizations are notorious for the absence of trust, for creating huge "silos" that impede cross-functional communication, and for penalizing the messengers of key messages. What is required then is some risk-taking, some training in how to listen and communicate, and sometimes even a new language or jargon that will permit a new mode of communication.[9] Finally, it takes some courageous leaders who can reward those who are forthcoming.

Information that places the need for change in the context of the outside environment is particularly useful, because this demonstrates to employees that change is not being dictated by internal mistakes—perhaps their own—but by a larger set of demands. Moreover, communication should not end once the initial announcement of change has been made. Rather, employees need to be kept well informed on an ongoing basis in order to understand and support the evolving process.

Finally, honesty is a critical part of involvement and good communication, particularly while employees try to understand and deal with the implications of a new way of working. If the members of an organization sense that they are not being told the truth, they will become suspicious of the entire process of change.

In one company, for example, an enthusiastic middle manager was charged with training employees in a new total-quality program. As part of the quest for total quality, he told workers, they would now be empowered to identify and fix problems in their own work environments. The initial response to the training was spirited, and a number of individuals proposed practical changes that would have improved their productivity. However, it soon became clear that despite the talk of empowerment and change, it was taking months to implement even the smallest changes suggested by workers. It was not long before cynicism replaced the initial enthusiasm, and the manager responsible for training eventually resigned from the job rather than continue to make promises he could not fulfill.

Communication is the opportunity to provide consistency, honesty, and realistic expectations. If done well it will further the change significantly. If done poorly it can derail the change entirely.

10. Monitor, Refine, and Institutionalize Change

All change efforts require careful monitoring of their progress and appropriate refinements. Midcourse calibrations occur for many reasons, including fatigue, cross-cutting priorities, plateauing, and changes in leadership. Indeed, it is often at the midpoint of a marathon-like four- to seven-year program of change that the "runners" experience the "heartbreak hill" of wondering whether they can finish.

But the world class runners ask another question at this stage: How can we accelerate our pace to the finish line? Thus, the challenge to dig deeper and find more strength is the key to making change last. What world class companies do then is rededicate themselves to the task, reset goals if necessary, and revisit their game plan.

Even more demanding, however, is to institutionalize change, for it is not a *specific* change that an organization should strive to institutionalize, but rather a mindset for continuous change. The real challenge for managers is to create an organization that is receptive to change, flexible enough to react to evolving environmental demands, and motivated to strive for continuing improvement.

MCI, the upstart telecommunications company that challenged AT&T, has tried to do this through a set of tenets that they developed.

1. We move fast. Individuals have the power to make decisions and take actions and must make a minimum of reports and studies.

2. We are countercyclical. Whatever is normal, expected, or traditional, we change.

3. We institutionalize change. Employees change jobs every two years, and there are no organizational charts, job descriptions, rule books, or policy pronouncements.

4. We encourage initiative. Individuals are given both responsibility and authority.

5. We like employee turnover. When people become stale in a job they should move on to another. They can find another job in another area or leave the company and return when the time is right and not lose any benefits.

6. We sometimes decide not to decide. Sometimes the pace of change is so fast it is better to watch and wait for the right opportunity or the right product to arise.

7. We are not pretentious know-it-alls. We know we cannot do everything well all the time. We will make mistakes, and we will learn from them. We are egalitarian.

8. We insist that work has to be fun. You must feel you can make a difference.

9. We encourage all thinking and we change styles. Diversity on the staff leads to more innovation.

10. We know that nothing is forever except change. We realize that decay sets in as soon as an idea or organization is born.

11. We learn more from the future than from the past. Imagine yourself five years from now and speculate about what you wish you did the year before.*

These tenets exemplify an orientation of making change their way of doing business. They do not want to be locked into organizational charts, procedures, personnel, or attitudes that provide comfort and routine. Rather, everything they do is premised on creating an ongoing readiness and capability for change.

Institutionalizing change requires both the rewiring of the organizational structures and systems described earlier and the rewiring of the organizational culture and mindset. Therein lies the power to routinize the management of change and expand the skill base throughout a company.

COPING WITH CHANGE AND RESISTANCE: UNDERSTANDING THE RECIPIENTS

Even if well implemented, these Ten Commandments will not transform change into an easy or painless process. In fact, I like to offer two reminders to managers who are implementing change: If your plans have not encountered resistance, you have not gone far enough; and if your plans do not include changes that you personally will undergo, if not resist, in doing your own work, you will not be part of the solution.

Thus it is important to understand how people typically react to change and how this can be managed. Let's not be Pollyanna-like about resistance. Some of it may be natural, legitimate, and even useful while some will be indicative of real barriers that must be overcome or eliminated. The "excuses" for not taking action are voluminous. Table 12-2, while amusing, is

---

*Jacquelyn Wonder and Priscilla Donovan, *The Flexibility Factor*, New York: Doubleday, 1989.

TABLE 12-2 Forty-four excuses for not making changes

1. We tried that before.
2. This place is different.
3. It costs too much.
4. That's beyond our responsibility.
5. We're all too busy to do that.
6. That's not my job.
7. It's too radical a change.
8. We don't have the time.
9. There's not enough help.
10. Our place is too small for it.
11. It isn't practical for operating people.
12. The folks will never buy it.
13. The union will scream.
14. We've never done it before.
15. It's against regulations.
16. It runs up overhead.
17. We don't have the authority.
18. That's too ivory-tower-like.
19. Let's get back to reality.
20. That's not our problem.
21. Why change it? It's still working okay.
22. You're right, but....
23. You're two years ahead of your time.
24. We don't have the personnel.
25. It isn't in the budget.
26. It's a good thought, but impractical.
27. Let's give it more thought.
28. Top management would never go for it.
29. Let's put it in writing.
30. We'd lose money in the long run.
31. It's never been tried before.
32. Let's shelve it for the time being.
33. Let's form a committee.
34. Has anyone else ever tried it?
35. What you are really saying is....
36. Maybe that will work in your department, but it won't in mine.
37. The executive committee will never....
38. Don't you think we should look into that further before we act?
39. Let's all sleep on it.
40. It won't pay for itself.
41. I know a fellow who tried that.
42. We've always done it this way.
43. It's hopelessly complex.
44. What would the president say?

also surprisingly realistic. Because change is not easy, some organizations do their best to postpone or deny the inevitable.

Resistance to change is as old a phenomenon as history itself. At its core, it reflects some universal human principles. After all, human beings are creatures of habit and so are the organizations they populate. And there is a natural tendency to resist change. Moreover, human beings tend to make rational choices, and therefore before they will embrace a change they want to be ensured that it will benefit them. In the absence of such assurance they will always choose the known over the unknown.

Yet, from these simple principles, we often infer erroneous conclusions that impede our ability to manage resistance and to overcome it. Here are some common myths:

Myth 1: You cannot teach an old dog new tricks. Since older employees are seen as the most habitual in their ways, we often assume that they are the least open to change. However, there is considerable evidence that some older people have anxiously awaited opportunities for change and have felt even more frustrated with the way things were. Moreover, although it may be difficult to teach new skills, it is by no means impossible. There is ample evidence in companies as varied as Motorola, Chemical Bank, and British Airways that new skills (such as customer and service approaches) can be taught to long-service employees.

Myth 2: Complaints and concerns about changes come from resisters. Labeling someone a "resister" can be a self-fulfilling prophecy. It has a pejorative connotation (old-fashioned, old guard, out-moded) and can turn someone into a real resister. Initial "concerns," though, may have been voiced out of a genuine desire to help, not hinder, the change. Such concerns are worth listening to because they often contain legitimate issues which might otherwise be ignored.

Myth 3: Either you are with the new "program" or you are not. (If they do not respond quickly, fire them.) Impatient change agents assume that others will see the benefits of the change as they do. What they forget is that it may have taken them time, information, and experience before they reached their conclusions. Becoming intolerant and forcing people into opposing camps can increase the level of resistance. And by taking such precipitous action as firing people, change agents risk losing valuable experience and resources.

Myth 4: Resisters are always other people than myself. There is a common tendency to identify resistance in others, but deny any resistance in oneself. In other words, sometimes we project our own resistance onto others, perhaps inflating theirs and usually under-acknowledging our own. This can be a dangerous trap in an era in which few changes do not require everyone to change in some way and to experience his or her own internal resistance.

Myth 5: Just change the reward system, and the hearts and minds of people will follow. The power of the financial and career incentive is undeniable, but we often overrely on its use and its timing. Although certainly resisters will be influenced by incentives to change, their behaviors may change without a corresponding change within their hearts and minds. Thus, the sustainability of a change becomes questionable. Moreover, it is rarely possible to make timely or sufficiently large changes in reward systems when change is initiated. Reward systems are more often utilized as reinforcers.

The above myths, if acted upon, can cause a variety of negative consequences, not only to the discredited individuals but to the integrity and success of the change effort itself. A more effective approach must begin with a fuller analysis of why individuals resist change.

Change, by its very nature, involves upsetting and disrupting routines, forcing people to reexamine their jobs, their performances, and how they fit into the new vision for the organization. Moreover, being a manager of change does not mean that you will not resist change yourself. In fact, regardless of your position in an organization, and regardless of the role you play in the change process, you will have to cope with change and experience the emotions associated with that. Indeed, part of the challenge of managing change is not only understanding the legitimate and often predictable reactions of the others who are being changed, but learning to manage your own reactions to the process.

In the literature on change, participants in organizational transformation are often exhorted to embrace change with open arms. Those who are managing change, as well as those who are most directly affected by it (whom I call the "recipients" of change), are urged to be flexible, to search endlessly for new ways to improve, to view change as an exciting adventure, and to "thrive on chaos."

But although these descriptions are inspirational they often bear little relationship to the way most people experience change, particularly those who have little say in the process. At the very least, organizational change stirs up a number of troubling questions: Am I doing my job right? Will I be able to do the new things asked of me? Will this still be a good place to work? Often, the questions raised are even more disturbing: Is it my fault we have to change? Will anything stay the same? Will I still have a job?

Even changes that are not job-threatening can produce a great deal of anxiety. Chris Argyris, who has written extensively on the subject, argues that people react to change as to a perceived threat. Faced with this threat, most people try to protect themselves by using defensive behaviors learned early in life.[10] They refuse to discuss key matters that bother them for fear there will be repercussions. While these behaviors may be a natural reaction, they often stand in the way of productive organizational change.

What, then, are the typical reactions to change? The following list summarizes some of the emotions and ways that employees may feel.[11]

- Sadness and a sense of loss of control, stability, security, friends, status, trust in boss and company, self-confidence, pride, self-esteem, satisfaction, authority, good working conditions, or simply the "old way of doing things."
- Anxiousness about their ability to handle new roles and responsibilities, fit in with new co-workers, satisfy new bosses, adapt to new environments, and know about their future or the future of the company.
- Anger (bitterness) from not being given warning of the change or a chance to make suggestions
- Confusion about their own self-worth or how to meet the new expectations and requirements

- Guilt about "surviving" when co-workers lose positions, money, or status
- Fear that their future may not really be secure and that additional changes may be on the way
- Disorientation and uncertainty about how to function in the new environment

These reactions are not really very surprising. Most people spend more hours on the job than at any other waking activity. Therefore, the satisfaction they derive from their jobs is crucial to how they feel about life in general. Not only that, many people base their self-image to a great extent on how well they feel they are performing at work; their sense of worth may become inextricably tied to their job. People who are laid off and unable to find other employment, therefore, may become deeply depressed or even suicidal.

Fortunately, most people do eventually adapt to change. Yet there are predictable stages that workers pass through in the process of assimilating change. One useful model presents a series of four phases similar to the stages of bereavement.[12] The first stage is shock, during which the employee typically denies that the change is occurring, pulls back from any risk-taking, and becomes timid and protective. The second stage is defensive retreat, characterized by continued unwillingness to change, accompanied by anger at the change or at those promulgating it. Next comes acknowledgment, which includes the mourning of what has been and the acceptance that something new is taking its place. And, finally, adaptation and change, in which doubt, resentment, and fear are replaced by growing enthusiasm and commitment.

Unfortunately, many companies discount these normal reactions to change. In their enthusiasm to embrace a new program and leave the old way behind, they want instant commitment to the cause. In the middle of the process, it is important for managers not to succumb to the sometimes understandable temptation to view resisters as enemies of change, or as people who are somehow bad. A closer look at the source of the resistance may reveal legitimate reasons for discontent and the various emotions described above, and therefore lead to shifts in direction or implementation that ultimately strengthen the entire change effort.

Furthermore, there are steps that organizations can take to prepare for these emotions and to help employees move beyond them. Following are some useful steps for managers to use in overcoming resistance.

1. *Listen, empathize, and acknowledge difficulties.* Many people simply want their concerns to be legitimized and acknowledged. Although they may realize that change is needed, they struggle to accept it. Dismissing their concerns and emotions outright will likely harden their resistance. In addition, it is important to listen to see what underlies the resistance. Is it a problem of will or of skill?

2. *Communicate key information.* When relevant information is provided, people are less anxious, less fearful, and better able to focus on the reasons for the changes. In particular, you should address concrete questions, such as how jobs, responsibilities, and reward systems will be affected by the changes. This includes negative changes. It is far better for employees to get a straightforward report from their managers, along with practical help in dealing with the effects of change, than it is for them to depend on rumors.

3. *Where possible, accommodate legitimate concerns. Provide training and support.* Concerns and issues about the change content or process may emerge that should indeed be factored in. Consider doing so, where appropriate. Moreover, the concerns may be related to the individual's confidence and capability for change. Additional training or coaching might be needed. Or, their concerns may be less with the content of the change than with gaining more of a role in the process.

4. *Involve skeptics.* Skeptics of change can often become supporters of the change when given a role in the process, particularly one in which they will find themselves having to be associated publicly with the change. For example, putting skeptics on steering committees can be very effective.

5. *Apply pressure through politically influential persons and incentives for change.* In order to create more motivation, it may be necessary to use more direct pressure tactics through influential opinion leaders or by sanctioning undesired behaviors. These hardball tactics should be used as a last attempt at "unfreezing" the individual.

6. *If all the above fails, resisters should be transferred or fired, in order not to impede progress in making the change.* If one has genuinely tried to increase both the readiness and the capability of an individual, and yet the individual cannot respond in one way or the other, he or she should be removed from the organization. The principle should be, "If you cannot change the person, change the person!" One who is ultimately not receptive to change must be replaced.

Overall, the kind of dialogue in the first steps is intended to involve people in the change process. When employees understand that they do have a say in what happens, they are more likely to have a stake in the outcome and to work for the program's success. Moreover, the sense of control that comes from involvement helps alleviate the normal stress associated with change. Involvement can range from open forums encouraging employee input in upper-management plans, to worker teams responsible for designing and implementing change.

Finally, honesty is an excellent way to defuse stress and to help people cope with change. It might seem self-evident that managers should be honest with employees, yet too often the fear of communicating unpopular news or of having to confront painful emotions causes managers to cover up important and relevant information, or to cut off communication entirely. What these managers fail to realize is that half-truths and coverups create their own pain and anxiety. Moreover, if managers are cagey about disclosing bad news, any good news that they share will also be seen as suspect. Some companies have allowed affected employees to "vent" themselves to each other while managers listen, which can help them move beyond their anxiety.

Underlying the foregoing discussion is the all-important need for employees to communicate and be heard. One of the hardest tasks for managers is to learn the fine art of listening in a nonjudgmental fashion. Although it can be threatening to managers to hear complaints, employees who are allowed to express their grievances and frustrations constructively and without fear of retribution typically find it easier to adjust to change.

Employees should have regular opportunities to identify problems, to suggest solutions, and to hear how the change is progressing. Managers who really listen to frustrations, rather than lumping them under the catch-all title of "resistance," will not only respond to employees in a more appropriate manner, but will learn about real issues whose resolution can make the change process smoother and more productive. (For more ideas on dealing with resistant individuals, see Chapter 4, by Stephen L. Fink, "Managing Individual Behavior.")

CONCLUSION

This advice so far has focused on how to make change less painful for the recipient. But, in fact, everyone in an organization is affected by change. Although as a manager you may have more control over the process, you will face the dual challenge of helping others cope with change at the same time that you are confronting unexpected events and emotions yourself. According to one observer, "To manage ambiguity and paradox, managers of the future will have to develop managerial philosophies and techniques that allow them to cope with messy, ill-defined situations that do not lend themselves to clear-cut interpretation, and have no ready-made recipes for action.[13]

Those who are change leaders may feel particularly uneasy, especially if they shoulder the blame for the reactions of others. Typical words used to describe the experience of being a change agent include stressful, uncertain, lone, isolated, confused, frustrated, threatened, afraid, vulnerable, villainized, and disappointed. One consultant working as a change agent confided in his journal that "he had learned more about asking for help during this time and more about why people wanted family to come home to than he had ever known before."[14]

Future change managers will face a much more complicated agenda than their counterparts of even a decade ago. The challenges laid out in this chapter make it clear that managing change is a demanding job. Implementors of change must be willing to take chances—to experiment with new structures, new systems, and new perspectives. They should be comfortable with uncertainty and change. They should involve others whenever possible. They should not become wedded to one particular approach or program, but should be willing to reexamine continually an organization's needs and goals. They should be patient and persistent. And throughout it all, they must remain pragmatic. No change process is flawless, no goal perfectly achieved. In fact, a good sense of humor could ultimately prove one of the finest characteristics for a change agent to possess.

Change is more likely to be a group project today. Rather than one person leading the way, change may well be driven by a top management team, or by a cadre of middle managers, or even by worker teams who have been empowered to analyze their jobs and their environments and to come up with better ways of doing things. This group approach demands a different kind of managerial sensibility, one that values the ability to collaborate, to let go, and to listen more than the ability to take charge.

Managing change, then, is not for the faint of heart. In the last few years the term "change agent" has become ingrained in common vocabulary. It is used more and more synonymously with the terms "manager" and "leader." What is required for managers to be successful in this? Along with the analytical and operational abilities that are an ordinary part of organizational life, the change agent needs the sensitivity of a social worker, the insights of a psychologist, the stamina of a marathon runner, the persistence of a bulldog, the self-reliance of a hermit, and the patience of a saint. And even with all those qualities, there is no guarantee of success.

Given this reality, managing change might seem a thankless task. Yet for many, implementing change can be not just an exciting growth experience, but a deeply satisfying venture, producing almost a feeling of euphoria. One manager who helped push through innovative and fruitful programs at a major airline described the experience this way: "I wouldn't have given it up for the world. It definitely changed the way I look at life and business, and how I handle myself." Another middle manager described his feelings during a productive period in his company's change process saying, "I've died and gone to heaven. I don't ever want this to end."

With the proper understanding of the challenges and possibilities involved, change managers can thrive on the very challenges and uncertainties that distinguish their role.

NOTES

1.   Jack Welch, "Managing Change" (Keynote address, Fuqua School of Business, Durham, NC, April 21, 1983), p. 2.

2.   G. Fuchsberg, "Quality Programs Show Shoddy Results," *Wall Street Journal* May 14, 1992, p. B-1.

3.   D. Dunphy and D. Stace, *Evolution or Transformation? Incremental versus Transformational Ideologies for Organizational Change* (Australian Graduate School of Management, University of New South Wales, 1989), pp. 317–334.

4.   J. Kotter and J. Heskett, *Corporate Culture and Performance* (New York: Free Press, 1992), p. 100.

5.   R. M. Kanter, *The Change Masters* (New York: Simon and Schuster, 1983), p. 216.

6.   M. Daniel and S. Schoonover, *Changing Ways* (New York: American Management Assoc., 1988), p. 112.

7.   Welch, "Managing Change," p. 2.

8.   T. Jick and L. Schlesinger, "Xerox: Leadership Through Quality," case study in *Managing Change*, ed. T. Jick (Chicago: Richard Irwin, 1983).

9.   For more on this topic, see R. Ashkenas and T. Jick, "From Dialogue to Action in GE Work-Out: Developmental Learning in a Change Process," in *Research in Organizational Change and Development*, vol. 6 (Greenwich, CT: Jai Press, 1992), pp. 267–287.

10.   C. Argyris, *Strategy, Change, and Defensive Routines* (Boston: Ballinger, 1985).

11.   "How Change Affects People and Organizations," *Trainer's Workshop*, vol. 4 (4) July–August, 1990.

12.   H. Woodward and S. Bucholz, *Aftershock* (New York: John Wiley & Sons, 1987).

13.   G. Morgan, *Riding the Waves of Change* (San Francisco: Jossey-Bass, 1988), p. 12.

14.   G. Shea and D. Berg, "Analyzing the Development of an OD Practitioner," *The Journal of Applied Behavioral Science* 23 (3) (1987): pp. 332–333.

FOR FURTHER READING

Beckhard, R. and W. Pritchard. *Changing the Essence*. San Francisco: Jossey-Bass, 1992.

Beer, Michael, R. Eisenstat, and B. Spector. *The Critical Path to Corporate Renewal*. New York: Free Press, 1990.

Bridges, William. *Surviving Corporate Transition*. New York: Doubleday, 1988.

Jick, Todd. *Managing Change: Cases and Concepts*. Chicago: Richard Irwin, 1993.

Kanter, R. M., B. Stein, and T. Jick. *The Challenge of Organizational Change*. New York: Free Press, 1992.

Morgan, Gareth. *Riding the Waves of Change*. San Francisco: Jossey-Bass, 1988.

CONCLUSION: FUTURE LEADERS MUST BE GLOBAL MANAGERS

Rosabeth Moss Kanter

If you had told most Americans in 1982 that currency issues in Germany would make the front pages of their local newspapers in 1992, they would have questioned your sanity. But by the mid-1990s the awareness of global economic interdependence has even spread to the backwaters of most regions of the industrialized world. In rural Ohio, in small towns so remote that they are many hours away from the nearest airport, town officials court Japanese manufacturers in hopes that they will locate a factory there. A French paper manufacturer brings its American plant managers to France for lessons. A regional British quality effort is led by a Japanese employer. In Indonesia, managers of branch banks on isolated islands view the latest management videos from the United States.

In the future, the leadership skills identified throughout this book will be practiced on a global playing field. *Globalization* is the extension of the geographic scope of business as national boundaries and barriers disappear. Because of political, economic, and technological changes, all of the factors of business can more easily move across borders: capital, labor, products, production, information, ideas, and sources of supply. Mobility and access provide more choices: where to buy, where to sell, whom to hire, where to locate, what to emulate.

Globalization brings managers two almost contradictory challenges. It increases the need for cooperation and coordination among businesses and among countries in order to find common standards, methods, languages, package sizes, transportation systems, or communications links. Indeed, to get access to all the cash, skills, goods, or markets the world can offer, globalization encourages companies to form relationships across traditional boundaries—alliances that can bring additional benefits quickly. But at the same time, as globalization increases cross-boundary contact it also increases peoples' awareness of their differences. Local pride seems inevitably to accompany global contact. And globalization clearly does not mean homogenization. Nor does it mean that national or regional differences in values, behaviors, and business practices disappear even as some of them converge. Global managers, therefore, must manage through far-reaching cooperative networks of people and companies that are independent and diverse.

The behavioral skills presented in this book—influence, negotiation, teamwork, creating vision, dealing with difficult subordinates, career management and change management—come into play in heightened form in the situations that global managers must manage. Let's take a look at three clusters of managers who must contend with global issues, and then we can better see the essential skills for managers of the future.

GLOBAL GOVERNANCE: OLOF LUNDBERG AND INMARSAT

Very few people will ever be in Olof Lundberg's position. His job contains about as much global complexity as any in the world and therefore illustrates many of the challenges associated with the global playing field. He is the director-general (chief executive) of Inmarsat, an international telecommunications satellite consortium. Inmarsat provides the satellite services for mobile communications at sea, by air, and on land throughout the world; CNN, for example, used its services to broadcast live during the Gulf War. Lundberg has been chief executive since the founding of Inmarsat, and he has helped lead it to a profitable place of preeminence in world telecommunications, expanding its services dramatically.

Inmarsat is owned by 64 telecommunications entities from 64 countries. The largest stakes are held by profit-making corporations such as the recently privatized Telecom of Britain and Comsat in the United States, for which Inmarsat-related services form a large portion of total revenue. At the other end of the organizational spectrum, Inmarsat shares are held by government PTTs (post, telegraph, and telephone ministries) in developing countries. Twenty-two owners, including the 18 largest, are represented on a governing council. On behalf of this diverse and numerous array of bosses, Lundberg leads a staff of 400 at Inmarsat's London headquarters; the staff is composed of 55 nationalities. Lundberg is Swedish; his own direct reports include British, Greek, German, and American-Egyptian managers.

Adjusting to the style differences when that many nationalities interact is the easy part of Lundberg's job. Shared technical orientations are often so strong among staff members that cultural origins are forgotten. But much more challenging is negotiating among the varied and sometimes divergent interests of the owners. The major owners are also Inmarsat's biggest customers, using the Inmarsat global system to provide local services to their customers in Canada, Japan, or Saudi Arabia; as mobile telecommunications spills across borders, some of them are in direct competition. In addition, some of the owners can also be suppliers, competing for contracts to provide technology for the entire system. The owners have different reasons for wanting to tap satellite capacity; for some, like Comsat, it is the major portion of their business, but for others it is trivial. And if these differences in interest are not enough, national pride is often at stake in Inmarsat decisions, because some of its owners are still government entities. Symbolism can sometimes be as important as economics in Inmarsat decisions. Questions of where to hold meetings or who is represented on committees can be matters requiring significant international diplomacy.

Skills in influence, negotiation, and conflict management are not optional for global managers like Lundberg—they are necessities. He must listen to widely varying needs and interests of his owner-customers and then determine a direction that will satisfy most of them. To manage change, he must patiently plant seeds of new ideas and then cultivate them through review and approval processes that are inherently slow and complex, while he builds coalitions of supporters from geographically distant places with diverse or even conflicting goals. He must win the respect of people from many nationalities who hold very different views about how they should be treated and how Lundberg, as a leader, should behave. For example, as Inmarsat staff members view it, Americans like decisiveness and fast action whereas Swedes are more patient and prefer consensus.

Lundberg himself sees his Swedish origins as an advantage for global management. "I grew up in a small country with the same number of people as New York City," he comments. "We never saw ourselves as dominating anyone else. As a small country, we knew we had to learn other languages, make relationships with other countries. We had to learn to listen."

GLOBAL DISTRIBUTION: AL NICHOLS, DICK DOZIER, AND NICHOLS INSTITUTE

For small companies, global management issues have a different character. Such companies may operate primarily within their home country but seek to export some of their products. For Dr. Albert Nichols, founder and CEO of Nichols Institute, in southern California, finding international distributors for his medical diagnostic kits is the first step toward the eventual international expansion of the company's clinical laboratory business.

Unlike some businesses, whose products can be licensed for distribution in other countries at arm's length and with contract renewals handled by fax, Nichols medical kits must have guaranteed exceptional quality. For example, time-sensitive chemicals need special handling, and distributors must work closely with the Nichols home office to ensure customer satisfaction. And as an entrepreneurial founder with his name on the door, Dr. Nichols is especially concerned about working with people who share his values— more difficult to determine when working outside of one's own country. The Nichols Institute's guiding vision stresses the application of state-of-the-art medical knowledge to patient care in the highest quality manner. Ensuring that the physician-patient interaction is enhanced by a Nichols diagnostic kit is more difficult through intermediaries, such as international distributors. Therefore, though the international side may be a small part of a small business, relationship management looms large. Trust is essential.

Dr. Nichols's first relationship-management accomplishment was finding a knowledgeable international representative in Richard Dozier, an American expatriate living in Switzerland who had appropriate industry experience. A joint project had provided confirmation of shared values, and over the next three years Dozier established relationships for distribution in 27 countries from his Geneva base. Soon Patty in California was in weekly phone contact with Marieluise in Switzerland or their distributors in Italy, Germany, and Japan, continuing to work out nuances of relationships: different billing and payments procedures in Italy or translation issues for product literature in Spain.

Dozier's ability to find and form the right relationships is artistry: a subjective process of seeing through language barriers, national regulatory differences, and differing business practices in order to find the values that drive a company and its leaders. The distributors must not only be well regarded by physicians in their countries, but they must operate their own businesses according to the highest medical standards, stressing scientific quality, respect for patients, and a highly professional staff. Organizational evaluation and relationship development are time-consuming because they involve many face-to-face meetings in each other's home territories. "Quite often an individual might make a favorable impression when he has traveled to a trade show or exhibition," Dozier says, "but once you get back to his country and meet the people he has hired and see how he treats his people, it can be quite a different story."

Dozier recognizes the importance of trust-building and negotiating stances that are appropriate to particular countries. To many Europeans, for example, friendships built up over the years are more important than contracts or profitability. Nichols and Dozier have to demonstrate their own trustworthiness, going out of their way to provide benefits for distributors, in order to compete with local products. "In international relationships the attitude and the approach often cause more problems than the substance," Dozier observes.

GLOBAL SOURCING: DAVID DWORKIN, LIZ BROUGHAN AND BhS

Even for businesses selling only locally, the global dimension is becoming more important. The ability to source globally, for example, provides a wider choice of parts or products. For David Dworkin, an American who became CEO of British retailer BhS in 1989, global buying was a clear part of a revitalization strategy for the chain. He needed to work with his buying directors, such as Liz Broughan, to make drastic changes in order to get better apparel merchandise into the stores faster and at lower cost. The changes meant a revamp of the supply base to allow working more closely with fewer suppliers and doing more direct buying in Asia.

Dworkin faced not only internal resistance—framed in criticism of the "American management style" as applied to a British company—but also external resistance: An outcry by small British suppliers that were to be displaced led to brutal media treatment. He laid the foundation for eventual success (and his promotion to CEO of the parent company, Storehouse) through excellent change-management skills: first getting the painful duties out of the way, such as cutting headcount and replacing weak managers; articulating a vision and creating a joint mission statement with the new team; and involving large numbers of people on task forces reviewing the appropriate shape of all parts of the business. Suppliers were then invited in to hear the new criteria and given an opportunity to meet the higher standards.

Liz Broughan's challenge is to make global sourcing a reality. Buyers inside BhS, many of whom had never traveled outside the United Kingdom, have to become attuned to unfamiliar business practices and cultural nuances. In small ways as well as large ways their work is different. They must become the linchpins of cross-boundary teams that includes BhS designers and supplier manufacturing experts, to speed up the process of getting fashionable merchandise to the stores and quickly replenishing the popular items obtained from factories halfway around the globe. They must learn to adjust their negotiating stances to the particular country with which they are dealing. They must know how country differences will affect their ability to get product made and delivered—from religious holidays to work force skills.

"We are looking at new markets for sourcing goods," according to Broughan, "and we need more preparation before entering them. We will need to know where to get fabric, buttons, trim, etc., in all those countries.

And the differences in the behavior of manufacturers can be a shock to some of the newer buyers. In India it is typical to receive reassurances that everything is on the boat when it hasn't even left the country yet. Korea and Japan, on the other hand, are very efficient and straightforward."

VARIETIES OF GLOBAL MANAGEMENT

Global management clearly comes in many varieties. It should not be equated with just the multinational firm that has subsidiaries in many countries, although that is the form that gets the most attention in treatises on managing across borders. As discussed in Chapter 8 ("Designing Effective Organizations," by Phyllis F. and Leonard A. Schlesinger), the problems of properly integrating the activities of such firms are complex variations on the problems of any large company with multiple units.

Organizations do not have to be large to think globally, and they do not even have to have offices or operations in many countries. Some might effectively conduct international business out of a single office. Guinness Peat Aviation, the aircraft-leasing firm that is Ireland's largest company, operates worldwide out of its headquarters at Shannon Airport. It closed its regional offices around the world because they added costs and interfered with teamwork; it was better for the company to send people temporarily to countries where deals were being negotiated.

Managers have to think internationally even if still operating just a local department in a local company—not because their *company* has locations elsewhere but because their *partners* do. They may be working with international suppliers, attracting capital from foreign investments, or selling to international markets. Or they may choose allies in other countries as a way to gain clout or ideas.

The European Retail Alliance (ERA) is a good example of the benefits of international cooperation for companies whose business scope is purely local. It was the brainchild of Pierre Everaert, chief executive of the Dutch food retail holding company, Ahold (Albert Heijn supermarkets). Everaert was born in Belgium and later became a U.S. citizen. Multilingual, he is at home all over the world. By forming the ERA with Argyll (Safeway stores) in the United Kingdom and Casino in France and then a larger marketing alliance with eight other European companies, Ahold can gain sufficient clout to encourage manufacturers to design standard products that all three companies can buy at lower cost. Furthermore, there are opportunities for the three ERA companies to learn from the others. Projects in information technology bring Argyll's competence to ERA members; Casino runs British food promotions. Now plans are underway to send staff on temporary assignments to other ERA companies, for "cross-fertilization" and idea exchange.

As organizations extend their reach across borders, there are three generic types of situations, relationships, and roles for their people, ranging from brief foreign visits to overseas assignment in a subsidiary to negotiating with foreign partners.

Temporary and ad Hoc Exchanges

Short-term exchanges include guest-host or foreign visitor-local target contacts, as well as those of external consultants with local clients or foreign information seekers with local experts or companies. Because the number of cross-border contacts of all kinds is increasing, the global manager is even more likely to be a *traveling* manager than an expatriate, assigned for long stints in another country. There are many short cross-border contacts as well as travel to sites for purposes of managing cross-border relationships—like the almost monthly meetings of the ERA partner CEOs in several different cities. Staying put in one place outside one's home country is a different experience from traveling to many places to manage many relationships. The latter involves skills in adjusting quickly to new places, absorbing new information, operating in unfamiliar territory, maintaining personal stamina, avoiding jet lag. Fatigue alone can alter judgment and lead to poor decisions.

In these relationships, differences of cultural backgrounds, practices, or knowledge may be known and may even be the reason for the contact. Many of these contacts are fleeting: They can be sufficiently superficial or confined to well-understood technical domains so that relatively few culturally based misunderstandings occur. Or participants can have limited expectations of needing to work together again anyway; they do not necessarily require deep immersion in the other culture. For one thing, "guests" or "visitors" are likely always to remain strangers and outsiders to their hosts. The foreigner is not actually permitted inside—even the consultant. If the relationships should go beyond the fleeting and superficial, then more compatibility or relationship-building elements must enter in.

Hierarchical Contacts

Hierarchical contacts include boss-subordinate or headquarters-field relationships, such as expatriate managers working in another country, or native country managers dealing with the headquarters staff in another country. These contacts should be distinguished as subtypes, depending on whether they involve geographic relocation, the length of time outside the native country, the number of other expatriates or locals similarly situated, and so forth. Because these relationships involve dominance and subordination, many things may be attributed to "culture" that really involve "power." In the past, Americans with "foreign contact" experience of this type were generally more likely to have been the boss or owner than to have been subordinates of foreign bosses. However, because of increased foreign investment in the United States, it is now more likely for managers from other countries to be thinking about the "problems of managing Americans."

Network Contacts

Network contacts include partner representative–partner representative or alliance/joint venture/supplier–customer relationships. These contacts definitely require deeper immersion, because the partners remain independent and are ostensibly relatively equal in many respects. It is important to the success of the relationship to identify areas of similarity and difference in business variables that could have influence. Such contacts require compatibility and the ability to work together over time. And since they are not hierarchically controlled by employment or full-ownership relationships, clear power cannot be exercised—persuasion and influence must prevail. It becomes more important to accommodate the "others" as well as have them accommodate you, which involves the need for greater mutual knowledge and perhaps acknowledgment of their core cultural identity.

Such network relationships involve a variety of skills and knowledge of organizational arrangements:

- Choosing the right partner
- Defining "compatibility" in business and organizational terms— understanding the needs and leverage that companies bring to their relationships with other companies
- Deciding how to distribute the economic benefits
- Establishing a governance system
- Understanding what can go wrong and negotiating changes in the relationship itself
- Modifying or revolutionizing internal systems to permit the coordination and transfer of learning necessary to take full advantage of external cooperation—the "infrastructure" for effective cross-boundary relationships

GLOBAL COMMUNICATION SKILLS: THE HUMAN DIMENSION

Globalism means that knowledge about other places and cultures is important—not just to sell to others but to learn from them. And to learn not just as a matter of noblesse oblige—to get along with the natives while privately feeling superior—but to be open to the possibility that they could have valuable skills or knowledge to impart. Respecting other cultures in this way is important not just to overcome differences for improving negotiations and establishing favorable cross-organizational relationships but also to get all the benefits from benchmarking, which involves learning from different ways of doing things. This parallels, with more complexity, the need for mutuality in operating with diversity raised in Chapter 11, "Managing Diversity," by R. Roosevelt Thomas, Jr.

Attention to cross-border and cross-company relationships leads directly to people issues—the role of differences in cultural values in different countries. How much cultural values matter is a subject with considerable controversy.

For some managers, cultural differences and their importance is clear and given. In the course of their work, they see that "cultural assumptions" affect national rules and business practices. They see that some managerial actions are more effective than others depending on the culture, that change strategies or influence strategies have to be culturally appropriate, and that negative cultural stereotypes can get in the way of cooperation toward mutual business ends. Furthermore, they acknowledge the special challenges for managers or professionals who are foreigners in a strange land.

But others feel strongly that cultural differences are not so important or should not deserve so much attention. They say that sound or shaky business actions are sound or shaky regardless of where they are found; that people are distinct individuals, and trying to understand their cultural assumptions produces meaningless, judgmental generalizations or distinctions; that invoking cultural differences can reflect sloppy thinking, not examining many other important situational business issues; that discussing cultural differences can lead people into "political correctness" traps; and that cultural value issues evoke emotional reactions.

This debate is a microcosm of debates that continue in the global economy itself. "Universalists" who ignore or downplay differences risk failure if such differences are important to those with whom they are dealing or if the differences show up in significant business practices. Some European observers have argued that Americans are particularly unaware of cultural differences because of the melting pot heritage, as well as the post–World War II experience of being a superpower nation in an increasingly English-speaking world. Such tendencies, when they exist, can handicap Americans in international negotiations. But "nationalists" or "culturalists," who are preoccupied with differences, run equal risks of failure if they attribute to cultural differences things that deserve deeper analysis or if they inappropriately generalize or stereotype. Historical rivalries between the British and the Germans or the British and the French can lead to a breakdown of negotiations (as in discussions of European monetary policy), especially if representatives feel their national pride wounded when asked to compromise or if they read "national interest" into every move made by their counterparts.

A good portion of effectiveness in cross-cultural management involves good common sense about managing people and relationships in general. But there are also some nuances and complexities added because of the cross-cultural dimension, including extra energy expenditures:

- There are more opportunities for strategically significant miscommunication, such as misinterpreting a key concept or misreading a cue.

- There is greater need for self-awareness, to understand the assumptions others hold about you and to modify behavior if necessary to counter such assumptions.

- There are more variables or issues to take into account as you develop a negotiating strategy or manage conflict or sell a proposal.

- And there is a greater likelihood of experiencing discomfort or fatigue from the additional mental or emotional effort—even the strain of listening to your own language spoken with an unfamiliar accent or speaking more slowly than usual to make yourself understood.

WHICH DIFFERENCES MATTER? THE NEED FOR SITUATIONAL ASSESSMENT

Cultural differences need to be seen in perspective. They can be a highly emotional matter, and people vary in their comfort at even mentioning such value-laden issues. Group affiliation and cultural compatibilities matter more to people when threatened, and they sometimes become a convenient label for the threat. Or they become a banner or rally cry for attempts to gain more power for one's own group and oneself. People who have never left their home culture or have been in a dominant majority may be particularly uncomfortable with encountering or discussing "difference" because it forces heightened self-awareness of taken-for-granted assumptions and behaviors.

Not all "cultural" issues, even if differences exist, are relevant from a business or managerial standpoint. But knowledge along some dimensions can be very helpful.

- *Attitudes toward authority.* How do people view hierarchy? And how important is the relative status of the people you are dealing with compared to your own?

  Feelings about authority affect how much information is disclosed and how honest others are likely to be (as opposed to respectful of someone with superior status and therefore overly polite and withholding of negative information). For example, as a culturally derived propensity, managers in Chinese business groups (regardless of the country in which they are situated) may want to please the expert and respect an older person, and they fear saying anything negative about bosses. Thus it is harder to get an accurate picture of business problems as reports or analyses are made much more respectful and less blunt or confrontational. Of course, authority differences in all cultures affect openness to some degree, but it is easier to take that into account within the culture one knows best; it is harder to deal with it across cultures.

- *Incentives and rewards.* What makes people look good to others or derive status in their community? What are the natures of the tangible career and monetary incentives for the people with whom you are dealing? How much are various kinds of rewards valued?

  How success is measured differs widely—for example, how important money is compared to face, or dignity. Knowledge of this sort tells you about what drives the other, what leverage you have in negotiations, what benefits you have to produce for the individuals with whom you are in contact and not just for their companies.

- *Politeness rituals and taboos.* How is respect (or disrespect) conveyed? It is easy to step on toes by not understanding the meaning of words or gestures or to offend by omission—failing to make an important gesture. Conveying respect is essential.

In dealing with other companies across national borders, there are eight general areas in which to gain knowledge, in order to assess and manage the differences that will influence the course of the relationship:

Objective ("Hard") Issues

1. National rules and regulations
2. Company economics and strategies
3. Relative company size, power, resources, roles
4. Company practices and systems

Subjective ("Soft") Issues

5. National cultural groups and values
6. Company cultures
7. Behavioral styles—such as negotiating posture
8. Stereotypes of others and cultural attributions

SUMMARY

Understanding and appreciating differences along these dimensions are necessities for the effective management of cross-cultural and cross-border issues. By asking "How are we different?" global managers can identify areas of compatibility or conflict. They can anticipate problems or areas about which they must learn, in order to succeed with foreign counterparts. They can see the constraints to change strategies. They can determine a negotiating posture, shape influence tactics, or find the key to relationships of trust. They can better design their organizations and manage their human resources strategically.

Despite all the technology that will link managers of the future into global networks—direct electronic interchanges, videoconferences, fax machines, supersonic jets, and overnight delivery—the fundamental basis for global success will still be one of the most ancient: direct human communication. All organizational life requires that members operate in a complex web of relationships; the global stage extends dramatically the scope and complexity of the web. Managers increasingly need to be able to thread their way, understanding the interconnections and players at each point while maintaining a sure sense of self. Success as a manager in the future will require no less.

FOR FURTHER READING

Adler, Nancy J. *International Dimensions of Organizational Behavior.* Boston: PWS-KENT, 1991.

Bartlett, Christopher, and Sumantra Ghoshal. *Managing Across Borders: The Transnational Solution.* Boston: HBS Press, 1990.

Hampden-Turner, Charles. "The Boundaries of Business: The Cross-Cultural Quagmire," *Harvard Business Review* September-October 1991.

Hofstede, Geert. *Cultures and Organizations: Software of the Mind.* London: McGraw-Hill, 1991.

Kanter, Rosabeth Moss. "Transcending Business Boundaries: 12,000 World Managers View Change," *Harvard Business Review* May-June 1991.

Kanter, Rosabeth Moss. *When Giants Learn to Dance: Mastering the Challenges of Strategy, Management, and Careers in the 1990s.* New York: Simon & Schuster, 1989.

Ohmae, Kenichi. *Managing in the Borderless World.* New York: Harper & Row, 1989.

ABOUT THE AUTHORS

David L. Bradford is Senior Lecturer in Organizational Behavior at the Graduate School of Business, Stanford University. He received his Ph.D. in Social Psychology at the University of Michigan and taught at the University of Wisconsin before joining the faculty at Stanford. Dr. Bradford was the founder and first executive director of The Organizational Behavior Teaching Society and is a past Board member of the NTL Institute. In addition to numerous articles published in professional journals, he has coauthored (with Allan R. Cohen) two major books on interpersonal and group processes in organizations (*Managing for Excellence: The Guide to Developing High Performance in Contemporary Organizations* and *Influence without Authority*, both published by John Wiley & Sons).

Dr. Bradford has served as a consultant in developing high-performing teams for such organizations as Allergan, Frito-Lay, IBM, Levi Strauss & Co., Raychem, and Syntex.

Anne Donnellon is an Assistant Professor at the Harvard Business School and a Research Associate at the Harvard Law School Program on Negotiation. Donnellon teaches *Power and Influence* and *Organizational Behavior* in the MBA program at Harvard. She has also taught team dynamics, interpersonal relations, organization communication, and leadership in the management development programs of several companies. She holds a Ph.D. in Organizational Behavior from Pennsylvania State University and an M.A. in Linguistics from Columbia University.

Professor Donnellon's research focuses on the interaction, work relationships, and effectiveness of decision-making groups. Her work has been published in *Organizational Dynamics, Administrative Science Quarterly, Journal of Productive Innovation Management,* and *Journal of Social Issues.*

Professor Donnellon is currently working on a book with the preliminary title of *The Meaning of Teamwork*. The book examines how teams construct the meaning of teamwork in their day-to-day interaction and what the implications of teamwork are—for identities and careers, for distribution of information and power, for organizational systems and structure, and for effective performance.

Stephen L. Fink is a Professor of Organizational Behavior at the Whittemore School at the University of New Hampshire. Previously he was an Associate Professor at Case Western University and a visiting lecturer at the University of Leeds,

England. Professor Fink received his B.S. from Union College and his Ph.D. from Western Reserve University. He is author of *High Commitment Workplaces* (Quorum, 1992) and coauthor of the widely adopted textbook, *Effective Behavior in Organizations* (Richard D. Irwin, 5th ed. 1992) and *Designing and Managing Organizations* (Richard D. Irwin, 1983). He has served as an organizational and management consultant to a wide range of public and private organizations.

Charles J. Fombrun is the Research Professor of Management and Organization at the Stern School, New York University, where he has been on the faculty since 1984. He completed his Ph.D. at Columbia University in 1980 and taught at The Wharton School from 1979 to 1984. Dr. Fombrun is the author of *Turning Points: Creating Strategic Change in Corporations* (McGraw-Hill). Dr. Fombrun is coauthor, with Noel Tichy and Mary Anne Devanna, of *Strategic Human Resource Management* (John Wiley & Sons, 1984). He has also written many articles for such publications as *The Journal of Business Strategy, The Sloan Management Review,* and *The Academy of Management Journal.* Dr. Fombrun is a frequent contributor to conferences and journals describing research on how organizations adapt to their environments, and he sits on the Editorial Boards of *The Academy of Management Review, Human Resource Planning,* and *Human Resource Management.*

Douglas T. Hall is a Professor of Organizational Behavior and Faculty Director for Masters Programs in the School of Management at Boston University. He is also the Director of the Executive Development Roundtable and a core faculty member of the Human Resource Policy Institute. He has also served as Acting Dean and Associate Dean of Faculty Development at the School of Management. He received his degree from the Sloane School of Management at M.I.T. He has held faculty positions at Yale, York, Michigan State, and Northwestern universities.

Professor Hall is the author of *Careers in Organizations* and coauthor of *Organizational Climates and Careers, The Two Career Couple, Experiences in Management and Organizational Behavior, Career Development in Organizations, Human Resource Management: Strategy, Design and Implementation,* and *Handbook of Career Theory.* He is currently a member of the Board of Governors of the Center for Creative Leadership. He has served on the editorial boards of five scholarly journals. His research and consulting activities have dealt with career development, women's careers, career plateauing, work/family balance, and executive succession. He has served as a consultant to organizations such as Sears, AT&T, General Electric, Price Waterhouse, Monsanto, Honeywell, Ford Motor Company, Eli Lilly, and the World Bank.

Drew Harris is a Ph.D. candidate in Human Resources Management at New York University and a coauthor (with R. Schuler) of *Managing Quality* (1992), as well as author of numerous articles published in professional journals.

Todd D. Jick was Associate Professor of Organizational Behavior/Human Resource Management at the Harvard Business School from 1984 to 1992. He is currently teaching at INSEAD (France). He has also taught at the Columbia University Graduate School of Business and York University (Toronto). Dr. Jick earned his M.S. and Ph.D. from Cornell University, New York State School of Industrial and Labor Relations, in organizational behavior. He has a B.A. in social anthropology from Wesleyan University.

Dr. Jick has been actively involved in executive education and consulting in areas such as leadership, organizational change, power and authority, managerial performance improvement, and human resources management. He has taught in Harvard's executive programs, and he has worked with numerous in-house executive education clients, including General Electric, AT&T, Bell Labs, Honeywell, Buick, Ameritech, Merck, and Allstate. European-based clients have included Ciba-Geigy, Volvo, Bull HN, and Finnair.

Dr. Jick's books include *Managing Change: Cases and Concepts* (Irwin, 1992), *The Challenge of Organizational Change: How Companies Experience It and Leaders Guide It* (Free Press, 1992) with Rosabeth Kanter and Barry Stein, and *Launching and Leading the Boundaryless Organization* (edited with Dave Ulrich and Len Schlesinger). He has also authored more than 20 cases on companies, including Apple Computer, Motorola, Walt Disney Europe, Continental Can, and Northwest Airlines and has published several articles on how to implement major organizational changes.

Rosabeth Moss Kanter has taught at Harvard Business School since 1986, holding the Class of 1960 Chair as Professor of Business Administration. Her current research and teaching center around globalization and the development of innovative, customer-directed companies. Before joining the Harvard Business School faculty, Dr. Kanter taught at Brandeis University and Yale University. She was also a Fellow in law and social sciences and a visiting Scholar at Harvard Law School. From 1989 to 1992, Dr. Kanter was editor of the *Harvard Business Review*, and she became Vice Chairman of the Board of the Harvard Business School Publishing Group in 1992. Dr. Kanter's books include *The Challenge of Organizational Change: How Companies Experience It and Leaders Guide It* (1992, coauthored with Barry Stein and Todd Jick); *When Giants Learn to Dance: Mastering the Challenges of Strategy, Management, and Careers in the 1990s* (1989), which received the Johnson, Smith & Knisely Award for new Perspectives on Executive Leadership and was translated into 10 languages; and *Men and Women of the Corporation* (1977), winner of the C. Wright Mills Award for the year's best book on social issues.

Harvey F. Kolodny is Professor in the Faculty of Management and the Department of Industrial Engineering at the University of Toronto. He earned a doctorate in business administration from the Harvard Business School, an MBA from the University of Sherbrooke in Quebec, and a B. Eng. in electronics from McGill University. His fields of interest are organizational design, high-commitment workplaces, and the management of technology. Professor Kolodny is also the Director of the Organization Design Program at the University of Toronto and a member of the Task Force on Work Organization of the Premier's Council on Economic Renewal (Ontario) and has been a visiting researcher with the Stockholm School of Economics in Sweden. Dr. Kolodny's current research includes a comparative international project to examine the relationships between new technology and organization design and their impact on the skills and knowledge of the workforce.

Roy J. Lewicki is Professor of Management and Human Resources at The Ohio State University. Professor Lewicki received his B.A. in Psychology from Dartmouth College and his Ph.D. in Social Psychology from Columbia University. Before coming to Ohio State, Professor Lewicki served on the faculties of Yale University,

Dartmouth College, and Duke University. In addition to his faculty appointment at Ohio State, Professor Lewicki also served as Associate Dean for Graduate Management Programs (1984–91) and Academic Director of Executive Education (1991–92) at the College of Business, The Ohio State University.

Professor Lewicki maintains research and teaching interests in the fields of negotiation and dispute resolution, managerial leadership, organizational justice, and ethical decision making. He is the author or coauthor of 14 books, including *Social Intervention: A Behavioral Science Approach* (Free Press, 1971), *Experiences in Management and Organizational Behavior* (John Wiley & Sons, 1975, 1982, 1988), *Negotiation: Readings, Exercises and Cases* (Richard D. Irwin, 1985 and 1992), *Research on Negotiation in Organizations* (JAI, 1986, 1990, 1991, and 1993), and *Organizational Justice* (Free Press, 1992). He is also the author of numerous research articles in these fields. Recently he was named as an Associate Editor of the *Academy of Management Executive*, a professional management journal.

Professor Lewicki has extensive experience in the design and teaching of executive education programs and in business consultation. Recent clients include Eli Lilly, Ross Laboratories, Marathon Oil Company, Price Waterhouse, Crowe Chizek, Red Roof Inns, The University of California San Diego, and university-based executive development programs conducted by The Ohio State University and Duke University.

Leonard A. Schlesinger is Professor of Business Administration at the Harvard Business School and Berol Foundation Faculty Research Fellow (1991–92). He teaches the MBA elective course on *Service Management,* for which he won the Excellence in Teaching Award in 1990, and he serves as faculty chairman of the *Achieving Breakthrough Service* executive program.

From 1985 to 1988, Professor Schlesinger served as Executive Vice President and Chief Operating Officer of Au Bon Pain Co., Inc.

Professor Schlesinger has consulted on major service improvement and organizational change efforts throughout North America, Asia, Australia, and Mexico; and has participated in the design and development of executive education activities for several *Fortune* 500 companies. The author of numerous articles and books (most recently *The Management Game,* Viking Press, 1987), he is Associate Editor of *Human Resource Management* and has served on the Editorial Boards of the *Academy of Management Review* and the *Academy of Management Executive.* He holds an A.B. in American Civilization from Brown University, an MBA in Corporate and Labor Relations from Columbia University, and a doctorate in Organizational Behavior from Harvard University.

Phyllis F. Schlesinger is currently an Assistant Professor of Management and Organizational Behavior at Babson College in Wellesley, Massachusetts, where she teaches undergraduate, graduate, and executive coursework in Organizational Behavior and Organizational Design and Change. She is the Faculty Director of the One Year MBA Program at Babson. She holds a bachelor's degree from Brown University, a master's degree from University of Wisconsin, and a doctorate in Organizational Studies from Boston University.

Dr. Schlesinger has consulted with several *Fortune* 500 companies, including NYNEX and the General Electric Company. She has been active in executive program design and delivery with a diverse base of organizations, including The

Electrolux Group, Digital Equipment Corporation, the Higher Education Resource Services, New York Life, and LIMRA. She has recently collaborated with Vijay Sathe, John Kotter, and Leonard Schlesinger on the third edition of *Organization: Text, Cases, and Readings in the Management of Organization Design and Change* (Richard D. Irwin, 1991).

Torbjörn Stjernberg is Associate Professor at the Stockholm School of Economics. He received his doctorate in Business Administration in 1977. His main research interests concern organizational change, quality of work life, and complex projects in networks of organizations. He has participated as an action researcher and consultant in several major projects and programs since 1970, focusing on alternative work organizations. He has published *Organizational Change and Quality of Life* and several articles.

R. Roosevelt Thomas, Jr., is founder and president of The American Institute for Managing Diversity, a non-profit organization affiliated with Morehouse College. The institute is a research and education enterprise with the objective of fostering effective management of employee diversity. Some of the institute's clients are American Airlines, Amoco, the Coca Cola Company, CBS, Goodyear Tire & Rubber, IBM, Procter & Gamble, Quaker Oats, and Shell Oil. Previously, Dr. Thomas served as Dean of The Atlanta University Graduate School of Business Administration, Assistant Professor at the Harvard Business School, and instructor at Morehouse College. Dr. Thomas received his MBA in Finance from the University of Chicago and his DBA in Organizational Behavior from Harvard University. Among Dr. Thomas's written works is *Beyond Race and Gender: Unleashing the Power of Your Total Work Force by Managing Diversity* (AMACOM, 1991). He is also the author of articles that have appeared in *The Harvard Business Review*.

Peter B. Vaill is Professor of Human Systems and Director of the Doctoral Program at George Washington University's School of Business and Public Management. He is the former Dean of this school. He has also served on the management faculties of Stanford University, the University of Connecticut, and UCLA. He holds a bachelor's degree from the University of Minnesota and MBA and DBA degrees from the Harvard Business School.

He is the creator of the theory of "high performing systems" and has been speaking and writing on this subject since 1972. In 1985 he was described in the *Training and Development Journal* as one of the top 10 organization development specialists in the country.

He has worked with many well-known corporations and with most of the major agencies of the U.S. government. He has also worked with various health systems, universities, and professional associations. Dr. Vaill is the author of *Managing as a Performing Art: New Ideas for a World of Chaotic Change* (Jossey-Bass, 1989), and he has contributed chapters to several books and articles to publications such as *Organizational Dynamics* and *Creative Change*. From 1985 to 1988 he was editor of the American Management Association's journal, *Organizational Dynamics*. He is a founding member of the NTL Institute and a member of the Board of Governors of the Center for Creative Leadership.

INDEX

386

Special Offer
available to
Portable MBA readers

...Turn page for details ☞